NIETZSCHE and the FEMININE

Feminist Issues: Practice, Politics, Theory

Alison Booth and Ann Lane, Editors

Carol Siegel
Lawrence among the Women: Wavering Boundaries in Women's Literary Traditions

Harriet Blodgett, ed.
Capacious Hold-All: An Anthology of Englishwomen's Diary Writings

Joy Wiltenburg
Disorderly Women and Female Power in the Street Literature of Early Modern England and Germany

Diane P. Freedman
An Alchemy of Genres: Cross-Genre Writing by American Feminist Poet-Critics

Jean O'Barr and Mary Wyer, eds.
Engaging Feminism: Students Speak Up and Speak Out

Kari Weil
Androgyny and the Denial of Difference

Anne Firor Scott, ed.
Unheard Voices: The First Historians of Southern Women

Anne M. Wyatt-Brown and Janice Rossen, eds.
Aging and Gender in Literature: Studies in Creativity

Alison Booth, ed.
Famous Last Words: Changes in Gender and Narrative Closure

Marilyn May Lombardi, ed.
Elizabeth Bishop: The Geography of Gender

Heidi Hutner, ed.
Rereading Aphra Behn: History, Theory, and Criticism

Peter J. Burgard, ed.
Nietzsche and the Feminine

NIETZSCHE and the FEMININE

Edited and with an Introduction by
PETER J. BURGARD

University Press of Virginia
Charlottesville and
London

The University Press of Virginia

First published 1994

Library of Congress Cataloging-in-Publication Data

Nietzsche and the feminine / edited and with an introduction by
Peter J. Burgard.
p. cm. — (Feminist issues)
Includes bibliographical references and index.
ISBN 0–8139–1494–9 (cloth). — ISBN 0–8139–1495–7 (paper)
1. Nietzsche, Friedrich Wilhelm, 1844–1900—Views on
femininity (Philosophy) 2. Femininity (Philosophy) I. Burgard,
Peter J. II. Series: Feminist issues (Charlottesville, Va.)
B3318.F45N54 1994
121′.68′082—dc20 93–34551
CIP

Printed in the United States of America

Contents

Contents

Acknowledgments

I would like to thank: the authors of these essays, for their work and their patience; Benjamin Bennett and Susan Bernstein, for critical readings as well as writings; my colleagues at Harvard, especially Maria Tatar, for their support and their interest in this project; Harvard University, for financing translations; colleagues in the German department at Princeton, for their counsel and for making me welcome during the year in which this volume was completed, and in particular Emery Snyder, for intellectual and technical assistance above and beyond the call of friendship; Alexander Nehamas, for his incisive reading of the introduction; my colleague Nadine Bérenguier, for her crucial and very generous help in the correspondence with the French contributors; Gary Shapiro and Mary Rorty, for reading the manuscript and recommending its publication; Nancy Essig of the University Press of Virginia, for her enthusiastic commitment to the project; Sylvia Schmitz-Burgard, for more than I could possibly mention here; and my students, for not letting me off the hook.

Sarah Kofman's essay originally appeared as a chapter entitled "Une généalogie fantastique" in her *Explosion I: De l'"Ecce Homo" de Nietzsche* (Paris: Galilée, 1992), pp. 189–213. It appears here, for the first time in translation, with the permission of Editions Galilée; permission to reproduce "Une généalogie fantastique" in English translation has been granted by Athlone Press. Luce Irigaray's "Ecce Mulier?," translated by Madeleine Dobie, was originally published in the *Graduate Faculty Philosophy Journal* 15, no. 2 (1991): 144–58 and appears here with the permission of the journal. The illustrations accompanying Susan Bernstein's essay, "Fear of Music?," are reproduced from the exhibition catalogue, *L'Estasi di Santa Cecilia di Raffaello da Urbino nella Pinacoteca Nazionale di Bologna* (Bologna: ALFA, 1983), and with permission of the Ministero per i Beni Culturali e Ambientali, Soprintendenza per i Beni Artistici e Storici di Bologna.

Note on Texts and Translations

Quotations from Nietzsche's works are documented in the text by a double reference: (1) to the volume and page of the *Kritische Studienausgabe;* (2) to section numbers (where the sections are numbered continuously from beginning to end in a text) and page numbers of published translations. In some cases, the contributors have chosen to use their own translations, but still provide references to published translations (preceded by *cf.*). In other cases, published translations have been used, but altered; such emendations are indicated by an asterisk following the reference. The absence of a reference to a published translation indicates that the text is not available in translation. Following is a list of the abbreviations used, together with sample references. Note that in some instances there is more than one abbreviation for a particular work; this is because the contributors were free to use the translation they prefer.

KSA	*Sämtliche Werke: Kritische Studienausgabe in 15 Einzelbänden,* ed. Giorgio Colli and Mazzino Montinari (Munich/Berlin: dtv/de Gruyter, 1988); e.g., KSA 5:175.
A	*The Antichrist: Curse on Christianity,* in *The Portable Nietzsche,* trans. Walter Kaufmann (New York: Penguin, 1976); e.g., A §59, p. 650. Kaufmann translates the subtitle, "Fluch auf das Christenthum," as "Attempt at a Critique of Christianity."
BGaE	*Beyond Good and Evil,* trans. R. J. Hollingdale (New York: Penguin, 1973); e.g., BGaE §232, p. 144.
BGE	*Beyond Good and Evil: Prelude to a Philosophy of the Future,* trans. Walter Kaufmann (New York: Vintage, 1966); e.g., BGE §232, p. 162.
BT	*The Birth of Tragedy, Or: Hellenism and Pessimism. New Edition with an Attempt at Self-Criticism,* in *The Birth of*

	Tragedy and The Case of Wagner, trans. Walter Kaufmann (New York: Vintage, 1967); e.g., BT §4, p. 44.
CW	*The Case of Wagner: A Musicians' Problem*, in *The Birth of Tragedy and The Case of Wagner*, trans. Walter Kaufmann; e.g., CW §8, p. 172.
D	*Daybreak: Thoughts on the Prejudices of Morality*, trans. R. J. Hollingdale (Cambridge: Cambridge Univ. Press, 1982); e.g., D §346, p. 165.
EH	*Ecce Homo: How One Becomes What One Is*, in *On the Genealogy of Morals and Ecce Homo*, trans. Walter Kaufmann and R. J. Hollingdale (New York: Vintage, 1967); e.g., EH p. 267.
EcH	*Ecce Homo*, trans. R. J. Hollingdale (New York: Penguin, 1979); e.g., EcH p. 75.
GM	*On the Genealogy of Morals: A Polemic*, in *On the Genealogy of Morals and Ecce Homo;* e.g., GM—III §27, p. 161 (= section 27 of the third essay of the *Genealogy of Morals*).
GS	*The Gay Science*, trans. Walter Kaufmann (New York: Vintage, 1974); e.g., GS §68, p. 126.
HATH	*Human, All Too Human: A Book for Free Spirits*, trans. Marion Faber and Stephen Lehmann (Lincoln: Univ. of Nebraska Press, 1984); e.g., HATH §417, p. 202.
HH	*Human, All Too Human: A Book for Free Spirits*, trans. R. J. Hollingdale (Cambridge: Cambridge Univ. Press, 1986); e.g., HH §417, p. 155.
MW	"On Music and Words," trans. Walter Kaufmann, in Carl Dahlhaus, *Between Romanticism and Modernism: Four Studies in the Music of the Later Nineteenth Century*, trans. Mary Whittall (Berkeley and Los Angeles: Univ. of California Press, 1980); e.g., MW p. 109.
NW	*Nietzsche contra Wagner: Out of the Files of a Psychologist*, in *The Portable Nietzsche;* e.g., NW p. 668.
T	*Twilight of the Idols*, in *Twilight of the Idols / The Anti-Christ*, trans. R. J. Hollingdale (New York: Penguin, 1968); e.g., T p. 34.
TI	*Twilight of the Idols, Or: How One Philosophizes with a Hammer*, in *The Portable Nietzsche;* e.g., TI p. 469.
TL	"On Truth and Lying in an Extra-Moral Sense," in *Friedrich Nietzsche on Rhetoric and Language*, ed. and trans.

	Sander L. Gilman, Carole Blair, and David J. Parent (New York: Oxford Univ. Press, 1989), pp. 246–57; e.g., TL p. 246.
TSZ	*Thus Spoke Zarathustra,* trans. R. J. Hollingdale (New York: Penguin, 1969); e.g., TSZ p. 91.
UM	*Untimely Meditations,* trans. R. J. Hollingdale (Cambridge: Cambridge Univ. Press, 1983); e.g., UM p. 127.
WP	*The Will to Power,* ed. Walter Kaufmann, trans. Walter Kaufmann and R. J. Hollingdale (New York: Vintage, 1968); e.g., WP §481, p. 267.
Z	*Thus Spoke Zarathustra: A Book for All and None,* in *The Portable Nietzsche;* e.g., Z p. 178.

P	Prefaces; e.g., BGE—P, p. 2 (for works with prefaces divided into sections, the reference reads, e.g., GS—P §2, p. 33).
E	Epilogues; e.g., CW—E, p. 191.

NIETZSCHE
and the
FEMININE

PETER J. BURGARD

Introduction: Figures of Excess

I

"You are going to women? Do not forget the whip!" What college student has not read or at least heard of this, one of the most familiar lines from one of the most familiar books of Western philosophy, *Thus Spoke Zarathustra*? Certainly none to whom the "superman," eternal return, and "God is dead!" are also known. And we needn't look far to find numerous other disturbing remarks on women in Nietzsche's writing. Remarks such as those in *Beyond Good and Evil* telling us that woman's "great art is the lie, her highest concern is mere appearance and beauty" and that "woman has much reason for shame; so much pedantry, superficiality, schoolmarmishness, petty presumption, petty licentiousness and immodesty lies concealed in woman"; that "when a woman has scholarly intentions there is usually something wrong with her sexually" and that "woman would not have the genius for finery if she did not have an instinct for a *secondary* role." In *Ecce Homo* we read that feminism closes the door, preventing entrance into the "labyrinth of audacious insights." And, again in *Zarathustra,* we learn that "everything about woman is a riddle, and everything about woman has one solution: that is pregnancy." The list could go on and on. In studying Nietzsche, there are two basic responses to the assault perpetrated on the reader by such statements. One is to say Nietzsche was a misogynist and leave it at that. The other is to wonder what place such statements, pervasive as they are, might have in his philosophy, to recognize that their very pervasiveness demands attention. And that such statements, taken together with other more ambiguous and even sympathetic ones—*and* contrasted with such surprising remarks as "in sum, one cannot be too kind about women"—establish "woman" and "the feminine" as a problem in Nietzsche's philosophy that cannot simply be ignored. Nietzsche, after all, also wrote of "the fundamental problem of 'man and woman'" and warned against underestimating the significance of this "most abysmal antagonism." It is the *problem* of woman and the feminine in Nietzsche that this collection of new essays addresses.[1] And quotation marks around "the feminine" should be taken as read both in the title of the book and in this introduction—quotation marks, because it remains undecided whether Nietzsche's treatment of woman and women amounts to the kind of essentialization of femininity that a phrase like "the feminine" suggests.

The first response to Nietzsche's sexist tirades—calling a misogynist a misogynist and leaving it at that—is still not uncommon. Such a response might be construed as implicit in the many studies of the philosopher appearing every year that treat issues in his work where woman and the feminine are at least in the neighborhood, but make no mention of the problem. But such avoidance sometimes also becomes explicit. In a study that appeared in 1990, we read: "Admittedly, Nietzsche emphasizes in a variety of ways the tentative character of his own claims, but this cannot change or justify the particularly dubious and often disturbing nature of some of his own politically significant ideas. His racial and genetic theories, for example, and *his views on women need no comment* except to say they are probably the most thoroughly discredited aspects of his thought."[2] And little more than a decade ago, another scholar introduced an extensive catalogue of Nietzsche's remarks on woman and women with a statement that the very catalogue it introduces belies: "Nietzsche's philosophical thought is entirely geared toward men."[3] In this country, the avoidance of the question of the feminine in modern Nietzsche studies can be traced back to Walter Kaufmann. Kaufmann, with his work on and translations of Nietzsche, did Nietzsche scholarship a great service. Indeed, the immense Nietzsche renaissance of the last twenty years is probably unthinkable without him; several generations of scholars have grown up reading his translations and his book *Nietzsche: Philosopher, Psychologist, Antichrist*. But Kaufmann also did Nietzsche and Nietzsche studies a disservice when he wrote there that "Nietzsche's writings contain many all-too-human judgments—especially about women—but these are philosophically irrelevant."[4] Kaufmann's influence allowed this remark to constitute an effective interdiction of further investigation.

This interdiction, together with the distastefulness of those "all-too-human judgments," has seriously hindered the advancement of our understanding of Nietzsche, a hindrance that has only begun to be overcome recently. We can trace the more serious treatment of the problem of the feminine in Nietzsche back to the late 1970s and France, to the publication of two seminal studies: Sarah Kofman's "Baubô" and Jacques Derrida's *Spurs: Nietzsche's Styles*. The latter, due to its almost immediate publication in translation and the extensive reception of the author's work in this country, generated numerous responses and with them the establishment and acceptance of the topic as one worthy of sustained investigation.[5] In addition to the various critical responses to *Spurs* by Mary Ann Doane, Alice Jardine, Kelly Oliver, Gayatri Spivak, and others, the subject has begun to receive attention in some monographs on Nietzsche in the last decade (e.g., those by Robert John Ackermann, Ofelia Schutte, Henry Staten, and R. Hinton Thomas) and has even had several books devoted to it. In addition to Luce Irigaray's recently translated *Marine Lover of Friedrich Nietzsche* and David Farrell Krell's *Postponements: Woman, Sensuality, and Death in Nietzsche,* two extended studies have appeared since the present volume was planned: Jean Graybeal's *Language and "the Feminine" in Nietzsche and Heidegger* and Gary Shapiro's *Alcyone: Nietzsche on Gifts, Noise, and Women*.[6] While the number of such studies has been growing considerably in the last few years, when we consider the hundreds of books and essays that have been published in the veritable Nietzsche boom of the last decade, we find that discussions of woman in Nietzsche are still few and far between.[7]

Taken together, and in some cases by themselves, the essays in this volume, including the introduction, will disclose, echo, and set into play the irreducible ambivalence in Nietzsche's attitude toward the feminine. As a result of that ambivalence, any discussion of the feminine in Nietzsche must take the form of debate. *Nietzsche and the Feminine,* building on (and sometimes tearing down) the foundation the studies mentioned above represent, is meant to galvanize debate on the topic and to be a debate. By offering multiple perspectives on the perspective on the feminine of this philosopher of perspectivism, by presenting a plurality of approaches to the question that together *cannot* yield a single answer, a final signified, this collection of essays as such can provide what the studies preceding it, embedded as they are in books on other or more general subjects or isolated in journals or in books by single authors, could not—a treatment of the topic *appropriate* to Nietzsche's repeated and troubling articulations of the feminine.

II

Nietzsche's misogynistic remarks are mitigated as simple misogyny when one considers that he also called attention to the self-hatred of misogynists: "*Misogynists.* —'Woman is our enemy'—out of the man who says that to other men there speaks an immoderate drive which hates not only itself but also its means" (KSA 3:238; D §346, p. 165*). At the beginning of this introduction I quoted a number of Nietzsche's statements on woman, but I quoted them in the way they are conventionally cited by those who avoid the problem of woman in his philosophy and dismiss him out of hand as a misogynist—in an abbreviated form and out of context. As soon as we begin to examine the statements in their immediate textual context or in their broader Nietzschean context, we discover the problematical complexity of the feminine in Nietzsche. It is perhaps this complexity—the ambivalences, ambiguities, and contradictions in his utterances concerning woman and women—that prevented Kaufmann from recognizing the magnitude and the philosophical significance of the problem, for his is a view of Nietzsche that, as Alexander Nehamas has pointed out, is "determined to show that Nietzsche's aphorisms are ultimately unified, that behind them 'there is a whole philosophy.' . . . Kaufmann's is an effort to find an underlying unity, at least of method and attitude."[8] And there is probably no area in Nietzsche's philosophy where one finds less unity and univalence than on the question of the feminine.

Let us return first to Nietzsche's most famous misogynistic utterance: "You are going to women? Do not forget the whip!" (KSA 4:86; Z p. 179). To quote Nietzsche properly, however, we have to add some punctuation: " 'You are going to women? Do not forget the whip!' " The admonition is a quotation and thus once removed from Nietzsche's voice. But it is actually further removed, for it is a quote within the quotation that is the voice of Zarathustra's narration: " ' "You are going to women? Do not forget the whip!" ' " And it is even further removed by virtue of being, first, a statement not in a straightforward philosophical discourse but in a fictionalized philosophy, and, second, uttered by a *woman.* Finally, the exclamation mark, which lends the remark its admonitory quality, is also at least potentially a mark of irony. Thus, this simple misogynism is hardly as simple as it seems.

Hinton Thomas has discussed the history and the ironies of the passage on the whip at length, but he goes too far in his conclusion: "What is certain is that the mention of the whip has no place in any discussion of Nietzsche's views on the treatment of women as such."[9] Regardless of the statement's multiple "filtration," Nietzsche still wrote it and included it in what is often considered, and in what he considered, his most important work. And even though the book is written in the voice of Zarathustra and that voice, like any fictional voice, cannot be held to be identical with the author's voice, Nietzsche *does* still allow Zarathustra—a philosophical voice after all—to speak for him, no matter how ironic this speaking may sometimes be. Furthermore, the distancing of the statement from Nietzsche through other voices is in part undermined by the text's rhetoric—by the way in which it is introduced: "And thus spoke the little old woman [*also sprach das alte Weiblein*]." Her remark could thus be seen to acquire a status approximate to the pronouncements of Zarathustra, especially since it is immediately followed by the line "Thus spoke Zarathustra [*Also sprach Zarathustra*]": if it could be Zarathustra's statement, it might also be Nietzsche's.[10]

In another text, *Beyond Good and Evil,* Nietzsche writes: "From old Florentine novels; also—from life: '*Buona femmina e mala femmina vuol bastone*'" (KSA 5:98; BGE §147, p. 89). Even though the fictional context, the fact that it is a quotation, and the fact that it is in another language once again tend to distance the remark from Nietzsche, with the words "also—from life" he presents it as a truth; and the parallelism between "good and bad women" here and the title of the section in *Zarathustra* where the whip passage appears, "On Little Old and Young Women," might be considered evidence that the truth of the aphorism from *Beyond Good and Evil* is being employed to validate the earlier admonition. On the other hand, while the Italian quotation, being in the form of a proverb, rather unambiguously means that good and bad women "want a stick" in the sense of "need to be beaten," it is not entirely unambiguous—it might be taken to mean that they "want a stick" "with which to beat (others?)"—especially given Nietzsche's various remarks on the relative violence of women and given the aphorism preceding this one by a page that claims women are more barbaric than men (BGE §139), which in Nietzsche's idiom is not necessarily a criticism.

The mitigations of Nietzsche's most famous misogynistic pronouncement cannot rescue him entirely from the implications of having written that line, but neither do the mitigations of those mitigations render him once again a simple misogynist. The point is that, even though we cannot excuse the remark, we also cannot decide finally what it says about Nietzsche's views on woman.

One way to get a sense of the problematic quality of Nietzsche's formulations regarding woman, without going into an involved discussion in every case, is simply to juxtapose one of those formulations to others on the same topic and thus place it in its broader Nietzschean context. For example, his discussions of woman's "secondary role" are at least problematized by other passages and other contexts in which woman is accorded a hierarchically superior position to man:

> Woman would not have the genius for finery if she did not have an instinct for a *secondary* role. (KSA 5:98; BGE §145, p. 89)

> It is man who creates for himself the image of woman, and woman forms herself according to this image. (KSA 3:427; GS §68, p. 126)

But:

> Woman is indescribably more evil than man; also cleverer. . . . the state of nature, the eternal *war* between the sexes, gives her by far the first rank. (KSA 6:306; EH pp. 266–67)

> The perfect woman is a higher type of human than the perfect man, and also something much more rare. (KSA 2:265; HATH §377, p. 195)[11]

We can see here how both perspectives are ambiguous; where Nietzsche places woman in a secondary role, it is sometimes in the context of a critique of men for forcing women into that role,[12] and in the latter remarks where he accords woman a higher rank, he gives with the one hand while taking away with the other.

Likewise, Nietzsche's comment on the many reasons woman has for shame acquires a somewhat different accent when we witness the way in which he repeatedly valorizes her "shame" (which, when valorized, Kaufmann translates as "modesty" or "bashfulness"; in the German, all of these remarks are related by the use of the word *Scham*):

> Woman has much reason for shame [*Scham*]; so much pedantry, superficiality, schoolmarmishness, petty presumption, petty licentiousness, and immodesty lies concealed in woman. (KSA 5:171; BGE §232, p. 163)

But:

> One should have more respect for the *modesty* [*Scham*] with which nature has hidden behind riddles and iridescent uncertainties. Perhaps truth is a woman who has reasons for not letting us see her reasons? (KSA 3:352; GS—P §4, p. 38)

> But perhaps this is the most powerful magic of life: it is covered by a veil interwoven with gold, a veil of beautiful possibilities, promising, resisting, bashful [*schamhaft*], mocking, pitying, seductive. Yes, life is a woman. (KSA 3:569; GS §339, p. 272*)

Even the outrageous claim, uttered by Zarathustra, that woman is a riddle solved by pregnancy loses something of its denigrative quality when brought into proximity with some of Nietzsche's other views on pregnancy and birthing and his sense of their relation to philosophical thought:

> "Everything about woman is a riddle, and everything about woman has one solution: that is pregnancy." (KSA 4:84; Z p. 178)

But in the pages that follow we read:

> "Marriage: thus I name the will of two to create the one that is more than those who created it." (KSA 4:90; Z p. 182)

> "Oh, my friends, that your self be in your deed as the mother is in her child—let that be *your* word concerning virtue!" (KSA 4:123; Z p. 208)

And elsewhere:

> All human intercourse revolves *only* around pregnancy. (KSA 10:32)

> Constantly, we [philosophers] have to give birth to our thoughts out of our pain and, like mothers, endow them with all we have in us of blood, heart, fire, pleasure, passion, agony, conscience, fate, catastrophe. (KSA 3:349; GS—P §3, pp. 35–36*)

> Spiritual pregnancy produce[s] the character of the contemplative type, which is closely related to the feminine character: it consists of male mothers. (KSA 3:430; GS §72, p. 129)

Finally, we must also hesitate to read Nietzsche's statement that woman's "highest concern is mere appearance and beauty" as straightforwardly misogynistic, since elsewhere Nietzsche explains that women, historically, *have had* to operate on the level of appearance: "Reflect on the whole history of women: do they not *have* to be first of all and above all actresses? . . . they give themselves out as, even as they give themselves"

(KSA 3:609; GS §361, p. 317*). In another passage, he seems to see this acting not as a negative quality but as a laudable ability: "Given the tremendous subtlety of woman's instinct, modesty [*Scham*] remains by no means conscious hypocrisy: she divines that it is precisely an *actual naive modesty* [*Schamhaftigkeit*] that most seduces a man and impels him to overestimation. Therefore woman is naive—from the subtlety of her instinct" (KSA 12:325; WP §806, p. 425). And in *The Gay Science* he even eulogizes this concentration on appearance: "Perhaps truth is a woman who has reasons for not letting us see her reasons? Perhaps her name is—to speak Greek—*Baubo?* Oh, those Greeks! They knew how to live. What is required for that is to stop courageously at the surface, the fold, the skin, to adore appearance, to believe in forms, tones, words, in the whole Olympus of appearance. Those Greeks were superficial—*out of profundity*" (KSA 3:352; GS—P §4, p. 38). One effect of these parallel formulations—"Therefore woman is naive—from the subtlety of her instinct" and "Those Greeks were superficial—*out of profundity*"—is to make woman as much the object of Nietzsche's high praise as the Greeks were. However, as much as these other perspectives on "appearance" might attenuate the misogyny apparent in the statement that woman's "highest concern is mere appearance and beauty," they still cannot completely overcome its derisive tone.

In all four cases—woman's secondary role, her *Scham,* pregnancy, and her devotion to appearance—the latter, apparently more positive comments I have quoted certainly do not fully undermine the former, negative ones. And one could of course discuss each of these passages at length (with a few exceptions, they are all treated in this volume). But the comparison alone should provide enough evidence to conclude that the "obviously" derogatory statements, when brought back into the context of Nietzsche's work, are not so straightforward as they might otherwise appear.

On two other issues—feminism and the incongruity of women and scholarship—Nietzsche is quite straightforward and consistent, but in both cases related passages reveal that his apparently belittling remarks need not be taken to derogate woman in particular. Among the countless pronouncements on feminism and what Nietzsche saw as its main goal, emancipation and equal rights, we read:

> Every human "feminism," too—also in men—is a closing of the gate for me; it prevents entrance into this labyrinth of audacious insights. (KSA 6:303; EH p. 264*)

> To go wrong on the fundamental problem of "man and woman," to deny the most abysmal antagonism between them and the necessity of an eternally hostile tension, to dream perhaps of equal rights, equal education, equal claims and obligations—that is a *typical* sign of shallowness, and a thinker who has proved shallow in this dangerous place—shallow in his instinct—may be considered altogether suspicious, even more—betrayed, exposed: probably he will be too "short" for all fundamental problems of life, of the life yet to come, too, and incapable of attaining *any* depth. (KSA 5:175; BGE §238, pp. 166–67)

> Woman, the more she is a woman, resists rights in general hand and foot. (KSA 6:306; EH p. 267)

> *Woman is retrogressing.* . . . and the "emancipation of woman," insofar as that is demanded and promoted by women themselves (and not merely by shallow males) is thus seen to be an odd symptom of the increasing weakening and dulling of the most feminine instincts. There is *stupidity* in this movement, an almost masculine stupidity of which a woman who had turned out well—and such women are always prudent—would have to be thoroughly ashamed. . . . what is the meaning of all this if not a crumbling of feminine instincts, a defeminization? (KSA 5:176–77; BGE §239, pp. 168–69)

> "Emancipation of women"—that is the instinctive hatred of the woman who *turned out wrong* [*missrathen*], who is incapable of giving birth, against the woman who turned out well [*wohlgerathen*]—the fight against the "man" is always a mere means, pretext, tactic. By raising *themselves* higher, as "woman in herself," as the "higher woman," as an "idealist" of woman, they want to *lower* the level of the general rank of woman; and there is no surer means for that than higher education, pants, and political voting-cattle rights. At bottom, the emancipated are *anarchists* in the world of the "eternally feminine," the underprivileged whose most fundamental instinct is revenge. (KSA 6:306; EH p. 267*)

Nietzsche here holds an ideal of femininity—elsewhere he suggests that he understands women better than others and deems himself "the first psychologist of the eternally feminine" (KSA 6:302/305; EH pp. 263/266)—that cannot be reconciled with feminism and equal rights. Of course, the one aspect of that ideal he specifies (what the "most feminine instincts" might otherwise be is not clear here)—woman as above all a procreator—can also be seen as degrading, even though, as we have already seen, he valorizes the pregnancy and birthing to which he reduces woman. Furthermore, as the final passage indicates, he associates feminism and emancipation with an essentializing tendency (" 'woman in herself' ") that he condemns not only here but throughout his work.[13] The irony, of course, is that precisely in espousing an ideal of femininity—"Woman, the more she is a woman"—and in identifying woman's ideal role, Nietzsche himself essentializes woman—a fundamental paradox throughout this antiessentialist philosopher's work, and one that Lynne Tirrell's essay examines. Thus, here as elsewhere, there are ambiguities in Nietzsche's treatment of woman that demand attention rather than a simple dismissal of some "all-too-human" blindness or malevolence.

Beyond the context of Nietzsche's views on femininity, we must also consider his consistent condemnation of feminism in light of its embeddedness in his pervasive critique of democracy and the democratic ideal, both being for him examples of a striving for equality that disregards difference and that characterizes the herd mentality of the weak. Among the many critiques of equality or sameness, Zarathustra for example declares, "'And "will to equality" shall henceforth be the name for virtue; and against all that has power we want to raise our clamor!' You preachers of equality, the tyrannomania of impotence clamors thus out of you for equality: your most secret ambitions to be tyrants thus shroud themselves in words of virtue. Aggrieved conceit, repressed envy . . . erupt from you as a flame and as the frenzy of revenge" (KSA 4:129; Z p. 212). Moreover, Nietzsche repeatedly portrays both feminism and democracy as maladies of the modern Europe that constitute new forms of slavery. Here, then, his antifeminism is not directed only against woman.

Nietzsche's berating of women scholars requires such contextualization as well. We already discover that it is not as simple as it seems when we consider as a whole the aphorism in which it appears: "When a woman has scholarly inclinations there is usually something wrong with her sexually. Sterility itself disposes one toward a certain masculinity of taste; for man is, if I may say so, 'the sterile animal'" (KSA 5:98; BGE §144, p. 89). Like feminism, scholarship closes the door to pregnancy and birthing, also to the spiritual pregnancy that produces the contemplative type. Indeed, Nietzsche takes every opportunity to deride scholars and scholarship and to assert that they fall far short of philosophy and the higher ranks of humanity. Besides referring to scholarship as "idiocy" (KSA 6:51; CW—E, p. 191) and writing of its "alliance with the barbarism of taste" (KSA 1:685), he also informs us that the scholar "is essentially infertile" (KSA 1:399; UM pp. 173–74*), "belong[s] to the intellectual middle class" (KSA 3:624; GS §373, p. 334*), and "is the herd animal in the realm of knowledge" (KSA 11:153; WP §421, p. 226). And he has Zarathustra warn the higher human being: "Beware of the scholars! They hate you, for they are sterile" (KSA 4:361; Z p. 402). Again, a derisive remark turns out to be not directed against woman per se but rather embedded in a more general critique of a phenomenon in which some women participate.

III

Thus far, we have been able to trace the attenuation (not the sublation) of Nietzsche's misogyny and the extent to which that attenuation through contextualization discloses the problem, the ambivalence, of woman and the feminine in his philosophy. In considering his association of woman with lying, however, we can come closer to an understanding of the *philosophical significance* of the feminine in his work and thus move from a horizontal to a vertical line of argumentation.

In *Beyond Good and Evil* we read that "[woman] does not *want* truth: what is truth to a woman? From the beginning, nothing has been more alien, repugnant, and hostile to woman than truth—her great art is the lie, her highest concern is mere appearance and beauty" (KSA 5:171; BGE §232, p. 163), and Nietzsche elsewhere repeats his identification of woman and lie, as for example in his many comments on woman's capacity for dissimulation.[14] But there are also instances where he identifies woman with truth. He opens *Beyond Good and Evil* with the lines "Taking for granted that truth is a woman—what then? Are there not grounds for the suspicion that all philosophers, insofar as they were dogmatists, have had little understanding of women?" (KSA 5:11; BGE—P, p. 2*), and in *The Gay Science* we read: "One should have more respect for the *modesty* [*Scham*] with which nature has hidden behind riddles and iridescent uncertainties. Perhaps truth is a woman who has reasons for not letting us see her reasons?" (KSA 3:352; GS—P §4, p. 38). Woman is thus inscribed on both sides of an opposition fundamental to the tradition in philosophy that Nietzsche made it his life's work to question and go beyond. Through the association of the figure of woman with both sides of this hierarchically inscribed binary opposition, we might say that woman comes to be a figure of Nietzsche's subversion of that opposition as such. Nietzsche's irreducible ambivalence about woman would thus reinscribe itself as woman's subversive ambi-valence—an ambi-valence that is crucial to his philosophical program.

In his early essay "On Truth and Lie in an Extra-Moral Sense," Nietzsche deconstructs the opposition of truth and lie by means of a critique of language. Portraying truths as illusions that we no longer recognize as such, as dead metaphors, he promotes, and in his writing practices, a return to metaphor as metaphor. Opposite the rationalism and science that operates on the basis of truth and lie he places and advocates intuition (with which he would later associate woman [KSA 2:274–75; HATH §417, p. 202]) and art. Nietzsche argues that the concepts on which traditional philosophy relies for the construction of systems actually have their foundation in metaphor, the metaphoricity of which has, however, been forgotten: "Whereas any intuitive metaphor is individual and unique and therefore always eludes any commentary, the great structure of concepts displays the rigid regularity of a Roman columbarium and has an aura of that severity and coldness typical of mathematics. Whoever feels the breath of that coldness will scarcely believe that even the concept, bony and cube-shaped like a die, and equally rotatable, is just what is left over as the *residue of a metaphor,* and that the illusion of the artistic transference of a nerve stimulus into images is, if not the mother, then the grandmother, of any concept" (KSA 1:882; TL pp. 250–51). Here woman, other than in the later works quoted above, is identified with neither truth nor lie but rather is associated with metaphor (and perhaps, implicitly, with intuition) and as such, in the terms of this text, can be seen to figure as the before but also the beyond of the philosophy that depends on the absolute distinction between truth and lie.[15]

My quoting from Nietzsche in these pages may seem excessive, but all of these quotations together, most of which will reappear in the essays in this volume, constitute only a fraction of the aphorisms and passages in his philosophy that address woman and women. And all of these quotations, all these contextualizations and attenuations of his misogyny—to each of which one could attach so many buts, howevers, and on-the-other-hands—do not begin to account sufficiently for the place of the feminine in his thought. However, what we can perhaps see by now is that when Nietzsche began two of his most important works, *Beyond Good and Evil* and *The Gay Science,* with (uncertain) inscriptions of woman as truth and when he wrote the critical third essay of *The Genealogy of Morals* under the sign of a statement from *Zarathustra* equating woman with wisdom, it was no accident. He includes woman, accords the feminine a central role, in the articulation of his philosophy, even as his extreme sexism excludes woman.

IV

Nietzsche is the philosopher of excess. Everywhere we turn, we are faced with excess, both in form and in content. In the most general terms, his philosophy is fundamentally concerned with *going beyond*—beyond good and evil, beyond all conventional values, beyond philosophy itself—and the *Über* of the *Übermensch* can also be understood to refer to a going beyond.[16] Related to this is what Alexander Nehamas demonstrates as a primary characteristic of Nietzsche's thought and writing—his perspectivism.[17] This perspectivism, which Nietzsche both theorizes and practices, entails numerous other manifestations of excess as well. The pluralism of Nietzsche's aphoristic style is, for example, one excessive aspect of the plurality of genres he employs. And "the figure of exaggeration or hyperbole [is the] single most pervasive feature of his writing. . . . Nietzsche's writing is irreducibly hyperbolic" (p. 22). Nehamas later relates this rhetorical excess and the fact that Nietzsche's texts "often say too much" to the content of those texts and grants it the status of an essential quality of his philosophy: "Nietzsche's writing, and his thinking, is *essentially* hyperbolic" (p. 31).

Nehamas' view is most succinctly borne out by one of the fragments that has been collected under the heading "The Will to Power": "Against positivism, which goes no further than the phenomenon—'there are only facts'—I would say: No, facts is precisely what there is not, only interpretations. . . . Insofar as the word 'knowledge' has any meaning, the world is knowable; but it can be *interpreted* differently, it has no meaning behind it, but rather countless meanings. —'Perspectivism' " (KSA 12:315; WP §481, p. 267*). In the declaration of what Sarah Kofman calls "a pluralism of interpretations" and of the countless possible meanings those countless interpretations yield, the idea of excess is at work.[18] But it also becomes explicit at many points from Nietzsche's earliest to his latest writings. Near the beginning of his first major work, *The Birth of Tragedy,* he defines one of his most important ideas, the idea of the Dionysian, in terms of excess:

> The effects wrought by the *Dionysian* also seemed "titanic" and "barbaric" to the Apollonian Greek. . . . And now let us imagine how into this world, built on mere appearance and moderation and artificially dammed up, there penetrated, in tones ever more bewitching and alluring, the ecstatic sound of the Dionysian festival; how in these strains all of nature's *excess* in pleasure, grief, and knowledge became audible, even in piercing shrieks. . . . The individual, with all his restraint and proportion, succumbed to the self-oblivion of the Dionysian states, forgetting the precepts of Apollo. *Excess* revealed itself as truth. (KSA 1:40–41; BT §4, p. 46; the emphasis is Nietzsche's)

In his philosophy of the beyond, *Beyond Good and Evil,* we read: "Let us admit that *measure* is alien to us; our thrill is precisely the thrill of the infinite, the unmeasured" (KSA 5:160; BGE §224, p. 153*). And in a very late fragment (Fall 1887) he identifies excess as the force that supports the cause of the "immoralists": "We immoralists. . . . the magic that fights for us, the eye of Venus that captivates and blinds even our enemies, is the *magic of the extreme,* the seduction that practices all that is excessive: we immoralists—we are *the excessive ones*" (KSA 12:510; cf. WP §749, p. 396). One could go on quoting practically forever, for Nietzsche's implicit and explicit formulations of the principle of excess, like his formulations of all principles and tendencies he held dear or scorned (or both), present themselves in excess.

It is in the case of woman that Nietzsche is perhaps most excessive. Both in the hyperbole, the extremity of his remarks on woman and in the multiple interpretations that attribute seemingly countless, competing meanings to woman. Moreover, a recurrent theme in those interpretations is the excessive character of woman, which appears sometimes threatening, sometimes repulsive, sometimes admirable:

> The perfect woman tears to pieces when she loves. —I know these charming maenads. —Ah, what a dangerous, creeping, subterranean little beast of prey she is! And yet so agreeable! (KSA 6:305–6; EH p. 266)

> So much . . . immodesty [*Unbescheidenes*] lies concealed in woman. (KSA 5:171; BGE §232, p. 163)

> The sick woman especially: no one excels her in the wiles to dominate, oppress, and tyrannize. The sick woman spares nothing, living or dead; she will dig up the most deeply buried things (the Bogos say: "woman is a hyena"). (KSA 5:370; GM—III §14, p. 123*)

> When we love a woman, we easily conceive a hatred for nature on account of all the repulsive natural functions to which every woman is subject. (KSA 3:422–23; GS §59, p. 122)

> What inspires respect for woman, and often enough even fear, is her *nature,* which is more "natural" than man's, the genuine, cunning suppleness of a beast of prey, the tiger's claw under the glove, the naïveté of her egoism, her uneducability and inner wildness, the incomprehensibility, scope, and movement of her desires and virtues. (KSA 5:178; BGE §239, p. 169)

Woman is inscribed in Nietzsche's first major articulation of the principle of excess—his formulation of the Dionysian principle—by way of the maenads, by way of the relation between Dionysus and Medusa, and perhaps also by way of his notion of woman's barbarity.[19] And woman, variously equated with life, nature, truth, lie, music, wisdom, etc., constitutes the or at least a moment of excessive identity in his philosophy. More significantly, woman, as we saw in the case of truth and lie, can be held to figure the *beyond* of philosophy that Nietzsche seeks. At one point he even locates woman beyond: "When a man stands in the midst of his own noise, in the midst of his own surf of plans and projects, then he is apt also to see quiet, magical beings gliding past him and to long for their happiness and seclusion: *women*. . . . The magic and the most powerful effect of women is, in philosophical language, action at a distance, *actio in distans;* but this requires first of all and above all—*distance*" (KSA 3:424–25; GS §60, p. 124).

If excess characterizes Nietzsche's philosophy, then we could say that woman is a figure of that philosophy by virtue of being a central figure of excess in it. However, Nietzsche's treatment of excess is not univalent. The Dionysian does not eradicate the Apollonian—the devotion to measure (*Maß*) and restraint—but is inextricably linked to it. Especially in connection with the Greeks, Nietzsche often praises a sense of measure, and his statement, quoted above, that "measure is alien to us" occurs in a passage that leaves his position on excess and measure unclear:

> Perhaps our great virtue of the historical sense is necessarily opposed to *good* taste, at least to the very best taste; and precisely the small short and highest strokes of luck and transfigurations of human life, which briefly light up here and there, we can reproduce in ourselves only poorly, hesitantly, and by force—those moments and marvels when great power voluntarily stopped this side of the immeasurable and boundless, when an excess of subtle delight in sudden restraint and petrification, in standing firm and taking one's measure, was enjoyed on still trembling ground. Let us admit that *measure* is alien to us; our thrill is precisely the thrill of the infinite, the unmeasured. Like a rider on a steed that flies forward, we drop the reins before the infinite, we modern men, like semi-barbarians—and reach *our* bliss only where we are most—*in danger.* (KSA 5:159–60; BGE §224, pp. 152–53*)

The ambivalence evident in the phrase "an excess of subtle delight in sudden restraint" is reflected in a fragment that lists some of the *problems* Nietzsche was most concerned about—including truth, certainty, the good, justice, and rank—and that includes "the problem of measure [*Maß*]" (KSA 12:311). Rather than undermining the figuration of his philosophy embodied by woman as a figure of excess, however, these moderations and modifications of the principle of excess can be seen to reinforce that figuration. For, on the one hand, Nietzsche's excessive portrayal of woman as excess (e.g., as immodest) is also moderated by the numerous passages we have already considered in which he writes of woman's modesty.[20] On the other, his ambivalence concerning excess recalls his fundamental ambivalence concerning woman as well as the role of woman in one of the central ambi-valences of his work. On woman as on excess, Nietzsche is both excessive and excessively ambivalent.

V

We have now had two encounters with woman as what might be considered a *figure* of Nietzsche's philosophy. One specific (the case of truth and lie), the other general (the case of excess). If we accept the view that the style of Nietzsche's philosophy is metaphoric and recall that in "On Truth and Lie" he promotes and practices the return to the metaphoricity of metaphor, then we discover another possible figuration of that philosophy in the figure of woman.[21] Nietzsche constantly identifies woman with critical components of his thought: with nature, with life ("Yes, life is a woman"), with wisdom ("wisdom . . . is a woman"), with truth ("truth is a woman"), with lie ("her great art is the lie"), with appearance, and with music ("for music is a *woman*"). Indeed, in "On Truth and Lie" woman even appears as metaphor itself, that is, as a metaphor for metaphor. Could we not then say that woman in Nietzsche—a metaphor for metaphor in a metaphoric philosophy—operates as a metaphor for that philosophy, as the eternally recurring figure (Nietzsche repeatedly comments on the "eternal feminine") in and of a figurative philosophy? And does not woman, as a kind of "floating signifier," introduce an excess of essentialism that *as* excess undercuts the very essentializing tendency it discloses? In other words, does not the simultaneous multiplicity of identities yield non-self-identity? In theory, yes. But in effect, Nietzsche's excessive metaphorization still excessively objectifies and thus reduces woman.[22] As much as he railed against hypostatizing "woman as such," Nietzsche, despite his multiplication of the as-suches, seems to have done just that.

VI

What I have tried to do so far in this introduction is not only to contextualize Nietzsche's pronouncements concerning woman and the feminine and to suggest briefly various possible responses to them, but, more generally, to provide a sense of the enormous complexity of the problem—a complexity that is confronted and articulated by the essays in this volume, to which I now turn my attention. My remarks have anticipated some of the arguments of these essays and also disagree with some of them. But this is as it should be, for *Nietzsche and the Feminine* was conceived as and is a critical symposium on the topic, a symposium where the perspectives are Nietzschean in their multiplicity, and sometimes in other ways as well. There is much disagreement here, but there is also a certain unity in the volume's diversity, in that all of the essays taken together do not rescue Nietzsche from his misogyny or apologize for it, but rather recuperate this aspect of his work—not only as one that is worthy of debate but also as a somehow "central" feature of his thinking and writing that *demands* discussion. Simultaneously, the volume as a whole can be seen to constitute an investigation of the relation between feminism and philosophy by focusing on one of its crucial flash points: Nietzsche.

Mothers

It seems appropriate that a volume on Nietzsche and the feminine should begin with essays considering the *genealogy* of Nietzsche's persistent and problematic judgments of woman and of their place in his philosophy. In the first piece, Sarah Kofman approaches this genealogy through an examination of the genealogy Nietzsche created for himself and offers the analysis of Nietzsche's reconstruction of his own lineage as a prolegomenon to further studies of the position of women in his work. Operating on the thesis that Nietzsche's image of his mother is essential to any understanding of his attitude toward women, Kofman compares two versions of the third section of the chapter in *Ecce Homo* entitled "Why I Am So Wise": the previously accepted version, in which Nietzsche marginally maintains his German origins in order to ennoble the paternal branch of his family and in which his only reference to his mother is to the effect that she is "in any case something very German" (although somehow not the carrier of nobility that the paternal grandmother was); and the currently accepted version, apparently suppressed by Nietzsche's mother and sister, in which all traces of Germanness have disappeared from his heritage in order to reveal the purity of his blood and the absence of any relationship to the "canaille" that his mother and sister are now held to represent and whom he now portrays as his most fundamental opposites. In constructing a fantastical genealogy that typologically establishes his nobility, Nietzsche creates a family romance in the Freudian sense, but in reverse: here the son has a stronger desire to free himself from the mother than from the father. Indeed, Nietzsche celebrates his father because he sees in him a means of construing his own noble distinction, which allowed him to understand Zarathustra and to create this counterideal to the ascetic ideal; and he rejects his mother as the carrier of "base instincts" foreign to him. There are two paradoxes at work here: first, that in exalting his father Nietzsche also "kills" him (by transforming him into part of a fantasmatically noble heritage not his own), and, second, that the violence of his rejection of both mother and sister, whom he calls "venomous vermin," and the "unspeakable horror" they arouse in him might also be interpreted as evidence of a forbidden, incestuous love. It is this radical ambivalence, Kofman argues, that is reflected in Nietzsche's many theoretical judgments of women. And it is that unspeakable horror which the thought of his mother and sister evokes that even led him to question the wisdom of and ultimately to modify his articulation of the doctrine of "eternal return," which might provide for *their* eternal return. His horror at his mother and sister, who represent the threat of castration, thus brings to mind horror at the head of Medusa, with which Nietzsche once associates eternal return. In defending himself against mother and sister, Nietzsche erects another head—the head of Dionysus—and thereby reformulates eternal return as the eternal return of *difference*. Thus Kofman demonstrates how one of the philosopher's most significant ideas is embedded in his image of woman as mother.

Wherever possible, I have organized the essays in this volume not only thematically (although the groupings should by no means be taken to suggest that the only relations among essays are among those that appear under the same heading), but also contestationally. The first pairing reflects this arrangement, which is designed to emphasize the sense of debate that must characterize any discussion of Nietzsche and the feminine. Kelly Oliver's examination of "Nietzsche's Abjection," like Kofman's essay, treats the philosopher's position on woman as a function of his relationship to his mother. But Oliver insists that we must keep in mind the difference between the feminine and the maternal. Arguing that past attempts to understand Nietzsche's relation to the feminine have overlooked this difference, Oliver undertakes, via Kristeva's separation of the feminine operation from the maternal function and her theory of abjection, to show that Nietzsche *reduces* woman and the feminine to the maternal, that is, that he is not able to make that crucial separation, and thus that his problematic relation to "woman" derives directly from his disturbed relation to the mother—a point seemingly similar to that made by Kofman, but actually quite different. Specifically, in an argument running counter to Kofman's, Oliver asserts that Nietzsche is caught at the stage of abjection, with no loving imaginary father to support his separation—that he is never able to separate the maternal function from the mother and thus to split the mother into the abject and the sublime, which would in turn enable him to develop an autonomous identity. It is as a result of this inability and of his reduction of women to the maternal that Nietzsche's relation to women remains a relation of abjection; it is thus also that Nietzsche can make such pronouncements as those claiming that women exist to be pregnant. The three "Nietzschean women" hypostatized by Derrida—castrated woman, castrating woman, and affirming woman—Oliver reads as the three faces of the mother. In essence, then, there is no "woman" or "feminine" in Nietzsche, insofar as they always remain inscribed in the maternal relation.

Figures of the Feminine

When Derrida wrote in *Spurs* that "the question of the figure is at once opened and closed by what is called woman," he opened the question of woman as figure to further debate.[23] For example, to Gayatri Spivak's argument, in response to *Spurs* and Derrida's writing of woman in Nietzsche's voice, that deconstruction inscribes woman as a figure of displacement;[24] or to Diana Fuss's contention that in Derrida's reading/writing of Nietzsche, "woman operates as the very figure of undecidability."[25] The three essays in this second section of the volume take up the debate concerning the issue, generally, of figuration in Nietzsche's philosophy, and, specifically, of the figurality of woman in his work. In his essay on "Castration Envy" Clayton Koelb examines the persistence of the figure of woman in Nietzsche. Addressing the question of castration that we have already seen, in the essays by Kofman and Oliver, as integral to Nietzsche's relation to his mother and thus to his relation to woman, Koelb argues that numerous crucial figures in his philosophy—the artist and the philosopher, that is, the contemplatives, the creators of the world, the male mothers—are all figures of castration and that all appear in the figure of woman. More significantly and surprisingly, all of these are linked to castration not through anxiety but through *desire*, since they draw their power from the absence of the phallus; as the figure of castration, woman thus becomes the object of castration envy. Koelb then delineates several of the more important figurations of woman through which Nietzsche addresses fundamental philosophical questions: the tropes of woman as nature, as veiled truth, and as life. In each of these tropes, castration is indispensable and itself becomes a trope for ultimate power—for example, nature as a dismembered but all-powerful woman—where the potency of the phallus is seen as insignificant when compared to the power its absence figures. Thus one of Nietzsche's central ideas, the will to power, instills envy for this void that represents absolute power. According to Koelb, then, woman in Nietzsche is a figure, indeed a pervasive figure. In this pervasiveness, however, woman functions as a figure that cannot be reduced to a simple figure, a simple equation that we might forget as such. And as a figure of castration, which Koelb argues is more purely a metaphor in Nietzsche than in Freud, woman is a figure once removed, a figure of a figure, and, so to speak, a nonfigural figure—a figure without concrete definition and outline. Perhaps in this intense play of figuration conventional figuration is destabilized.

The problematics of figuration implied by Koelb's analysis, and specifically those of woman as figure, are taken up in a different vein by Bianca Theisen's essay, "Rhythms of Oblivion." Questioning whether in his numerous derisive remarks on women Nietzsche is even writing about real women or the concept of "woman," Theisen argues in the first part of her paper, on Nietzsche's treatment of the distinction between truth and lie, that he excludes woman doubly—from both the male and the female realms, and from both truth and lie. Non-self-identical (both wom*e*n and wom*a*n), woman figures as a simulated truth that plays on the very distinction between truth and lie—a logical third that calls attention to this distinction as such and thus calls into question bivalent logic. As a *tertium datur,* woman in Nietzsche's text reveals *as* distinction the distinctions that determine cognition. If we are to see woman as a figure in Nietzsche's work at all, Theisen implies, then it is not as a figure of any particular position in an opposition within a philosophical argument but as that which moves beyond a philosophy of binary oppositions—a figure of Nietzsche's subversion of traditional philosophy, a figure of Nietzsche's philosophy itself. In the second part of her essay, Theisen turns to the poem "Ariadne's Lament," showing how Nietzsche reinscribes in the voice of woman the magician's song from *Thus Spoke Zarathustra,* and from this book's staging of the undecidability between truth and deception, and how this reinscription, together with the addition of Dionysus' response, leads to a mingling of figures—Ariadne, Dionysus, woman—to a "third sex" that dissolves gender boundaries and with them other fundamental paradigms of distinction as well. The poem reveals the shift from a negation that operates within a yes/no, true/false distinction to an affirmation that is no longer based in such distinctions. Ariadne's sublime experience—in the torment of thinking eternal return (but, as in Kofman's analysis, not of the same)—results from a movement *through* negation that *affirms negativity* and that therefore also subverts the Kantian notion of the sublime along with a logic of opposition. Working through the figuration of woman, Nietzsche inscribes a figure of woman as antifigure, as that which does not operate within the "figure's" economy of identity but rather calls into question systems of identity.

In "Fear of Music? Nietzsche's Double Vision of the 'Musical-Feminine,'" Susan Bernstein takes as a starting point the destabilizing force of the figures of woman and music in Nietzsche's writing, in order then to show how the means by which he inscribes those figures lends them tenacity and ultimately allows them to restabilize what they were supposed to undermine. In the first part of her argument, Bernstein calls attention to the role played by "woman" in Nietzsche's critique of the concept of truth and to Derrida's conclusion that woman is a term that destabilizes a philosophical discourse inextricably linked to the search for truth. But Bernstein goes on to investigate the manner in which the critique of truth continues to depend on the stability of the figures named "woman," "truth," and "music" and argues that the opacity of these figures—their bodily form, their quality as tropes or conceptual masks, their clear outlines—prevents the actual ruin of philosophy. (Bernstein also reminds us that Nietzsche's inscription of "woman" does not silence his pejorative statements on women, indeed that wherever terms such as "woman" and "truth" are employed—even as philosophical figures—women and truth are necessarily part of the discussion.) To point to the obstruction of transparent conceptual thought effected by figuration, Bernstein then shifts her attention from "truth" and "philosophy" in Nietzsche to the more opaque terms of music and painting. In close readings of Nietzsche's critique of Wagner, of his essay on "Music and Words," and of a painting about music to which Nietzsche refers in that essay—Raphael's *The Ecstasy of St. Cecilia*—Bernstein is able to show how Nietzsche relies on figuration, how he repeatedly enlists images in lieu of argumentation, how he calls attention to the tenacity of figures and the materiality of signifying bodies, and how his figural manner of exposition is embedded in an economy of desire and castration anxiety. Figuration in Nietzsche—in which "woman" and "music" figure an "other" discourse but at the same time reintroduce stability precisely where they are meant to undermine it—comes to be associated with the "feminine operation."

Beyond Antifeminism

In the face of such severe judgments of feminism as those treated earlier in this introduction—or many others, including the equation, in the *Genealogy of Morals,* of feminism with "moral mawkishness and falseness" (KSA 5:386; GM—III §19, p. 137) and with indecency, dishonesty, weakness, and cowardice (KSA 5:410; GM—III §27, p. 161)—any attempt to enlist Nietzsche in the cause of feminism might come as a surprise. But this is precisely what Janet Lungstrum and Lynne Tirrell, albeit from quite different perspectives, argue we can and perhaps should do.

In her essay "Nietzsche Writing Woman / Woman Writing Nietzsche: The Sexual Dialectic of Palingenesis," Lungstrum takes as a starting point the problems caused for feminism by the very discussion of figuration and examines the ways in which Nietzsche's extreme statements on women have led to the kind of feminist double bind Alice Jardine describes, whereby one either rejects "the feminine" or "woman" as figurations and thus runs the risk of falling back into metaphysical and anatomical delineations of sexual identity, or accepts such figuration and thereby risks the absence of women as subjects. Lungstrum's essay stakes out a third position that approaches Nietzsche from the perspective of eroticism-as-creativity rather than gender-as-identity, in order then to be able to show that feminist self-empowerment can be attained through the woman that Nietzsche writes into existence. In contrast to a poststructuralist view, deriving from Deleuze's seminal study, of Nietzsche as antidialectical, Lungstrum deploys Pautrat's reinscription (as nonsynthetical) of the dialectical aspect of Nietzsche's philosophy, in particular of the incessant and insistent sexual opposition that grounds his creativity. On this view, Nietzsche sets into play a sexual *agonistics* in which woman acts as catalytic muse in a self-renewing creativity. While acknowledging that, in societal terms, Nietzsche silences female sensuality, Lungstrum argues that when viewed through the lens of art it is rehabilitated, since the sexual dialectic can be just as empowering for woman as for man, and, indeed, woman as written by Nietzsche is endowed with a potentially greater power of creative dissimulation than the male artist. Furthermore, his formulation of feminine narcissism and of woman's self-distancing veiling of herself—two lightning rods for feminist critiques of Nietzsche—can be seen as the means by which, respectively, the woman he writes can rewrite her otherness and the creative tension between the masculine and the feminine is kept alive within the self. To what she sees as a refusal to acknowledge or a dissolving of Nietzsche's (sexual) dialectics in Irigaray and Derrida, Lungstrum opposes Lou Salomé's originary feminist reading of Nietzsche as inherently bisexual, of his philosophy as fundamentally oppositional, and concludes that his contradictions about woman form part of a more basic contradiction between masculine and feminine forces within himself. Nietzsche's dialectical articulation of the feminine in his writing allows woman to (re)create herself; the feminist rewriting of Nietzsche is thus already contained in Nietzsche.

In "Sexual Dualism and Women's Self-Creation: On the Advantages and Disadvantages of Reading Nietzsche for Feminists" Lynne Tirrell argues that, despite the philosopher's virulent misogyny, which cannot be explained away, there are areas of shared concern for Nietzsche and feminists and that certain elements of his work are worthy of feminist appropriation. Indeed, his own writings carry the potential for a subversion of his misogyny—for example, he condemns women for their nature, thus revealing an essentialist conception of woman's nature, but his philosophy is at the same time thoroughly antiessentialist. The three areas in that philosophy that Tirrell identifies as anticipating contemporary feminist concerns regarding women's articulation of their own lives are (1) his antidualism, (2) his perspectivism, and (3) his views on the power of naming. While Nietzsche abandoned his early dualism and by the time of *Beyond Good and Evil* was questioning "whether there are any opposites at all" (KSA 5:16; BGE §2, p. 10) and suggesting that the values placed on such supposed opposites are really only provisional perspectives, he nevertheless maintained, as Lungstrum demonstrates, one particular dualism—the sexual dualism apparent in his insistence on the "eternally hostile tension" (KSA 5:175; BGE §238, p. 166) between man and woman. This insistence can be seen to explain his various attacks on equal rights and feminism, which he saw as threatening the collapse of that fundamental opposition. But Tirrell does not stop at this contradiction; rather, she proceeds to articulate the irony of Nietzsche's sexual dualism in the context of his far-reaching critique of all dualisms. She also shows how Nietzsche actually does challenge this last dualism, even as he appears to uphold it, in that he recognizes the extent to which men and women as such are created by social interpretations, interpretations that create an opposition on the basis of assigned values, the accuracy of which he draws into question. In the very act of stating woman's secondary status, Nietzsche reveals that status as the socially determined result of men's perspective. Thus Tirrell shifts the recuperation of Nietzsche's potential feminism back to the social terms of gender-identity that Lungstrum argues such recuperation must avoid. In the second half of her essay Tirrell addresses what she sees as Nietzsche's surprisingly insightful discussions of women's situation under the rule of sexual dualism. Tirrell detects in these discussions, particularly in those of *The Gay Science*, a nonmisogynist conception of woman that recognizes her disadvantage in a sexual economy that forces her to take a role written by man, gradually to adapt this role as her own reality, and thus to inhibit the development of her own perspective. Nietzsche himself reveals the cruelty of a male/master morality that perilously objectifies woman, leading her to "close her eyes to herself" (KSA 3:429; GS §71, p. 128), and he articulates the power by which man creates woman as he creates his world—the power of naming which, so exercised by man, robs woman of the power of self-articulation. Tirrell is careful to remind us, however, that neither Nietzsche's (unfinished) attack on dualism nor his unexpected sensitivity to the deplorable situation of women should lead us to label him a feminist, for neither is able to silence his otherwise vast misogyny. The combination of these two facets of his treatment of women precludes any final resolution of the question of his sexual politics. Still, significant elements of his philosophy can serve feminism well, and throughout her essay Tirrell repeatedly calls attention to aspects of modern feminist theories—including those of Mary Daly, Audre Lorde, and especially Simone de Beauvoir—that are anticipated by or echo Nietzsche's own formulations.

Feminist Philosophy

The question of the relation between Nietzsche and feminist philosophy, in particular the French feminists, is posed, at least implicitly, by most of the essays in this volume. The three pieces in this section address that (sometimes confrontational, sometimes reciprocal, sometimes confrontational *and* reciprocal) relation directly. "To the Orange Grove at the Edge of the Sea," David Farrell Krell's contribution, is a fragmentary reading of Luce Irigaray's fragmentary reading of Nietzsche in *Amante marine: De Friedrich Nietzsche*. Krell reads Nietzsche with Irigaray and Irigaray with Nietzsche, revealing the provocative and problematic intermingling of their voices in her text. In an increasingly resistant reading of Irigaray's resistance to the figure of woman in Nietzsche's writing, Krell outlines what he perceives as the troubling blind spots, precisely from a feminist point of view, of Irigaray's feminist reinscription. Approaching her sea-lover perspective on Nietzsche by way of Bachelard's portrayal of the philosopher as an ascensional poet who resists the spongy, moist receptivity of earth and sea, Krell examines the three parts of *Amante marine* in an attempt to discover whether Irigaray ever allows Nietzsche to descend back into the sea (of woman) to which she invites him. To Irigaray's formulation, in "Speaking of Immemorial Waters," of the challenge presented by the sea/woman/other to Nietzsche's thought of the eternal return of the same, Krell counters, first, that Nietzsche himself recognized the abrogation of the idea of the same entailed by the very thought of recurrence and, second, that the Irigarayan sea itself might be considered the locus of the eternal return of the same thought as metaphysical consolation. In "Veiled Lips," where Irigaray's rhapsody of the lips posits the perfect self-embrace of woman and her capacity to feel without feeling ressentiment, Krell sees the arrow of ressentiment being shot back at Nietzsche and detects a repetition of Nietzsche's thoughts on woman "giving herself out as, even as she gives herself." For Irigaray's description of ressentiment as something entirely foreign to woman might well be taken as a case of woman giving herself out *as if* without ressentiment. Krell's greatest resistance to Irigaray's reading emerges in his response to the third section of her book, where he senses a tension between her scorn for the phallus, which he suggests we might after all consider the sea-creation of woman, and the phallic quality of her refutation—the phallicy of her claims of womanly perfection and self-embrace, of her insistence on the self-sufficient womanly body, and of what might be seen as an unwitting return to metaphysics and morals. At the end of his remarks, however, Krell allows his own resistance to flow into and be consumed by a Nietzschean-Irigarayan rhapsody—a revery of Nietzsche the sea-lover and the sea-lover of Nietzsche written not contra Irigaray but in the neighborhood of her thought.

In reading Irigaray's reading of Nietzsche, Krell rewrites an already written dialogue between Nietzsche and feminist philosophy. Alan Schrift, on the other hand, brings forth and explicates a dialogue that until now has remained only implicit. "On the Gynecology of Morals: Nietzsche and Cixous on the Logic of the Gift" examines a recurrent theme in Nietzsche—the economies of exchange and giftgiving—which Nietzsche did not inscribe in terms of gender, but which, when regarded through the lens of Cixous's writing, discloses a gender distinction and intimates an unacknowledged feminine aspect of Nietzsche's economic discourse. To a notion of justice originating in the economy of exchange between buyer and seller, creditor and debtor, and understood as the law of an eye for an eye that operates between individuals in positions of equal power, Nietzsche juxtaposes his vision of an age when justice will no longer be predicated upon such equality, when the law of equal return will no longer constitute society's principle of justice. From these two types of justice emerge two competing types of economy: a slave economy that depends on the rule of exchange and where it is not possible to give gifts freely, because the expectation of reciprocity is always already assumed; and a "nobler" economy of "expenditure" in which the strong, out of the fullness of their power, can give of themselves and expect nothing in return. Such an economy is enacted in Zarathustra's gift of his teachings; and Nietzsche himself tries to realize this nobler economy by treating his own writings as gifts to his readers that demand no return, but rather encourage them to disseminate his writings by rewriting them in their own terms. Cixous articulates such an economy of generosity when she envisions a postpatriarchal future no longer constrained by the law of return. Schrift argues that, in outlining divergent economies, Cixous rewrites Nietzsche by abandoning his valorization of strength and by casting those economies in terms of gender and intersubjective relations. The economy grounded on the law of return she reveals as based in the notion of property and the phallocentric desire to appropriate the other. This "masculine" economy—founded on the fear of castration, of losing what one already possesses—does not allow true giving, for, in order to prevent loss, it always requires something in return. A "feminine" economy, on the other hand, can bear separation—giving up what is its own—and promotes giving for the sake of establishing relationships that neither maintain the division of self and other nor effect the appropriation of the other. Cixous, like Nietzsche, links this economy of generosity to writing: *écriture féminine* becomes possible once the proprietary constraints on subjectivity have been cast off. Schrift's argument suggests, then, that Cixous is the kind of reader Nietzsche sought—one who accepts his gift, but does not feel obliged to return it in kind, one who acts on his writing, one who carries it on by transformatively deploying it.

If the pieces by Krell and Schrift articulate the dialogue between Nietzsche and feminist philosophy, Arkady Plotnitsky's essay can be seen (or *heard*) to show how that dialogue might put the very notion of feminist philosophy into question. "The Medusa's Ears: The Question of Nietzsche, the Question of Gender, and Transformations of Theory" begins by discussing, first, the ways in which transformations in the history of theoretical thinking in the twentieth century—marked, for example, by the writings of Bataille, Deleuze, and Derrida—have occurred under the sign and by way of Nietzsche, and, second, the decisive role these changes have had in feminist thought as well as, conversely, the effect of (post)modern feminism on those changes. Plotnitsky approaches this matrix of relations and transformations—which provides insight into the effect gender difference can have on the theoretical fields it infiltrates—via the question of the Medusa, which (as we have already seen by this point in the volume) informs much feminist thinking after Nietzsche, and the question of the ear (of the other), which figures prominently not only in Nietzsche but also in postmodern and feminist readings that relate to Nietzsche. Arguing that the question of Nietzsche's woman must be posed in relation to the question of the Dionysian and suggesting that the entire economy of the feminine in Nietzsche is related to the ear (of the other, of Medusa), the essay traces the focus on a Medusan/Dionysian economy of the ear in some of the most prominent readers of the feminine in Nietzsche: Cixous, Derrida, Irigaray, and Kofman. But the essay also suggests that readings inscribed at the juncture of post-Nietzschean theory and feminism, but still operating in a (deconstructive) field more or less within the closure of philosophy, might not sufficiently address the problems posed by the disturbing simultaneity in Nietzsche of apparently feminist propositions and vociferous antifeminism. The central question then becomes whether one can perform as powerful a critique of philosophy/ontotheology as Nietzsche and his deconstructive readers do *and* at the same time successfully approach the questions of woman, feminism, and gender—the suggestion being that such an approach might require first moving beyond that critique to a more radical departure from philosophy. In Cixous's call to "break out of the circles" Plotnitsky detects the (Nietzschean) intimation of such a move, of the idea that the question of gender and its history may be located outside the economy of philosophy, and he asks the question: Can there be a *philosophy* of gender? Thus Nietzsche, despite the gender-trap he built for himself, might still prove useful for feminism, since he, more even than his readers, offers the strategies for a radical break with philosophy.

"Digression"

Given the determined focus of this volume on the question of Nietzsche and the feminine, Laurence Rickels's essay may be taken to be a digression. "Insurance for and against Women: From Nietzsche to Psychotherapy" begins with a discussion of Sabina Spielrein's contribution to Freud's theories and to psychotherapy; it proceeds through investigations of Jung's notion of collective guilt in his response to Nazism, of the rise of the insurance industry, of the role of war in the formation and formulations of psychoanalytic theory, of Marx and Engels, of Mickey Mouse, of the relation among group psychology, war, and homosexuality, and of Adler's defense of equal rights for women; it ends by turning its attention to Kafka's insurance work; and there are many other stations along the way. However, the essay is also *not* a digression. Through his exploration of Nietzsche's significance for the development of psychoanalysis and psychotherapy, Rickels articulates a relation that the many references to Freud throughout the volume intimate as in some way critical to the question of Nietzsche and the feminine. This (Nietzschean) articulation is generated by the early inscription of Nietzsche into psychoanalytic theory via the voice of woman (Spielrein) and via his fixation on one figure of woman—the mother. In considering the consequences of that inscription, Rickels shows how psychotherapy both provides insurance *for* women—by including them in its institutional group—and at the same time, from the position of a masculine bias, theorizes neurosis as insurance *against* women—as a reflection of the need to protect the (masculine) self from the threat of difference/death represented by the (feminine) other. Woman introduces Nietzsche into the history of psychotherapy, and psychotherapy, in the name of Nietzsche, includes woman in its theory and practice.

Supplements

Benjamin Bennett's essay, "Bridge: Against Nothing," constitutes a commentary on what most of the essays preceding it might at least appear to do—namely, attempt to elucidate in one way or another the "meaning" of "woman"/"the feminine" in Nietzsche or the relation between Nietzsche's meaning and the meaning of feminism. Bennett's argument is that as long as we speak in terms of meaning, we are speaking within an established male discourse and precluding any feminist *use* of Nietzsche. "Bridge: Against Nothing" is about revolution; it operates on the premise that feminist thought is pointless if it is not revolutionary and that the various theoretical positions it assumes, because they are embedded in institutionalized discourse, bring feminism into complicity precisely with that which it is up against. Bennett echoes Nancy Miller's question—of what it means "to read and write as a woman within the institution that authorizes and regulates most reading and writing"—and asks whether there is any location within this institution that provides leverage for revolutionary feminist thought, for thought that would take feminism truly out on a limb with respect to the institution. Bennett argues that Nietzsche provides such leverage because

> in all of Nietzsche, the question of the reader's historical situation is crucial, and the question of the reader's *use* of the text in history. In later Nietzsche, however, this question becomes unanswerable. Precisely the situation of being a qualified reader, a reader addressed by

> the text and in a position to understand it, *denies* one the possibility of making any reasonable historical use of one's understanding. The text therefore becomes useless, except perhaps, paradoxically, from the point of view of the *disqualified* reader, the reader who is excluded from the text's projected community of understanding, the reader whom the text never speaks *to,* but only *about,* which means the (or a) woman. Thus the relation of women to the Nietzschean text occurs at exactly that point where the text develops . . . its free revolutionary leverage, the point of divorce . . . between the text's *use* and its understanding . . . between use and *meaning.*

The meaning of Nietzsche—for example, his many sexist remarks in *Beyond Good and Evil*—disqualifies woman as a reader of Nietzsche and thereby opens up his work to use by feminists. After outlining the disruption of the contiguity of meaning and use in the later Nietzsche, Bennett sets into play different readings (Derrida's and Sontag's) in an attempt to discover how Nietzsche can be used by feminists in a way that is divorced from any hypostatizable meaning of his texts. Such a use is achieved by Irigaray in *Amante marine*—to the extent that she, like Nietzsche, maintains the exclusionary force of an "I" that resists subsumption into an interpretive community and its hermeneutic order and that maintains the gender difference that disqualifies her as a reader. Bennett's essay itself, in its constant play of paradox and in its articulation of the hermeneutically impossible divorce of use from meaning, is, like the writing it addresses, out on a limb. "Bridge: Against Nothing" might be said to reinscribe this volume deconstructively; but when Bennett concludes that "only the multiple game of readings can conceivably liberate the revolutionary energies in Nietzsche," he also, in a sense, summarizes the volume.

Nietzsche and the Feminine begins and ends with *Ecce Homo.* It begins with Sarah Kofman's reading of *Ecce Homo* and its implications for Nietzsche's relation to woman, and it ends with Luce Irigaray's rewriting of *Ecce Homo* in the voice of (a) woman: "Ecce Mulier?"—a text *de* Nietzsche, but not his text. Many of the essays in the volume, particularly those that seem to go beyond commentary, resist introduction and outline, and I have resisted that resistance for the sake of the reader, or at least the reader's convenience. In the cases of Rickels and Bennett my resistance to allowing the texts to speak for themselves began giving way—for one I give a brief and uncharacteristically general summary, for the other a summary that succumbs to direct quotation from the text it summarizes. In Irigaray's case—the case of a text that goes to commentary's beyond—I give . . . up. Perhaps for my convenience. Perhaps because in a sense all of the essays in *Nietzsche and the Feminine,* especially the immediately preceding one, serve as introductions to Irigaray's text. Perhaps, and more likely, because *Ecce Mulier* must speak for itself.

Notes

1. Two of the essays, written for this volume, have in the meantime appeared elsewhere. Luce Irigaray's "Ecce Mulier?" appeared in an issue of the *Graduate Faculty Philosophy Journal* devoted to Nietzsche; the translation has been revised for publication here. Sarah Kofman's "A Fantastical Genealogy" is a chapter in her new book, *Explosion I* (1992), and appears here for the first time in translation.

2. Bruce Detwiler, *Nietzsche and the Politics of Aristocratic Radicalism* (Chicago: Univ. of Chicago Press, 1990), p. 193; my emphasis.

3. Manfred Thiel, *Nietzsche: Ein analytischer Aufbau seiner Denkstruktur* (Heidelberg: Elpis, 1980), p. 675.

4. Walter Kaufmann, *Nietzsche: Philosopher, Psychologist, Antichrist,* 3d ed. (Princeton: Princeton Univ. Press, 1968), p. 84.

5. It should be noted that the studies mentioned here are not the first that attempted to establish the question of woman in Nietzsche as a significant philosophical topic. Long before Kaufmann dismissed Nietzsche's statements on women as "philosophically irrelevant," Hellmut Brann, in 1931, called attention to the way in which early Nietzsche scholarship, as well as his contemporary Alfred Baeumler, had simplistically dismissed the importance of woman in Nietzsche's philosophy and he offered his book on *Nietzsche and Women* as proof of its significance: Hellmut Walther Brann, *Nietzsche und die Frauen* (Leipzig: Felix Meiner, 1931); for Brann's critique of Baeumler and the tendency to ignore the problem of woman in Nietzsche, see pp. 5–7.

6. Most of this work is described or commented on in one way or another in the course of this volume. For bibliographical references to the texts by Kofman, Derrida, Doane, Jardine, Oliver, Spivak, Ackermann, Schutte, Staten, Thomas, Irigaray, Krell, Graybeal, and Shapiro, see the Bibliography at the end of the volume.

7. This statement might seem to be contradicted by the fifty–one studies listed in the Bibliography, a number of which have appeared since this volume was first planned. However, many of these scattered studies address the issue only briefly, some even quite cursorily, and the number shrinks in significance when one considers that the MLA Bibliography for the last decade includes over a thousand studies that list Nietzsche as a subject.

8. Alexander Nehamas, *Nietzsche: Life as Literature* (Cambridge: Harvard Univ. Press, 1985), p. 15. While we cannot finally excuse Kaufmann for dismissing the philosophical relevance of Nietzsche's comments on woman, it would be fair to point out that part of the reason for that dismissal is that, when he wrote on Nietzsche, "woman" was not the issue for philosophy that it is today, due to the impact of feminism and poststructuralism in the intervening years.

9. R. Hinton Thomas, *Nietzsche in German Politics and Society, 1890–1918* (Manchester: Manchester Univ. Press, 1983), p. 140. See also: Henry Staten, *Nietzsche's Voice* (Ithaca: Cornell Univ. Press, 1990), pp. 171–72.

10. Indeed, in a later section of *Zarathustra,* "The Other Dancing Song," it is the

voice of Zarathustra himself that reminds us of the whip: " 'Keeping time with my whip, you shall dance and cry! Or have I forgotten my whip? Not I!' " Immediately following this, however, the voice of life, a woman's voice, admonishes Zarathustra not to crack the whip too ferociously: " 'Then life answered me thus, covering up her delicate ears: "O Zarathustra, don't crack your whip so frightfully! After all, you know that noise murders thought—and just now such tender thoughts are coming to me" ' " (KSA 4:284; Z p. 338).

11. This passage and the one preceding it call into question absolute statements, such as Thiel's, that for Nietzsche men occupy a higher rank than women (pp. 675–76).

12. The entire passage reads: "Someone took a youth to a sage and said: 'Look, he is being corrupted by women.' The sage shook his head and smiled. 'It is men,' said he, 'that corrupt women; and all the failings of women should be atoned by and improved in men. For it is man who creates for himself the image of woman, and woman forms herself according to this image' " (KSA 3:427; GS §68, p. 126).

13. The critique of essentialism, which is in line with Nietzsche's radical perspectivism, might also attenuate the virulence of one of his other famous misogynistic pronouncements: "Woman wants to become self-reliant—and for that reason she is beginning to enlighten men about 'woman as such': *this* is one of the worst developments of the general *uglification* of Europe" (KSA 5:170; BGE §232, p. 162).

14. On woman's deception in Nietzsche and in Derrida's reading of Nietzsche, see Mary Ann Doane, "Veiling Over Desire: Close-ups of the Woman," in *Feminism and Psychoanalysis,* ed. Richard Feldstein and Judith Roof (Ithaca: Cornell Univ. Press, 1989), pp. 119–26.

15. For more extensive discussions of the relation between woman and truth in Nietzsche, see the essays by Susan Bernstein and Bianca Theisen in this volume, the latter of which also addresses the essay "On Truth and Lie."

16. On the notion of going beyond philosophy, see the essay by Arkady Plotnitsky, and on the revolutionary quality of Nietzsche's thought, Benjamin Bennett's.

17. See especially the first chapter of *Nietzsche: Life as Literature:* "The Most Multifarious Art of Style," pp. 13–41.

18. Sarah Kofman, *Nietzsche et la métaphore* (Paris: Payot, 1972), p. 168.

19. For a discussion of the relation between Dionysus and Medusa, see Sarah Kofman's essay in this volume.

20. Another example of Nietzsche's moderation of his portrayal of woman as excess occurs in the passage from *The Gay Science* on the "*actio in distans*" that he calls women's "most powerful effect." Here Nietzsche locates women "beyond," but at the same time, in the lines I omitted when I first cited the passage, he brings women back from beyond: "When a man stands in the midst of his own noise, in the midst of his own surf of plans and projects, then he is apt also to see quiet, magical beings gliding past him and to long for their happiness and seclusion: *women.* He almost thinks that his better self dwells there among the women, and that in these quiet regions even the loudest surf turns into deathly quiet, and life itself into a dream about life. *Yet! Yet! Noble enthusiast, even on the most beautiful sailboat there is a lot of noise, and unfortunately much small and wretched noise.* [emphasis added] The magic and the most powerful effect of women is, in philosophical language, action at a distance, *actio in distans;* but this requires first of all and above all—*distance*" (KSA 3:424–25; GS §60, p. 124*). This simultaneous location of women both beyond and not beyond

reflects the conflation of excess and moderation contained in the phrase "an excess of subtle delight in sudden restraint."

21. On the metaphoricity of Nietzsche's philosophy, see, for example, Kofman's *Nietzsche et la métaphore.*

22. Cf. Ackermann, who addresses the complexity of Nietzsche's treatment of women, but in effect rescues him from his misogyny by arguing that he assigned no essence to woman: "If Nietzsche had assigned an essence to woman, the structural core of any misogyny, he would have fallen into contradiction with his views on Dionysian process and affirmation. Consistency with those views required Nietzsche to make the complex observations concerning women that he does" (Robert John Ackermann, *Nietzsche: A Frenzied Look* [Amherst: Univ. of Massachusetts Press, 1990], pp. 136–37).

23. Jacques Derrida, *Spurs: Nietzsche's Styles / Eperons: Les Styles de Nietzsche,* trans. Barbara Harlow (Chicago: Univ. of Chicago Press, 1979), p. 41.

24. Gayatri Chakravorty Spivak, "Displacement and the Discourse of Woman," in *Displacement: Derrida and After,* ed. Mark Krupnick (Bloomington: Indiana Univ. Press, 1983), pp. 169–95.

25. Diana Fuss, *Essentially Speaking: Feminism, Nature, and Difference* (New York: Routledge, 1989), p. 13.

PART ONE

Mothers

SARAH KOFMAN

A Fantastical Genealogy: Nietzsche's Family Romance

Everyone carries within him an image of woman that he gets from his mother; that determines whether he will honor women in general, or despise them, or be generally indifferent to them.

—Nietzsche, *Human, All Too Human*

The above aphorism from *Human, All Too Human* invites us to try to define Nietzsche's own image of his mother as decisive to the question of his relation to women. For such an inquiry, section 3 of *Ecce Homo*'s "Why I Am So Wise" is of primary importance and should in fact serve as a prolegomenon to any further reflection on the position of women in Nietzsche's work.

For the reader long accustomed to reading this passage entirely differently, the first reaction it produces is surprise. Until the recent edition made available to us by Colli and Montinari, the version now relegated to the notes was the only one known. The current text is from the manuscript found among the papers of Peter Gast, while the former version corresponds to a separate manuscript that had been more or less falsified by Nietzsche's sister, who censored, among other things, the venomous remarks—irreverent to say the least—that Nietzsche "spit" at her and her mother.[1]

In this text, to more firmly establish his "nobility" in the typological sense, Nietzsche attempts to anchor it in what he calls "race" (*Rasse*)[2]—precisely the concept that requires clarification here. On the one hand, in raising the so-called question of race (*die Frage der Rasse*), he at first seems to be speaking of a biological inheritance, which he refers to three times in the passage as "blood": "I am a noble *pur sang* Pole: not a drop of bad blood is mixed in my veins [*nicht ein Tropfen schlechtes Blut beigemischt ist*], and above all no German blood [*am wenigsten deutsches*]" (KSA 6:268). He insists on the purity of this blood, unadulterated by even a drop of the bad blood (typified by German blood) that might threaten its purity and quality. But on the other hand, the rest of the passage shows that the racial perspective overlaps with the typological, since by the expression "bad blood" he means the plebeian type, which he calls (in French, as he does the term *sang pur,*) *la canaille,* "the rabble";[3] and by the expression "good" and pure blood, he means the nobility.[4]

Nietzsche in fact slides from the issue of purity of blood to purity of instincts (his "Polish" atavism).[5] The purity of instincts amounts to the same thing as the "sovereign sense of distinction" (*ein souveraines Gefühl von Distinktion*) (KSA 6:268), which is to say, nobility in the typological sense. It is precisely this sense of refinement or distance that prevents him from limiting himself to a biological perspective, to blood or race in the common and racist sense of the words (even if the usage of these terms is not innocent—the terms "linger" as such and are susceptible to misinterpretation when taken up by a type of force less noble than Nietzsche). His sense of distinction constrains him to reject all kinship with his physiological relatives: this kind of relation would be physiological nonsense and a sign of baseness, of the absence of blood purity. "Kinship" is not a physiological "given" but something that rests on the will to be or not to be in a rapport of closeness or identification with those to whom one is closest physiologically: "It is with one's relatives that one has the *least* kinship [*Man ist am wenigsten mit seinen Eltern verwandt*]: being related to one's relatives [*seinen Eltern verwandt zu sein;* the French translation adds, "*wanting* to be related"] would be the worst sign of baseness" (KSA 6:268–69).

The corollary to this rejection is the invention of an entirely different kinship, the fiction of a fantasmatic genealogy, a true family romance in the quasi-Freudian sense of the term, since it is always a question, for Nietzsche as for the child making up a romance, of creating a more "noble" and illustrious family than the one from which one derives physiologically.[6] The elaboration that permits Nietzsche to pass from a physiological to a philosophical framework and to believe in his romance (or to make of it something other than a romance) hinges on the substitution of economic for "physiological" factors, which authorize him to confer upon himself the highest and oldest origin there is. But not without a certain note of humor, or irony, emphasizing that he is not the dupe of his own rationalizations, that he is noble enough to keep a distance from his own "familial" romance and its elaboration.

At first glance, however, the element that differentiates the Nietzschean "romance" from the neurosis described by Freud is that according to Freud the boy is much more likely to have hostile feelings against his father than his mother, and thus to have "a far more intense desire to get free from *him* than from *her*" ("Family Romances," p. 42). Whereas Nietzsche's text—at least in what it states openly—manifests a rejection of kinship above all with the mother and the maternal side of the "family." This rejection is formulated in terms so violent that it becomes suspect, and all the more surprising because in the former version of "Why I Am So Wise" it is the mother who is said to have bequeathed him life: he owes his father, according to the former version of the third section, all of his privileges with the exception of "life, the great Yes to life" (KSA 14:473; EH p. 226).

In rejecting his mother, then, is Nietzsche passing up life and its affirmation in favor of decadence and paternal morbidity? Hardly. First of all, the currently accepted version says nothing about his owing the affirmation of life to his mother. His mother, like his sister, is typologically classified on the side of the rabble, of "the immeasurable baseness of instincts" from which Nietzsche feels himself to be at the opposite pole. Furthermore, Nietzsche here pays homage to his father, a priest who was compared to an angel by the peasants to whom he preached, a delicate being representing God on earth, more celestial than terrestrial.[7] Nietzsche claims to have received his divine nature—which his mother and sister would blaspheme in their too terrestrial baseness if he did not deny all kinship with them—from his father, from whom he also claims to have received the system for evaluating decadence. He affirms that it is "a great privilege" (*ein grosses Vorrecht*) to have had such a father (the former version even says that this explains all his other privileges), despite the fact that the previous section ended by claiming that he was "the *opposite* of a decadent," and thus the opposite of his father.

A privilege is a right accorded to the nobility and to it alone: paradoxically, the source of Nietzsche's noble distinction is identified as paternal morbidity. The former version of the text specified that the father had unintentionally given him the gift of forthright entry into a world of delicate and lofty things where he would be truly "at home" (*zu Hause*), where his most intimate passions would have free range. This privilege of being "at home," exalted, nearly cost him his life, because the identification with the sickly father (Nietzsche at one point states that he is simply a new edition of his father)[8] led him to the lowest points of his vitality, reduced him to a shadowlike state. If he had not been basically healthy, the system of decadence might, for his sins, have had the best of him. Nevertheless, for Nietzsche the risks incurred do not represent too high a price for the privilege acquired in compensation: namely, that he, and *only* he, had understood Zarathustra and everything represented by this unheard-of ideal—the figure of the superman living in the crystallized air of the summits, at heights inaccessible to terrestrial beings. Nietzsche owes to his father, the pastor (who, in a certain sense, had gotten him pregnant), the fact that he had been able to bring into the world the inventor of the only counterideal sufficiently potent to combat the dominant ascetic ideal. Only someone who, like himself, had kept one foot *beyond* life by incorporating the father could have pushed the ascetic ideal and its moral code far enough to make them reverse direction and transform into their opposites. Someone who, initially, had been secretly wounded by each of the words of Zarathustra and thus was capable of understanding them. The original Zarathustra could transform himself into the new one—into Nietzsche's Zarathustra, the child of love, child of sin, who weighs on his conscience because, far from paying his debt to his father through him, he denies the father at the very moment when he seems to be filled with gratitude toward him. *Zarathustra* is the work of a regenerate, of someone who had already had one foot in the tomb and then finds himself cured of a long illness. Thus he does not owe the passion of the "Yes" par excellence to his mother but to his father, and precisely because his father had not given it to him as such. In the chapter consecrated to *Zarathustra* he asserts that in order to understand this ideal he needs a single but essential thing: *triumphant health*. Is this contradictory? In fact, being triumphantly healthy implies having been ill and having been able to overcome the illness. A conquest to be endlessly reconquered. The paternal legacy is the inheritance of the values of everything great and lofty, even if the son does not mean the same things by the same words, and perhaps even the opposite of what the father had meant. The preservation of the old words is like a path, a remnant of the system of paternal evaluations that Nietzsche, after having pushed them to their extremes, reverses.

While his mother is trampled underfoot and made party to the basest values, his father is positioned on the side of everything exalted, and of everything that had taught the son the true meaning of loftiness. But Nietzsche only exalts his father the better to "kill" him, because in making use of the term *loftiness* he gives it an entirely opposite meaning. Furthermore, he can only conserve his kinship with his father by reconnecting him genealogically to more or less fantasmatically noble stock. Which is to say that Nietzsche's family romance actually is true to Freud's understanding of the term. Freud distinguishes a second stage that takes place when the child learns of the difference between the father and the mother with respect to sexuality: "When presently the child comes to know the various kinds of sexual relations between fathers and mothers and realizes that '*pater semper incertus est,*' while the mother is '*certissima,*' the family romance undergoes a peculiar curtailment: it contents itself with exalting the child's father, but no longer casts any doubt on his maternal origin, which is regarded as something unalterable . . . the motive force behind this being his desire to bring his mother (who is the subject of the most intense sexual curiosity) into situations of secret infidelity and into secret love-affairs" (Freud, "Family Romances," pp. 43–44).

When Nietzsche rejects his mother, it is not to ennoble her. In the former version of the text he says that his mother, Franziska Oehler, is "*certainly* something extremely German" (KSA 14:472; EH p. 225*; my emphasis), while the present version assimilates German blood to the *canaille* or "lowlife," to "the immeasurable baseness of instincts" (KSA 6:268). If he cannot deny his kinship with her, because *semper mater certissima est,* he denies all typological kinship, claiming to be of noble Polish descent (and not, we can be sure, of Jewish origin, since, as *The Antichrist* reveals, he feels no racial affinity with the Polish Jews, who smell as bad, he asserts, as Christians).

What proofs does Nietzsche bring forward to support the "truth" of his romance? First, a typological proof that actually begs the question: he recognizes in his blood many instincts that can only have been passed down to him by a noble race. But why the Polish race? Because, he asserts, it fundamentally possesses the instinct of *liberum veto* as it had been exercised by the nobles in the Polish Diet, where a single veto had the right to reverse the vote of the entire Diet. In *Beyond Good and Evil,* a similar right is said to have been exercised already by "the Pole Copernicus," who, with a single word, changed the course of the stars. Something of Copernicus apparently came down to Nietzsche in his blood, since he took as his own task and destiny the reversal of values and the beginning of a new era for humanity. The other proof furnished (again in the former version) is purely factual and empirical: that he was often taken for a Pole (even by Poles themselves) while traveling, whereas he was rarely taken for a German.[9] One Pole apparently even suggested that he came from the family of the Nietzki counts, banished from Poland for political and religious conspiracy. This argument was bolstered in Nietzsche's eyes by the fact that he was born in a region of Thuringia that had been separated from the Saxon kingdom in 1815. Prussian by virtue of a thirty-year-old annexation, Nietzsche was a Thuringian Saxon from the upper Saxony wrested from three Slavic peoples, including the Poles, by Germanic colonists. The important thing here obviously is not the "reality" but the fantasy of such an origin on the paternal side, at the expense of the German side, the undeniable and intolerable "something extremely German" in his mother. To be German at the time was essentially to be a subject of the Reich—by which he means, to be limited to a purely local and national parochialism, a single and narrow perspective—while his own origin gives him at least a double, if not a triple, outlook. This distance with regard to any single perspective permits him to be an *antipolitical* German, a man without a country, a "good European." What is inconceivable for the Germans of the day is not so for Nietzsche, who thereby enjoys a special connection to the one European German for whom he can feel respect: Goethe.[10] Therefore, while he rejects his rigidly German mother, he makes much of his paternal grandmother, Erdmuthe Krause, who, although also German, was able to transcend the strictly national limitations: having grown up in Weimar she had had some contact with the circle surrounding Goethe. Nietzsche even considers it plausible that the name "Muthgen" in Goethe's journal may have referred to his grandmother. It is from his grandmother that Nietzsche would have inherited his admiration for Napoleon: after her second marriage to the superintendent Nietzsche in Eilenburg she gave birth, probably in the grip of emotion, to Nietzsche's father on the day that Napoleon entered Eilenburg in 1813. True or not, Nietzsche emphasizes this coincidence in order to associate the birth of his father (on October 10, while Nietzsche was born October 15—a temporal proximity that reinforced the possibility of identification) with the arrival of the great man who would be one of the models of the superman and whom Nietzsche, parodying theology, calls an *ens realissimum*. The coincidence and the association betray the fact that for the child Nietzsche, his father also must have been an *ens realissimum*, a great man or a superman, ennobled and aggrandized in the typological sense by the presence of this other great man the day of his birth, as though he had been infected by the type Napoleon represented.

The brief narrative of Nietzsche's father's life particularly underscores his contact with nobility, with the four princesses whom he taught before becoming a pastor. Nietzsche revels in enumerating their names and titles, as if the contact with these queens and duchesses had granted his father something of their distinction and their sense of greatness, etiquette, and hierarchy, which Nietzsche then inherited. All the more so in that, just as the father's birth had occurred under the sign of the great man, the son's coincided with the anniversary of the birth of King Frederick William IV, from whom his father had received his pastorship and whom he particularly venerated. Given the almost obsessional importance accorded by Nietzsche to dates of birth, it is not surprising that he should have emphasized such a quasi-miraculous coincidence: not only because during his childhood his birthday was a school holiday, but above all because the dates facilitate his identification with the royal personage and his nobility, and especially because he had also received one of the king's given names.

Thus everything played out for Nietzsche as if his father's birth and his own were connected to great men through nonaccidental links. As if life's coincidences had grafted the body of Nietzsche's father onto the body of Napoleon, and Nietzsche's onto that of Frederick William IV, king of Prussia, inscribing the father into the lineage of great men and the son into a lineage of kings. In both cases, such "grafts" helped to erase the purely German character of Nietzsche's origins. The mention of Napoleon, Frederick William IV, and Goethe together in one section of *Beyond Good and Evil* underscores one of the points they had in common for Nietzsche: the shared opinion that true Germans, worthy of the name, no longer existed, because true men no longer existed. King Frederick William IV looked for men and said "*men were lacking*." His own son did not escape his suspicion. On which point he was mistaken, Nietzsche notes: the king had confused the virility of his son's skepticism (of the same character as Nietzsche's skepticism) with "the great blood-sucker, the spider skepticism," even though, according to Nietzsche, "the skepticism of audacious manliness, which is related most closely to the genius for war and conquest . . . first entered Germany in the person of the great Frederick." He was characterized by "intrepidity of eye," "bravery and sternness of dissecting hand," and a "tenacious will for voyages of discovery," and was described as a fatalistic, ironic, and Mephistophelean spirit, capable of rousing Europe from its " 'dogmatic slumber.' " At the end of the same passage Nietzsche cites Napoleon's comment about Goethe: " '*Voilà un homme!*' " (KSA 5 : 142; BGE §209, p. 133). (Napoleon's astonishment was not surprising, since he knew the Germans above all through Madame de Staël, whose book *De l'Allemagne* described them as pleasant, inoffensive, easy-going and poetic rustics.)

While in the first version of the text Nietzsche's German origins are not completely denied, this is only because he had started out by trying to ennoble the paternal branch of the family. He could only accept his affiliation to this branch after having transformed it, through an extensive game of coincidences judged to be noncoincidental, from the German into the European and then the European into the complete man, the superman. Which is to say, only after emphasizing the distance separating the Germans in his family from the Germans of the contemporary Reich.

This transformative gesture applies beginning with the generation of his paternal grandparents, to whom he can recognize his relatedness without feeling demeaned. Thus his family "history" or "romance" permits him to induce a general law: "One is much more the child of one's four grandparents than of one's two parents" (KSA 12:359).

In the Colli and Montinari version, the "double" character "flecked" with the Germanic that Nietzsche attributes to his double heritage, and which provides access to a double series of experiences and to two antipodal worlds, is effaced to support the "purity" of his blood, allegedly free of even a drop of German blood, of "bad" blood, of the *canaille*. (This term, coined by the French nobility at the time of the Revolution to register the depth of its scorn for the populace and its vile origins, is taken up by Nietzsche against his mother and sister to establish an immeasurable distance between them and himself, as a nobleman distinguished by a divine nature.) Just as, despite his divine nature, Christ was crucified between two robbers, blasphemed by the Jews who condemned his divinity to a torture "which was in general reserved for the *canaille* alone" (KSA 6:213; A §40, p. 614*), the divine Nietzsche would feel ridiculed, blasphemed, and crucified in the bosom of his biological family. In contrast to Christ's willingness to be assimilated into the rabble, Nietzsche is compelled to protect himself from this form of torture and its attendant risk of contamination by rejecting all kinship with his mother and sister. Yet he disqualifies them in terms whose violence could unknowingly betray his relatedness to this *canaille* or "venomous vermin" (*giftiges Gewürm*) from which he is trying to defend himself; all the more so since it is with them that the proximity is greatest and the most dangerous.

Because of the *baseness* of their instincts, his mother and sister are his antipodes. Taken in the moral sense, this would signify that they are incapable of any moral "exaltation," that they are interested only, like the robbers flanking Christ, in satisfying their drives, their bodily needs, the belly, sex.[11] Yet nothing justifies acceptance of this sense of the term. Everything indicates, on the contrary, that the expression "baseness of instincts" should be read in the typological sense, the sense meant in noble morality: in this context the mother and sister represent a froglike worldview, flattening everything lofty and great. Not that Nietzsche settles for a mere typological disqualification. Mother and sister are not treated as frogs but as "venomous vermin." Despite the fact that Nietzsche had always described the perspective of the low to the high in terms of "crawling," with the expression "venomous vermin" he seems to shift to another register. More than the simple description of a point of view with which he is in opposition, it amounts to an outright insult referring back to an entire fantasmatic framework. The term *vermin* evokes a swarming and proliferating population of which one must, with great difficulty, rid oneself. Hitler found no better image to justify the total extermination of the Jews, as repugnant to his eyes as lice to be crushed. To be sure, the term *venomous* added on to "vermin" does displace this meaning somewhat. More than just lice, Nietzsche evokes dreadful-tongued serpents who wound cruelly and infallibly, disarming the victim of any strength for self-defense. Nietzsche sees himself, basically, as the victim of a plot hatched by the two women against him: the sureness of their sting, of their choice of the optimal moment to penetrate his vulnerability, implies a truly "infernal machination" (*Höllenmaschine*). In their "venomous" aspect they are fearsome and dangerous; as "vermin" they arouse repugnance and horror above all. This "horror" is so "unspeakable" (*unsägliches Grauen*) that it can only be the flip side of a more or less forbidden love, for which it functions as a counterinvestment. Among other writings, Nietzsche's correspondence, from his youth but also from his last years, testifies to this love.

In a letter to his sister of 23 March 1887, Nietzsche says that for him to marry would be an "act of *folly*" because he had not found a woman suited to his temperament. With no transition, he moves on: "The Lama was a good housemate for whom I can find no substitute, but it wanted to vent its energy and to sacrifice itself. For whom? For a miserable foreign race of men, who will not even thank her—and not for me. And I would be such a grateful animal, and always ready for merry laughter. Are you still able to laugh at all?"[12]

Nietzsche alludes to his sister's pan-German activities, tinged to a greater or lesser degree with anti-Semitism, which for him would always reveal "ressentiment" rather than spontaneous aggressive force.[13] His declaration of horror thus can be understood as a product of his disappointment in the face of family conduct for which he would not want his name to serve as backing, from which he attempts to dissociate himself by denying all "kinship" with his mother and sister. But he experiences such violent negative sentiment only because he loves his sister in such a way that, at the thought of marriage, his "dear Lama" comes to mind. His incestuous love for his sister and mother is replaced by an unspeakable horror that serves as its conscious *Ersatz.* But beyond this split in Nietzsche's affect, ambivalence also resurfaces in the "theoretical" judgments he makes concerning women, and which originate, he claims, in decisive images of the mother: "Whenever a cardinal problem is at stake, there speaks an unchangeable 'This is I'; about man and woman, for example, a thinker cannot relearn but only finish learning—only discover ultimately how this is 'settled in him' [*feststeht*]. . . . After this polite gesture, which I have just made at my own expense, I shall perhaps be permitted more readily to state a few truths about 'woman as such'—assuming that it is now known from the outset how very much these are after all only—*my* truths" (KSA 5:170; BGE §231, p.162*); "Everyone carries within him an image of woman that he gets from his mother; that determines whether he will honor women in general, or despise them, or be generally indifferent to them" (KSA 2:265; HATH §380, p. 195).[14]

In *Ecce Homo,* the violence of Nietzsche's statements against his mother and sister was sufficiently unbearable for them that they attempted censorship. For only Nietzsche's negative feelings and his insistence on the insurmountable difference between the two women and himself, beyond (and because of) their excessive closeness, were emphasized. In order to defend himself from a hyperprotective symbiotic relationship (it was his mother, after all, who offered him his first umbrella, advising him not to forget it, especially when it rained!),[15] Nietzsche is compelled to establish a distance that is marked empirically by the forgetting of his umbrella, and philosophically by a theory in which, parodying Leibniz, he institutes what he calls a "*disharmonia praestabilita*" between his mother and sister and himself.[16]

If we are to believe an aphorism from *Human, All Too Human,* this disharmony with the clan of women is the repetition of an unresolved disharmony between the two parents; as such it marks, once again, the Nietzschean will to protect his father's life within himself. "Unresolved dissonances in the relation of the character and disposition of the parents continue to reverberate in the nature of the child, and constitute his inner sufferings" (KSA 2:265; HATH §379, p.195).

The world in which Nietzsche could coexist with his mother and sister would not be, as in Leibniz, the best of all possible worlds: Nietzsche could never desire the eternal return of such a world. In fact, he gets to the point of wishing to retract his concept of "eternal return"—his most profound, most "abysmal" thought (*eigentlich abgründlicher Gedanke*)—at the very idea that his mother and sister could also return eternally: *horribile visu!* He recoils, seized with an unspeakable horror, exactly as Zarathustra shuddered at the idea of the eternal return of the weak: "'Alas, man recurs eternally! The small man recurs eternally!'" (KSA 4:274; Z p. 331).

"Exactly as"? This comparison, in fact, begs to be nuanced: his mother and sister are not a neutral example among others; within the "human, all too human" type they are, properly speaking, not "small men" but "small women," who seek to emasculate him, to castrate him, leaving him without strength or defense in his "highest moments," which they cannot help but reduce to the measure of their baseness. This indicates that Nietzsche's horror at his mother and sister is akin to the horror experienced at the sight of Medusa's head, the symbol of castration according to Freud, who uses the same term as Nietzsche: *Grauen*.[17] As if devastated by these two women, Nietzsche recoils at the idea that such a vision of horror could return eternally. But it is not only Freud's text with the usage of the same term *Grauen* that leads to the evocation of Medusa's head: a draft of *Zarathustra*, nothing of which remains in the definitive text, relates the concept of eternal return to Medusa's head.[18] This capital concept would threaten to decapitate Nietzsche if he did not defend himself immediately through the erection of another head, that of Dionysus, which functions apotropaically,[19] and about which he says, as if joking, that he has received one at the very moment at which he is writing, by mail (KSA 6:269).[20] A head of Dionysus for a head of Medusa. The concept of eternal return, understood as the eternal return of the same, in which the mother and sister would return as they were, eternally, cannot, any more than woman's sex or the Medusa, be regarded head-on without threat of annihilation. Only another truly Dionysian concept of eternal return, in which the world of becoming is conceived as the eternal return of difference, can surmount the horror provoked by the idea of the eternal return of the same, which goes hand in glove with death in that it annihilates all thought of the future, of newness, and of selection in the return. Only the head of Dionysus thus erected can triumph over Medusa's head. It is remarkable that this text from *Ecce Homo* reverses the relation established in *The Birth of Tragedy* between Dionysus and Medusa's head. There, Medusa's head plays an apotropaic role of defense against the terrifying and brutal depth of the Dionysian. Apollo, in order to triumph over his brother/enemy Dionysus, confronts him with Medusa's head: this alone, reflected in the mirror of Apollonian beauty, can vanquish Dionysus, petrified by his own image as reflected in his double. Only an artistically veiled Medusa, perceived as if in a dream or in a mirror, could combat a horrific Medusa, shorn of all veils and thus as one with Dionysus. Thus, Apollo against Dionysus would be the combat of one Medusa against another, in their intimately related enmity.[21]

One understands after this how it is that in *Ecce Homo,* Dionysus, who is as one with the Medusa shorn of every Apollonian veil, is able, in his turn, to play the apotropaic role against Medusa's head, against a notion of eternal return which, conceived of as a return of the same, still remains an excessively Apollonian cover-up of the "truth," protecting against its terrifying abyss, against the world of differences, of contradictions, and of death.

Thus Nietzsche defends himself against his mother and sister by exhibiting a head of Dionysus as a defensive shield against all kinship with them, claiming as a last resort that his only "real relative" is Dionysus. The whole conclusion of the passage consists, in effect, of an attempt to cancel out the atrocious evocation of his mother and sister by establishing an immeasurable distance, both spatial and temporal, between them and himself, through the fiction of an "origin going back infinitely further" (*Ursprung unendlich weiter zurück*). He goes back to his Polish atavism to emphasize the truly exceptional character of his nobility. It would be necessary "to go back centuries" (*Jahrhunderte zurückzugehn*) to find the equivalent of the nobility and kinship of instincts that he incarnates, marked not by a physiological or social trait but by a typological characteristic: his sovereign sense of distinction. This places him much higher than what in his own day calls itself "noble," whether in Poland or Germany, noble only in name (and for Nietzsche the name itself, "*noblesse,*" only expresses its real meaning when heard in French).

As if by bravado he compares himself to the highest in the land, the young German emperor William II, asserting that in terms of nobility the emperor would not be worthy of being his coachman, in other words, of carrying out the most subordinate of functions, generally reserved for the populace. (Just as he had stated that the poets of the Veda were not worthy of untying the sandal straps of a Zarathustra [KSA 6:343; EH p. 304]. And for the same reasons: Nietzsche's grandeur or nobility, like that of his "son," cannot be measured by any other grandeur or nobility, even by the greatest of the great, the most noble of the noble.)

However, after having distanced himself from everyone because of his singular nature, unrelated to anything human (he had alluded, previously, to his divine nature), Nietzsche then extends a gesture of reconciliation to the only human beings with whom he can accept closeness, kinship, a certain reciprocity—as if he had gone too far in the exhibition of his singular pathos. He feels he can "share parity" (*meines Gleichen anerkenne*) without degradation with, first of all, a woman, *Frau* Cosima Wagner, "by far" (*bei Weitem*) "the most noble nature" (*die vornehmste Natur*); and then, even if the avowal is costly for him, with Richard Wagner, the man to whom he is "by far" (*bei Weitem*) the "most closely related" (*verwandteste Mann war*) (KSA 6:268). This fantasmatically reconstituted parental couple with which Nietzsche surrounds himself is set in desert solitude, standing up to its full height far from everyone, like a building of grand style. Putting his "parents" at such an exalted height permits the child to have them all for himself, to isolate them from the rest of the world—concerning which silence is the best response, since to "speak about it" would already mean being contaminated, vulgarized, by this "scum." Within the couple, despite the repetition of certain terms emphasizing the symmetry established between the substitutive "mother" and "father" (they are both *bei Weitem,* "by far," the most noble and the nearest to Nietzsche), Nietzsche nevertheless introduces a dissymmetry in favor of Madame Cosima Wagner. She is cited first and spoken of in the present tense: she "is" (*ist*) still and always the most noble nature, while Richard Wagner comes up second and in the past; with a kind of melancholic nostalgia not only because he is no longer living and thus can only be spoken of in the past, but because this confession on Nietzsche's part (following his frequent assertions that Wagner, as an example of the decadent type, was his antipode) can only emphasize his denial of this man who, as if under the effect of old age and Schopenhauer at the end of his life, had taken for his own usage the mask of the ascetic ideal. It must be added that this "confession" concerning the kinship with Wagner, placed at Cosima's side, conceals, even in revealing, the love rivalry between the two men, both taken with this woman who was quite possibly the real cause of Nietzsche's rupture or divorce with the man he claims as his closest relation. It is to Cosima, the only woman he admits to having venerated in his life, that Nietzsche sends the first copy of *Ecce Homo*. This narrative written to "himself" was above all written as a gift to her, a token of gratitude.[22] It is to her, under the name of the fiancée of Dionysus, the Princess Ariadne, his beloved (KSA—Briefe 8:572),[23] that he sends a declaration that is no longer of veneration but of love: "Ariadne, I love you." Ariadne of whom he says in *Ecce Homo,* in the section on Zarathustra, that he is the only one who understands her, who possesses the key to this enigma, because he is the only one to have suspected that there was an enigma behind this name: that of the suffering of the god Dionysus and his "solar solitude" (KSA 6:348; EH p. 308).

After jumping from his Polish atavism to his relation with the Wagners (who are more noble than the most noble Poles), Nietzsche continues to distance himself from his physiological kin in developing the fiction of an origin "loftier still," farther away in time, more ancient. He sets it in the most exalted Greco-Roman antiquity, where Julius Caesar or Alexander, which is to say Dionysus, since Alexander is allegedly the very incarnation of this god (*oder Alexander, dieser leibhafte Dionysos*),[24] could be his father. Certainly, Nietzsche does not present this genealogy *seriously,* as is stressed in the choice offered between Caesar and Alexander (the "or," *oder,* is in italics) and in the identification of these great men with Dionysus, as well as in the ironic avowal that he "doesn't really understand" how it is that one of his heroes could be his "father" (KSA 6:269). If one takes this term seriously, in the sense of "real" kinship, it would be essentially incomprehensible. But, enigmatically, and as if making a mockery of himself and his pretention to such a lofty and distant origin, Nietzsche wants to make it understood that true kinship is not of a physiological but a typological order. If he comes from a line of descent that dispenses him from any need for glory,[25] it is because he has, through identification, inscribed himself into the most exalted stock, passing over geographical frontiers and breaking with any spatiotemporal coordinates: he has given himself as ancestors Zoroaster, Moses, Mohammed, Jesus, Plato, Spinoza, Heraclitus, Goethe, and Pascal, in addition to Caesar, Alexander, and Dionysus. What does this say if not that he had always preexisted in them, that he lived in them in an embryonic state before being born as himself? Before surging forth to the light and to maturity as "Nietzsche," many a thing needed to ripen, elsewhere, for some thousands of years. Nietzsche the individual represents great individuality because he is the explosion into daylight of a huge quantity of accumulated forces, amassed and held in (*gesammelt, gespart, gehäuft*) over the centuries, elsewhere: the most exalted natures can have only the most distant origins. Conversely, the basest natures can feel related to those with whom they share the closest blood bond in time and space: they needed no ripening.

In order to deny all connection and affinity with those closest to him, in favor of exclusively "elective affinities," Nietzsche substitutes an economic hypothesis for biological or racial hypotheses of kinship. Birth is conceived as the result of an accumulation of energy necessitating the build up of a capital that will burst forth or explode all the more strongly for the time it is kept in check. Time permits the selection of the most forceful force, and the elimination of all the rest. In earlier writings, to present himself as a well-formed individual, Nietzsche already used the metaphor of capital; he instinctively amasses his own capital in everything that he sees, hears, and experiences; he is an active principle of selection, eliminating much along the way. In effect, "ontogeny" recapitulates "phylogeny." In the course of any particular life, the individual undergoes a process of accumulation and selection that permits him to mature into himself, just as the accumulation and selection of forces over the course of time permit the coming into maturity, the explosion, of great men, of what Nietzsche calls "genius," his conception of which is described in *Twilight of the Idols* (KSA 6:145–46; TI pp. 547–48).

Here, Nietzsche goes against both the Hegelian idea in which the genius is called forth by the spirit of the time and the era and the metaphysical idea of the genius as a perfectly original being: Nietzsche's economic hypothesis allows him to affirm that the great man is an outcome and an endpoint, and that a long work of accumulation was necessary for his coming: "*My conception of genius.* Great men, like great ages, are explosives in which a tremendous force is stored up; their precondition is always, historically and physiologically, that for a long time much has been gathered, stored up, saved up, and conserved for them—that there has been no explosion for a long time. Once the tension in the mass has become too great, then the most accidental stimulus suffices to summon into the world the 'genius,' the 'deed,' the great destiny" (KSA 6:145; TI p. 547). The example used is Napoleon.

Because the birth of a work of art is also the birth of a gifted child, Nietzsche uses the same economic hypothesis to understand it. Thus, against Schopenhauer, he shows that the work of art draws on all the reserves and supplements of the force and vigor of animal life: aesthetic creation does not result from a suspension of desire, particularly of sexual desire; nor is it the result of sublimation, although it does involve accumulation and retention, selection; the strongest force, in this case the aesthetic drive, putting the weaker at its service.[26]

The "economic" conception allows comprehension of the apparently incomprehensible: that Nietzsche could have Julius Caesar or Alexander (Dionysus) as a father. It is obviously not just chance that Nietzsche chooses these two ancestors rather than other "great individuals" of equal antiquity. Perhaps he does so, not without irony, to stress a secret kinship with Hegel, whose conception of the "genius" he opposes, but not the choice of those he names as geniuses; Hegel also, in his *Lessons on History,* cites Caesar and Alexander among the great men used by the cunning of reason to reach its ends. In any case, the Nietzschean texts in which Caesar and Alexander appear as privileged figures of superhumanity are numerous indeed, most often associated with Napoleon, although here they are isolated from Napoleon, probably because for Nietzsche to attach his origins to Napoleon would not permit him to go back far and high enough.[27]

Perhaps this is also because, if Napoleon is a Caesar in Nietzsche's eyes, he is a Caesar gone bad, corrupted by the means he had to employ, and thereby shorn of the nobility of his character. Despite the "splendid radiance of the individual," and despite the fact that Nietzsche approves of Napoleon sufficiently to pardon him this corruption by attributing it to the men who surrounded him, he could not make this "*ens realissimum*" an equal of Caesar and Alexander, an incarnation of Dionysus.

Or perhaps, ultimately, it was because Napoleon didn't like women enough . . .

Translated by Deborah Jenson

Notes

1. Tracy B. Strong informs me that he has taken this new version into account and has translated it in an article entitled "Oedipus as Hero: Family and Family Metaphors in Nietzsche," in *Why Nietzsche Now? A Boundary 2 Symposium*, ed. Daniel O'Hara, *Boundary 2* 9, no. 3 and 10, no. 1 (1981): 311–35 [Strong's translation can be found at 327–28. —Ed.]. [Translator's note: For Mazzino Montinari's remarks on the "new" section 3 of *Ecce Homo*'s "Why I Am So Wise," which Kofman makes the centerpiece of this essay, see his "Ein neuer Abschnitt in Nietzsches *Ecce Homo*" *Nietzsche-Studien* 1 (1972): 380–418. References here to the new version in English are my translation.]

2. "I consider it a great privilege to have had such a father. . . . Which leads me to the question of race" (KSA 6:267–68).

3. "To believe that I am related to these *canaille* or lowlife types would be blasphemy of my divine nature" (KSA 6:268).

4. This call to purity of race and blood, isolated from the typological context that displaces its "racial" and indeed racist import, could bolster the biologizing interpretations and exploitation of Nietzsche by the Nazis. Yet they differ from him, at the very least, in their reversal of the relation of good to bad, since for them it is German blood that is fundamentally pure and good.

5. "But also as a Pole I embody a formidable atavism. One would have to go back centuries to find this most noble of the world's races in a state as pure of instinct as I represent it" (KSA 6:268).

6. See Sigmund Freud, "Family Romances" (1908), in *The Sexual Enlightenment of Children* (New York: Collier, 1963), p. 43: "The child's imagination becomes engaged in the task of getting free from the parents of whom he now has such a low opinion and of replacing them by others, occupying, as a rule, a higher social station." And, further on: "a phantasy in which both his parents are replaced by others of better

birth." Further references to Freud's "Family Romances" will be given parenthetically in the text.

7. "The peasants to whom he preached—for after having lived some years at the Court of Altenburg, he was a pastor in the last years of his life—said this is what an angel must be like" (KSA 6:267–68).

8. "I am merely my father once more and, as it were, his continued life after an all-too-early death" (KSA 6:271; EH p. 228).

9. See Nietzsche's letter to Georg Brandes of 10 April 1888 (*Sämtliche Briefe: Kritische Studienausgabe in 8 Bänden,* ed. Giorgio Colli and Mazzino Montinari [Berlin/Munich: de Gruyter/dtv, 1986], 8:288; cited hereafter as KSA—Briefe). For a more general background on Nietzsche's alleged Polish ancestry, see Charles Andler, *Nietzsche, sa vie et sa pensée* (Paris: Gallimard, 1958), vol. 1.

10. See §4 of "What the Germans Lack," in *Twilight of the Idols* (KSA 6:106–7; TI pp. 508–9). See also the "Introduction" to my *Explosion I: De l'"Ecce Homo" de Nietzsche* (Paris: Galilée, 1992), pp. 11–43, especially pp. 19–20.

11. According, at least, to Pasolini's very interesting and striking film "La Ricotta."

12. *Selected Letters of Friedrich Nietzsche,* ed. Oscar Levy (Garden City, N.Y.: Doubleday, 1921), pp. 193–94. [This letter of 23 March 1887, from Nietzsche in Nice to his sister in Paraguay, was published by Elisabeth Förster-Nietzsche in her edition of her brother's letters to herself and her mother—*Friedrich Nietzsches Briefe an Mutter und Schwester* (Leipzig: Insel, 1909), 2:715–17—and has been included in various editions and translations, such as that by Levy cited here. However, Schlechta omitted the letter and pointed out that it is among those for which there is no original, but rather only texts written in the sister's hand or based on her editorial activity; see the appendix to *Friedrich Nietzsche: Werke in drei Bänden,* ed. Karl Schlechta (Munich: Hanser, 1956), 3:1410–11. Following Schlechta, Colli and Montinari omit the letter from their edition of Nietzsche's complete letters; see KSA—Briefe 1:vii. —Ed.]

13. "*Ressentiment* . . . this plant blooms best today among anarchists and anti-Semites" (KSA 5:309; GM—II §11, p. 73).

14. For a commentary on these passages, see Sarah Kofman, "Baubô: Theological Perversion and Fetishism," in *Nietzsche's New Seas: Explorations in Philosophy, Aesthetics, and Politics,* ed. Michael Allen Gillespie and Tracy B. Strong (Chicago: Univ. of Chicago Press, 1988), pp. 175–202.

15. See Nietzsche's letter to his maternal grandparents of 1 November 1857 (KSA—Briefe 1:12) and the letter to his mother of 2 February 1871 (KSA—Briefe 3:180).

16. See the aphorism "I have forgotten my umbrella" (KSA 9:587) and Derrida's reading of it in *Spurs: Nietzsche's Styles / Eperons: Les Styles de Nietzsche,* trans. Barbara Harlow (Chicago: Univ. of Chicago Press, 1979), pp. 122–43.

17. See Freud, "Medusa's Head," in *Sexuality and the Psychology of Love* (New York: Collier, 1963), pp. 212–13: "To decapitate: to castrate. The terror of Medusa is thus a terror of castration that is linked to the sight of something. . . . Medusa's head takes the place of a representation of the female genitals."

18. See Bernard Pautrat, "Nietzsche médusé," in *Nietzsche aujourd'hui? (Colloque de Cerisy)* (Paris: Union générale d'éditions, 1973), 1:9–30.

19. "The sight of the Medusa's head makes the spectator stiff with terror, turns him to stone. . . . For becoming stiff means an erection. Thus in the original situation

it offers consolation to the spectator: he is still in possession of a penis, and the stiffening reassures him of this fact. . . . it may be recalled that displaying the genitals is familiar in other connections as an apotropaic act. . . . To display the penis (or any of its surrogates) is to say: 'I am not afraid of you. I defy you. I have a penis.' Here, then, is another way of intimidating the Evil Spirit" (Freud, "Medusa's Head," pp. 212–13).

20. Bernoulli relates Kurt Hezel's account of the "Dionysian" Rosalie Nielsen, one of Nietzsche's acquaintances from the period in which he lived in Basel: "As a souvenir of my student days I still possess a photograph dedicated to me by Madame Nielsen, of a curious head of Dionysus (a photo of a sculpture). . . . Madame Nielsen claimed to have received this photograph from Nietzsche in person" (Carl Albrecht Bernoulli, *Franz Overbeck und Friedrich Nietzsche: Eine Freundschaft* [Jena: Diederichs, 1908], 1:117; cf. also Curt Paul Janz, *Friedrich Nietzsche: Biographie* [Munich: dtv, 1981], 1:549).

21. See section 2 of *The Birth of Tragedy* (KSA 1:32; BT §2, p. 39), as well as section 3 of the essay "The Dionysian Worldview" ("Die dionysische Weltanschauung," KSA 1:568).

22. See Nietzsche's letter to Cosima Wagner of (ca.) 25 December 1888: "Revered lady, the only woman I have ever revered . . . please deign to accept the first copy of this, *Ecce Homo*. Everyone, basically, is mistreated therein, with the exception of Richard Wagner—and also Turin. Malwida is also there in the guise of Kundry . . . [signed:] The Antichrist" (KSA—Briefe 8:551).

23. Kurt F. Leidecker, ed., *Nietzsche: Unpublished Letters* (New York: Philosophical Library, 1959), p. 154.

24. In his 1875 lectures at Basel, recently translated into French under the title *Le Service divin des grecs* (Paris: L'Herne, 1992), Nietzsche already noted that the Greeks identified Alexander with Dionysus: "The people crowded around him [Alexander] as if around a new Dionysus (as the Athenians called him [Diogenes Laertius VI, 63])" (p. 161).

25. "My pride . . . consists in the fact that I have *origins*—that is why I have no need of glory. . . . in me some things first come to light maturely that remained embryonic for millenia" (KSA 9:642).

26. See chapter 8 of the third essay of *The Genealogy of Morals* (KSA 5:351–56; GM—III §8, p. 108–12).

27. On Caesar's greatness see, for example, the posthumous fragments located at KSA 11:588; 12:419 (WP §776, p. 407); 12:428 (WP §380, p. 205); 12:550 (WP §544, pp. 292–93); 13:273–74 (WP §751, p. 397).

KELLY OLIVER

Nietzsche's Abjection

> With the riddle-solving and mother-marrying Oedipus in mind, we must immediately interpret this to mean that where prophetic and magical powers have broken the spell of present and future, the rigid law of individuation, and the real magic of nature, some enormously unnatural event—such as incest—must have occurred earlier, as a cause. How else could one compel nature to surrender her secrets if not by triumphantly resisting her, that is, by means of something unnatural? It is this insight that I find expressed in that horrible triad of Oedipus' destinies: the same man who solves the riddle of nature—that Sphinx of two species—must also break the most sacred natural orders by murdering his father and marrying his mother. Indeed, the myth seems to whisper to us that wisdom, particularly Dionysian wisdom, is an unnatural abomination.
>
> —Nietzsche, *The Birth of Tragedy*

Nietzsche's troubled relation to "the feminine" continues to fascinate his critics and multiply their interpretations of his writing. Interpretations of Nietzsche's relation to the feminine range from David Krell's claim that Nietzsche "writes with the hand of woman" to Ofelia Schutte's insistence that Nietzsche "maintains what can be characterized fundamentally as an antifeminist position both on gender difference and on the issue of social and political equality."[1] As I have argued elsewhere, these interpretations overlook an important difference in Nietzsche's writings between the feminine and the maternal.[2] Some of the ambiguity in Nietzsche's relation to the feminine can be explained by separating the feminine from the maternal and analyzing the position of the mother in Nietzsche's writings.

Kelly Oliver

The Mother Is Not a Woman

Much of the recent Nietzsche scholarship in the United States that emphasizes a distinction between the feminine and the maternal employs interpretative frameworks developed by French psychoanalyst Julia Kristeva.[3] Kristeva suggests that woman and the feminine operate independently of what she calls the maternal function.[4] By identifying the maternal as a function, she unhinges the child's relationship to its mother qua mother from its relationship to its mother qua woman. The maternal function cannot be reduced to either woman or femininity. Kristeva maintains that the mother "is alone of her sex"; she is neither masculine nor feminine.[5] As a mother she has a relationship to the child that is preoedipal and operates before any sexual difference. To conflate the feminine, woman, and the mother is to overlook the uniqueness of the mother-child relationship and to subject both woman and the feminine to an "abjection" that is appropriate only to the mother fulfilling the maternal function.

Kristeva introduces the notion of abjection in *Powers of Horror*.[6] She develops the term *abjet* in its ambiguity; it can mean to jettison, repel, repulse, throw out, or to be revolting, disgusting, repulsive. The abject, that which is abjected and gives rise to the experience of abjection, is related to the mother: "Defilement is the translinguistic spoor of the most archaic boundaries of the self's clean and proper body. In that sense, if it is a jettisoned object, it is so from the mother" (*Powers*, p. 73). Kristeva maintains that it is necessary for every child to "abject" its mother to become an autonomous subject. The child abjects the mother in the process of weaning and separation. Through this process the mother herself is made abject. In other words, because she is seen as abject she can be abjected.

The abject is disgusting and it makes you want to vomit. It is repulsive and yet it both attracts and repels. It is fascinating. So when the child finds the mother abject, abjects her, it finds her body as it fulfills the maternal function, both attractive and repulsive. The child is fascinated with this body that has met all of its needs. To separate from this body, to be weaned, however, the child must find the maternal body repulsive. The child must feel continued dependence on the "maternal container" as a threat to its autonomy.

In fact it is the child's intimate relation to its mother's body that both makes it possible and necessary to abject the mother and makes the experience of abjection troubling. The experience of abjection, or the abject, challenges the very possibility of autonomy. The abject is what is on the border, what does not respect borders. It is not a "lack of cleanliness or health that causes abjection but *what disturbs identity,* system, order" (*Powers,* p. 4; emphasis added). The abject threatens identity. It is neither good nor evil, subject nor object, ego nor unconscious, but something that threatens the very distinctions themselves. In the child's relation to the mother, abjection shows up as the struggle to set up borders between the maternal body, the maternal "container," and itself.

This abjection that calls the child's primary narcissism to account is founded in birth itself (*Powers,* p. 10). Human life, human society, is founded on the abject separation of one body from another at birth. Separation that founds and prefigures subsequent separations is labored but necessary. It is at the birth of the child, and not before, that the identity of the human subject is most visibly called into question. Before the umbilical cord is cut, who can decide whether there are one or two beings?

If the abject "is a jettisoned object, it is so from the mother." The child is this jettisoned object, violently expelled from the mother's body. The "subject" discovers itself as the impossible separation/identity of the maternal body. It hates that body, but only because it cannot be free of it. It is a horrifying, devouring body.[7] It is a body that evokes rage and fear. The child, the male child, feels rage against his mother because her carrying him in her womb compromises his identity. How can he become a man when "he" was once a woman? He was once part, now the expelled waste, of a woman's body. Even more curiously, how can he become a man and love a woman, that abject and threatening hole "represented" by his mother? This is why, according to Freud, fetishism is not a denial of *woman's* castration, but a denial of the *mother's* castration—"If mom is castrated and I was once her, then I too am castrated."

In *Powers of Horror* Kristeva describes how the child, there always the male child, must split his mother to take up his masculine gender identity. The mother is split in two: the abject and the sublime (*Powers,* p. 157). Making the mother abject allows the male child to separate from his mother and become autonomous. But if the mother is only abject, then she becomes the phobic object and the child himself becomes abject. The oedipal situation is thrown out of alignment. If the mother remains abject, she never becomes the object, and certainly not the object of love. The phobic substitutes the sign, in a denial of sexual difference, for the absent object (*Powers,* p. 45). Within the heterosexual narrative, the mother must also be made sublime so that the male child can take her, a woman, as an object of love. Part of the experience of abjection is an attraction and fascination with the repulsive. In addition to this fascination, the child sees its mother as divine beauty, as sublime. If she is only sublime, however, the child will not separate from her. He will have no subject or object identity whatsoever, no primary repression and thus no secondary repression. In other words, the Other will have been completely foreclosed, never set up, and the child will be psychotic. He will still be unable to love a woman, or anyone else. For the psychotic, there is no one else, no object, no other(s).

When the child does not properly go through the stage of abjection and take its mother as a proper object, when the child remains at the stage of abjection and abjects itself, then the maternal body becomes a phobic "object." The phobic is on the "borderline," on the edge of psychosis, but not mad. Whereas the neurotic has displaced or denied the Other to maintain its ego, and the psychotic has foreclosed the Other and therefore the possibility of an ego, the phobic has confused the Other with itself and upholds its "ego" within the Other (*Powers*, p. 15). In some sense, the abject "subject" is too precocious. It realizes that it can be constituted as a subject only by virtue of the Other—that its identity rests on separation—even before it undergoes this process. Still on the level of drives, the abject sublimates the "object" before it is an object proper. The abject sublimates it by taking its place, or, more properly, by taking the place of the undecidable.

For Kristeva, the child can only properly go through the stage of abjection with the support of what she calls a loving "imaginary father." Without the loving "imaginary father" the child abjects itself rather than separating from the mother. If we do not have some imaginary construct that enables us to both separate from her and separate the maternal function from the mother, then we misplace abjection. Rather than perceive the "maternal container" as a horrible threat from which we must separate, we perceive women as a threat. Without the imaginary wherewithal to turn the threat into a representation of mother as Other, we turn women into the Other. Here it is important to reconsider the difference between mother and woman.

What a representation of maternity provides that a representation of woman does not is alterity within identity. Kristeva's analysis in "Stabat Mater" in particular suggests that maternity provides an example of radical alterity within identity. The mother provides a case of the other *as* the self and the other *in* the self. As such, only she can provide the necessary sense of separation within union that grounds subjectivity. A representation of the mother as a subject-in-process, as an open subjectivity that contains alterity, sets up a model of autonomy that still allows for connection, identity, ethics, and love. The woman as radical other, completely exterior to the self, does not. She is not reachable, loveable, or even identifiable, let alone "identical."

Nietzsche's Abject Mother

Perhaps the ambiguity in Nietzsche's writings toward the feminine and even woman can be read through his ambiguous relation to the maternal. Perhaps Nietzsche can be read as the phobic who is caught at the stage of abjection, with no imaginary loving father to support his separation from an overbearing mother. Nietzsche can be read as fascinated with the figure of the mother because he is both attracted and repulsed by the maternal body. In his writings he desperately tries to separate from this devouring body, the horrible womb of being, and yet he relies on his identification with its procreative powers. Kristeva's account of the abject mother can be useful in diagnosing Nietzsche's ambiguous relation to the feminine and woman in his writings as an ambiguous relation to the maternal.

Jean Graybeal, in *Language and "the Feminine" in Nietzsche and Heidegger,* uses Kristeva's notion of abjection to analyze Nietzsche's relation to his mother. Graybeal argues that Nietzsche abjects his mother, Franziska.[8] She reads the opening line of the first chapter of *Ecce Homo*—"The happiness of my existence, its uniqueness perhaps, lies in its fate: I am, to express it in the form of a riddle, as my father already dead, while as my mother I still live and grow old" (KSA 6:264; EH p. 222*)—as Nietzsche's failed attempt to articulate his relation to the feminine, specifically his relation to his mother. Graybeal points out that there are two versions of this section of *Ecce Homo*. There is a revised version that was discovered only relatively recently because it had been suppressed by Nietzsche's friend Peter Gast after Nietzsche's collapse in January 1889. As she explains, Nietzsche collapsed very shortly after sending this revised version to his publisher. After the collapse, Peter Gast edited the manuscript and omitted the revised version. Graybeal suggests that there could be a correlation between this later version of the chapter of *Ecce Homo* and Nietzsche's collapse.

Graybeal describes the significant differences between the earlier and later version of the first chapter of *Ecce Homo*. She maintains that both versions are Nietzsche's attempts to come to terms with the influence of his mother on his life. She argues that his first attempt to look directly at his mother paralyzes him, whereas the second attempt plunges him into rhetorical excess and frenzy. In the first version, after his riddle, Nietzsche says only that his mother is "very German." The rest of that version describes his father. In the later version, however, Nietzsche launches a miniature diatribe against his mother and sister, calling them "rabble" and a "hell-machine" (KSA 6:268). Graybeal concludes that, had Nietzsche been able to articulate the sublime and the horror that he experienced in relation to his mother, he might have retained his sanity longer: "As his father he is dead, beyond life, and as his mother he is abjectly implicated in the horrors of 'human, all-too-human' existence" (Graybeal, pp. 92–93).

Graybeal does not develop her thesis that Nietzsche might have retained his sanity had he been able to articulate his relationship to his mother. But taking off from Kristeva's theory of abjection, it is an intriguing hypothesis. Kristeva claims that if the child cannot abject the mother through the support of a loving father, then the child abjects itself. The mother becomes a phobic object because the child cannot separate itself from her. When Nietzsche tried to face the mother, he could not separate himself from her. After all, if the abject is a jettisoned object, "it is so from the mother." As the phobic, Nietzsche abjects himself when he abjects the mother; the identification is too strong. Her abjection was his abjection. Unable to separate from the mother, teetering on the edge of psychosis, his failed attempt to articulate his relationship to the mother might have sent him over the edge.

So in his writings Nietzsche continually struggles to separate from the maternal. He struggles with the boundaries between individuals, between categories, between opposites. His struggle often returns to the boundary between the child and the mother during birth. Birth is a process of individuation. Through birth, the child is separated from the mother and becomes an individual. For Nietzsche, individuation always covers over the chaos and arbitrariness of what was before individuation. The Dionysian womb of being gives birth to the Apollonian individual only through Apollonian control: "I see Apollo as the transfiguring genius of the *principium individuationis* through which alone the redemption in illusion is truly to be obtained; while by the mystical triumphant cry of Dionysus the spell of individuation is broken, and the way lies open to the Mothers of Being, to the innermost heart of things" (KSA 1:103; BT §16, pp. 99–100).

The Dionysian womb of being, however, creates *without* individuation. Nietzsche's maternal womb is a fetishized womb that does not give birth. For Nietzsche, individuation, like childbirth, is too painful. Therefore, he invokes Silenus' wisdom: it is best not to be born at all (KSA 1:35; BT §3, p. 42). If, however, one must be born, it is necessary to forget the repellent aspects of that separation. To enjoy the child, one must forget the more repellent and painful aspects of pregnancy. It is necessary to forget the womb out of which one is born (KSA 5:343; GM—III §4, pp. 100–101). One must revel in the sublime and forget the abject. One must struggle for separation.

In addition to the bizarre effects on the body in a literal pregnancy, in Nietzsche's metaphorical pregnancy we have a bizarre unassimilated unity between the creator and the created. The pain of childbirth, says Nietzsche, is the pain of creating (KSA 4:111; Z p. 199). It is this chaos, which both creates and destroys, that constitutes the terror of nature. It is the terror that must be forgotten. Ultimately, it is the womb itself, this creative/destructive force, which must be forgotten in order to enjoy the child, or more precisely, so that the child can enjoy. The child (Nietzsche?) cannot bear to imagine its unity with its mother. He cannot tolerate an identification with the abject mother. The undifferentiated fusion is horrifying. The indeterminate identity between mother and child is too much to bear, especially for the male child. How can this child be a man if he was once part of a woman? In order for the child to be autonomous, he must forget that he was once part of the mother, expelled from her womb. This masculine phobia that takes the mother's pregnant body as its "object" is Kristeva's abject.

Nietzsche is repulsed and yet fascinated by the abject, the in-between, especially as it is associated with pregnancy and birth. It is the inability to distinguish that fascinates him. He is troubled by borders. He argues that procreation is a reactive process because it is the inability, "impotence," to deal with excess (KSA 12:38; WP §654, p. 345). This excess can only be tolerated if it is broken off, if it is separated into another individual, if it is born and the process through which it is born is forgotten. In fact, Nietzsche suggests that this is how truth is born. Truth is born out of chaos that we forget was once chaos. For him, it is Apollonian individuation that cures the eye hurt from staring at this chaos, the womb of being. Only individuation can make this creative/destructive life bearable. For Nietzsche, the relation to the womb of being is abject. Thus, he is both fascinated and repulsed by the process of individuation.

Yet it is only the weak who need to make life bearable. Nietzsche's Dionysian *Übermensch,* on the other hand, is a strong new type who can bear the excesses of pregnancy without individuation. The *Übermensch* has no need for truth or individuation. These are for the weak who cannot bear life's excess, for those who cannot affirm pain and difference. The *Übermensch* is truly *eternally pregnant:* the one who does not need to give birth; the creator without creations; the artist without works of art; life become creative; son become mother, both sublime and abject.

Nietzsche's Fetish

In *Human, All Too Human* Nietzsche says that our relationship to women is determined by our relationship to our mothers (KSA 2:265; HATH §380, p. 195). If Nietzsche's relation to the figure of the mother is a relation of abjection, then, according to Nietzsche, his relation to the figure of woman will also be a relation of abjection. Regardless of Nietzsche's actual relationship with his own mother, his writings are evidence of an abject relationship to a metaphorical mother, a fetishized woman.

Freud says a fetish is a substitute for the mother's missing penis that allows the fetishist to maintain the fantasy of the phallic mother. The womb becomes, for Nietzsche, a symbol of the phallic mother, the force of life, of life's potency. He fetishizes the mother's womb. He repeatedly figures the will to power using metaphors of pregnancy and the "eternally creative primordial mother" (KSA 1:108; BT §16, p. 104). His Dionysian type *is* the "eternally pregnant mother"—she affirms herself continually through procreation.

In addition to the figures of the maternal in Nietzsche's writing, there is also the suggestion that women exist to be pregnant. "Everything about woman," says Nietzsche's Zarathustra, is a "riddle" solved by "pregnancy," and you can "cure" a woman by giving her a child (KSA 4:84; Z p. 178; KSA 6:306; EH p. 267). Women's profession, says Nietzsche, is "to give birth to strong children" (KSA 5:177; BGE §239, p. 169) and feminine love is "maternal love" (KSA 2:267 and 276; HATH §392 and §421, pp. 197 and 203). He cannot face a feminine love that is not maternal, a love that is not dependent on man, a love that does not create a child. His relationship to the figure of woman and the feminine must be read through this relationship to the maternal. Both his attraction to and repulsion from the feminine and woman revolve around the maternal and a misplaced abjection. Nietzsche reduces woman and the feminine to the maternal. His woman is the fetish of eternal pregnancy, eternal nourishment, eternal potency, the phallic mother: as a mother she is revered, but as a sexual being she is feared. Nietzsche's fetish, like all others, is a way of denying maternal castration.

Masculine sexuality is threatened by an identification with the mother; so if the boy cannot both abject his mother and overcome that abjection, then his sexual identity is threatened because he continues to identify with maternal castration. The mother's sex is not only threatening within Nietzsche's texts because it represents castration, a castration with which he identifies, but also because it actively castrates. Nietzsche is afraid not only of the castrated mother, but also of the castrating mother who will cut him to pieces. Unless she is domesticated in her pregnancy, the mother is dangerous. Nietzsche says that the tragedy of woman "tears to pieces as it enchants" (KSA 5:178; BGE §239, p. 170). He worries that like Dionysus he will be torn apart by his own mother: "May I here venture the surmise that I *know* women? That is part of my Dionysian dowry. Who knows? Perhaps I am the first psychologist of the eternally feminine. They all love me—an old story—not counting *abortive* females, the 'emancipated' who lack the stuff for children. —Fortunately, I am not willing to be torn to pieces: the perfect woman tears to pieces when she loves. —I know these charming maenads. —Ah, what a dangerous, creeping, subterranean little beast of prey she is! And yet so agreeable!" (KSA 6:305–6; EH p. 266).

In spite of Nietzsche's identification with women, or perhaps because of it, he claims that he cannot be ripped apart by them. Fertile women, mothers, love him because he knows them. He identifies with these mothers. Yet, unlike Dionysus, he will not be torn apart by his mother in some phallic frenzy. While Nietzsche identifies with the phallic mother, reveres her as the sublime metaphor for the will to power, he is afraid that she will tear him apart. She is the terrifying abject mother who threatens his unity and autonomy. She threatens to tear up his unified self. She threatens to dismember him. The beloved phallic mother becomes the feared castrating mother.

Graybeal argues that Nietzsche feared castration from his own mother. She quotes the latest version of the first chapter of *Ecce Homo:* "Here works a perfect hell-machine, with unfailing certainty about the moment when one can bloodily wound me—in my highest moments . . . for there all strength is lacking to defend oneself against poisonous vermin" (KSA 6:268). Graybeal interprets this passage as a sign of Nietzsche's fear of a castrating mother: "This hell-machine has unfailing (hence inhuman) certainty about the *Augenblick,* the precise instant 'when one can bloodily wound me.' When could this be but in his *highest Augenblicken?* Association of erection and castration are suggested by this entire fantasy. The hellish perfection and inhuman, unfailing certainty of this female machine, a machine that knows exactly when to attack, when the victim is at the height of his exaltation. . . . A castrating mother awaits him at the bottom of his ladder of life" (Graybeal, p. 87).

We can move Graybeal's analysis from the level of personal psychology to the level of textual positionality. If Nietzsche's metaphorical mother is not castrating, then she is not the all-powerful phallic mother of his fantasies. And she cannot be the revered sublime mother. If she is not the castrating mother, then she is the castrated mother. She is the mother against whom the fetish becomes a shield. When Nietzsche looks at the mother whom he has created—the masculine mother, the *Übermensch,* Zarathustra—he sees that she is not the all-powerful mother of his fantasies. He can no longer deny the mother's castration; she is not the phallic mother. But to admit it is too much for him to bear because of his narcissistic identification with his mother. He cannot separate himself from her; if she is castrated then so is he.

Nietzsche's poststructuralist critics, starting with Derrida, have emphasized, perhaps overemphasized, Nietzsche's identification with woman. Derrida argues that Nietzsche performs the feminine operation by identifying with three different types of women: the castrated woman, the castrating woman, and the affirming woman. "At once, simultaneously or successively, depending on the position of his body and the situation of his story, Nietzsche was all of these."[9] Derrida describes Nietzsche's relationship to these three woman as ambiguous: he identifies with them yet dreads them. Are these three women just any women? Or are they three faces of the mother? The castrated mother, the castrating mother, and the phallic mother? Perhaps behind all of the masks of Nietzsche's women we find the mother with whom Nietzsche struggles. Perhaps it is Nietzsche's inability to separate from the mother that troubles his writing on the feminine and woman. Much of his writing can be read as an attempt to escape his mother, his motherland, his mother tongue, and maternal security in order to give birth to himself. He envisages a motherless child, the *Übermensch,* that gives birth to itself as a dancing star, a self-propelled wheel.[10] His free spirit is one who flies alone without women, without his mother (KSA 2:279–80; HATH §426, p. 205):

> The free spirit will always breathe a sigh of relief when he has finally decided to shake off the maternal care and protection administered by the women around him. What is the harm in the colder draft of air that they had warded off so anxiously? What does one real disadvantage, loss, accident, illness, debt, or folly more or less in his life matter, compared with the bondage of the golden cradle, the peacock-tail fan, and the oppressive feeling of having to be actually grateful because he is waited upon and spoiled like an infant? That is why the milk offered him by the maternal disposition of the women around him can so easily turn to bile. (KSA 2:281; HATH §429, p. 206)

The free spirit flies free of the women around him only if he can abject his mother, only if for him her sweet milk turns to bile. Nietzsche abjects all women and femininity because he cannot abject the maternal. He misplaces abjection onto women and femininity in general as a defense against his own identification with the maternal body. Nietzsche is not the free spirit. He cannot completely leave the safe haven of the maternal body. Without the support of a loving father, haunted by a perfect dead father, Nietzsche cannot imagine a creativity that is not an identification with the mother: "To be the child new-born, the creator must also be the mother who gives birth and endure the pangs of the birth-giver" (KSA 4:111; Z p. 199*). He feels guilty for his mother's pain and for the "matricide" necessary to separate from her. He must experience her pain, the pain that he caused her to feel. He cannot abject the mother and make her abhorrent; he feels too guilty. And since love is associated solely with the maternal, to abject the mother is to live without love.

The Dead Father

Kristeva diagnoses problems with abjecting the mother and then overcoming this abjection as the lack of any loving father to support that process. The father figure in Nietzsche's writings seems to be characteristically stern and demanding, Caesar or Napoleon.[11] Nietzsche's writings are full of hard warriors, fathers who demand the impossible from their sons, fathers who demand that the son separate from the womanly mother to become manly: "Truths that are *hard* won, certain, enduring, and therefore still of consequence for all further knowledge are the higher; to keep to them is *manly,* and shows bravery, simplicity, restraint. Eventually, not only the individual, but all mankind will be elevated to this *manliness,* when men finally grow accustomed to the greater esteem for durable, lasting knowledge" (KSA 2:25–26; HATH §3, p. 15; emphasis added).

Here Nietzsche identifies with the eternal *manly* truth and looks forward to the day when all of mankind is manly. In the *Gay Science,* he welcomes signs of a more "virile, warlike age" (KSA 3:526; GS §283, p. 228). In "How to Philosophize with a Hammer," he orders us to become "hard!" And Zarathustra tells others, or is told, to become "hard," to become "manly" (KSA 4:268; Z p. 326). He tells us that all creators are "hard" (KSA 4:116; Z p. 202).[12] Zarathustra maintains that "brave, unconcerned, mocking, violent—thus wisdom wants us: she is a woman and always loves only a warrior" (KSA 4:49; Z p. 153).[13] Nietzsche envies this warrior, this conqueror, this image of the manly hero. For Nietzsche impotence is the real enemy of life. "One is today ashamed of hardness," he says (KSA 5:358; GM—III §9, p. 114). It is no wonder that he chooses the god of fertility, Dionysus, whose symbols are blood red wine and the tumescent phallus, to represent life's force. And, repeatedly, degenerate life is figured in terms of castration, emasculation, effeminacy, and impotence.

But Nietzsche cannot become the potent warrior as long as he is identified with the mother. If the son identifies with the mother and the mother is abject, then the son must be abject, too. Kristeva suggests that if the child cannot separate from the mother it will abject itself. In fact, in some cases the child will abject itself so that it does not have to abject its mother. To hate the mother is to hate yourself, hating yourself so that you will not have to hate the mother. Even Nietzsche claims that misogynists really hate themselves (KSA 3:238; D §346, p. 165).

Nietzsche feels a disgust at himself because he cannot separate from his abject culture, a culture that he associates with his "very German" mother.[14] German culture makes Nietzsche nauseous because German culture abjects life. German culture, Western culture, in its nihilism, is sick. Its longing for another world, a higher purpose, is the result of a nausea with life. Nausea at life and the mess of the body, its finitude, leads to Christian or other types of redemption. And any type of redemption that denies the finite life of the body overcomes the nausea at life by denying life.

Nietzsche identifies another nausea, however, his own nausea, Zarathustra's nausea: " 'The great disgust with man—*this* choked me and had crawled into my throat' " (KSA 4:274; Z p. 331). Christian redemption itself makes Nietzsche sick. His is the "great nausea" at man's nausea; his nausea is overcome through another "redemption," Dionysian redemption, a redemption of the earth, the *Übermensch*'s redemption: "He must yet come to us, the *redeeming* man of great love and contempt, the creative spirit whose compelling strength will not let him rest in any aloofness or any beyond. . . . This man [*Mensch*] of the future, who will redeem us not only from the hitherto reigning ideal but also from that which was bound to grow out of it, the great nausea, the will to nothingness, nihilism" (KSA 5:336; GM—II §24, p. 96).

Out of nausea grows something beyond nausea: out of man's nausea at life grows the life beyond, Christian redemption. Out of the nausea at man's nausea grows the beyond man, the *Übermensch,* Dionysian redemption. "Close beside this sickness stand signs of an untested force and powerfulness of soul. *The same reasons that produce the increasing small-*

ness of man drive the *stronger and rarer individuals up to greatness*" (KSA 11:496–97; WP §109, p. 68).

This nausea is a pregnancy that gives birth to something beyond it. Nietzsche describes this pregnancy as an illness out of which something grows, nausea as self-overcoming. "Bad conscience," he says, is "an illness but . . . as pregnancy is an illness" (KSA 5:327; GM—II §19, p. 88). The nausea of pregnancy is necessary to get beyond sickness, to give birth to health. The purpose of Zarathustra's nausea is to sire, to give birth to, the new healthy Dionysian type, the *Mensch* of the future, the *Übermensch*.

Nausea produces both smallness (Christian redemption) and greatness (Dionysian redemption). Nietzsche is both fascinated and repulsed by this nausea, this morning sickness, that is a necessary part of pregnancy. Again he is oscillating between reverence for the pregnancy out of which something is born and horror at the same process. Even while he identifies with the process, he finds it repellent. He maintains that these bizarre and repellent aspects of creativity, of birth, of individuation, must be forgotten. And yet he cannot forget them. He is obsessed with them. He is obsessed with the bizarre and repellent aspects of his own culture, of himself, that he associates with the "very German" mother.

He cannot separate from the mother by abjecting her, however, without the support from a loving father. But his is a stern, threatening father who will not protect him from his devouring mother. Nietzsche is caught in abjection. Because of his narcissistic identification with his mother—"as my mother I still live and grow old"—Nietzsche cannot abject her without abjecting himself. He cannot face her without facing his own abjection. He cannot face her without facing the fact that he was once part of this woman's body. So he fetishizes the abjection itself. He fetishizes the womb of being where there are no borders between truth and falsity, good and evil, creation and destruction, mother and son, masculine and feminine.

Notes

1. David Farrell Krell, *Postponements: Women, Sensuality, and Death in Nietzsche* (Bloomington: Indiana Univ. Press, 1986), p. 10; Ofelia Schutte, "Nietzsche on Gender Difference: A Critique," *Newsletter on Feminism and Philosophy* 89, no. 2 (1990): 64.

2. See my "Woman as Truth in Nietzsche's Writings," *Social Theory and Practice* 10 (1984): 185–99; "Woman's Voice, Man's Language: A Reading of Gender and Language in Nietzsche," Ph.D. diss., Northwestern University, 1987; "Nietzsche's

'Woman': The Poststructuralist Attempt to Do Away with Women," *Radical Philosophy* 48 (1988): 25–29; "Who Is Nietzsche's Woman?," in *Modern Engendering: Critical Feminist Readings in Modern Western Philosophy,* ed. Bat-Ami Bar On (Albany: SUNY Press, 1994).

3. See, for example, Alison Ainley, " 'Ideal Selfishness': Nietzsche's Metaphor of Maternity," in *Exceedingly Nietzsche: Aspects of Contemporary Nietzsche-Interpretation,* ed. David Farrell Krell and David Wood (New York: Routledge, 1988), pp. 116–30; Jean Graybeal, *Language and "the Feminine" in Nietzsche and Heidegger* (Bloomington: Indiana Univ. Press, 1990); and my studies of 1987, 1988, and 1991.

4. Julia Kristeva, "Motherhood according to Giovanni Bellini," trans. Thomas Gora, Alice Jardine, and Leon S. Roudiez, in *Desire in Language: A Semiotic Approach to Literature and Art,* ed. Leon S. Roudiez (New York: Columbia Univ. Press, 1980), pp. 237–70.

5. Julia Kristeva, "Stabat Mater," in *Tales of Love,* trans. Leon S. Roudiez (New York: Columbia Univ. Press, 1987), pp. 234–63.

6. Julia Kristeva, *Powers of Horror: An Essay on Abjection,* trans. Leon S. Roudiez (New York: Columbia Univ. Press, 1982).

7. Kristeva argues that becoming abject is the body's defense against cannibalism. If it is disgusting, it will not be eaten (*Powers of Horror,* pp. 39, 78–79).

8. I find Graybeal's argument that Nietzsche abjects his own mother Franziska problematic. Although psychoanalysis can provide an interesting and useful way to read texts, I am wary of extending that analysis to a diagnosis of the author's actual psychological problems.

9. Jacques Derrida, *Spurs: Nietzsche's Styles / Eperons: Les Styles de Nietzsche,* trans. Barbara Harlow (Chicago: Univ. of Chicago Press, 1979), p. 101; Krell claims that Derrida and Nietzsche save real women from dogmatic philosophy by writing with the hand of woman: "Writing now with the other hand, as it were, both Nietzsche and Derrida record the plaint of women against 'the foolishness of the dogmatic philosopher' " (Krell, pp. 10–11).

10. Luce Irigaray makes a similar argument in *Marine Lover of Friedrich Nietzsche,* trans. Gillian C. Gill (New York: Columbia Univ. Press, 1990). For an analysis of Irigaray's text see my "Plaint of Ariadne," forthcoming in *Nietzsche and Feminism,* ed. Keith Ansell-Pearson and Howard Caygill (Aldershot [England]: Avebury, 1994).

11. For passages in which Nietzsche praises war and conquering, see KSA 2:311–312; HATH §477, pp. 230–31 and KSA 5:120–21; BGE §200, pp. 111–12 (also: WP §§53, 125, and 975). Also in *The Genealogy of Morals* Nietzsche argues in favor of the master morality; for places where he praises Napoleon and Caesar, see, for example: WP §§27, 41, 104, 128, 129, 380, 422, 544, 665, 684, 740, 751, 776, 829, 877, 975, 1017, and 1026; BGE §§199, 209, 232, 244, 245, and 256; and HATH §164.

12. Krell quotes an unpublished note in which Zarathustra tells the cat maidens: "Weep no more Pallid Dudu! Be a man, Suleika!" (Krell, p. 77; see also pp. 24, 27, and 58).

13. In his preface to *On the Genealogy of Morals,* Nietzsche maintains that the rest of the third essay, "What Is the Meaning of the Ascetic Ideal?," is an exegesis of this aphorism. In the third essay of *On the Genealogy of Morals,* Nietzsche attacks the sickness, seriousness, and impotence of the ascetic ideal. The ascetic ideal is not the mocking warrior loved by wisdom. The ascetic ideal is impotent. It is not

manly. It is not hard enough to love a woman. Opposed to the serious, sickly, impotent ascetic ideal is the playful, healthy, potent Dionysus. See my "Dagger through the Heart: The Ethics of Reading Nietzsche's *On the Genealogy of Morals*," *International Studies in Philosophy* 25, no. 2 (1993): 13–28.

14. See Jean Graybeal's analysis of Nietzsche's association of his mother with German culture (pp. 77–93).

PART TWO

Figures of the Feminine

CLAYTON KOELB

Castration Envy: Nietzsche and the Figure of Woman

It would be difficult nowadays to approach the topic of woman as metaphor in Nietzsche without crossing through the formidable terrain of Derrida's *Spurs*. My particular formulation of the topic in fact situates its discourse squarely within the territory explored by that essay, though perhaps paradoxically; for Derrida announces specifically that the phrase "figure of woman" (*figure de la femme*) does *not* belong in his discussion. He speaks of the "question" and not the "figure" of woman "precisely because we shall bear witness here to her *abduction*, because the question of the figure is at once opened and closed by what is called woman."[1] I wish to pursue the question of the figure, not by any means to refute Derrida's claim, but on the contrary to explore (in perhaps a somewhat different vein) its ramifications.

One of those ramifications is Derrida's demonstration of a powerful connection in Nietzsche's thinking between the notions of "woman" and "castration." The connection both affirms and puts in abeyance the questionable figure of the woman as a man-without-a-penis and focuses attention on the issue of weakness, the ethos of power-in-powerlessness that Nietzsche finds in Christianity. Derrida shows how Nietzsche's characterization of the early Christian church is explicitly linked on the one hand to the realm of the feminine (Nietzsche calls it *weiblich*) and on the other to an ethos of extirpation and denial he refers to as *Kastratismus* in a passage Derrida quotes from *Twilight of the Idols*.[2] From his reading of this and other Nietzschean discourses on women, Derrida claims to have found a "principle [*règle*], which might be resumed in a finite number of typical and matrical [*matricielle*] propositions" (*Spurs*, pp. 94/95). He offers three of them. We need not cite the first two; we need only note that "woman, up to this point then, is twice castration: once as truth and once as nontruth" (*Spurs*, pp. 96/97). In Derrida's third formulation of the Nietzschean principle of woman, he finds something different: "In the instance of the third proposition, however, beyond the double negation of the first two, woman is recognized and affirmed as an affirmative power, a dissimulatress, an artist, a dionysiac. And no longer is it man who affirms her. She affirms herself, in and of herself, in man. Castration, in the sense I just spoke of, does not take place" (*Spurs*, pp. 96/97*).

Derrida is very careful here: he does not say that castration in every sense does not take place, but only that it does not take place "au sens que je disais tout à l'heure." His careful language is entirely obligatory in this instance because there is good evidence that even this third, more positive proposition about woman carries with it strong associations with castration in some sense. Here is a poem from "Joke, Cunning, and Revenge"—the collection of verses that opens *The Gay Science*—that will serve as a case in point:

Lost His Head

She now has spirit—how did it happen that she found it?
A man recently lost his reason over her,
His head was rich before this pastime:
His head went to the devil—no, no! to the woman!
(KSA 3:364; cf. GS p. 63)

The woman with intellect and spirit (*Geist*), the "affirmative" woman of Derrida's third proposition, appears in this little drama as the beneficiary of a man's dismemberment. He is intellectually castrated by his love for her, whereas she miraculously gains the potency he has lost. The castration anxiety is displaced in the poem's imagery from the penis to the head, but the nature of that anxiety—the fear of a loss of male power associated with bodily dismemberment—reveals its fundamental sexual nature. Nietzsche suggests here that love brings about a reversal of gender roles that essentially moves the phallic power from man to woman.

One might argue, however, that the poem offers an example not so much of castration as of anticastration: the woman's intellectual/spiritual power seems to be the result of her acquisition of a male body part, not its loss. The male seems indeed to be castrated, but he is also no longer spirited. There is an association of castration with spiritual power here, but it is an association of opposition. Is there any evidence to suggest that Nietzsche believes the association could be more complex and more intimate?

Derrida himself cites some of the best evidence of such a complex relationship when he quotes another passage from *Twilight of the Idols* that follows almost directly the one mentioned above: "The same means in the fight against a craving—castration, extirpation—is instinctively chosen by those who are too weak-willed, too degenerate, to be able to impose moderation on themselves. . . . Just look at the whole history of the priests and philosophers, including the artists" (KSA 6:83; TI pp. 487–88*; quoted in *Spurs,* pp. 92/93). We must not overlook the fact that Nietzsche seems to count among the weak-willed and degenerate adherents of *Kastratismus* not only priests, as we would expect, but also artists and philosophers. These are the very groups with which Nietzsche regularly associates himself (carefully constructing his own persona as both artist and philosopher) and with which Derrida understands him to associate the notion of woman in his third and more affirmative "proposition." We may not, then, understand Nietzsche to be setting up a simple opposition such as, say, "potent artist vs. castrated priest" any more than we may suppose that "woman" is excluded from the company of philosophers. Woman, priest, and philosopher/artist all have something in common. Oddly enough one of these common traits is complicity in an ethos of castration.

An association of woman with the castration syndrome of self-effacement is clearly present even when Nietzsche seems to be stressing the positive, powerful fecundity which women share with artists: "Pregnancy has made women kinder, more patient, more timid, more pleased to submit; and just so does spiritual pregnancy produce the character of the contemplative type, which is closely related to the feminine character: it consists of male mothers" (KSA 3:430; GS §72, p. 129). Here are some familiar notions in a somewhat different context. Patience, timidity, and submission are traits Nietzsche regularly associates with the feminine, but more often with the "negative" feminine; that is, they belong to the ethos of castration. Here, though, he brings them in contact with the "contemplative type," a concept perhaps in need of further specification. Nietzsche speaks of the contemplative type often, and in the broad category of contemplatives we find not only priests and hermits but also the artist/philosophers among which he numbers himself. Another passage makes the explicit connection: "We who think and feel at the same time are those who really continually *fashion* something that had not been there before: the whole eternally growing world of valuations, colors, accents, perspectives, scales, affirmations, and negations. . . . Only we have created the world *that concerns man!* —But precisely this knowledge we lack, . . . we fail to recognize our best power and underestimate ourselves, the contemplatives, just a little" (KSA 3:540; GS §301, pp. 241–42). The "we" who create the world are the contemplatives who appear otherwise as male mothers; that is, they appear in the figure of woman. They are immensely powerful, but their power is not phallic potency. On the contrary, it appears to depend critically on the absence of the phallus. It depends on a constellation of elements that include all of the negatives linked elsewhere with *Kastratismus:* self-effacement, the affectation of weakness, and the paradoxical power which weakness exerts.

The woman/artist of Derrida's third proposition, then, does not by any means escape the rhetoric of castration. Derrida is surely right, though, in wanting to make a distinction between those instances in Nietzsche's discourse where "woman" appears to be equivalent to "castration" and this one, where castration is present but is not part of any such direct equation. A careful scrutiny of the argument in the passage from *Twilight of the Idols* under discussion makes clear that priests, philosophers, and artists (and also, by implication, the figure of woman that stands for and explains them) are not linked to castration by a logic of equivalence or of similarity; they are linked by a logic of desire. Their weakness and degeneracy are not a matter of their having practiced castration upon themselves or others but rather part of a psychic constellation that includes a kind of wish for castration. If we examine "the whole history" of the priests, philosophers, and artists, Nietzsche tells us, we will discover in them not the impotent themselves, not genuine ascetics, but instead "those who might really have needed to be ascetics" (KSA 6:83; TI p. 488*). The priests, artists, and philosophers in question here are "impossible ascetics" who advocate and perhaps even long for an "extirpation" they are incapable of achieving.[3] The denial of a "craving" (*Begierde*) involves a craving of another sort, a craving for the extirpation of cravings. Nietzsche's language even acknowledges this strange double edge of desire when he says that those who are too weak-willed to impose moderation on themselves choose castration "in the fight with a craving." Nietzsche's original German (*wird instinktiv im Kampfe mit einer Begierde von Denen gewählt*) allows an instant of uncertainty as to whether the phrase *mit einer Begierde* modifies the noun *Kampf* or the verb *gewählt,* an uncertainty therefore as to whether the "craving" in question is something the weak-willed oppose or possess. When one considers the rest of Nietzsche's argument, it is clear that both alternatives are affirmed. The choice of the preposition *mit* allows and even encourages the suspicion that desire remains a powerful force even as it is being denied. The uncertainty may be easily resolved on the syntactic level, but on the conceptual level it remains in force, strengthened at last by the admission that these weak-willed folk are not full-fledged eunuchs but only those who "might really have needed to be ascetics."

Nietzsche does speak elsewhere of a certain religious figure—an ideal figure, to be sure—as actually achieving the castration that these others only dream of. "The saint with whom God is well pleased," he declares, "is the ideal eunuch [*Castrat*]" (KSA 6:85; TI p. 490*). But the concept of "saint" is not coextensive with that of "priest." The saint embodies what the priest may wish to be but falls short of achieving. He is precisely the "ideal *Castrat*" whose castration is understood paradigmatically as an object of emulation, and not as a metaphor of achieved reality. His castration represents the standard toward which others, the others referred to as "impossible ascetics," aspire. Granted Nietzsche's irony, granted even his evident contempt for "saints" such as this, the use of the term *ideal* is both instructive and appropriate.

It is even consistent with Nietzsche's own view of himself. At times he sees himself as participating in just such a longing for self-abnegation and extirpation. Consider these closing lines from the poem "On the Poverty of the Richest," a piece he thought highly enough of to use twice. It serves as the conclusion of both the *Dionysus Dithyrambs* and *Nietzsche contra Wagner* and expresses an unmistakable longing for a (probably impossible) self-effacement:

> You must become *poorer*,
> wise Unwiseman,
> if you want to be loved.
> People love only those who suffer,
> they give only to those who starve:
> *first give yourself away,* O Zarathustra!
> —I am your truth.
> (KSA 6:410 and 6:445)[4]

Zarathustra's "truth" sets him the goal of a radical self-abnegation. He must extirpate his "excess" (*Überfluss*), his wealth (*Reichthum*), the source of both his pride and his pain, in order to attain the power to attract love. Nietzsche dramatizes himself (in the persona of Zarathustra) as one of those "impossible ascetics" often found among the contemplatives, one of "those who might really have needed to be ascetics." He presents the divestiture of spiritual "wealth" not as (or not only as) a loss but as a goal toward which Zarathustra should strive.

Here as elsewhere he characterizes this "ideal" condition to which contemplative types look with longing, this extirpation of the phallus, as at once an almost impossible transcendent goal and the most frightening, the lowest condition imaginable. He also, of course, understands it as the mysteriously permanent condition of woman. Woman is the alternative version of the saintly ideal, the other paradigm of Christian morality, who shares with the saint the whole constellation of (often contradictory) values gathered under the term *Kastratismus*.

Nietzsche's complex rhetoric thus places two related but somewhat different versions of "woman" on *both* sides of the relationship of desire: since she is in one guise a kind of artist, she is the desiring subject; but because she may also appear in another form as the embodiment of impotence, as the already-castrated body, she is also the object of desire. In this second guise she is the object of something one might call, if the reader will forgive the impertinence, "castration envy."

I ask for the reader's indulgence here on three counts: first because I insist on the implausible notion that something so self-evidently undesirable as castration could be an object of desire; second because I propose that Friedrich Nietzsche (of all people!) was an advocate of this notion; and third because I am playing fast and loose with Freudian terminology. The first count I will deal with shortly. On the second count I offer in defense the evidence already presented. I believe it substantiates the claim that Nietzsche's texts urge us to think of "desire" and "castration" as compatible concepts. These texts link elements explicitly identified as part of the syndrome of *Kastratismus* with a rhetoric of an "ideal" self-effacement that is part of the writer's own system of values. On the third count I can only plead guilty and throw myself on the mercy of the court. I am indeed playing fast and loose with Freud's notion of "penis envy." But I venture to suggest that "castration envy" is not, when all is said and done, much more outrageous an idea than the one it plays upon. If "castration envy" seems a paradoxical and ridiculous notion, especially perhaps to many men, "penis envy" has seemed no less so, especially perhaps to many women. If we are willing to entertain the one, then, we had better not dismiss the other. And since the issue of penis envy has become an open and indeed vexed question in the light of its reexamination by feminist criticism, we might welcome rather than reject the possibility that it could have a hitherto unsuspected opposite.

Now let me address the question of the ostensible implausibility of the very idea of "castration envy." In the first place, we must recognize that the notion of "castration" as it appears in Nietzsche is rather different from the concept worked out by Freud. Nietzsche's "castration" is not so much a psychological as a philosophical metaphor, and it figures in a discourse that aims to account for cultural, not individual, behavior. Freud uses castration anxiety and penis envy primarily as part of an attempt to explain the psychohistory of particular persons, while Nietzsche looks to explain the genesis of ethical and epistemological categories. One might say that Nietzsche's "castration" is more purely a metaphor than Freud's, for Nietzsche is rarely if ever concerned with actual sexuality or actual body parts. He uses sexuality in general and the penis in particular as figures, principally for generative power in the intellectual realm, but also in other ways.

That having been granted, however, it remains to show also how and why this evidently negative notion could be turned into a positive value and to demonstrate that "castration envy" forms a coherent part of Nietzsche's thinking.

It is necessary to return first to the figure of woman, a figure both castrated and castrating, who appears regularly as the trope through which Nietzsche approaches the most enduring and perhaps most fundamental questions in philosophy. We can start with one of the most traditional and recognizable of these tropes, in which nature appears as a (usually nurturing) woman. Nietzsche proposes a variation on this old chestnut of a figure when he describes the Greek view of her in *The Birth of Tragedy:* "In these Greek festivals, nature seems to reveal a sentimental trait; it is as if she were heaving a sigh at her dismemberment into individuals" (KSA 1:33; BT §2, p. 40). Nature is thus a dismembered woman, but mysteriously still whole, still complete, and still powerful. Her completeness *as body* is stressed in another passage from the same work: "The essence of nature is now to be expressed symbolically; we need a new world of symbols; and the entire symbolism of the body is called into play, not the mere symbolism of the lips, face, and speech but the whole pantomime of dancing, forcing every member into rhythmic movement" (KSA 1:33–34; BT §2, p. 40).

As Nietzsche reconstructs the Greek figuration of nature, then, it appears as a female body that is on the one hand subject to dismemberment but on the other enormously powerful. One of the principal arguments of *The Birth of Tragedy* hinges upon the power of that body and its effects on the Greek mind: "That overwhelming dismay in the face of the titanic powers of nature . . . was again and again overcome by the Greeks with the aid of the Olympian *middle world* of art; or at any rate it was veiled and withdrawn from sight" (KSA 1:36; BT §3, p. 42).

This last formulation is particularly interesting in that it links the rhetoric of one female body, *natura,* with another, the veiled *veritas.* Both are stock figures, but by bringing them together Nietzsche moves them in a new direction. We recognize the trope of "veiled truth" not only from its frequent appearance elsewhere in Nietzsche's writings (about which more below) but also from its extensive use by theologians and rhetoricians from the middle ages onward. Augustine used it to describe the way in which truth is clothed in figurative language in the Bible, and Boccaccio reformulated it in his defense of secular poetry: "*Fabula* is a way of speaking under [the cloak of] a figure/fiction so as to serve as a pattern or point something out; and if its surface [lit. "husk"] is penetrated, the intention of the author shows forth. And so if something sensible is ascertained under the veil of fiction, it cannot be superfluous and useless to compose fictions."[5] In all of these versions, part of the argument is that an unmediated vision of the bare truth, *nuda veritas,* is neither safe nor proper for mere mortals. There is an implication, sometimes stated and sometimes only implied, that looking at the naked truth would be just as difficult and dangerous as looking directly at the sun and just as improper as gazing at actual naked women. The veil that covers the body of the truth is thus a matter of moral decency as well as epistemological necessity. Boccaccio says that the goal of literary invention is "to cover the truth with a marvelous *and seemly* veil."[6] When Nietzsche uses the trope, he calls upon this tradition with all its implications. One of the most often-cited passages in *The Gay Science* suggests that he did so quite consciously: " 'Is it true that God is present everywhere?' a little girl asked her mother; 'I think that's indecent'—a hint for philosophers! One should have more respect for the bashfulness with which nature has hidden behind riddles and iridescent uncertainties. Perhaps truth is a woman who has reasons for not letting us see her reasons? Perhaps her name is—to speak Greek—*Baubo?*" (KSA 3:352; GS—P §4, p. 38). The naked truth is not attainable because the woman who is truth (and nature) chooses to keep it concealed. It is not desirable because what she conceals is something we would not wish to see. The clear implication is that *veritas/natura* is hiding something downright repulsive.

That there is something unpleasant, even repellent, about the female body is surely one of Nietzsche's more offensive notions, but (in this version at any rate) it may tell us at least as much about the writer's view of nature as it does about his misogyny. It is important to realize that Nietzsche's negative attitude toward the body of woman is linked to his sense of woman's closeness to nature. "Woman is more closely related to nature than man," he wrote on one occasion, and on another: "When we love a woman, we easily conceive a hatred for nature on account of all the repulsive natural functions to which every woman is subject. We prefer not to think of all this. . . . We artists! We ignore what is natural" (KSA 3:422–23; GS §59, pp. 122–23). It is probably not possible to decide here whether woman is repulsive because she is nature or nature is repulsive because she is female. All we can say for certain is that Nietzsche's rhetoric binds together the notions of woman, truth, nature, and revulsion into a single idea.

One cannot avoid the conclusion that for Nietzsche the scandal of the female body is not only or even primarily the "natural functions" of menstruation, lactation, and so forth, but the absence of a visible organ. What Mother Nature needs so urgently to hide from view is not so much what she has as what she lacks. Nietzsche suspects a void at the center of the body of nature. He does not name that void "castration" in his early writings; he names it instead with other figures: Moira, the vulture devouring Prometheus, the curse of the house of Atreus, the wisdom of Silenus; but it is the same dismembered body with a gap in the middle.[7] It is the abyss from which the Greeks sheltered themselves by creating their own veil, the golden world of the Olympian gods. For the most part, though, we do not have to weave veils for ourselves; nature herself withholds from us the sight of her castrated body by offering only mediated visions of the scandal at her center.

There is anxiety—indeed stark terror—that comes with the recognition of the abyss, but it is not exactly castration anxiety. The revulsion that comes from a recognition of nature's appalling dismemberment does not arise from a fear that something similar could happen to us. A sufferer of castration anxiety fears the loss of power that accompanies the loss of the penis. But in Nietzsche's figuration of nature, the castrated body is not the locus of a loss of power; quite the contrary, the feminine body of nature is the most potent force imaginable—and not merely in spite of but to a large extent because of the void at its center. The anxiety Nietzsche depicts in the Greek facing the uncovered body of Mother Nature is not the fear that he might become like her; it is rather a fear that comes from the knowledge that he can never have a power anything like hers. He is in awe of the overwhelming negativity that defines her, a negativity which she ordinarily graciously hides from view.

The potency of the penis is negligible in comparison to the irresistible might figured by its absence. Castration is the trope that stands for the ultimate power, an object as much of envy as of fear. All the positive values of life, all of life's powerful magic, indeed even life itself, are subsumed under the figure of the veiled female body: "I mean to say that the world is overfull of beautiful things but nevertheless poor, very poor when it comes to beautiful moments and unveilings of these things. But perhaps this is the most powerful magic of life: it is covered by a veil interwoven with gold, a veil of beautiful possibilities, sparkling with promise, resistance, bashfulness, mockery, pity, and seduction. Yes, life is a woman" (KSA 3:569; GS §339, pp. 271–72). Consider also figuration of life as a seductive woman (Helen) in the following: "We hear nothing but the accents of an exuberant, triumphant life in which all things, whether good or evil, are deified. And so the spectator may stand quite bewildered before this fantastic excess of life, asking himself by virtue of what magic potion these high-spirited men could have found life so enjoyable that, wherever they turned, their eyes beheld the smile of Helen, the ideal picture of their own existence, 'floating in sweet sensuality' " (KSA 1:35; BT §3, p. 41).

One might imagine that such a powerful figure—woman-as-nature, woman-as-truth, woman-as-life, not to mention woman-as-artist and woman-as-philosopher—could evade the ethos of castration. But she does not, because power resides in the place of castration. The artist and the philosopher, the lovers of nature and truth and life, recognize this, and so castration haunts their dreams. They dream such disquieting dreams, Nietzsche suggests, even more often and more vividly than do the priests. But they are dreams indeed, not nightmares. The "impossible ascetics," the artists and philosophers, do not fear the extirpation of the sensual any more than the priest does: they long for it. If woman is an artist, then she too longs for the castration which—as a figure—she represents.

The philosopher, the woman, and the poet are of imagination all compact, though as imagined bodies they are radically different. The figure of woman stands for the fulfillment of an imagined impossibility. No one can truly know her (sexually or intellectually), since to know her would undo knowledge.[8] She is the locus of absolute power. Because her power is an infinite void, an irremediable absence, she is appalling; but because her power is enormous, all those who possess a will to power must envy the void that is its source.

Notes

1. Jacques Derrida, *Spurs: Nietzsche's Styles / Eperons: Les Styles de Nietzsche,* trans. Barbara Harlow (Chicago: Univ. of Chicago Press, 1979), pp. 40/41.

2. "The church resists passion with extirpation in every sense: its practice, its 'cure' is *Kastratismus*" (KSA 6:83; cf. TI p. 487).

3. "Just look at the whole history of the priests and philosophers, including the artists: the most poisonous things against the senses have been said not by the impotent, nor by ascetics, but by the impossible ascetics, by those who might really have needed to be ascetics" (KSA 6:83; TI p. 488*). See also *Spurs,* pp. 92/93.

4. [Kaufmann omits this poem from his translation of *Nietzsche contra Wagner.* —Ed.]

5. Giovanni Boccaccio, *Genealogie deorum gentilium libri,* ed. Vincenzo Romano, 2 vols. (Bari: Gius, Laterza & Figli, 1951), 2:706. This is my translation of the following: "Fabula est exemplaris seu demonstrativa sub figmento locutio, cuius amoto cortice, patet intentio fabulantis. Et sic, si sub velamento fabuloso sapidum comperiatur aliquid, non erit supervacaneum fabulas edidisse."

6. "Velamento fabuloso atque decenti veritatem contegere" (*Genealogie,* 2:699; translation and italics are mine).

7. See section 3 of *The Birth of Tragedy* (KSA 1:34–38; BT §3, pp. 41–44).

8. Derrida speaks of a similar effect of what he calls the "question" of woman: "The question of woman suspends the decidable opposition of true and non-true" (*Spurs,* pp. 106/107). Nietzsche's usual term for woman, *Weib,* even suspends the opposition between male and female, as it possesses neither masculine nor feminine (grammatical) gender. Because *Weib* is both grammatically neuter and sexually female, the word can be the antecedent of either feminine or neuter pronouns, a possibility which Nietzsche's rhetoric occasionally exploits.

BIANCA THEISEN

Rhythms of Oblivion

To remember forgetfully: again, the outside.
—Maurice Blanchot

I

It requires a "third ear" (KSA 5:189; BGaE §246, p. 159) to listen to what Nietzsche writes about women. Most of his remarks at first seem unquestionably derisive: he scorns feminists who try to enlighten us about "woman as such," he mocks female writers like Madame Roland, Madame de Staël, or "Monsieur George Sand" as "the three *comic* women as such" (KSA 5:172; BGaE §233, p. 145), and he denounces emancipation as one of "the worst developments in the general *uglification* of Europe" (KSA 5:170; BGaE §232, p. 144). Not only does he characterize female attempts to gain access to a male-dominated world—to aim for autonomy, education, and equal rights—as a corruption of instincts and as the paragon of bad taste, Nietzsche also questions woman's right in her traditional realm: woman is incompetent as a cook, since she has not grasped the significance of food and of physiology (KSA 5:172–73; BGaE §234, p. 146); certain female character traits like "pedanticism, superficiality, schoolmarmishness, petty presumption, petty unbridledness and petty immodesty" (KSA 5:171; BGaE §232, p. 144) show themselves especially in woman's behavior with children. Nietzsche's judgments on "woman" were already challenged by his feminist friend Malwida von Meysenbug.[1] In her autobiography she reports on her talks with Nietzsche: she renounced his generalizing judgments on "woman," because he hardly knew any women.[2]

But is Nietzsche writing about real women at all, is he even writing about the concept of "woman"?

Excluding woman from both the traditionally male and the traditionally female realm—excluding her doubly, as it were—Nietzsche praises woman's art of deception and simulation. Women are prodigies of mockery and masquerade: "What is truth to a woman! From the very first nothing has been more alien, repugnant, inimical to woman than truth—her great art is the lie, her supreme concern is appearance and beauty" (KSA 5:171; BGaE §232, p. 145). What at first simply seems to be a metaphorical endorsement of the philosophical opposition appearance/being changes when read against Nietzsche's parody of philosophy's traditional outlook on woman and truth. "Supposing truth to be a woman—," Nietzsche surmises in the introductory paragraph of *Beyond Good and Evil,* then the suspicion would be "well founded that all philosophers, when they have been dogmatists, have had little understanding of women." The "gruesome earnestness" and "clumsy importunity" with which they approached her precluded their beholding truth, this most evasive of "females" (KSA 5:11; BGaE—P, p. 13). In relation to truth, then, "woman" figures on the one hand as the object of inquiry, when philosophers pursue her as truth, on the other hand as the inquiring subject, when she favors the lie—a simulated truth, a play on the distinction between truth and nontruth. Excluding "woman" both from the traditionally male and the traditionally female realm and including "woman" in his philosophical discourse as both truth and deception (the negative side of truth), Nietzsche undercuts a bivalent or Aristotelian logic that operates on distinctions like male and female, truth and deception, or being and appearance.

Nietzsche confronts us with paradoxes, then, if "woman" is situated neither in the male nor the female realm, or if she is posited as truth and deception simultaneously. His statements are contradictory as long as we argue from within the distinction truth/lie and try to locate "woman" in any of these two positions. We cannot seek the truth of "woman" as such since there is no truth "as such," as Nietzsche persistently informs us. But we also cannot simply proclaim the supremacy of deception. To ascribe truth value to deception, by merely reversing positions and privileging deception as the "truer" term of the distinction, would still draw on the distinction truth/deception and borrow its terms from the operation of "truth" within that distinction. Nietzsche's paradox on "woman," then, leads bivalent reasoning into indistinction and self-referentiality.[3] Deceptive truth and truthful deception become even more intertwined when women are observing it: "Whatever women write about 'woman,'"

Nietzsche states—and this statement must certainly also apply to women writing about "woman" in Nietzsche—"we may in the end reserve a good suspicion as to whether woman really *wants* or *can* want enlightenment about herself" (KSA 5:171; BGaE §232, p. 144). When women claim to reveal the "truth" about "woman" (for instance, the "truth" about "woman" in Nietzsche: that woman cannot but deceive), they cannot but deceive. Even if "woman" were honest enough to state, "I am deceiving," this would not mean that for once she was telling the truth. Characterizing "woman" as deceptive, Nietzsche offers another version of the self-referential circularity known as the liar's paradox: the statement "all Cretans are liars" by the Cretan Epimenides is false, if it is taken to be true; it is true, if it is taken to be false. Simultaneously true and false, "woman" (just as Epimenides) violates the very distinction between truth and lie.

This deadlock of undecidability, brought about by paradox and self-reference, appears to be Nietzsche's subterfuge to undercut a bivalent logic that dates back to Aristotle. According to this tradition of logic, something either is or is not; something either is true or it is not true (false). This logic is based on two values that are mutually determined through negation: A (truth) is designated through not-A (nontruth) and not-A through A. Bivalent logic obviously cannot allow for paradox or self-reference: A cannot simultaneously occupy the position of not-A—as Nietzsche suggests, when "woman" stands in for both truth and nontruth. Also, this logic has to exclude a *tertium datur,* since A and not-A are posited to be each identical with itself. If Nietzsche, however, differentiates between "woman" and "women," singular and plural, a concept and a phenomenon (of language), he introduces a split into what seems to be identical to itself, whether it functions as the subject (woman simulates truth) or as the object (woman is pursued as truth) of inquiry in relation to truth. This splitting, which doubles one of the positions, enters a third value of a different logical type into bivalent logic and marks the transition to many-valued logic as it has been formulated by distinction theory.[4] The "logical" third or *tertium datur* that thus dislocates logic in a moment of transition, is not a "given": I would like to suggest that, similar to "woman" in Nietzsche, this given third always only gives itself *as,* even when it *gives* itself (KSA 3:609; GS §361, p. 317). The operation of splitting and doubling one of the positions, I shall claim, shifts the movement of negation on which all bivalent logic is based; in its transitoriness, this operation could be compared with what Derrida has described as "desistance." The "logic" of desistance occasions a dis-identification of the subject through a redoubling of negation that, however, entails nothing negative.[5] Nietzsche's insistence on female simulation seems to "desist" Aristotelian logic with regard to both its *tertium non datur* and its necessary negation. Before investigating Nietzsche's concept of affirmation, which he associates with a woman, namely Ariadne, let us consider the shift in logical type that allows for arguing beyond true and false—in an "extralogical" sense, as it were.

The inclination to deceive and the power to simulate, for which Nietzsche both blames and praises women in his later aphorisms, are held to be intrinsic to the nature of the human intellect in general in his early essay "On Truth and Lying in an Extra-Moral Sense." The distinction between truth and deception is not a necessary presupposition of reasoning, Nietzsche argues, but a contingent effect of convention. With man's deceptive consciousness as a means of self-preservation, all kinds of simulation are "so much the rule and the law" that it seems almost incomprehensible that a "desire for truth" should have developed (KSA 1:876; TL p. 247). The conventional distinction between truth and deception coincides with instituting social order; Hobbes's "war of all against all" is suspended by a peace pact that according to Nietzsche first establishes what shall become truth: "For what 'truth' will be from now on is fixed; a uniformly valid and binding terminology for things is invented and the legislation of language also enacts the first laws of truth. For now, for the first time, the distinction between truth and lying arises. The liar uses the valid terms, the words, to make the unreal appear real. For instance, he says, 'I am rich,' when 'poor' would be the right term. He misuses established conventions by arbitrary substitutions and even reversals of names" (KSA 1:877–78; TL pp. 247–48). Truth is not the essential quality of an "as such" or a "thing-in-itself" (KSA 1:879; TL p. 248) but rests upon a linguistic convention: "to be truthful, i.e., to use the customary metaphors, or in moral terms, the obligation to lie according to an established convention" (KSA 1:881; TL p. 250).[6] The liar, in turn, inverts conventional designations (rich and not rich, to use Nietzsche's example). The effect of lying is that it blurs distinctions until they reach a point of undecidability. Thus, lying paradoxically undercuts a linguistic convention that is founded on lying, because it recalls what has been forgotten: the contingency of the *distinction* between truth and lie.[7] Truths are but subliminal lies. If intellect and language are basically deceptive, "truth" is but a deception about deception. Nietzsche calls the process of deception that underlies truth "forgetting": "Truths are illusions about which it has been forgotten that they *are* illusions" (KSA 1:880–81; TL p. 250). To forget this forgetting, to remember forgetfully, would entail reintroducing deception (as a shifting and collapsing of distinctions) into a moral, linguistic, or cognitive system that had confined distinctions to a logic of exclusion.

It requires a "third ear," then, to listen to Nietzsche's statements on woman; they cannot be read only on the level of *énoncé,* where this conventional bivalent logic is valid. Every sentence is misunderstood, Nietzsche observes, that we only read for its meaning on the level of *énoncé;* to misunderstand is to read a sentence without listening to its tempo or rhythm, without perceiving a fracturing of language that subliminally undercuts all symmetries, without perceiving an asemantic stratum underlying the semantic and logical levels of language (KSA 5:189; BGaE §246, p. 159). The "third ear" Nietzsche asks for would try to perceive this asemantic, rhythmic stratum as a scansion of language, a split between enunciation and *énoncé;* a rhythmic scansion to which our perception is usually oblivious because it rests upon it. Rhythm here could be defined as liminality: within the parameters of distinction theory it could be called form, that is, the fact *that* a distinction is drawn.[8] Analogous to a "third ear" that would perceive a certain scansion, a logical third or *tertium datur* would allow one to recognize the distinctions upon which cognition necessarily operates *as* distinction (that is, not as the distinction *true/false,* but as *distinction*). And if gender difference can be seen as one of the more fundamental paradigms of distinction, then a "third sex," as it were, would be necessary to generate a rebirth of philosophy out of philosophy. This third sex manifests itself on the one hand in what Nietzsche tries to describe as a male mother—the philosopher should neither distinguish body from soul, as everyday reasoning does, nor should he divide soul from spirit: "Constantly, we have to give birth to our thoughts out of our pain and, like mothers, endow them with all we have of blood, heart, fire, pleasure, passion, agony, conscience, fate, and catastrophe" (KSA 3:349; GS—P §3, pp. 35–36). The metaphors of pregnancy and procreation that pervade Nietzsche's writings are intricately linked to his notion of life as both production and sickness. Again, Nietzsche calls this ambivalent simultaneity "woman": *vita femina,* life is a woman (KSA 3:568; GS §339, p. 271). This metaphor has led Eric Blondel to speak of Nietzsche's "onto-gynecology": "One could indeed characterize Nietzsche's 'ontology' as feminine, or even as gynecological, for this ontology speaks of being as a woman who has no being, as appearance and disguise."[9] On the other hand, besides its metaphorical condensation in the intellectual pregnancy of a male mother, a third sex emerges from a constant and subliminal shifting of distinctions. Woman is here not so much grasped in terms of life, creation, or instinct, but she is rather enacted in a theater of simulation.

As masked actress she plays on the appearance and disappearance of distinctions. In fact, Nietzsche himself seems to be miming this feminine art of delusion when he simulates bivalent distinctions like truth/deception, being/appearance, appearance/disappearance, pleasure/pain up to a point at which they dissimulate. Nietzsche thus empties out the values of, for instance, truth/deception, but keeps them operative as value-positions. In a simulation and dissimulation of these empty value-positions, distinction *as* distinction appears and disappears. Nietzsche situates the displacement of a bivalent logic in aesthetics and, especially where the problem of negation is at stake, in the aesthetics of the sublime. His poem "Ariadne's Lament" illustrates a shift from negation to affirmation and finally, with the epiphany of Dionysus, to simulation and dissimulation.

II

With the poem "Ariadne's Lament," one of his *Dionysus Dithyrambs,* Nietzsche reedits the magician's song from *Zarathustra.*[10] He only changes masculine pronouns into feminine ones, thereby transforming the magician into Ariadne, and he adds Dionysus' answer to the monological lament. Reinhardt believed this change of gender to be almost singular in literary history and compared the play of roles that turned a no into a yes and a masculine into a feminine form to character-drama; for him the poem represented the "intricate problem of the mask that observes itself as mask or of the text that interprets itself as interpretation."[11]

The fact that Ariadne could be substituted for the magician clearly does not derive from autobiographical circumstances alone: the magician as Wagner, Ariadne as Cosima Wagner, Dionysus as Nietzsche, and Theseus as Wagner again. The magician and Ariadne both appear in a context of deception. The magician acts out the torments of forsakenness so as to seduce Zarathustra into pitying him. The Ariadne myth is already a story of betrayal. Minos had Daedalus construct the labyrinth in order to hide the double-natured Minotaurus, the monstrous proof of his wife's adultery. Ariadne, Minos' daughter, betrays her kin when she shows Theseus how to escape from the labyrinth with a thread and then runs off with him after he has defeated her monstrous half brother. Finally, Theseus deceives Ariadne, abandoning her on Naxos. According to most versions of the myth, Dionysus then approaches Ariadne, who is still lamenting her loss, and marries her.

In fact, what the magician has in common with "woman" is his art of delusion. Like woman, who gives herself *as* (who plays a role) even when she *gives* herself, the magician is an actor (KSA 3:609; GS §361, p. 317). Moreover, he confronts the spectators and interpreters of his deceptive art with the liar's paradox. Zarathustra is not seduced by the magician's convulsions and his wailing about being forsaken. When Zarathustra calls him a "liar from the bottom," the magician honestly, it seems, confesses that he only acted the "*ascetic of the spirit,*" that he only played the part of him "who at last turns his spirit against himself" (KSA 4:317–18; Z p. 368). But he takes the impossible unmasking of his own mask even further; the lie of having tried to represent a great human being is breaking him, he avows: "O Zarathustra, everything about me is a lie; but that I am breaking—this, my breaking, is genuine" (KSA 4:319; Z p. 369). It is undecidable whether there is truth-value to the magician's statement: if he is a liar, even his apparently utmost genuineness—the confession that he has always been lying and that this is breaking him—could be yet another lie.

Embedded in a theatrical undecidability between truth and deception in *Zarathustra,* the poem itself deals with the blurred distinction between inside and outside. Both the magician and Ariadne are tortured by an unknown, veiled, unnameable god who is but a projection of a thought that pursues them. But the Dionysus Dithyramb enigmatically adds the epiphany of this "god," as if the thought projected outside had assumed a gestalt that could finally be named—Dionysus:

Ariadne's Lament

Who warms me, who loves me still?
Give hot hands!
give hearts burning like coal-pans!
Stretched out, shivering,
Like someone half-dead whose feet one warms,
stricken, alas! by unknown fevers,
shaking with sharp icy frost-arrows,
hunted by you, Thought!
Unnameable! veiled! terrible one!
You hunter behind clouds!
Flashed at by your lightning,
you scornful eye that stares at me from the dark!
Thus I lie,
bending myself, twisting myself, tormented
by all eternal tortures,
hit
by you, cruelest hunter,
you unknown—*god* . . .

Hit deeper!
Hit yet One Time more!
Split, splinter this heart!
Why this torture
with blunt-toothed arrows?
Why do you stare again
not weary yet of human agony,
with gods' lightning-eyes that are pleased by pain?
Not killing it is that you want,
only torturing, torturing?
Why—torture *me,*
pleased by pain, you unknown god?

Haha!
You are sneaking up
in such a midnight? . . .
What do you want?
Speak!
You are pressing me, harassing me,
Ha! too close already!
You hear me breathing,
you listen to my heart,
you jealous one!
—jealous of what?
Away! Away!
why the ladder?
do you want to come *in,*
into the heart, climb in,
climb into my most secret
thoughts?
Shameless one! unknown one! thief!
What do you want to get by stealing?
What do you want to get by listening?
What do you want to get by torturing,
you torturer!
you—hangman-god!
Or should I, like a dog,
roll about before you?
Yielding, passionately beside myself
wag—love to you?
In vain!
Pierce on!
Cruelest spur!
No dog—only your prey I am,

cruelest hunter!
your proudest captive,
you robber behind clouds . . .
Speak at last!
You, veiled in lightning! unknown one! speak!
What do you want, waylayer, from—*me?* . . .

What?
Ransom?
How much ransom do you want?
Ask for Much—my pride advises!
and speak briefly—my other pride advises!

Haha!
Me—you want? me?
me—entirely? . . .

Haha!
And you torture me, fool that you are,
torture my pride?
Give *love* to me—who warms me still?
who loves me still?
give hot hands,
give a heart burning like coal-pans,
give me, the loneliest one,
your ice, alas! sevenfold ice
teaches yearning for enemies,
even for enemies,
give, yes give in
cruelest enemy,
to me—*yourself!* . . .

Gone!
Then even he himself fled,
my only companion,
my great enemy,
my unknown one,
my hangman-god! . . .
No!
come back!
With all your tortures!
All my tears are running
their course to you
and my last flame of heart
is glowing for you.

Oh come back,
my unknown god! my *pain!*
my last happiness! . . .

Lightning. Dionysus appears in emerald beauty.

Dionysus:

Be clever, Ariadne!
You have small ears, you have my ears:
put a shrewd word into them! —
Must one not first hate oneself if one is to love oneself? . . .
I am your labyrinth . . .
(KSA 6:398–401; cf. Z pp. 364–67)

Dionysus' enigmatic advice about an interlocking of love and hate ("Must one not first hate oneself if one is to love oneself?": "Muß man sich nicht erst hassen, wenn man sich lieben soll?"), is not as unequivocal as my translation has rendered it. The German pronoun "man" can designate both "people" and "one," an impersonal plural and an impersonal singular. Hillis Miller has pointed out that Dionysus' "shrewd word" is undecidable and that the sentence has several possible readings: Must people not first hate each other if they are to love each other? Must people not first hate each other if each is to love himself? Must one not first hate oneself if one is to love people? Must one not first hate oneself if one is to love oneself?[12] My "decision" for this last option is based on the following interpretation of the poem that reads the undecidability between one and other, between inside and outside, first as a question of distinctions *within* a subject (Ariadne).

The poem sketches a development: Ariadne moves through externalization—an attempt to grasp as "outside" what is "inside," to understand as "other" what is "herself"—to a final state in which the reciprocity of self and other, inside and outside is realized. The simultaneity of the impersonal plural and singular at the end, for instance ("muß man sich nicht erst hassen, wenn man sich lieben soll"), corresponds to Ariadne's invocation first of people, in the plural, who are to give her warmth and love ("Gebt heisse Hände" [KSA 6:398]), and its subsequent repetition, identical but for its singular address of her torturer ("gieb heisse Hände" [KSA 6:400]). Throughout the poem, physical states merge with states of mind. Ariadne first personifies as the hunter, "thought," what pursues and tortures her; she then projects this "thought" outside of herself as an "unknown god" who delights in a spectacle of agony. Thus, she invents a cause for her suffering, something to justify, to make more bearable the senselessness of suffering: a god who "roams even in secret, hidden places, sees even in the dark, and will not easily let an interesting painful spectacle pass unnoticed," as Nietzsche put it in *The Genealogy of Morals* (KSA 5:304; GM—II §7, p. 68). The god is the witness and spectator of suffering—Zarathustra plays this part for the magician. But this god is also identified, both by the system of religious justification and in the poem, as the reason for suffering. Again, we are faced with a circular kind of reasoning: what seems to be the cause (god) is but the effect of its effect (suffering). Just as truth turned out to be an illusion whose illusoriness has been forgotten, the "god" as invented cause of suffering demands forgetting that he is but an invention. His lightning-bolt glance, as it were, leaves a blind spot. Because of this forgetting, suffering functions as a mnemotechnique. Social order, moral and religious systems are constituted through the infliction of pain that creates memory: " 'If something is to stay in the memory it must be burned in: only that which never ceases to *hurt* stays in the memory' " (KSA 5:295; GM—II §3, p. 61). The piercing arrows, the cruel spur, the "shrewd word" Ariadne is to put into her ear, could be seen as metaphors for imprinting memory. "Ariadne's Lament" is the printout of this imprint in its typographical particularities: indentation of certain lines, alternation of upper and lower case at the beginning of lines, and the disruptive use of punctuation marks.

The thought that had been projected outside as the unknown god then returns and tries to penetrate the inside. The ladder with which he seems to climb into Ariadne's innermost recesses is reminiscent of "the ladder of religious cruelty" (KSA 5:74; BGaE §55, p. 63). Its three rungs represent three stages in the development of sacrifice: in times of archaic religion people sacrificed humans to their gods; in times of moral belief people sacrificed their strongest drives and instincts to their gods; in a time yet to come people will sacrifice god himself (representative of any belief in consolation and salvation) as a final cruelty against themselves. Ariadne can be situated between the second and third rung of this ladder: between the painful pleasure of the ascetic who expels her drives and the violent jouissance of a nihilist who worships total loss, sacrificing god to a nothing (Nietzsche lists: a stone, stupidity, gravity, fate). This last abjection will be the "paradoxical mystery of the ultimate act of cruelty," a cruelty against oneself, for in discarding the god one will have disposed of oneself (KSA 5:74; BGaE §55, p. 63). As a "thief"—but what does he want to steal?—the god is in fact situated in a realm of loss; as a "waylayer" he demands Ariadne herself as ransom. But the demarcation between Ariadne and her "god" fades more and more with the distinction between god, human, and animal; when Ariadne is literally "outside" of herself ("ausser mir"), panting love to her god like a dog, while the god hunts her as his prey, the demarcation is erased between the domesticated and the wild, that is, the very foundation of social and symbolic order.

It was typical of Dionysus to instigate confusion and to erase borders: his devotees lose their sense of identity and of circumscribed social roles; the frontiers that separate god, human, and animal constantly shift; the distinctions that define class, age, and gender fade. Through the god's epiphany, Vernant states, the bivalent distinctions that seem to stabilize social order lose their distinctiveness. Wildness and civilization merge ambiguously: on the one hand, Dionysus invented the cultivation of wine and established civilized life; on the other hand, Dionysus drives his devotees out of the city and out of civilized life into the wilderness. Near and far merge; Dionysus promises no transcendence, no salvation beyond this world; he transforms immanence. Moreover, Dionysus blurs gender difference: male and female fuse, since Dionysus is a male god with a female appearance.[13]

With the fading of distinctions we seem to enter the labyrinthine maze of indistinction. What first had been rejection (Ariadne wards off the god when he comes "too close," penetrating her inner being) changes into affirmation: she welcomes her "cruelest enemy" *with* all his tortures. Ariadne's lament turns into a dithyramb as she comes to affirm the pleasure in the tormenting pains of "thought" as her "last happiness." Some critics have claimed that the thought pursuing Ariadne stands for Nietzsche's most terrible thought, eternal recurrence.[14] What keeps recurring, however, could not be a recurrence of the same, if sameness is constituted by our recognition of distinct positions and fixed designations. Sameness rests upon the logic of negation and thus precludes Nietzsche's emphatic notion of affirmation implicit in his idea of eternal recurrence. Deleuze therefore argues that eternal recurrence emerges from a union of Dionysus and Ariadne in a movement *through* negation to affirmation; he sees in Ariadne a figure of doubled affirmation.[15] What keeps recurring in the poem is not a particular "thought" but a pain that accompanies the insistence of the unthinkable in thought. Pain is the disruptive moment that undercuts the perception of what to us appears as sameness over time. This disruptive moment temporarily suspends the logic of contradiction from within which we cannot perceive what inscribes those distinct positions that guarantee "sameness." Nietzsche employs graphic markers in his poem to grasp this disruptive moment eluding perception; the *Gedankenstriche*—the dashes as figures of elision—literally mark thoughts

(*Gedanken*) which have been erased (*gestrichen*) by a dash (*Strich*) that stands in for them. Dionysus' enigmatic statement, "you have small ears, you have my ears / put a shrewd word into them," calls on a different kind of perception that would try to grasp what eludes perception. Are Ariadne's small ears "the same" as Dionysus'? Or are these ears simultaneously his and hers, a *tertium datur* of perception, as it were, corresponding to what Nietzsche calls the "third ear"? The "shrewd word" to be perceived would then be something that eludes perception: the inscription of distinction *as* distinction. This distinction cannot be represented "as such." It can only be simulated and dissimulated; like Dionysus in his epiphany, it appears only in disappearing.

In a flash of lightning, a stage direction tells us, Dionysus, who had remained offstage throughout the poem, at last appears "in emerald beauty." For the Greeks, Dionysus' epiphany was different from that of other gods: he showed himself, but as a masked god; he revealed himself, but only by concealing himself. Vernant does not trace Dionysus' bearing on tragic theater back to religious origins that remain obscure; rather, he sees the manifestation of the masked god in what he calls the most modern aspect of Greek theater: in dramatic simulation the distinction between reality and illusion disappears, but at the same time remains conscious as fiction.[16] The Dionysus of Nietzsche's dithyramb has more in common with the god Vernant describes (derived from Greek tragedies) than with Nietzsche's metaphysical figure for the "original One" (*Ur-Einen*) in *The Birth of Tragedy,* a figure in a state prior to its transfiguration into appearance through theater and art. In the dithyramb, however, appearance is grafted onto being, when Dionysus appears on stage and "is" Ariadne's labyrinth; even when he finally gives in to Ariadne's invocation and gives himself, he gives himself "as." But Dionysus' appearance in disappearance dissimulates the negative aspects of simulation for which Nietzsche blames women. A third sex emerges with the configuration of Ariadne and Dionysus: the female, Ariadne, and Dionysus, the male god who appears *as* female, together manifest a *tertium datur* of gender difference.

III

Nietzsche draws on an aesthetics of the sublime to describe what escapes perception, to represent what eludes representation—not as sublime unrepresentability, however, but as this *tertium datur,* a distinction *as* distinction.[17] "Ariadne's Lament" first conforms to the sublime attempt to unveil truth—she beseeches the veiled, unknown, and unnameable god to speak and to show himself, and she tries to fathom his will at all costs, even that of death or self-sacrifice—but then moves through the negative pleasure of sublime kinesis to a forgetting of the sublime.

Sublime unrepresentability is best captured in the story of the veiled idol in the temple at Sais. The veil does not hide the goddess, only her idol; the goddess herself (truth "as such") can neither be seen nor represented. The veil marks a demarcation that is not to be transgressed. In Schiller's version of that story a youth disregards the taboo, uncovers the veil, falls unconscious in the very moment he expects to see the truth, and dies without having been able to tell anyone what he saw.[18] There is maybe nothing more sublime, Kant notes in his *Critique of Judgment,* than the inscription on the temple of Isis: I am everything that is, that was, and that will be, and no mortal has ever lifted my veil.[19] Truth cannot be seen or perceived; for as soon as it *appears* (in the form of an idol, for instance), truth no longer *is;* as soon as we can perceive truth *as* something, truth is no longer truth *as such*. Nietzsche mocks this sublime quest for truth and the problematics of its unrepresentability; it betrays the bad taste of "those Egyptian youths who endanger temples by night, embrace statues," and want to unveil whatever is concealed "for good reasons":

> We no longer believe that truth remains truth when the veils are withdrawn; we have lived too much to believe this. Today we consider it a matter of decency not to wish to see everything naked, or to be present at everything, or to understand and "know" everything. "Is it true that God is present everywhere?" a little girl asked her mother; "I think that's indecent"—a hint for philosophers! One should have more respect for the bashfulness with which nature has hidden behind riddles and iridescent uncertainties. Perhaps truth is a woman who has reasons for not letting us see her reasons? Perhaps her name is—to speak Greek—*Baubo?* Oh, those Greeks! They knew how to live. What is required for that is to stop courageously at the surface, the fold, the skin, to adore appearance, to believe in forms, tones, words, in the whole Olympus of appearance. Those Greeks were superficial—*out of profundity.* (KSA 3:352; GS—P §4, p. 38)

If truth has reasons for not letting us see her reasons, she hints at a similar doubling of logic from out of itself, as does Dionysus, who appears in disappearing (he is absent and masked even when he is present); and if her name is Baubo (instead of Isis), truth is just as "obscene" as Dionysus was "off-scene" in "Ariadne's Lament." Baubo reveals the so-called "naked" truth when she lifts her skirts; displaying her sexual organs, Baubo reveals a truth, as psychoanalysis has taught us, that we both perceive and yet cannot perceive as gender difference, a quandary that can be solved only through the denegations of the castration complex or of fetishism.[20] But whereas the unveiling of Isis grants the view of a terrible nothingness, a sublime intimation of death (as "castration"), as petrifying as the view of Medusa's head, the unveiling of Baubo presents the "naked" truth only as another mask. Baubo displays her genitals, which in turn display a figure: thus, she causes Demeter to laugh, who consequently gives up her asceticism and her mourning due to the loss of Persephone. Since she reestablishes Demeter in her functions and properties of fecundity, Baubo has been interpreted as another figuration of eternal recurrence besides Dionysus.[21] Nietzsche blames the "sublime ones" for not yet having learned how to laugh (KSA 4:150; Z p. 229); the comic overcomes the sublime as the sublime aesthetically overcomes the terrible. But Nietzsche does not only subvert the sublime by turning its aesthetic rendering of the terrors of cognition into the comic aspects of the mask;[22] he also shifts the problematics of liminality at stake in the sublime.

When the magician acts as "an ascetic of the spirit" to seduce Zarathustra with his lament, he is also an actor of the sublime, hunting in "the woods of knowledge" for his "ugly truths" (KSA 4:150; Z pp. 228–29). The ascetic and the "sublime one" both turn their spirit against themselves.[23] Like Ariadne, they are suspended between the rungs of the "ladder of cruelty": the ascetic turns against himself with the painful pleasure of expelling his drives; the sublime one turns against himself with the negative pleasure of violating the limits of his imagination; the most radical version of turning against oneself, however, is offered by the violent jouissance of the nihilist who rejects "god" for nothingness. The ascetic, the sublime one, and the nihilist struggle with a problem of borders: what they turn back against themselves is a distinction; their subjectivity swallows what threatens this subjectivity and is at the same time its precondition. Abjection resembles the sublime, as Kristeva has pointed out, in that both have no object.[24] Their "object" is a border, a demarcation, a distinction *as* distinction—something we cannot think, because reasoning operates on it; something we cannot perceive, because it inscribes perception.

Already Kant had radically altered the concept of the sublime when he stated that sublimity was not to be found in natural objects themselves (like the ocean) but "merely in ourselves and in our attitude of thought, which introduces sublimity into the representations of nature."[25] In the sublime, inspiring awe through magnitude and boundlessness, we experience "something" that eludes our perception. "Ariadne's Lament" revolves around pleasure and pain and thus seems to correspond to Kant's notion of the sublime as negative pleasure; but the poem then transforms this negativity by affirming it. In his *Anthropology,* Kant defines pain (displeasure) as that which incites us to abandon a given condition and pleasure as that which incites us to maintain a given condition. Because of our perception of time, pleasure cannot be positive but only negative; time drags us from one instant to the next so that we constantly have to abandon a given condition: "But we are incessantly moved by the stream of time, and the change of sensations resultant from it. Even if the abandonment of one instant, and the occurring of another, is one and the same act (of change), it is, nevertheless, in our thought and in our awareness of change, a temporal sequence conforming to the relation of cause and effect."[26] Both the awareness of abandoning a present instant and the anticipation of entering a future instant can incite only negative pleasure; the former would be nothing more than an ending of pain, the latter could only be something positive if this future instant were definite—but it is indefinite "since time drags us from the present to the future (and not the other way around)" so that we are always first compelled to abandon a present instant without any certainty about the following instant. Only the fact *that* this following instant or future condition will be a different one can be a condition of pleasure. Pleasure thus always rests upon the displeasure of having to abandon a given condition: it cannot be but negative pleasure. Kant infers that pain precedes pleasure. Pain is a discontinuous moment that disrupts what to our perception seems to be continuous: "Actually small checks [*Hemmungen*] on our vital power, with interspersed advancements, constitute the state of health which we erroneously take for a continuously felt condition of well-being, since it always consists only of erratic sequences of pleasant feelings (constantly interspersed with pain)."[27]

A necessary error of our perception, Kant believes, is to perceive as continuous what becomes continuous only by virtue of a discontinuity. What eludes our perception is the distinction between the two, the moment of disruption. This dialectics of pleasure and pain, continuity and discontinuity, is also realized in the sublime. The feeling of the sublime is "a pleasure that arises only indirectly; viz. it is produced by the feeling of a momentary checking [*Hemmung*] of the vital powers and a consequent stronger outflow of them."[28] This checking again marks a painful moment of disruption that induces negativity into the continuous flow of the vital powers. The sublime (a magnitude beyond comparison, an infinite series in the case of the mathematical sublime, an indefinite and overwhelming force in the case of the dynamical sublime) incites negative pleasure because it urges us to grasp something ungraspable. In a magnitude that overstrains our perception we experience a violation of the limits of our perception; because our senses and our imagination fail in comprising this magnitude as a unity, our faculty of reasoning turns back upon the inadequacies of imagination, makes its limits of perception the "object" of reasoning and thus expands these limits. In this process, the disruptive aspect of the sublime experience is counteracted by what Kant calls apperception; it is a perception of perception that is to conceive of the inconceivable (the sublime "object" that is no object: the limit or distinction that eludes perception) by way of achieving a comprehension or conceptual unity. The task of apperception is to conceive of the distinction between continuity and discontinuity as continuity, that is, from within the distinction and by virtue of one of its terms.

For Nietzsche, the sublime is no longer an experience that violates the limits of imagination in order to conceptualize an inconceivable disruption, to represent the unrepresentable, or to make conscious what, like truth, cannot be an object of conscious reflection. He subverts the Kantian notion of the sublime in three respects.

First, even though Nietzsche ridicules the sublime as *will* to truth, he retains its moment of disruption, thereby dissolving the sublime into a subliminal rhythm of oblivion. In one of his posthumous fragments, Nietzsche suggests that pleasure could be defined as a rhythm of small stimuli of displeasure (KSA 13:38). Nietzsche affirms Kant's "momentary checking [*Hemmung*] of the vital powers"; he affirms the painful disruption in its negativity and thus transforms it into a "positive checking." What Nietzsche calls forgetting is the scansion marked by these repeated discontinuous moments. "Forgetting is no mere *vis inertiae* as the superficial imagine; it is rather an active and in the strictest sense positive faculty of repression [*positives Hemmungsvermögen*], that is responsible for the fact that what we experience and absorb enters our consciousness as little while we are digesting it (one might call the process 'inpsychation') as does the thousandfold process, involved in physical nourishment—so-called 'incorporation'" (KSA 5:291; GM—II §1, p. 57). Forgetting as a "positive faculty of repression" is double; it operates both as a negative, reactive force, a kind of repression—a faculty of checking or blocking—and as a positive, active force. Truths, which are but forgotten lies, for instance, rest upon the repression necessary for the inscription of a symbolic order; a concept like truth can function only if the distinction truth/lie is presupposed and if the contingency of this presupposed distinction is forgotten. To forget the *will* to truth, however, implies an active form of forgetting beyond the opposition truth/lie.

Second, Nietzsche revives the physiological implications of the sublime. In its necessarily reactive aspects, forgetting corresponds to what Freud describes as negation: the "no" of an intellectual judgment is "the hall-mark of repression."[29] For Nietzsche, as later for Freud, negation rests upon the physiological processes of internalizing and externalizing. The function of judgment, Freud supposes, derives from a yes or no to incorporation: " 'I should like to eat this,' or 'I should like to spit it out.' . . . That is to say: 'It shall be inside me' or 'it shall be outside me.' "[30] When Nietzsche describes perception, consciousness, and cognition as physiological processes, he does not undercut Kant's transcendental enterprise by reestablishing an empirical approach akin to Burke's. Burke had pictured the sublime experience as a cathartic outlet, a clearing of the body's constipated fibers, and was criticized by Kant for his empiricism. Beyond the opposition of transcendental and empirical, Nietzsche tries to show how judgment and thinking arise out of a reiterated moment of disruption, to which conscious thinking is necessarily oblivious.

Third, with his conception of time as eternal recurrence, Nietzsche tries to transform what according to Kant is necessarily negative pleasure into positive pleasure by affirming the process of negation—by simulating and dissimulating it. Simulation is already implied in the Kantian sublime in that the sublime entails earnestness (not play of the imagination as does the beautiful), a kind of earnestness, however, that is defused in fictionality; force and magnitude can be sublime only as long as they appear "as-if." This simulated peril occasioned by the sublime could in fact be called the "actio in distans" (KSA 3:425; GS §60, p. 124) of the sublime (Nietzsche "hears" in it the effect of woman). But because this kind of simulation still draws on negation—epitomized in the falsehood, deception, lying, and acting Nietzsche ascribes to woman—it has to be doubled and supplemented by dissimulation. The negativity inherent in the sublime experience—the painful moment of checking and disruption—cannot be simply inverted into something positive, because every affirmative positing is determined by what it is not. Logically, affirmation is based on negation and includes it. An inversion of negation into affirmation, then, could only end up with an affirmation which paradoxically tries to "negate" negation. This simple inversion is the shortcoming of the "higher men" in *Zarathustra:* their "Ja" (yes) only reproduces the "I-A" of the ass, and this affirmative braying fails, because it remains within the given system of thought and its logic of negation. Correspondingly, Nietzsche mocks the long ears of the ass, ears that fail to perceive what eludes perception. And Nietzsche's Dionysus compliments Ariadne on her small ears, but also teases her for her long ears. Thus, Ariadne appears to figure the interrelated issues of affirmation and perception. For Deleuze, Ariadne stands for a doubled affirmation that overcomes negativity and a logic of opposition: "We cannot think of affirmation as 'being opposed' to negation: this would be to place the negative within it. Opposition is not only the relation of negation with affirmation but the essence of the negative as such."[31] The problem Nietzsche's concept of affirmation poses is that it cannot be conceived within the parameters of bivalent logic—what Deleuze refers to as "opposition." Within bivalent logic, affirmation and negation are basically the same operation: every affirmation can be affirmation only by virtue of negating that which it is not. Because affirmation and negation are still operative in bivalent logic and presuppose the concepts of identity and *tertium non datur,* they have to be superseded by simulation and dissimulation; operations that suspend logic in the transitory moment that introduces a *tertium datur* and thus leads to a different logical type or a second order of logic. What Nietzsche calls affirmation, then, seems to be a threefold operation. A simple affirmation remains within bivalent distinctions that have been drawn already and it implies negation. Simulation affirms what is not, dis-simulation negates what is being simulated. This threefold process of affirmation redoubles negation, thus opening up bivalence to the contingency of the fact *that* distinctions are drawn—a contingency that entails nothing negative. The problem of negation is linked to that of time. The negativity of that moment of disruption when distinction appears and disappears is dissimulated as soon as time not only "drags us from the present to the future," as Kant stated, but also "the other way around." When time becomes reversible, as it does in eternal recurrence, the distinction between pleasure and displeasure, continuity and discontinuity, can be drawn anew. Eternal recurrence, Vaihinger suggested, is a useful fiction or a lie in the positive sense: if Nietzsche's concept of time functioned as a positive lie, one could add, it would transform the negativity of that moment of disruption which constitutes and deconstitutes our perception of time.[32] I read the prodigious "female" in Nietzsche's writings as a (negative) reaction to and an (affirmative) acting upon this repeated and repetitive moment of disruption. "She" is also a useful fiction, a positive as well as negative lie, "an old story": in *Ecce Homo* Nietzsche wishes for readers who recognize him as an unprecedented psychologist, readers who recognize that propositions like "pleasure and displeasure are opposites" belong to the "falsifications in psychologica." In this context of being read as an "unprecedented psychologist," Nietzsche surmises that he *knows* women and that this is part of his "Dionysian dowry": "Who knows? Perhaps I am the first psychologist of the eternally feminine. They all love me—an old story" (KSA 6:305; EH p. 266).

Notes

1. Although Nietzsche scorned feminists in his writings, he surrounded himself with educated feminist women like Malwida von Meysenburg, Meta von Salis, Resa von Schirnhofer, or Helene Druscowitz, whom he encouraged to write about these writings; see the biography by Curt Paul Janz, *Friedrich Nietzsche: Biographie,* 3 vols. (München: Hanser, 1978), 2:376.

2. Malwida von Meysenbug, *Memoiren einer Idealistin,* ed. Renate Wiggershaus (Frankfurt: Insel, 1985), p. 348.

3. Paradox in general can be characterized by self-referentiality and indistinction; see Niklas Luhmann, "Tautology and Paradox in the Self-Descriptions of Modern Society," in *Essays on Self-Reference* (New York: Columbia Univ. Press, 1990), pp. 123–43; Elena Esposito, "Paradoxien als Unterscheidungen von Unterscheidungen," in *Paradoxien, Dissonanzen, Zusammenbrüche: Situationen offener Epistemologie,* ed. Hans Ulrich Gumbrecht and K. Ludwig Pfeiffer (Frankfurt: Suhrkamp, 1991), pp. 35–57.

4. This transition from bivalent to many-valued logic has been described by Gotthard Günther; see, for instance, his essays "The Tradition of Logic and the Concept of a Trans-Classical Rationality," "Information, Communication, and Many-Valued Logic," or "Life as Poly-Contexturality," in *Beiträge zur Grundlegung einer operationsfähigen Dialektik,* 3 vols. (Hamburg: Felix Meiner, 1979), 2:116–22, 2:134–48, and 2:283–306. Distinction theory (*Unterscheidungstheorie*) refers to Niklas Luhmann's application of the logical calculus developed by G. Spencer Brown to the description of social systems. On the possible impact of distinction theory on feminism, which could reformulate the (often essentialized) distinction male/female as contingent, see Niklas Luhmann, "Frauen, Männer und George Spencer Brown," *Zeitschrift für Soziologie* 17 (1988): 47–71.

5. Jacques Derrida, "Introduction: Desistance," in Philippe Lacoue-Labarthe, *Typography: Mimesis, Philosophy, Politics,* ed. Christopher Fynsk (Cambridge: Harvard Univ. Press, 1989), pp. 1–42. If I stress the transitoriness of the splitting and doubling operation of a logical third, it is to extricate it from a dialectics in which Gotthard Günther still seems to situate it.

6. On the rhetoricity of logic in Nietzsche, see Paul de Man, "Rhetoric of Tropes (Nietzsche)" and "Rhetoric of Persuasion (Nietzsche)," in *Allegories of Reading: Figural Language in Rousseau, Nietzsche, Rilke, and Proust* (New Haven: Yale Univ. Press, 1979), pp. 103–18 and 119–31.

7. On a systems-theoretical interpretation of Nietzsche's critique of history and on forgetting as one of its premises, see David E. Wellbery, "Contingency," in *Neverending Stories: Toward a Critical Narratology,* ed. Ann Fehn, Ingeborg Hoesterey, and Maria Tatar (Princeton: Princeton Univ. Press, 1991), pp. 237–57.

8. See Hans Ulrich Gumbrecht, "Rhythmus und Sinn," in *Materialität der Kom-*

munikation, ed. Hans Ulrich Gumbrecht and K. Ludwig Pfeiffer (Frankfurt: Suhrkamp, 1988), pp. 714–29. On rhythm as form—in a different sense of "form"—see also Emile Benveniste, "La notion de 'rythme' dans son expression linguistique," in *Problèmes de linguistique générale* (Paris: Gallimard, 1966), pp. 327–35.

9. Eric Blondel, "Nietzsche: Life as Metaphor," in *The New Nietzsche: Contemporary Styles of Interpretation,* ed. David B. Allison (New York: Delta, 1977), p. 156.

10. I have interpreted this poem differently—with regard to the question of mnemotechnics—in "Die Gewalt des Notwendigen: Überlegungen zu Nietzsches Dionysos-Dithyrambus 'Klage der Ariadne,'" *Nietzsche-Studien* 20 (1990): 186–209.

11. Karl Reinhardt, "Nietzsches Klage der Ariadne," *Die Antike* 11 (1935): 85–109.

12. J. Hillis Miller, "Ariadne's Thread: Repetition and the Narrative Line," *Critical Inquiry* 3 (1976): 57–77.

13. Jean-Pierre Vernant and Pierre Vidal-Naquet, *Myth and Tragedy in Ancient Greece,* trans. Janet Lloyd (New York: Zone, 1988), p. 398.

14. See, for instance, Adrian Del Caro, "Symbolizing Philosophy: Ariadne and the Labyrinth," *Nietzsche-Studien* 17 (1988): 125–57 and Philip Grundlehner, *The Poetry of Friedrich Nietzsche* (New York: Oxford Univ. Press, 1986).

15. Gilles Deleuze, "Mystère d'Ariane," *Philosophie* 17 (1988): 67–72; on Ariadne as doubled affirmation, see also Gilles Deleuze, *Nietzsche and Philosophy,* trans. Hugh Tomlinson (New York: Columbia Univ. Press, 1983), pp. 186–89.

16. Vernant and Vidal–Naquet, *Myth and Tragedy,* p. 391.

17. On a discussion of the sublime on the basis of a theory of distinction, see Dirk Baecker, "Die Kunst der Unterscheidungen," in *Im Netz der Systeme,* ed. Dirk Baecker et al. (Berlin: Merve, 1990), pp. 7–39.

18. Friedrich Schiller, "Das verschleierte Bild zu Sais," in *Schillers Werke: Nationalausgabe,* ed. Norbert Oellers et al. (Weimar: Hermann Böhlaus Nachfolger, 1943–), 1:254.

19. Immanuel Kant, *Critique of Judgment,* trans. J. H. Bernard (New York: Collier Macmillan, 1951), p. 160.

20. Jacques Derrida has shown the correlation between the nontruth of truth that Nietzsche addresses as "woman" and castration as the problem of gender difference; see Jacques Derrida, *Eperons: Les Styles de Nietzsche* (Paris: Flammarion, 1978). On a psychoanalytic reading of the sublime, see Thomas Weiskel, *The Romantic Sublime: Studies in the Structure and Psychology of Transcendence* (Baltimore: Johns Hopkins Univ. Press, 1976) and Neil Hertz, *The End of the Line: Essays on Psychoanalysis and the Sublime* (New York: Columbia Univ. Press, 1985).

21. Sarah Kofman, *Nietzsche et la scène philosophique* (Paris: Union générale d'éditions, 1979), pp. 294–99; the figure of Baubo also signifies, according to Kofman, that a "simple logic" of oppositions cannot comprehend life which is neither surface nor profundity, because behind the veil there is yet another veil.

22. On Nietzsche's overcoming of the sublime, see Norbert Bolz, "Die Verwindung des Erhabenen—Nietzsche," in *Das Erhabene: Zwischen Grenzerfahrung und Größenwahn,* ed. Christine Pries (Weinheim: VCH Acta Humaniora, 1989), pp. 163–69.

23. Werner Hamacher has described this figure of turning against oneself as the

problem of a self-referential will that necessarily turns against itself in manifesting itself, that unfolds only within a certain scission; see Werner Hamacher, "Das Versprechen der Auslegung: Überlegungen zum hermeneutischen Imperativ bei Kant und Nietzsche," in *Spiegel und Gleichnis: Festschrift für Jacob Taubes,* ed. Norbert W. Bolz and Wolfgang Hübener (Würzburg: Königshausen & Neumann, 1983), pp. 252–73. On the necessary aspects of self-negation and its overcoming in an aesthetics of affirmation, see David E. Wellbery, "Nietzsche—Art—Postmodernism: A Reply to Jürgen Habermas," *Stanford Italian Review* 6 (1986): 77–100.

24. Julia Kristeva, *Powers of Horror: An Essay on Abjection,* trans. Leon S. Roudiez (New York: Columbia Univ. Press, 1982), p. 12.

25. Kant, *Critique of Judgment,* p. 84.

26. Immanuel Kant, *Anthropology from a Pragmatic Point of View,* trans. Victor Lyle Dowdell (Carbondale: Southern Illinois Univ. Press, 1978), p. 131.

27. Kant, *Anthropology,* p. 132.

28. Kant, *Critique of Judgment,* p. 83.

29. Sigmund Freud, "Negation," in *The Standard Edition of the Complete Psychological Works of Sigmund Freud,* trans. James Strachey, 24 vols. (London: Hogarth, 1961), 19:236.

30. Freud, "Negation," p. 237. Cf. Nietzsche on pleasure and displeasure as appropriation and rejection, as faculties that originate in the central sphere of the intellect and presuppose an acceleration of perception, ordering, and inferring (KSA 13:33).

31. Deleuze, *Nietzsche and Philosophy,* p. 188.

32. Hans Vaihinger, "Nietzsche and his Doctrine of Conscious Illusion," in *Nietzsche: A Collection of Critical Essays,* ed. Robert C. Solomon (Notre Dame: Univ. of Notre Dame Press, 1980), p. 103 n. 27.

SUSAN BERNSTEIN

Fear of Music? Nietzsche's Double Vision of the "Musical-Feminine"

In paragraph 17 of *Beyond Good and Evil,* Nietzsche performs an interesting exercise on the concept of thinking defined as an operation of predicative logic. In this passage he corrects the "logical superstition" that the phrase "I think" (*ich denke*) implies, namely, that "the subject 'I' is the condition of the predicate 'think.' *It* thinks: but that this 'it' is precisely the famous old 'I' is, to put it mildly, only an assumption." Rather, "a thought comes when 'it' wants, and not when 'I' want it to" (KSA 5:30–31; BGE §17, p. 24*). In Nietzsche's revision, the "I" loses its position of control, and thoughts are autonomous agents. Rejecting the metaphysical interpretation of predication, Nietzsche compares his reformulation of thinking as a nonsubjective process to the research of atomists, who finally could do away with the last remnants of matter and focus strictly on the "force" at work. Similarly, Nietzsche suggests: "Perhaps some day we shall accustom ourselves, including even the logicians, to get along without the little 'it' (in which the good old I has taken refuge)" (KSA 5:31; BGE §17, p. 24*). Nietzsche is working to excise the "I" as a substance separate from and prior to its activity. But even though the "I" is banished, and all that is left is the verb, nevertheless the verb is still *thinks* (*denkt*).

While Nietzsche seems to advocate the abduction of the subject, he postpones its disappearance into the future, protecting its space with the neuter subject "es," or simply in the conjugated verb form "denkt." But maybe the problem lies just as much with *denken* ("to think") as with "I" or "it." At the beginning of *The Case of Wagner,* Nietzsche sketches a different model of thinking, perhaps resembling the not yet existent sort indicated in the above passage. He describes this "thinking" that is not exactly thinking in his reaction to the music of Bizet: "And, oddly, deep down I don't think of it, or don't know how much I think about it. For entirely different thoughts are meanwhile running through my head. . . . Has it been noticed that music liberates the spirit? gives wings to thought? that one becomes more of a philosopher the more one becomes a musician? — The gray sky of abstraction rent as if by lightning; the light strong enough for the filigree of things; the great problems near enough to grasp. . . . And unexpectedly answers drop into my lap, a little hail of ice and wisdom, of *solved* problems. —Where am I?" (KSA 6:14; CW §1, p. 158*). This kind of "thinking," though highly philosophical, is not the abstract thinking—the gray sky—of predicative logic; instead, it carouses as figurative language, the winged speech that liberates the "spirit" from the dead "letter." The "I" is distracted, its boundaries fluid between "philosopher" and "musician." Abstraction is rent by simile, thoughts replaced by metaphoric hailstones. The shift into figurative language, enacted through rhetorical questions rather than positive assertions, accompanies the relative disorganization and relaxation of reflexive control attending the absencing of the "I." The real agent here is not the "I," but music, although the explicit link between the music and the thoughts it induces is obscured or simply deleted. The "I" is not in control and does not know "where" it is.

In this alternative "thinking," then, the (still) philosophical subject comes close to disappearing; but it is slyly reappointed in the concluding question: "Where am I?" The subject-position and the figure of the "I" remain intact even in their suggested withdrawal. The past tense of Nietzsche's narrative keeps the state of mind he describes at a safe distance; the distraction indicated by ellipses and rhetorical questions introduces the nondiscursive condition, but these techniques hold it within a controllable frame. Thus the stable character of the "I" is reasserted in the circumscription of its figurative activity, even as it states its own inability to control and circumscribe itself.

The named figure, "I," holds, even when its place is put into question. In this essay, I shall examine more closely this tenacity of the figure installed by its name. The critique of the "I" continues to rely on the stability of the very terms it thematizes as destabilizing. In particular, I shall consider how the names *woman* and *music* come to stand in for the subject put into question. While "woman" and "music" are invoked to figure "other" or altered discourse, they nevertheless tend to reinstate stability at the very moments when they are enlisted to undo it.

Woman, Truth, and Music

Given the two following passages, consider the relationship between "woman" and truth:

> Given that truth is a woman . . . (KSA 5 : 11; cf. BGE—P, p. 2)

> There is no such thing as the essence of woman because woman averts, she is averted of herself. Out of the depths, endless and unfathomable, she engulfs and distorts all vestige of essentiality, of identity, of property. And the philosophical discourse, blinded, founders on these shoals and is hurled down these depthless depths to its ruin. There is no such thing as the truth of woman, but it is because of that abyssal divergence of the truth, because that untruth is "truth." Woman is but one name for that untruth of truth. (Derrida, *Spurs*)[1]

Nietzsche, of course, is not really speaking of "woman" in the first quotation above.[2] Rather, "das Weib," as the quote from *Spurs* suggests, plays a role in a critique of the concept of truth, in the destabilization of that ideality that is the object of the philosopher's gaze and desire. "Das Weib" stands in for distance and spacing, undoes the opposition between castration and noncastration (pp. 88/89), reveals the truth as the operation of revealing or unveiling ("the truth"), and points to the nonessentiality of the whole operation. Nietzsche associates "woman" with all those seemingly negative terms that are so revealingly essential in the critique of truth as a stable center. As Derrida writes, "All the emblems, all the shafts and allurements that Nietzsche found in woman, her seductive distance, her captivating inaccessibility, the ever-veiled promise of her provocative transcendence, the *Entfernung,* these all belong properly to a history of truth by way of the history of an error" (pp. 88/89). Derrida's purpose in *Spurs* is not to define "woman" but rather to trace out a process that defies conceptual stability (*Spurs,* pp. 70/71) with a view toward altering the style of philosophical inquiry and, perhaps, whatever we call "thinking" in general. Writing about "woman" in *Spurs,* then, Derrida speaks not of an essence but of a term destablizing philosophical discourse. He writes, for example, "Truth, woman is scepticism and veiling dissimulation; this is what it would be necessary to be able to think" (pp. 56/57*).

While the "conjoined confabulation" of "truth, woman" here is immediately alluring, I would like to draw attention instead to the final phrase: "*This is what it would be necessary to be able to think*" (pp. 56/57*, my emphasis). Perhaps it is not just the theme but the verb which must be altered here. For does this exigency of thinking not already install a scaffold that will direct us to "truth," in whatever perverted and untrue aberration? Even if the position of truth has been "undone," it is not clear that this "think," this *penser,* is not still its hidden advocate. For some, the emphasis on thinking and its orientation toward truth defines the philosophical project per se. In "Nietzsche Medused," for example, Bernard Pautrat writes: "Should you want a philosophical translation of this, or simply something 'a little more' philosophical, let us say that I will be inquiring into the rapport of philosophic discourse to truth, to the referent 'truth,' without which one couldn't define philosophy as such, nor the desire to philosophize."[3] This falls in line with Derrida's exigency, as well as the irresistible temptation indicated in the following: "The questions of art, style, and truth cannot be dissociated from the question of woman. But the simple formulation of their common problematic suspends the question, 'what is woman?' One can no longer seek woman or the femininity of woman or feminine sexuality. At least one cannot find them working according to any known mode of the concept or knowledge, *even if one cannot resist looking for them*" (*Spurs,* pp. 70/71, my emphasis). Who is this "we" or "on," this "ich" or "es"? Why *must we think* toward the referent "truth"? Why can we not resist the temptation to seek conceptually? Is there no other way to read?

In this essay I am interested in how the critique of truth outlined above continues to rely on the stability of the named figures of "woman," "truth," and, I will add, "music." What is important is not their conceptual content but rather their opacity as figures, in all the various senses—from a bodily form to a trope to a conceptual mask. The clarity of their outlines allows the blindness and ruin of philosophical discourse to remain metaphoric—that is, it can still be produced and is not ultimately obliterated. For the feminism of *Spurs,* is there not still a figure to be abducted, even if we say there is not? Must woman, and truth, be continually reinscribed as figures in order to be disfigured?

Derrida's rereading of "la femme," "woman," like Nietzsche's dip into a nondiscursive "musical" philosophy, creates a space of writing which the narrative voice can occupy and then abandon. This position, held in place by the figures of "woman" and "music," suggests a kind of alternative thinking that is not self-conscious or conceptually controlled: a nice place to visit, but one wouldn't want to live there, for it could, in principle, produce no text. In escaping philosophical entrapment, the excursion into uncontrolled discursivity out of which no "I" would reemerge allows the philosophical subject to step briefly into an "other" position, a position freed of the obligation and responsibility to understand itself: an obligation that is not deleted, but perhaps made all the more pressing, by the suggestion that such self-understanding may be impossible.[4]

This position—of a discourse that is blind to itself and also does not care—is explicitly held by the figure of the female in the following passage in *Beyond Good and Evil:* "And whatever women write about 'woman,' we may in the end reserve a healthy suspicion whether woman really *wants* enlightenment about herself—whether she *can* want it. . . . But she does not *want* truth: what is truth to woman? Nothing is more alien, repugnant, and hostile to women in the first place" (KSA 5:171; BGE §232, p. 163*). Women should not, or cannot, be interested in truth, nor, according to Nietzsche, carry on an intelligible discourse illuminating themselves; and there is something fundamentally perverse about their self-disclosure. Women ought to conceal and obscure themselves, not unfold in a discourse "about" themselves. Whatever we may do with these lines, the pejorative statements about women vis-à-vis philosophical discourse resound in this text and are not thoroughly silenced by a rereading of "truth," "woman," and "philosophy." In the same way that Nietzsche's "I" does not quite get lost enough in its musical oblivion, but is always recuperable, the figure of "woman" cannot be thoroughly abducted; its referential residue remains. As long as terms like *woman* and *truth* are used, one cannot escape, somehow, also speaking about women and truth, and women remain defined by and confined to an unphilosophical position. This statement should be qualified; for it is made from a position no longer favoring a traditional concept of philosophy and thus represents an advance rather than a defeat. Nevertheless, the potential isolation of these kinds of statements makes it impossible to fully neutralize their derogatory overtones, and the lines between men and women, philosophy and literature, along with endless oppositions, are redrawn even if withdrawn. For this reason, it is important to read figures of femininity (etc.) critically but temporarily—that is, to track their critical potential, yet not attach to them and privilege them as reliable substantive terms. Such stasis invites confusion between the figure "woman," meaning the "feminine operation," and the referent "women."[5]

Shall I, then, hang, suspend, and pull down more veils around the "truth" as *aletheia?* No, I think not; instead, I will try to find a slightly different "optic" or "perspective." Here, I would like to investigate a little bit the problem of the "perspective" on this problem and ask whether it is possible to "think" perspective at all. I will shift my attention a little away from "truth" and "philosophy" and focus instead on some aesthetic questions about painting and music. Or—to echo Pautrat—I will give here a reading that is "something a little less" philosophical. Maybe these arts will have something slightly different to say about "perspective," or maybe just a slightly different way of saying it. This shift toward more material terms, in turn, brings into relief the "bodily" aspects of exposition, figuration, and representation that pose an obstacle to the transparency of conceptual thinking. It is these intrusions and blocks that will be of interest here.

In a passage in *Nietzsche et la scène philosophique* (p. 278), Sarah Kofman, arguing convincingly that Nietzsche introduces a genuine alteration and not simply a reversal of Platonism, refers to the following lines from *Beyond Good and Evil:* "For one may doubt, first, whether there are any opposites at all, and secondly whether these popular valuations and opposite values on which the metaphysicians put their seal, are not perhaps merely foreground estimates, only provisional perspectives, perhaps even from some nook, perhaps from below, frog perspectives, as it were, to borrow an expression painters use" (KSA 5 : 16; BGE §2, p. 10). The problems of perspective, reversal, opposition, alteration, etc., are clearly elucidated by Kofman. But why this emphatic borrowing from painters? Why the explicit reference to this particular art here?[6] I am not asking about the whole network of visual metaphors, nor what the concept of perspective means, but am interested in the shift of vocabulary registers. Perhaps the intrusion of particular arts covers over a point that precisely cannot be thought; perhaps these arts insert an opacity that thinking can neither penetrate nor unravel. This is indeed what Derrida suggests in pointing out how Heidegger significantly maintains silence about "woman" in his analysis of "History of an Error." Derrida writes: "Heidegger cites this sequence . . . but in his commentary (as seems generally to be the case) he skirts the woman, he abandons her there. Much as one might skip over a sensible image in a philosophy book or tear out an illustrated leaf or allegorical representation in a more serious volume, Heidegger analyzes all the elements of Nietzsche's text with the sole exception of the idea's becoming-female (*sie wird Weib*). In such a way does one permit oneself to see without reading, to read without seeing" (*Spurs,* pp. 84/85). Derrida uses a flagrant simile to point to a blind spot in Heidegger's text toward women, explicitly comparing this blindness to the theoretical rejection of a sensible image, an allegorical representation, a picture—another loan from the painters.

These similes suggest that painting stands in for the concreteness of an allegorical sign and the materiality of the signifier. The borrowing from painting in the above examples both enacts and indicates an exchange of currency meant to give off a sense, but one that does not evaporate into a meaning or a concept. Much more, these references to painting point to a communicative effect that remains linked to the materiality of what has generated it. The explicit comments about simile and transfer in both Nietzsche and Derrida point to the nonconceptual ("literary" or "figurative") aspects of their own exposition that cannot be conceptually dissolved—the scriptural remnant. Painting draws attention to the relationship of exchange between the visible sign or image and its sense. It may be strange to insist on painting here, especially when we all know that there is, of course, another art with which Nietzsche was considerably more preoccupied. For Nietzsche, music, in contrast, puts into operation the self-erasure that allows sense to emerge. The "truly" musical, as opposed to the painterly, is always in flight even as it is glimpsed. Nietzsche writes contra Wagner: "Every truthful, every original music is a swansong" (KSA 6:423–24; cf. NW p. 668), leaving no painted bird behind.

But Wagner, Nietzsche says, will not allow the swan to fly away. This is why Nietzsche's critique of Wagner's music, which falls in line with many of the issues of "the feminine," ultimately claims that Wagner, somehow, is not really a musician, but a *painter*. Despite Wagner's apparent desire for the gigantic, Nietzsche writes, Wagner is actually a specialist in the small working within painterly confinement: "He is master of the minuscule. But he doesn't want to be! Much more, his character loves vast walls and bombastic wall-paintings. . . . He doesn't notice that his spirit has a different spirit and pull—an opposite *optic*—and really prefers to sit silently in the corners of collapsed houses. There, hidden away, hidden away from himself, he paints his real masterpieces" (KSA 6:418; cf. NW p. 663). Wagner's attachment to plastic and effect, and his manipulation of the exchange between them, are precisely his downfall, in Nietzsche's view; the problem with Wagner originates in his "thirst for ecstatic sensuousness and desensualization [*Sinnlichkeit und Entsinnlichung*]—this whole give and take of Wagner's regarding material, images, passion, and nerves clearly enunciates the *spirit of his music*—given that this itself, like any music, would not know how to speak unambiguously about itself: for music is a *woman*" (KSA 6:424; cf. NW p. 668). By definition, music, like "woman," actually *should not* be able to speak clearly about itself. It would seem that both "woman" and "music" operate in such a way as to elude the concept and even any self-reflective discursivity; both manage to avoid the confines of the "about." But the prohibition of the self-disclosure of music/woman/whatever, with its potentially pejorative overtones, maintains a fundamental ambivalence. Within its critical context, it grants these figures the power to elude the concept and warp "phallogocentric" discourse in a decisive way. In isolation, though, such statements still outline the garbled discourse of an "other" which "this" text need not fall into. The naming and framing of an "other" position both presents it and protects against its potential power of disarticulation. This ambivalence is lodged not in the referents "woman" or "music" but in the manner of their figuration and inscription.

I would like now to return to some of Nietzsche's ambivalent remarks about music in their connection with the delineation of the female figure/position. As the passage on musically inspired thinking showed, in Nietzsche's positive evaluations of music, the connections between the music and its effect must remain unperceived, unarticulated, disjointed. Wagner is still partially capable of this, as Nietzsche remarks in "Where I admire" (NW): "He knows a sound for those canny-uncanny midnights of the soul, where cause and effect seem to have come off their hinges [*aus den Fugen gekommen zu sein scheinen*] and, at any moment, something can emerge out of nothing" (KSA 6:417; cf. NW p. 663). What Nietzsche most objects to in Wagner, finally, is the calculated logic and mechanics, turning around this "Fug," or hinge, that allow the two poles of cause and effect to remain visible. Because of the visibility of this mechanics, Wagner is classified as a dissimulating actor—and note how the lack of subtlety is allied with an exchange system: "What occurs to him first is a scene with an unconditionally certain effect, a real *actio* with a *hautrelief* of gestures, a scenario that overwhelms and *throws* people [*umwirft*]—this he thinks through in depth, and from this he then derives his characters. The rest all follows from this, in accordance with a technical economy that has no reason to be subtle" (KSA 6:32; CW §9, p. 174*). Wagner's art exposes its own exchange and convertibility—*Sinnlichkeit und Entsinnlichung*—sensuousness and desensualization. The blatancy of the reversal comes forth in a reference to the visual arts (*hautrelief*) linked with the three-dimensionality of the bodily gesture. Three networks emerge here in critique of Wagner: the exposure of the system of allegorical signification, the resemblance to the visual arts, and the intrusion of the body. The economic calculation of these systems makes Wagner an actor directly threatening to the presentational standards of truth. Nietzsche writes:

"One becomes an actor by having *one* insight in advance of the rest of the people: what is supposed to have the effect of being true is not allowed to be true. . . . Wagner's music is never true" (KSA 6:31; CW §8, p. 173*).

So like "la femme," Wagner's music is not, but clearly ought to be, true; and like women who try to write about "woman," Wagner does not maintain the proper "pudeur," or modesty, but instead exposes—not the naked body that must recede in order to remain what it is (not)—but a mechanics. This lack of subtlety, the *hautrelief* of gesticulation, is associated with the bodily quality of the visual arts; "real" music should leave nothing in its trace, just as philosophical discourse would tear out allegorical illustrations and visual interruptions.

Nietzsche criticizes the overtly allegorical qualities in Wagner's music that define it as a mark of something more, of something "beyond," and as a production of meaning.[7] "And indeed," Nietzsche writes, "his whole life he repeated *one* sentence: that his music did not signify only music . . . therefore, he *was compelled* in principle to bring the 'it means' into the foreground" (KSA 6:35; CW §10, p. 177*). More specifically, Nietzsche objects to the preservation of the two poles of *Sinnlichkeit* and *Entsinnlichung* that this reified allegorism implies—to the separation between signification and what is signified implicit in "the need for redemption" satisfied by Wagner, a release and dissolution that could neither be needed nor satisfied without the division of spheres it supposedly connects.

Wagner himself becomes the mark of this allegorical dissolution—an allegorical sign of his own activity, a mark unable to speak "*unzweideutig*" about itself or anything else, since its very definition is to relate by division—a mark that is duplicitous in principle. "If Wagner remains the name for the *ruin of music,* still he is not its cause" (KSA 6:46; CW—E, p. 186*), Nietzsche writes.[8] In the same way, "woman" may be the name for the *ruin of Truth,* and no woman its cause. It is thus not surprising that Wagner's gender is itself unclear, though Nietzsche resorts to Latin formality to say so: "For in his old days, Wagner was thoroughly feminini generis" (KSA 6:51; CW—E, p. 191*).

Wagner is a "woman," but only if we understand "the feminine genre or gender" to mean a duplicitous mode of signification that exposes the mechanics that its result is meant to conceal. Moreover, Wagner and women, like the allegorical ruin and "the beyond" this ruination indirectly exposes, stand in a mutual interdependence. In the following passage, there is a telling interconnection between the allegorical release of meaning from the materiality of its sign and the corresponding function of constructed embodiment that allegory would presuppose: "Wagner has redeemed woman; and for this, she built him Bayreuth. . . . Woman impoverishes herself for the benefit of the master, she becomes touching, she stands naked before him. —The [female] Wagnerian—the most charming ambiguity that can be found today; she *embodies* the cause of Wagner—in her sign his cause *triumphs*" (KSA 6:44–45; CW—Postscript, p. 185*). Here, ambiguity (*die anmutigste Zweideutigkeit*) stands naked before the master's eyes; and this nude body *incarnates,* thus completes and gives form to, Wagner's "femininity." But this woman's body, like Wagner's music, remains a vehicle, a conveyor; for no sooner does it incarnate than it immediately turns into a sign for a male victory.

Thus it might be possible to attribute to Nietzsche a feminist critique of Wagner's instrumentalization of female figures, who literally become a part of his operatic architecture. Nietzsche laments this openness between Wagner and his women, Wagner and his gestural signs laid bare—the abduction and exposure of "our women" who ought not to reveal or speak of themselves: "Oh, the old robber! he steals our young men, he even steals our women and drags them into his cave. . . . Oh, the old Minotaur!" (KSA 6:45; CW—Postscript, p. 185*). On the other hand, perhaps another scenario has been put into play at the same time. Nietzsche gazes on a dyadic spectacle from a third point of exclusion; and the tone of grudging jealousy is suggestive of Nietzsche's own unfulfilled desire, the door shutting on his gaze rendering the objects of desire inaccessible. The interplay between the dyad and the triangle, with its psychoanalytic overtones, repeats the ambiguous status of allegorical representation. Aligned with the painterly, the opacity of the painted figure or material remnant protects the "I" who criticizes it. Music, on the other hand, allows this "I" to slip into its metaphor without a trace, but provides no path for return.

Figuring Fear and Desire

Both music and "the feminine" set a limit point to the self-figuration of the writing philosophical subject, a limit or blind spot that eludes the grasp of the predicative text. The alliance of music and figures of femininity, in fact, has a wide cultural history, from the seductive and threatening songs of a Circe or Lorelei to the nurse's indoctrinating rhythms in Plato's *Republic.*[9] Rousseau, too, is first exposed to and indelibly marked by music through the half-forgotten songs of his Tante Suzon.[10] In more recent semiotic theory, the musical is associated with "signifiance" and the femininity of "écriture."[11] According to Julia Kristeva, for example, music becomes the generalized metaphor for the direct infusion of semiotic drives into a work of art, disrupting the communicative and phallocentric organization of language toward "meaning." It is then a small step to connect "music" with the femininity of "écriture," according to which the "bodily" and uncontrolled aspect of writing is aligned with a "femininity" opposed to the "masculinity" of an articulated subject in charge of a transparent discourse.[12]

The fear named in my title indicates the anxiety about the passive subject's lack of control when placed at the receiving end of music. This anxiety is linked with the danger of rhetorical manipulation and erotic seduction, both resulting from the bodily workings of music on the "soul" or "the nerves." Even Hegel gives way to music's persuasion and is tempted to throw away the text in a passionate outburst; for in the experience of musical performance, one is presented not only with a completed work, but with artistic production itself. "In this completely living presence," Hegel writes, "one forgets all external conditions, location, occasion, the particular place in the church service, the content and meaning of the dramatic situation, one no longer needs, indeed, one no longer even wants any text, nothing remains but the universal tone of feeling in general."[13] The fear of the attack on the nerves, which transgresses the boundaries of the subjective receiver, is tremendously apparent in Adorno's critique of Wagner and, of course, in his condemnation of jazz.[14] Sexual seduction and rhetorical disempowerment are names for the intrusion of the "musical-feminine" other and its manipulation of a passive receptive subject. In an essay entitled "L'Echo du sujet," Philippe Lacoue-Labarthe sets up an interesting connection between "the autobiographical compulsion"—a desire for self-representation and exposure—and what he calls "la hantise musicale," a haunting obsession with music.[15] The first pertains to "the constant preoccupation with its own subject" characteristic of philosophical discourse, a preoccupation linked with the perhaps unavoidable "desire of and for 'figurality' " (p. 225) which, Lacoue-Labarthe argues, becomes most powerful where it is most in question. He writes: "In Nietzsche, as after him (and in his wake), the active destruction of the *figure*, whatever the mode (through exhibition or ostentation, or just as much through retreat, the cult of anonymity, of the secret, of silence), contrary to all expectations, will have aggravated the weight of agonistic mimeticism in philosophy" (p. 224). Lacoue-Labarthe's text brings together the problems of philosophical self-presentation, self-conception (with its ambiguity), obsession with music, and relations of rivalry. The ambivalence of desire and anxiety is simultaneously legible in the registers of rhetoric, representation, and psychoanalytic structures. Lacoue-Labarthe asks: "Or, is it perhaps necessary to presume that there is something necessary—a constraint inherent to being and to the very structure of the subject, to its desire to attain itself, to represent itself, to conceive itself; and inherent to the impossibility in which the subject finds himself, at the same time, of capturing himself or even catching a glimpse of himself, etc.—something necessary that, in fact, connects autobiographical compulsion and musical obsession?" (p. 226). The desire for self-displacement into music, Lacoue-Labarthe suggests, is a reaction to the "*affolement*" ("madness") in the dissolution of the specular model of self-production and representation. We have seen Nietzsche's desire to replace the discursive with the musical, as well as the potential danger this implies.

For Nietzsche, "the feminine" and music—at least Wagnerian music—share a number of features and, moreover, stand in a kind of unabashed conspiracy. Wagner's allegorism installs a fundamental ambiguity that allows Nietzsche to link rhetorical manipulation, emasculation, and intoxication—all forms of the receptive subject's loss of control. It is, in fact, the rhetorical duplicity, structured as allegory, that makes Wagner into a seducer. In *The Case of Wagner,* Nietzsche writes: "He is distinguished by every ambiguity, every double sense, everything quite generally that persuades those who are uncertain without making them aware *of what* they have been persuaded. Thus Wagner is a seducer of the grand style" (KSA 6:42; CW—Postscript, p. 183*). The allegorical manipulation of signs translates and conceals its communicative intent, working instead directly on the senses; Wagner communicates "*not* in formulas: Wagner is too shrewd for formulas—but by means of a persuasion of sensuousness which in turn makes the spirit weary and worn out. Music as Circe . . ." (KSA 6:43; CW—Postscript, p. 183*). So here we see the dangerous drawback of the uncontrolled quasi thinking suggested by Nietzsche's response to Bizet, if it were really to get out of control and lead to a feminized impotence, an infinite graphic proliferation that Nietzsche tries to both represent and halt by the three dots of his own ellipsis. Wagner, Nietzsche writes, is a master in "all that trembles and is effusive, all the feminisms from the *idioticon* of happiness! —Drink, O my friends, the philters of this art! Nowhere will you find a more agreeable way of enervating your spirit, of forgetting your manhood under a rosebush. —Ah, this old magician!" (KSA 6:43; CW—Postscript, p. 184).

So there seems to be a general overlap between the condemnation of exposed allegorism, the fear of erotic seduction, and loss of discursive control. All are based in the *Zweideutigkeit* (duplicitous meaning or ambiguity) characteristic of the "feminine operation." Repeatedly, a dyadic spectacle is established and a third position inserted, meant to both give access to, yet protect from, the absorption operative in the figured relationship between two. The thematics of seduction, impotence, and the structure of a specular triangle suggest that some psychoanalytic terms may enrich the reading of the problem of allegory and signification already laid out.

To examine further this ambivalence and connection, the "musical feminine operation," let us say, I will turn now to a fragmentary text, "On Music and Words," written by Nietzsche in 1871 (during the era of *The Birth of Tragedy*). Carl Dahlhaus writes that, although Nietzsche wrote this text during the time of great admiration for Wagner, nevertheless "it contains the outlines of his later critique of Wagner."[16] It would not be surprising if Nietzsche's love for and subsequent turn against Wagner might hinge around the same ambivalence, or *Zweideutigkeit,* delineated by "the feminine operation."

In this text, Nietzsche is primarily concerned with establishing the priority of music over verbal accompaniment. He relays this priority to the relationship between "the will," "the most general form of appearance," and the "primeval ground," on the one hand; and, on the other, any particular crystallizations of this ground—whether in gesture, word, image, or representation. The aesthetic debate over the relation between music and language (in opera and song, for example) is a subset of another cleavage, a "duplicity in the essence of language" (KSA 7:360; cf. MW p. 107), distinguishing a universally comprehensible subtending tonal ground (*Tonuntergrund*) from the representations in which it comes to expression. While verbal accompaniment, or other forms of representation, may be the only means of disclosure of the tonal generality, they can never generate, but only transmit, their musical origin. Nietzsche is adamant about this ordering: "Imagine . . . what an undertaking it must be to write music for a poem, that is, to wish to illustrate a poem by means of music, in order to secure a conceptual language for music in this way. What an inverted world! An undertaking that strikes one as if a son desired to beget his father! Music can generate images [*Bilder*] that will always be mere schemata, as it were examples of its real universal content. But how should the image, the representation, be capable of generating music?" (KSA 7:362; MW p. 109). To maintain the hierarchical order between the musical origin and the representational symptom, Nietzsche dismisses the power of images to generate sense; they can never stand in the position of the origin of transmission. Images are marked similes of their musical origin ("as it were"). But despite his rejection of the force of images, Nietzsche immediately paints a striking picture to keep the order in place: "While it is certain that a bridge leads from the mysterious castle of the musician into the free country of images—and the lyric poet walks across it—it is impossible to proceed in the opposite direction, although there are said to be some people who have the delusion that they have done this" (KSA 7:362–63; MW p. 109). This medieval scenario, operating through unmarked metaphors, places "the musician" in an internal chamber of entrapment; he is then transformed into a lyric poet by walking across the bridge into the freedom of representations. "We" spectators are protected from the inner sanctum by this fellow who, like the bridge itself, simultaneously provides distance from and proximity to the interior. We are connected to, but not absorbed by, the mysterious inside, as a third party is called in to make the passage through the corridor—to be born—at the same time that a prohibition is set up against returning. This little scene, which by the way also preserves the generational order of father and son, suggests birth trauma, the desire to return to the womb whether by "death drive" or intercourse, and the prohibition against return indicative of castration anxiety.[17]

Like any fetishized representation, this image both reveals and conceals, protects against and reinstitutes castration.[18] Since Nietzsche's castle metaphor is really not very logically compelling—why *can't* one walk back over the bridge?—it would seem that it is the metaphoric frame of the castle scene itself—the rather abrupt intrusion of an architectural and topographic figure reminiscent of "the dark ages"—that sets up a defense against the absorption into the dark inside. Resisting the temptation to solve this problem by translating it glibly into the concepts of the "Dionysian" and "Apollonian"—as if we knew what these were—I will instead read the next sentence in Nietzsche's text, which relates the "imagistic" element of Nietzsche's language to the more concrete imagery of painting.

In the following passage Nietzsche refers to Raphael's painting *The Ecstasy of St. Cecilia*.[19] The painting shows St. Cecilia, patron saint of music, with John the Evangelist, Augustine, Paul, and Mary Magdalene. St. Cecilia, in the center of the scene, gazes decidedly upwards, where a hole opens in the blue of the sky to expose an angelic choir. A number of broken instruments lie scattered at the saints' feet, and St. Cecilia herself is holding an organetto (about which there will later be something strange to say). Here is the reference:

> Populate the air with the imagination of a Raphael and contemplate, as he did, how St. Cecilia is listening, enraptured, to the harmonies of angelic choirs: no sound issues from this world though it seems to be

Figure 1. Raphael, *The Ecstasy of St. Cecilia*, ca. 1515. (Photograph courtesy Soprintendenza per i Beni Artistici e Storici di Bologna)

> lost in music. But if we imagined that this harmony did actually acquire sound by virtue of a miracle, whither would St. Cecilia, Paul, and Magdalene, and even the singing angels, suddenly have disappeared from us? We would immediately cease to be Raphael, and even as the instruments of this world lie broken on the ground in this painting, our painter-vision [*Malervision*], conquered by a higher one, would pale and vanish like shadows. (KSA 7:363; MW pp. 109–10*)

In this passage, the same elements reappear: the middle man becomes Raphael, and the one-way direction of the bridge is stabilized in the image of a painting. Raphael holds the position of both creator (painter) and observer—a position that can be borrowed by any spectator who can step into it and create figures through a metaphor of prosopopoeia ("populate the air"), yet still remain at a safe enough distance to simply gaze upon them. Thanks to this space, comparable to the musician–lyric poet's bridge, the loss of self in music is contained and held at bay by the reference to the painting itself: that is, both by the female figure figured there, and by the figure of a painting per se. At the same time, Nietzsche's prosopopoeia is displaced, handed over to the painter to keep guard, so to speak.

In Raphael's painting, the painted figure of Cecilia stands visibly as the conduit between the literal musical instruments and that metaphoric music of which earthly music is but a distant and feeble echo or shadow.[20] One might say the painting represents allegory itself, opening the corridor from the wreckage of material signs to their invisible transcendent counterparts. But part of the scene's character as a *painting* is precisely that the invisible is indeed visible; the transcendent music is given visible form in the angelic choir. At the same time, the earthly signifiers are hardly erased. Our gaze remains directed toward the rubble of instruments at the saints' feet: the inverted organetto Cecilia is holding points directly and emphatically downward at them. The materiality of these instruments is maintained and reasserted in the foreground, even as the plot line of the painting seems to advocate their rejection. The materiality of the painting itself thus contradicts the transcendence of the mundane it implies. Thus the passage from image to (heavenly) music is halted, and the painting can be brought into line with Nietzsche's claim: "Music can generate images out of itself. . . . But how should the image, the representation, ever be able to generate music out of itself?" (KSA 7:362; MW p. 109*). The allegorical flip into the music of the spheres is only represented and does not actually occur. For if it did, Nietzsche dramatizes, there would be no position from which to gaze; all finite subject positions would disappear.

I would like to stress especially the last point in Nietzsche's scenario: "our painter-vision [*Malervision*], conquered by a higher one, would pale and vanish like shadows." The painter-vision that ensures distance and protection would itself extinguish (*verlöschen*). In the hypothetical subjunctive, the viewer momentarily stands blind and castrated, sucked into the heavenly hole of Cecilia's music. "But how could such a miracle ever happen!" (KSA 7:363; cf. MW p. 110). The danger is indeed great, but can be shrugged off by the choice of the painting as an example—that is, of course the painting does not begin to emit music. So Nietzsche has himself fictionalized the castration scene he wards off, using Raphael's Cecilia as his fictional instrument and figure. It would seem that Cecilia is a kindly Medusa, in fact one so well concealed as to appear a Medusa in reverse; for it is she who is frozen and whose stability prevents the blindness of the observer.[21]

Who is this St. Cecilia, this rather marginal saint? Thomas Connolly, outlining her legend, explains that she was a Roman pagan goddess who treated eye disease; even her name derives from *caecitas* (blindness) (*La Santa Cecilia,* p. 121). She both cures blindness and is blindness, and in any case operates as a figure of reversal and conversion. A pagan virgin, her absorption into Roman liturgy causes a gender reversal; her legend, Connolly describes, "selects a reading, again for the only time in Roman liturgy, from the book of Esther. . . . The reading, moreover, distorts scripture by putting the text on the lips of a woman, Esther, whereas in the Bible it is clearly attributed to a man, Mordechai—again an undoubted reference to the rites of Bona Dea, from which men were strictly banned, she being a goddess of women" (p. 122). Cecilia confounds gender, excludes men, blinds them in their reading of the scripture, yet heals their blindness. Her rather late association with music is usually traced back to this line from her legend: "Cantantibus organis Cecilia in corde suo soli Domino decantabat: Fiat cor meum et corpus meum immaculatum ut non confundar" (p. 130). This prayer is uttered at Cecilia's wedding, perhaps a bit too reminiscent of Brunhilde's wedding night. She prays that she *not be confounded,* asking for the preservation of her virginity. If she confounds and reverses, she is not herself confounded or reversed, and maintains a barrier against the intrusion of men.

The male observer cannot crawl into Cecilia's painted skin; and it's a good thing, too. For otherwise the inverted world of the painting would exceed its bounds, the son would beget the father and the protective shield of representation would shatter. "But how could such a miracle ever happen!" Nietzsche exclaims; "How could the Apollonian world of the eye, wholly absorbed in visual contemplation, be able to generate a tone which after all symbolizes a sphere that is excluded and overcome by the Apollonian abandonment to appearance? The delight in appearance [*die Lust am Scheine*] cannot generate out of itself the delight in nonappearance [*die Lust am Nicht-Scheine*]. The delight of seeing is a delight only because nothing reminds us of a sphere in which individuation is broken and annulled" (KSA 7:363; MW p. 110*).

I am not interested so much in the relation between music and word (as Nietzsche explores it here) as in the two examples I have just discussed which Nietzsche enlists in lieu of argumentation. How beautifully Cecilia removes the venom of Medusa's snakes; yet perhaps the broken instruments—"organa"—*do* remind us, after all, of "die Lust am Nicht-Scheine," "the pleasure in nonappearance," of a different and rather threatening order. The broken organs and the pleasure in nonappearance evoke the two-sided effect of Freud's scene of the origin of castration anxiety, combining the pleasure of viewing the mother's genitals with the anxiety of the potential absence of the penis it implies. Therefore, it is probably best that Cecilia does not or will not speak clearly about herself and tell the tale of castration and exclusion. Instead, she emblematizes an endless series of reversals and, as a fetish, holds them at bay.

Raphael's painting, in maintaining both poles of the allegorical exchange, duplicates Wagner's error, leaving open the possibility of return and descent that ought to be blocked by Nietzsche's one-way bridge. Despite the beautiful idealization of Raphael's painting in Nietzsche's reading, the center is held by Cecilia's *reversed* and inverted organetto; it is both upside down and backwards. Connolly argues that this reversal might further symbolize the turn from material to heavenly music. The common explanation hypothesizes that Raphael

> had copied a woodcut or print where the process of printing had simply reversed the original incision. Though this is surely true in some cases, it should not be accepted too readily. Certainly in the case of Raphael's Cecilia there seems an excellent reason for adding the symbolism of reversed pipes, of "back-to-front" music, to that of earthly music cast aside, but the interpretation is far from certain, and cannot be insisted upon. The whole question of the reversed instruments, in fact, deserves much closer study. The inadequacy of the explanation that derives them from the process of printing is evident from the existence of such images before printing was used in the West. (p. 136)

If this reversal is ultimately mysterious, perhaps it is because the organ is in the wrong hand. In any case, the technical aspect of the reversal reminds

Figure 2. Detail: Raphael, *The Ecstasy of St. Cecilia,* ca. 1515. (Photograph courtesy Soprintendenza per i Beni Artistici e Storici di Bologna)

Figure 3. Organ. Palazzo Ducale, Urbino. (Photograph courtesy Soprintendenza per i Beni Artistici e Storici di Bologna)

us of the persistent centrality of the image, needed for any further transport, referring us downward to the technical means of reproduction—a reproduction allowing for a "reversal of the original incision"—and visually, to the broken "organa" in the foreground which still bear the mark of castration.

Both the examples I have discussed rely on figuration. In the first, Nietzsche draws a metaphoric scenario to which he does not explicitly draw attention; and in the second, the same kind of metaphorization is enacted upon the example of a painting. Nietzsche enlists these examples in lieu of argumentation; both work by implementing and foregrounding the tenacity of figures and the materiality of signifying bodies, whether these be literal painted figures or written tropes. Nietzsche's manner of exposition thus imitates the painterly and does not erase itself. This is why conceptual translation cannot unravel these passages without repeating the same fetishization of the thematized figure within the economy of philosophical desire and castration anxiety.

A Literary Revision

So—the figure holds. The figure of St. Cecilia both reveals and conceals the desire for and the dread of castration, protects against and repeats the danger. The Christian interpretation of her legend, which brings her into the strictly upward movement toward celestial music, makes palatable her pagan prehistory, covering over the always present possibility of the reversed movement. But fears of regression, exclusion, and castration are just more names for the potential reversibility of sign and meaning—of closure, suffocation, and the collapse of the difference of signification.

But as I began by suggesting, there may be no further to go with this image within the confines of a theoretical exposition. This is why I have shifted my view from the thematized figures of "truth," "woman," to the modes of signification allied with painting and music; what I have been reading are rhetorical ripples and snags that come up in the discontinuities between specificities and generalities. So I will turn now to "St. Cecilia or the Power of Music (a Legend)" ("Die heilige Cäcilia oder die Gewalt der Musik [eine Legende])"—a short story by Heinrich von Kleist in which the dire consequences of Cecilia's reversals are more clearly exposed.[22]

The story begins with the rather dry report of an aborted attack on a cloister of St. Cecilia in Aachen toward the end of the sixteenth century. The opening relates how three brothers from the Netherlands, together with a friend, organize an iconoclastic movement against this Catholic stronghold, this retrograde nunnery maintaining a link to the past that ought to be broken. They plan to gather at night, provided with "all sorts of instruments of destruction," to smash the cloister's windows, painted with Biblical stories. On the appointed night, however, the expert orchestra of nuns performs a mass so powerful that the iconoclasts fail in their mission and, the narrator concludes, the cloister survived the whole Thirty Years War. The story then picks up six years later, when the mother comes to Aachen in search of her still missing sons.

Already the title of Kleist's story underscores and connects Cecilia, power, and music in a specifically written form—a legend, presented as an authorless tale supplementing the Christian legend of the saint. There would be much to say about the narrative structure, which in its detours and displacements duplicates the protective framing I have already discussed; but unfortunately I cannot develop this here. However, the violence latent in Raphael's painting is fully released in Kleist's story in the clash between the men's attempt to destroy the image and the self-protective violence exercised by the nunnery. The nuns are closed off and self-sufficient—not only in their cloistered virginity, but also in their ability to manipulate instruments: "As is well known, in the cloisters the nuns, proficient in playing all kinds of instruments, execute their own music; often with a precision, an understanding, and a sensibility one misses in male orchestras (perhaps because of the feminine gender of this mysterious art)."[23] Whether the feminine gender of music be grammatically or otherwise determined here, this taking into their own hands of the "feminine art" becomes the nuns' source of power; they, too, can wield the deadly instrument. On the night in question, the abbess has planned the performance of an "ancient Italian Mass of an unknown master, with which the orchestra had achieved the greatest of effects" (p. 217). Unfortunately, Sister Antonia, the only nun able to conduct the piece, falls ill and cannot perform. Despite the imminent danger of the iconoclasts, waiting outside with axes and hammers, the abbess orders that an ordinary piece of music be played nevertheless. But at the last moment, Sister Antonia inexplicably appears, and conducts the mysterious and authorless work, playing the organ in the lead.

Through a series of narrative steps backwards, and into a first person flashback, we eventually discover what happened during this performance to dissipate the planned attack. As the music begins, the four leaders are so *struck* as to be instantly *converted:* they remove their hats, fall to their knees praying, and fail to give the sign of attack. Even after the music ends, the four iconoclasts remain prostrate and frozen. The reporter describes:

"But how can I describe my horror, dear lady, when I saw these four men just as they were, with folded hands, as if they were frozen into stone, kissing the ground, with their breasts and heads prostrate before the altar of the church, with the most heated ardour!" (p. 222).

The attempt to break the images containing the Cecilian nuns, to penetrate this cloister, is countered by musical Medusification, converting the men to stone and to the ancient faith. Moreover, the condition is permanent; the formerly sociable brothers continue an eccentrically ascetic lifestyle ("a desolate, ghostly cloister life" [p. 224]), mumbling prayers to the cross and virtually robbed of speech. Every night at midnight, they interrupt their gestures and begin to howl the Gloria of the mysterious masterpiece with disturbing volume and effect. Thus they continue to transmit the violence by which they were struck, but merely as ghosts, as automata compelled to repeat at the sound of the midnight bell.[24] Though they are not unhappy, they end up in the local insane asylum, where their mother finds them six years later.

This "conversion," also a regression and a silencing, is due not only to the nuns' mastery of their instruments but also to the dubious identity of the conductor, Sister Antonia. The abbess explains to the mother that the nun was dying and could not possibly have performed, concluding: "On that miraculous day, God himself protected the cloister from the insolence of your sorely deluded sons. Since you are a Protestant, the means He used to do so must be a matter of indifference to you" (p. 227). The archbishop of Trier and the pope confirm " 'that St. Cecilia herself effected this miracle, at once terrible and glorious.' "

The miracle at hand rests not in the nameable figure but in the power of figuration, of incarnation and embodiment—whether it be "God" or "St. Cecilia" who descends, or whether one of them is responsible for a miraculous resuscitation or dissimulation of Sister Antonia; for this point remains unclear. This power, then, is not specifically "female," though perhaps the violent workings of a hidden and ultimately unnameable agency through musical instruments may resemble what Derrida calls "the feminine operation." And Kleist's story indeed shows a case where the embodied image (*Bild*) produces music, the very reversal prohibited by Nietzsche's example. The power of embodiment, in turn, reappears in the magical quality of the musical text in question. The mere image of the scriptural induces the same effect as the performed music. The mother happens to glimpse the score and falls prey to the same vertigo and insanity as her sons: "She observed the unknown magical signs, in which a terrible spirit seemed to be circling about, and felt as if she were sinking into the earth, happening to find the score open precisely to the Gloria in Excelsis. It seemed to her as if the whole art of sound that had ruined her sons came pouring over her head with a great din; she thought she would lose her senses at the mere sight of the score" (p. 226). She, too, later converts to Catholicism. This struggle between the old and the new, the upward movement and the reverse, which privileges the materiality of the sign—whether as music, painting, or writing—is thus not gender-specific, though gendered positions make emphatic the hierarchical organization of representational power of the system that produces them. Unlike "woman" or "music," the "feminine operation" is not a figure, but something about which one can neither say that it is nor that it is not.

Kleist's text gives us the inverse movement already in place in Raphael's painting and in Nietzsche's hypothetical reference to it: allegorical passage upwards compulsively repeats what it ought to leave behind and thus reinstates the possibility of the disastrous movement downward. The descent results in petrification, castration, blindness, insanity, exclusion, or even disappearance, overturns the priority of sense over sign, father over son, of end over instrument. St. Cecilia is a fetish; thus her visibility is always a reminder of what is not visible, and neither the attempt to destroy images, to skip over them in a philosophical text, nor to contain them within a gilded or narrative frame can control this memory.

Thus Nietzsche's early writing about music, written during his pro-Wagner years, sets up a structure that can be reversed and programs his own turn. This is indeed what happens when, later, Nietzsche apparently holds himself outside the Wagnerian spectacle. It is not surprising that Nietzsche's critique of Wagner should center around *Verfall*—decadence, decline, and feminization. In "The Case of Wagner" (*Der Fall Wagner*, of course), Nietzsche describes the general decadence of art as "an expression of physiological degeneration (more precisely, a form of hystericism) like every single corruption and infirmity of the art inaugurated by Wagner: for example, the visual restlessness [or anxiety, distress: *Unruhe*] of its optic, which requires that one changes one's position before it at every moment" (KSA 6:27; CW §7, p. 169*). The fall into feminized physiological degeneration is allied with the vertiginous *optic* that makes it difficult to see or speak *unzweideutig*. Nietzsche explicitly aligns this fall with the reversal of the music/image hierarchy: "For Wagner, in the beginning is the hallucination: not of tones, but of gestures. Then he seeks the right sound semiotic for them" (KSA 6:27–28; CW §7, p. 170*). And of course, Wagner's biggest fans are either women or castrated converts:

"Just look at these young fellows—rigid, pale, breathless!" (KSA 6:29; CW §8, p. 172*).

I would like to end—and not to conclude—with a mention of the often-quoted passage in the forward to *The Gay Science* allying "truth" with a woman who, perhaps, ought not to be stripped bare.[25] Toward the beginning of the paragraph, in which Nietzsche is describing his "recovery" from Wagner, Nietzsche writes: "One returns from such abysses . . . born anew" (KSA 3:351; cf. GS—P §4, p. 37). The passage conveys not only a critique of "truth," but also the desire to "conceive oneself," give birth to oneself and thus do away with women, or perhaps (m)others, altogether; to be born again with no threatening and enticing memory of a dangerous past; and the desire for the power to refigure necessity as if it were a free choice, a choice "not to see everything naked, not always to have to be present at everything" (KSA 3:352; cf. GS—P §4, p. 38). Perhaps this "choice" is the compensation and mastery regained after a forced exclusion and rejection—painful, perhaps, but not nearly so dangerous as the chaos induced by inclusion. The same passage, by the way, with only a few differences, appears in the epilogue to *Nietzsche contra Wagner.*

Notes

1. Jacques Derrida, *Spurs: Nietzsche's Styles / Eperons: Les Styles de Nietzsche,* trans. Barbara Harlow (Chicago: Univ. of Chicago Press, 1979), pp. 50/51.

2. In *Spurs,* Derrida is explicit about this; he does not essentialize this "woman" that cannot even be called a "figure," since it tampers with the structures of identity underlying what could be called a figure. Derrida writes: "It is perhaps because 'woman' is not some thing, not the determinable identity of a figure which announces itself from a distance. . . . Perhaps she is, as a non-identity, a non-figure, a simulacrum, the *abyss* of distance, the distancing of distance" (pp. 48/49*). Sarah Kofman gives a similar reading of femininity in *Nietzsche et la scène philosophique* (Paris: Union générale d'éditions, 1979), especially pp. 263–304; she also reconnects the philosophical ambivalence toward the feminine with the more concrete question of Nietzsche's misogyny, but does not collapse the two issues.

3. Bernard Pautrat, "Nietzsche Medused," in *Looking after Nietzsche,* ed. Laurence A. Rickels (Albany: SUNY Press, 1990), p. 159.

4. I am pointing here toward a particular "fort/da" relationship—see Sigmund Freud, *Jenseits des Lustprinzips,* in *Gesammelte Werke,* 18 vols. (London: Imago, 1941), 13:1–69—to an "other" writing that is not exclusively necessary; it is not self-evident that this is the only "other" nor the only possible relationship to it. The work of Luce Irigaray, for example, presents an "other" writing that does not reproduce this same structure, most relevantly in *Amante marine: De Friedrich Nietzsche* (Paris:

Minuit, 1980) and of course in her other very well known works. I am not implying that Derrida and Nietzsche, for example, do not themselves engage in what they designate as "other," "feminine," etc. On the contrary, both do so, most notably through their style and manner of exposition. I am pointing, instead, to a framing of limits that allows both to "return" while digressing.

5. Alice A. Jardine outlines the variety of issues often confused in discussions of "the feminine," "femininity," empirical structures of power, etc. in *Gynesis: Configurations of Woman and Modernity* (Ithaca: Cornell Univ. Press, 1985). Her neologism, "gynesis," seems to indicate what I am calling, along with Derrida, "the feminine operation"; see p. 25.

6. Particular arts do not tend to be included in the general cataloguing of Nietzschean thematics. Alexander Nehamas, for example, opens his *Nietzsche: Life as Literature* (Cambridge: Harvard Univ. Press, 1985) with a list of the grand themes of the content of Nietzsche's writing: "It includes, for example, his view of the will to power, the eternal recurrence, the nature of the self, and the immoral presuppositions of morality" (p. 1).

7. Here I am referring to the conventional (and of course reductive) definition of allegory subordinating sensuous presentation to a guiding concept. While this structure is promoted by Winckelmann, for example, as the necessity for rational control, it is of course subsequently rejected by Goethe, Coleridge, and many others as a cold dissociation of "idea" and "material." To this extent, Nietzsche remains within a certain tradition privileging the organic unity of idea and material in the material over the overtly rationalized manipulation of matter by an independent concept. This is, of course, only a superficial and reductive view of one strain in the interpretation of allegory; I shall return to more of its complexities below.

8. Walter Benjamin examines the relationship between the ruin and allegory in *Ursprung des deutschen Trauerspiels* (Frankfurt: Suhrkamp, 1974). Here, the ruin indicates the plastic and fabricated presence of the degeneracy of history, thus functioning as a sign of a "beyond" opposed to "this" realm of history and death. Interestingly, not only does Nietzsche criticize the allegorical manner of Wagner's work, but he also makes Wagner an allegorical example of a larger historical development. Wagner comes to occupy a position similar to that of the death skull in Benjamin. In this passage, Benjamin contrasts symbol and allegory: "While in the symbol, with the transfiguration of decline, the transfigured visage of nature fleetingly reveals itself in the light of redemption, in allegory the *facies hippocratica* of history lies before the eyes of the observer as a petrified primordial landscape. History, in all the untimeliness, suffering, and failure that it has from the beginning, expresses itself in a face—no, in a skull" (p. 145). His description of the symbol echoes Nietzsche's designation of music as a swan song; and one might say the "facies hippocratica," invoking also the art of dissimulation, applies both to Wagner and to his operatic characters.

9. Plato's restrictions on the musical modes in book 2 of *The Republic* are, of course, well known. For Plato, of course, the actual musical phase—a preconceptual phase of education—is possible because it is grounded in an intelligible system of harmony based on mathematical relations; these, in time, will replace the musical imprints on the child. Further, music is delineated as a preparatory stage of education, imprinting a preconceptual disposition toward truth. From music, as from proper poetry, "our young men . . . may receive benefit from all things about them, whence the

influence that emanates from works of beauty may waft itself to eye or ear like a breeze that brings from wholesome places health, and so from earliest childhood insensibly guide them to likeness, to friendship, to harmony with beautiful reason. . . . education in music is most sovereign, because more than anything else rhythm and harmony find their way to the inmost soul and take strongest hold upon it, bringing with them and imparting grace, if one is rightly trained, and otherwise the contrary" (*The Collected Dialogues,* ed. Edith Hamilton and Huntington Cairns [Princeton: Princeton Univ. Press, 1961], book 3 §§401c–402a, pp. 645–47). But if the musical stage is not transcended, the soul remains too "soft": "Now when a man abandons himself to music, to play upon him and pour into his soul as it were through the funnel of his ears . . . [and] continues the practice without remission and is spellbound, the effect begins to be that he melts and liquifies till he completely dissolves away his spirit, cuts out as it were the very sinews of his soul and makes of himself a 'feeble warrior' " (book 3 §411b, p. 655). The "true" music is not that practiced by musicians, which bears with it the threat of emasculating dissolution; instead, it is the harmonious relation of body and soul which allows music to play a part in development, but must be limited (book 3 §412a, p. 655).

10. Jean-Jacques Rousseau, *Les Confessions,* 2 vols. (Paris: Garnier-Flammarion, 1968), 1:48–49.

11. Emile Benveniste examines *signifiance,* the process of signifying in general, in its relation to music especially in "Sémiologie de la langue," in *Problèmes de linguistique générale,* 2 vols. (Paris: Gallimard, 1974), 2:43–66. Because music, according to Benveniste, has a syntax but no semiotic, "signifiance" emerges through the selection and arrangement of an individual work and cannot be relayed through a conventional set of signifying codes. In *Le Langage, cet inconnu: Une Initiation à la linguistique* (Paris: Seuil, 1981), Julia Kristeva agrees with Benveniste that music is not a system of signs, and thus: "Music leads us to the limit of the system of signs" (p. 306). In *La Révolution du langage poétique: L'Avant-garde à la fin du XIXe siècle: Lautréamont et Mallarmé* (Paris: Seuil, 1974), "music" is actually a metaphor used to describe the "properly" poetic function of disrupting hierarchies of signification (p. 62). In *L'Obvie et l'obtus: Essais critiques III* (Paris: Seuil, 1982), Roland Barthes similarly points to an "other" discourse modeled on music, one which is both individual and bodily; he clearly connects the "musical" to the "otherness" of textuality as *écriture.* Barthes elucidates in an interesting way how he interprets music as a metaphor for text, concluding, "Perhaps this, then, is the value of music: to be a good metaphor" (p. 252).

12. Jardine makes this connection explicit when addressing the question of the author's gender with respect to "femininity" and "masculinity." She writes: "The assurance of an author's sex within this whirlpool of decentering is problematized beyond recognition. The policing of sexual identity is henceforth seen as complicitous with the appropriations of representation; gender (masculine, feminine) is separate from identity (male, female). The question of whether a 'man' or a 'woman' wrote a text . . . becomes nonsensical. A man becomes a woman (*devient femme*) when he writes, or, if not, he does not 'write' (in the radical sense of *écriture*)" (p. 58). What I have called the referential residue indicates only that, despite whatever degree of "devient femme" has taken place, neither Nietzsche nor Derrida, as examples, has undergone mystical transsexual surgery.

13. Georg Wilhelm Friedrich Hegel, *Aesthetik*, 2 vols. (Berlin: verlag das europäische buch, 1985), 2:325.

14. Adorno is an interesting case, since his critique of Wagner in many ways echoes Nietzsche. His analysis is especially directed at the gestural aspect of the composer-conductor's manipulation of the scenario, as well as at the illusory plasticity of the operatic characters; see "Versuch über Wagner," in *Gesammelte Schriften*, ed. Gretel Adorno and Rolf Tiedemann (Frankfurt: Suhrkamp, 1970–86), 13:7–148. In "Zeitlose Mode: Zum Jazz" (in *Prismen*), Adorno displays an inordinate anxiety at the "false individuality" of improvisation, which he compares to illiteracy as a menace. The "jitterbugs'" regression into bodily gesticulation and other aspects of jazz are explicitly related to castration anxiety: "The aim of jazz is the mechanical reproduction of a regressive moment, a castration symbolism. 'Give up your masculinity, let yourself be castrated,' the eunuchlike sound of jazz proclaims, 'and you will be rewarded, accepted into a fraternity which shares the mystery of impotence with you'" (*Prisms*, trans. Samuel and Schierry Weber [Cambridge: MIT Press, 1981], p. 127). He criticizes the modern consumption of music along similar lines in "Über den Fetischcharakter in der Musik und die Regression des Hörens" (in *Dissonanzen*, in *Gesammelte Schriften*, 14:14–50). Referring directly to the Greek tradition linking music to chaos and seduction—the danger to which Plato offers an antidote—he stresses the manipulative rhetoric in modern music and the correlative extinction of critical awareness in "the mass public," inducing the illusion of an infantile regression into a mythic prehistory (especially pp. 16–19).

15. Philippe Lacoue-Labarthe, "L'Echo du Sujet," in *Le Sujet de la philosophie: Typographies I* (Paris: Aubier-Flammarion, 1979), pp. 217–303.

16. Carl Dahlhaus, *Between Romanticism and Modernism: Four Studies in the Music of the Later Nineteenth Century*, trans. Mary Whittall (Berkeley and Los Angeles: Univ. of California Press, 1980), p. 20. Thanks to Paul Fleming's unpublished work on Nietzsche's "On Music and Words."

17. See Freud, *Jenseits des Lustprinzips*.

18. On the fetish, see Freud's essay "Fetischismus," in *Gesammelte Werke*, 14:309–17, and Sarah Kofman's interesting essay "Ça Cloche," in *Les Fins de l'homme: A partir du travail de Jacques Derrida*, ed. Philippe Lacoue-Labarthe and Jean-Luc Nancy (Paris: Galilée, 1981), pp. 89–116.

19. Schopenhauer mentions this painting at the end of the third book of *Die Welt als Wille und Vorstellung*, in *Sämtliche Werke*, ed. Wolfgang Frhr. von Löhneysen, 5 vols. (Wiesbaden: Eberhard Brockhaus, 1949), 1:315–16. Interestingly, it is precisely in describing the manner in which the artist, while presenting images freed from primordial pain, still remains within this suffering and is afforded only momentary solace through artistic production. He names Raphael's painting as an image (*Sinnbild*) of the end of aesthetic play and the beginning of moral gravity; the painting itself stands as the image of this *Uebergang*. Since Nietzsche is clearly working from Schopenhauer in the fragment in question, it is noteworthy that Nietzsche uses the same example, but does not allow the transition beyond the aesthetic to take place. Thanks to Peter Fenves for pointing out this passage in Schopenhauer.

20. The painting is generally interpreted allegorically, highlighting the virgin St. Cecilia as a figure who rejects the earthly for the celestial, the musical attack on the nerves for the higher purity of the music of the spheres. For such readings, the history

of the painting, and detailed reproductions, see especially Stanislaw Mossakowski, "Il significato della 'S. Cecilia' di Raffaello," Thomas H. Connolly, "The Cult and Iconography of S. Cecilia before Raphael," and other essays in *La Santa Cecilia di Raffaello: Indagini per un dipinto,* ed. Andrea Emiliani (Bologna: ALFA, 1983) and *L'Estasi di Santa Cecilia di Raffaello da Urbino nella Pinacoteca Nazionale di Bologna,* ed. Francesca Valli, Maurizio Armaroli, and Gianpiero Cammarota (Bologna: ALFA, 1983).

21. See Sigmund Freud, "Das Medusenhaupt," in *Gesammelte Werke,* 17:45–48. Neil Hertz gives an interesting reading of the intertwined problematics of castration, the Medusa figure, representation, and politics in "Medusa's Head: Male Hysteria under Political Pressure," in *The End of the Line: Essays on Psychoanalysis and the Sublime* (New York: Columbia Univ. Press, 1985), pp. 161–93. Carol Jacobs's reading of Shelley's poem "On the Medusa of Leonardo da Vinci," in *Uncontainable Romanticism: Shelley, Brontë, Kleist* (Baltimore: Johns Hopkins Univ. Press, 1989), pp. 3–18, is both complementary and contrasting to my reading here. The case she discusses is also a literary presentation of a painting; but as Jacobs argues, Shelley's version exposes the infinite regression that is blocked off in Nietzsche's rendition. Jacobs points directly to the endless oscillation I have suggested above. "As in the 'Medusa,' " Jacobs writes, "where the beholding subject, the producing subject, and the object produced can never coincide, where all takes place under the aegis of an endless mirroring in which thought no more can trace, poetry or Imagination can never close definitively on that to which it makes its internal adjustment" (p. 18). A comparison of Shelley's poem and Nietzsche's reference would, I think, give some insight into the explicit vs. implicit position of this instability, perhaps related to the difference between the "poetic" and "theoretical" determinations of these texts. In "Nietzsche Medused," Bernard Pautrat makes an argument to which mine is in many ways parallel, but with a more explicit orientation toward the relationship between "truth" and its philosophical exposition.

22. In *Nietzsche contra Wagner,* Nietzsche lists Kleist among several authors martyred by a "break" in need of healing (KSA 6:434–35; NW p. 678). These broken souls, Nietzsche says, appeal specifically to the female sensibility, suggesting that the masculine reader tends to avoid such figures of castration.

23. Heinrich von Kleist, *Sämtliche Erzählungen und Anekdoten* (Munich: dtv/Hanser, 1978), p. 217.

24. The connection between automata, repetition compulsion, and castration anxiety has of course been much discussed, especially in the many readings of Freud's essay "Das Unheimliche" (in *Gesammelte Werke,* 12:227–68); see especially Neil Hertz, "Freud and the Sandman," in *The End of the Line,* pp. 97–121, and Samuel Weber, "The Sideshow, or: Remarks on a Canny Moment," *MLN* 88 (1973): 1102–33. Music plays a more crucial role within similar configurations of castration and automatization in many Hoffmann stories besides "The Sandman," such as "Die Automate," "Der Unheimliche Gast," along with others in E. T. A. Hoffmann, *Die Serapions-Brüder,* 4 vols. (Frankfurt: Insel, 1983). Lacoue-Labarthe also develops the relationship between the uncanny, music, and repetition compulsion in "L'Echo du Sujet."

25. Derrida analyzes this passage and the complex relation between "woman" and "truth" in *Spurs,* especially pp. 54/55–62/63.

PART THREE

Beyond Antifeminism

JANET LUNGSTRUM

Nietzsche Writing Woman / Woman Writing Nietzsche: The Sexual Dialectic of Palingenesis

Nietzsche's philosophy of the Greek agon is both the condition for his creativity and the acting-out of his will to power in self or text. As an energy requiring a transformed intersubjectivity with an Other, it is acted out on multiple levels, such as in the Bloomian framework of anxious influence between writers and their tropes.[1] The latter gesture of creativity is in fact a derivative notion of Nietzsche's insight into the Heraclitean movement of repeated creation and destruction, into physiological struggle against and for sickness and health, and Dionysian self-loss coupled with Socratic self-gain. Since the agon for Nietzsche is above all a metaphor of vitalism, it is worth investigating his most blatant use of it, namely *la ronde* of sexuality. Such a dialectical structure of Nietzsche's creative agonistics is at its most extreme, and hence potentially most insightful, in his writing on woman. Warlike difference is the paradigm of the masculine/feminine struggle for Nietzsche, who speaks in favor of a "most abysmal antagonism" between man and woman, of the "necessity of an eternally hostile tension" between the sexes (KSA 5:175; BGaE §238, p. 166).

A consequence of Nietzsche's extremity regarding woman has resulted in a Scylla and Charybdis problematic arising in postmodernist and feminist critical responses. On the one hand, feminist theory has, quite understandably, taken issue with Nietzsche-the-misogynist positing woman's will to power—and woman's will to write—in the camp of the degenerate metaphysicians, a move by which he would appear to exclude woman from his discourse of becoming.[2] The suspicion has arisen that Nietzsche's creativity maintains its sexual power, its Foucauldian *ars erotica,*[3] by restraining woman to such notorious images as a self-distancing feint, as a desirable and controllable animal-other, or at best as the mother of the *Übermensch* who gives birth but cannot recreate herself.[4] Zarathustra's explicit command to woman is: "Let your hope be: 'May I bear the Superman!' " (KSA 4:85; TSZ p. 92). But, on the other hand, Derrida and others in his wake have interpreted the Nietzschean sexual rhetoric as a covert, and (pro)creative, feminism: in depicting woman as subversive metaphor, as a liberating, deceitful *différance,* Nietzsche is thereby shown to propose the creation of a metafeminine, namely, the figure of a woman who is supremely—if perhaps somewhat too neatly—transvalued beyond all passive, castrated good as well as overactive, castrating evil.

The above resulting contradiction of views in Nietzsche criticism has produced a specific dilemma for those whose reading strategies toward self-creation utilize both feminist *and* postmodernist approaches. The situation is akin to, but less comfortable than, what Richard Rorty, in *Contingency, Irony, and Solidarity,* locates as the compartmentalization between "public" liberalism and "private" irony—but for Rorty, Nietzsche is totally inappropriate for the former sphere.[5] For the feminine can be read as the feminist keynote to Nietzsche's philosophy, or the woman-in-Nietzsche can be equally rejected outright as a rehypostatized image by and for man, namely as *das Weib,* with all its wenchlike connotations. It is a case in point of what is quite possibly the most crucial predicament for feminism in modern and postmodern philosophy, as noted by Alice A. Jardine in *Gynesis:* "To refuse 'woman' or the 'feminine' as cultural and libidinal constructions (as in 'men's femininity') is, ironically, to return to metaphysical—anatomical—definitions of sexual identity. To accept a metaphorization, a semiosis of woman, on the other hand, means risking once again the absence of women as subjects in the struggles of modernity."[6] At issue here is the call for a new subjectivity, a feminist "semiosis," that yet would not remain beholden to metaphysical identity, nor inactive in social relations.

It is the endeavor of this essay to chart an alternate course through the critical waters of the Nietzschean woman and to highlight the creative potential of the Nietzschean sexual agon. The specific context of my response to Nietzsche's writings regarding woman will be to demonstrate the fluidity of his notion of *eroticism-as-creativity* rather than to delineate any fixed gender-as-identity, the latter approach having typically, and somewhat too obviously, resulted in a dead end for Nietzsche in recent feminist enquiry.[7] The Nietzschean text simply does not respond well to a critic imposing her own politically preordained set of feminist values. I argue, however, that a feminist self-empowerment is indeed attainable within the woman that Nietzsche creates—less in his societal or metaphorical images of her than in his discourse on the metonymic, antagonistic desire between the sexes. It is a desire that Nietzsche internalizes, or bisexualizes, within his own text—and, as has been noted by his biographers, within his own life.[8] Nietzsche may write woman into existence, but this virulent staging of woman occurs above all within himself as a necessary contradiction of an overt virility and as a key part of his undoubtedly homoerotic mode of self-creation. Underlying the controversy of the Nietzschean woman is, above all, a new dialectical art of *palingenesis:* a creativity of self-renewal that demands a male-female symbiosis, a bisexual agon without resolve and without synthesis.[9] Viewing Nietzsche's economy of sex and of writing in this manner may indeed help provide a more flexible vocabulary for a feminist creativity that would assertively welcome rather than avoid or elude a renewed, transvaluing sexual agon, as a more authentic depiction of the modus operandi in (discursive) desire. In the manner of Rorty's proposed "liberal ironist," then, the woman written by Nietzsche may in fact simultaneously redescribe and reinvent herself via Nietzsche's "final vocabularies," which are themselves already less than final (*Contingency,* p. 73).

An extradilemmatic move begins with a consideration of the repeated sexual oppositions in the Nietzschean text, the various positions from which woman is endowed to act as catalytic muse. Even here, as he stereotypes woman's role as an aide-mémoire to the male pen, Nietzsche upsets his own reification of woman in the creative process. The female body lends itself to a sexual "antagonism," states Nietzsche in *The Gay Science,* out of which the male body and perspective profit absolutely on the collective level: this admittedly immoral "natural opposition," he insists—somewhat unexpectedly, given his generally condemnatory tone for woman in her genderized roles—is the source of social injustice for woman, an inequity that is played out in interpretations of the sexual act itself, for a woman making love is seen to "give herself away," while man "acquires more" thereby (KSA 3:611–12; GS §363, p. 319). In fact, the sexual difference is, Nietzsche claims in a note of 1882, not one of hierarchy but of asymmetry, the varying sensual tempos easily leading to mutual misinterpretation (KSA 10:56; also, KSA 13:240; WP §799, p. 420). Nietzsche is hence not correlating woman's societal domination by man with her actual sexuality. The enigma of *Weib*-woman is radically situated against man-Nietzsche, but not in a regular dichotomy; neither category is a static eternal unto itself. In his rabid need to put woman in her place, he is far from recreating the myth of woman-in-herself—since he mocks the "eternal feminine" as man's metaphysical creation "out of a rib of his god, his 'ideal' " (KSA 13:477). This is not to say, however, that woman-as-difference in Nietzsche somehow escapes her dialectical location in regard to man; rather, she represents an Other, a negative identity, who does not (and physically and sociologically is highly unlikely ever to) simply go away in a puff of smoke to a realm beyond good and evil (that is, beyond man's anxieties about her). Determined, however, to create out of this struggle, Nietzsche writes in praise of a sexual agonistics in which no single pairing is ever predetermined, since the art of sexual desire is to reconceive itself in new alignments. In this way, woman is not genderized—rather, she designs and desires the male as Other, precisely as he desires her, and each sex gives and acquires. Moreover, the asymmetry of loss and gain that Nietzsche detects in the sexual act between masculine and feminine desire is precisely the dialectical agon operating in his creative writing.

At this point, however, one will recall that much of postmodernist Nietzsche criticism has grown around the figurehead of an absolutely *anti*dialectical Nietzsche: the debt of influence here is owed to Gilles Deleuze's tide-turning book of 1962, *Nietzsche and Philosophy*.[10] Deleuze's crucial thesis, so influential for Derrida, is focused on demonstrating how Nietzsche effectively crushes the Socratic-Hegelian dialectic in favor of a multiplicity of difference (pp. 195–96).[11] Deleuze explains this overcoming of dialectical oppositionality by concentrating on the transvaluing *Übermensch* (pp. 162–64), but it should be noted that he achieves this at the cost of omitting woman from his analysis, except to locate her as the fettered spirit of ressentiment (thus most definitely and always a genderized *Weib*)—or, conceivably, as Ariadne, the affirming, labyrinthine lover of Dionysus (pp. 187–88), but as a marginal figure hardly able to compete with the Overman.

In contrast to Deleuze, Bernard Pautrat's *Versions du soleil* (1971)[12] offers a more mediatory path, while still belonging to the Derridean circle;[13] for he identifies the "Nietzschean dialectic" to be a new parodic reversal of, and yet a constant responding to, its Hegelian ancestor (p. 32). For Pautrat this new dialectic is the very mechanism by which Nietzsche achieves his "reverse Platonism" (p. 84)—an unfortunate choice of term, given Heidegger's demonstration of Nietzsche's limitations via a mechanism of "overturning" Plato.[14] However, Pautrat's main observation of an unsynthesized dialectic is still sound.[15] The Nietzschean agon is one of transvaluation (*Umwertung*) of values, not a Heideggerian tactic of reversal (*Umdrehung*). The (feminine) Other in Nietzsche thus enjoys a new alterity. The generational gap between the dialectic as it is formulated by Hegel and subsequently revamped by Nietzsche is one of contradiction supplanting unification of difference. Pautrat can thus permit himself to consider in detail the disturbing role of the woman-metaphor: he sees in the Nietzschean text not only an explosion of dichotomies into metaphor and difference but also a continuing round of oppositional sexual attraction and rejection between interchangeable masculine and feminine elements, as in the act of Apollonian-Dionysian copulation creating the experience of tragedy (p. 120).

The asymmetric axis of separation in the Nietzschean creative dialectic finds its qualifying characteristic in stimulative contradiction, one which Nietzsche needs in order to write. Hence his disgust, in *Beyond Good and Evil,* at those emancipatory women who would blunt the sexual difference and dissolve the natural power of their femininity by becoming " 'woman as clerk,' " as boringly Socratic and cultured as most men (KSA 5:176; BGaE §239, p. 167). Adrian Del Caro rightly stresses Nietzsche's concern with the "threat of the neuter" arising if the male-female will-to-antagonism were to be eliminated.[16] Such a societal "defeminizing" operates like a case of repressive overcivilization to deprive Nietzsche of the fundamentally sexual "*force of the will*" that he requires in woman and within himself to validate the artwork—"her *nature,* which is more 'natural' than that of the [Socraticized] man, her genuine, cunning, beast-of-prey suppleness, the tiger's claws beneath the glove"; hence the nature of "this dangerous and beautiful cat 'woman' " is to be encouraged as an antidote to male Socratism (KSA 5:177–78; BGaE §239, pp. 168–69). Here is a philosopher who transvalues woman's *physis,* by insisting in *Ecce Homo* that the "state of nature, the eternal *war* between the sexes" is one which in fact "puts her in a superior position by far," sexually and creatively speaking (KSA 6:306; EcH pp. 75–76): this is woman as and at the locus of becoming.

From the necessity of woman-as-contradiction in Nietzsche's sexual dialectic arises an uncontrollable sadomasochism. In this war zone with both sides pursuing and eluding, Nietzsche writing the woman within himself is not for the faint at heart. He admits to his desire for and yet fear of contact with a Pygmalionesque perfect woman: "Happily I am not prepared to be torn to pieces: the complete woman tears to pieces when she loves . . . I know these amiable maenads" (KSA 6:306; EcH p. 76).

Indeed, his sister and mother are depicted in the currently accepted version of section three of *Ecce Homo*'s "Why I Am So Wise," first published in 1969, as a "perfect hell-machine" (*die vollkommene Höllenmaschine*), a "disharmonia praestabilita" or poisonous, parasitic worm threatening to wound his deepest thought of eternal return (KSA 6:268). As Gary Shapiro states, Nietzsche's claims to mastery over binary oppositions (as in *Ecce Homo*) are a transparent cover for himself written by the text as a "*function* of a play of doubles that he cannot control."[17] Ostensibly feminine, these dialectical Others effectively emasculate their purported master—in the case of mother and sister, by actually censoring the statement out of the text, or by seeking to end Nietzsche's relationship with the as yet unmarried Lou von Salomé. And yet Nietzsche's concept of self and desire evidently thrives on the pain; in the "Tautenburg Notes" composed explicitly "for Lou von Salomé" (KSA 10:9) during the high point of their friendship in July and August of 1882, Nietzsche proposes a pre-Freudian explanation of sadomasochistic desire: "How do contradicting sensations work, therefore a duality? As related, as a duality?" (KSA 10:29). As a response to this, he cites the highest self-love as having an heroic desire for self-destruction, or "self-rape" (*Selbst-Vergewaltigung*), just as those who love humanity the most will also hurt people the most; likewise, "self-spite" (*Trotz gegen sich*) characterizes two types of (male) lovers, he who (masochistically) longs to give himself over to suffering and he who (sadistically) tyrannizes himself by tyrannizing the beloved (KSA 10:29). Cruelty to the person one loves brings a certain "*pleasure* in pitying": for Nietzsche's lover—interpretable as himself loving Lou or himself fantasizing about being loved by such a (wo)man—achieves his or her best love by pitying the beloved (s)he is simultaneously torturing (KSA 10:29). Nietzsche is effectively creating out of these painful differences in the structure of desire; he does not merge them in any higher truth or easy machismo. Following this logic of open contradiction emerges another dictum of the sexual will: "Self-mutilation and lust next to each other is the same. Or clearest consciousness and leadweight and immovability after opium" (KSA 10:29). This is the sadomasochistic "*contradiction* of two opposed strong drives, which functions here as the *highest stimulus* [*höchster Reiz*]" (KSA 10:29)—that is, the only way Nietzsche can love and write. Thus it is that the highest Nietzschean self-love involves a desire for self-violation in an acting-out of creative self-alterity.

At this stage it would be cautious to read *against* Nietzschean sexual difference in order to ask whether Nietzsche is, after all, inventing woman too absolutely in the profitable pursuit of inspirational, agonistic relations.

One must consider whether his new design for woman is intrinsically any better *for her* than her usual garb of idealization by Socratic man, that is, of being "*wrapped up*" in the motifs of the eternal feminine (KSA 5:177; BGaE §239, p. 168). The following passage in Nietzsche's notes, of which only the first part appears in *Twilight of the Idols* (KSA 6:62; T p. 34), posits how he patents the otherness of his complete woman: "The perfect woman [*das vollkommene Weib*] perpetrates literature in the same way as she perpetrates a little sin: as an experiment, in passing, looking around to see if someone notices and *so that* someone may notice: she knows how well a small spot of degeneracy and brown depravity suits the perfect woman, —she knows even better how all literature-making affects woman, as a questioning of all *other* female *pudeurs*" (KSA 13:29). Positioned differentially and yet intimately related to her, is literature: whether as writing or as reading, it functions as that ornamental little sin or transgression, as the pudendum or putrefaction (*ein kleiner Fleck Fäulniß und brauner Verdorbenheit*) (KSA 13:29) with which the perfect woman daringly adorns herself, beginning thereby a nonstop, unfolding *mise-en-doute* of accepted female mores and metaphysical values. This subversive proposition is an outfit made to enhance narrative life as much as it is made to "suit" the perfect woman, who may be just a metaphorical vehicle for the decoration.

The passage cited above would certainly apply well to Nietzsche's self-denigrating announcement that his comments on woman are "*my* truths" only (KSA 5:170; BGaE §231, p. 163), but such perspectivism nonetheless asserts a position of inflammatory influence. Since he recognizes only too well that "what things *are called* is incomparably more important than what they are" and that the task for a strong creator, as he says in *The Gay Science,* is one of designing a new "dress" to "throw over things" in order to create these things anew (KSA 3:422; GS §58, pp. 121–22), one must probe his strict policy of differentiating her from man in the name of a creative dialectic. As the textual clothier par excellence, he knows precisely how to drape a suggestive garment over his perfect reader-woman for his own ends, leaving her little choice but to parade herself in his stylistic show of antimetaphysics. At times, Nietzsche castigates *das Weib* as if she were synonymous with the growth of Christianity and its fable-like unreality (KSA 6:80; T p. 50); but, since he also ranks genderized woman alongside Christianity as a decadent, hysterical consequence of overcivilization, she is not, then, sick-in-herself, but has been made such. In the face of such metaphorical slippages, how should the recipient of Nietzsche's text respond to his aggressive redefinition? Sublimate, vilify, or identify? In what way can one read Nietzsche's prime modus vivendi, namely the enormously seductive power of recreating oneself textually and sexually via woman, and yet avoid the complicitous feeling of having acquiesced voyeuristically to sexism? When, indeed, is the woman written by Nietzsche no longer just a reessentialized *Weib*—no matter how perfectly postmodern the dress?

It is time, then, to seek out woman's voice in Nietzsche, to ask if she indeed can have a room, or a garment, of her own making. If viewed through a societal lens, female "*sensuality* in its disguises" appears silenced, idealized, reified, as a "concave image" of man's own subliminal drives, as Nietzsche states in notes of 1887 (KSA 12:324; WP §806, p. 424). Through the transferential lens of art, however, it becomes less clear just which sex is doing the image-creating: "The sensuality of the artist puts into one object everything else that he honors and esteems—in this way he *perfects* an object ('idealizes' it). Woman, conscious of man's feelings concerning women, assists his efforts at idealization by adorning herself, walking beautifully, dancing . . . she divines that it is precisely an actual naive modesty that most seduces a man and impels him to overestimate her. Therefore woman is naive—from the subtlety of her instinct. . . . A deliberate *closing of one's eyes to oneself*—Wherever dissembling produces a stronger effect when it is unconscious, it *becomes* unconscious" (KSA 12:324–25; WP §806, pp. 424–25). It is the task of the Nietzschean voyeur-artist to fall for an illusion that he realizes to be such, to parody idealism from within, to effectively close his eyes to himself, just as woman is doing to her own artifice.[18] But here the sexual dialectic is, potentially at least, just as empowering for the woman as it is for her lover; if anything she is granted more originary powers of creative feigning than is the artist. Nietzsche posits woman as "conscious of man's feelings" about her, but instigating her own form of self-blindness so as to make her beauty (the artwork) more effective; in creating her own image of herself, she fakes her own ignorance about her art of attraction. The will to power in woman as artwork, as desirable catalytic beauty, consists in her vaguest hint of self-knowledge regarding her pose and her strategies of self-creating finery. As Nietzsche jokes in *The Gay Science*, woman is an act, "giving herself" to a performance even when she gives herself to a (real *or* faked) orgasm (KSA 3:609; GS §361, p. 317*). She is both naive and self-ador(n)ing, with or without a lover to seduce or be seduced by.

The feints and power plays between Nietzsche's (male) artist and (female) catalyst are always those of seduction. They form the dialectic of self-overcoming. Here it is appropriate to refer to Jean Baudrillard's

Seduction (1979), in which an authentically creative mode of being is defined as a "*transubstantiation*" of sex into a signifying art of sexual attraction—an art which, for Baudrillard, lends itself to the feminine but is not gender-specific.[19] Baudrillard's provocative thesis is implicitly Nietzschean throughout;[20] in both texts, "to seduce" becomes an intransitive verb for the experience of creating. "It is the power of the seductive woman who takes herself for her own desire, and delights in the self-deception in which others, in their turn, will be caught" (p. 69)—such is the illusory snare of art. With the advantages of this semiconsciousness, woman enjoys, states Baudrillard, an "ironic," diversionary space of play and defiance against the (socratically) commodified "referentiality of sex" (p. 21). Thanks to a crucial move "from ethics to aesthetics"—although here Baudrillard separates what is joined in Nietzsche (p. 114)—woman can afford "that minimum reversibility which puts an end to every fixed opposition" (p. 104). Baudrillard's playful poetics of seduction is unimaginable without the Nietzschean sexual dialectic.

In his description of woman's seductive ability as that of creating dissimulation, or dissimulating creatively—both of which lead man on to create in his turn—Nietzsche is portraying a pre-Freudian condition of *narcissism*. It is a crucial concept in that the Nietzschean woman's narcissism is the tool by which she can rewrite her agonal otherness. According to Freud in his 1914 essay on the subject,[21] most men tend—after an initial narcissism—toward object-love, while women, especially the young and pretty ones, develop "self-contentment" to such a degree that they are fulfilled loving and decorating simply themselves—and this very indifference excites thereby the "greatest fascination" among men (p. 89).[22] Now, it is possible to see this representation of woman's self-love as a curable stage on the path to psychical maturity—Freud suggests a cure in pregnancy (p. 89), while Lacan relativizes it as the imaginary joys of childhood in the mirror stage—or, on feminist grounds, reprehensible as yet another male version of the eternal feminine, substituting man's own lost narcissism, as Sarah Kofman indicates.[23] However, it is also possible, and ultimately more liberating, to view the narcissistic display of the Nietzschean woman as a creative state of literal self-sufficiency, and indeed as Nietzsche's highest aim of self-engendering.

One such woman for both Freud and Nietzsche was Lou von Salomé (later Andreas-Salomé). Kofman suggests the possibility of Salomé having acted as a physical mediator of the theory of narcissism between Nietzsche and Freud (*Enigma*, p. 53). However, Kofman does not mention Salomé's own paper on narcissism, "Die in sich ruhende Frau" (1899).[24] Evidently

Salomé may have influenced Freud textually in her own right, despite the Nietzschean inspiration for her essay. Salomé was the only philosophical-erotic focus of Nietzsche's otherwise essentially celibate (and, if indeed attempted, very likely syphilitic)[25] experience of women; he saw in her a role reversal from his former tutelage to Wagner. In her refusal to be his wife or his devotee, she inevitably served as venomous inspiration for his dialectic of feminine creativity. Transference was two-way: their philosophical discussions (including co-written aphorisms on woman)[26] influenced Salomé's subsequent writings on woman and on Nietzsche himself.

In particular, Salomé's essay, "Die in sich ruhende Frau," while engaging in an undeniably metaphysical essentialization of woman's reproductive function, brings to light a theory of female narcissism (literally: "woman resting in herself") which not only offsets misogynistically motivated understanding of late nineteenth-century genetic science, but also unabashedly celebrates woman's intrinsic gift for self-fulfillment and self-(re)creation. In a most Nietzschean move, Salomé's creative woman as life-force is positioned in opposition to the truth-seeking theoretical man (p. 298). Indeed, if the (male) artist is lucky, he can aspire to the creative skills of woman: creativity makes him "more whole, more organic, fused . . . with what he creates, just as woman is, and maintains him as it were in a joy of spiritual pregnancy, which lives deep within itself" (pp. 295–96). In matching woman's innate gift with that of the genius, Salomé is evidently drawing here on Nietzsche's aphorism in *The Gay Science* on male spiritual pregnancy, which is itself based on Schopenhauerian genius: "Spiritual pregnancy produce[s] the character of the contemplative type, which is closely related to the feminine character: it consists of male mothers" (KSA 3:430; GS §72, p. 129). Pregnancy, as the physical female reproduction of life, is what Nietzsche and Salomé instance as the feminine creativity most akin to artistic creation, more fruitful indeed than even the sex act—because of the inherent act of narcissistic self-seduction during the process of internal germination.[27] Creative narcissism is sustained by the growth of the egg of male and female parents within one's own body, be the pregnancy literal or literary. After conception or inspiration, so to speak, comes one's real and most fruitful transformation: a palingenesis within the womb, a reunion with the artwork within.

A caveat: Nietzsche's metaphor of the birthing process of narcissistic palingenesis should not be equated with a philosophy of motherhood. Nietzsche's—and Salomé's—emphasis is not on the offspring; this is not a philosophy of the maternal-materialistic instinct for art-as-product. The last thing Nietzsche would ask for would be to be called the spokesman of an essentialization of maternity in the name of some utopic, asexual femininity. While the Nietzschean artist must be able to fill the role of the "birther" (*Gebärerin*) and her pains in order to give birth to a child of spiritual becoming (KSA 4:111; TSZ p. 111), the maternal metaphor is not all-consuming in this philosopher's creative stance. Zarathustra's male warrior actually prefers the ongoing, dialectical combat-play with the "bitter" fruit that woman is for him (KSA 4:85; TSZ p. 91). The pregnancy that provides the "cure" to woman's riddle must be repeated in the artist (KSA 4:84; TSZ p. 91) as a problematical *re*production rather than a single production.

One may, of course, turn against Nietzsche for having thus turned against the maternal origin, for "vomiting up," as Irigaray puts it in her *Marine Lover of Friedrich Nietzsche,* "that first nurse whose milk and blood he has drunk."[28] Irigaray goes so far as to threaten Nietzsche that his creativity via woman is doomed to impotency: "You will never have pleasure [*jouir*] in woman, if you insist on being woman. If you insist on making her a stage in your process" (p. 39). Like Salomé, Irigaray seeks to rewrite the Nietzschean text on woman, but unlike Salomé, she reads the Nietzschean woman as essentially *re*active, and hence seeks a corrective measure in the maternal metaphor of "unceasing birthing" (p. 86). The result of this overwriting is that Nietzsche becomes a stage in *her* process. *Marine Lover* is a text written by a would-be bride of Zarathustra, who would yet prefer her own, strictly *un*veiled, lips in a self-embrace. Irigaray's suggestion of *faire la noce* with Nietzsche is made ostensibly to improve upon what she sees as his failed mission of self-overcoming. She cannot forgive him for having dared—without her—to narcissistically create himself as woman, for his "self-marriage" of being both "bride and groom" (p. 32). Irigaray's view of Nietzsche's self-seduction as a culpable inversion or misuse of woman refuses to acknowledge the creative dialectic of "you in her, and her in you" (p. 73).

The Nietzschean creative paradox here, absent in Salomé's as well as in Irigaray's more unified view of woman as *physis,* is that a "spiritual pregnancy," or germination toward palingenesis, insists upon (Dionysian) integration in conjunction with a degree of (Apollonian) *separation from itself,* in order for representation of the artwork to be born. Nietzsche, wanting to stress the opposite of synthesis in his dialectic of creativity, later reproached his *Birth of Tragedy Out of the Spirit of Music* for having implied too smooth and final a "rebirth" of tragedy, in a burst of Wagner-influenced Hegelian *Aufhebung* (KSA 6:309; EcH p. 78). Within his description of the Dionysian and the Apollonian, however, there is still a constant emphasis on the oppositional process of becoming rather than on the actual product. As Nietzsche states in his 1871 notes, the Dionysian genius, immediately upon fusing in orgiastic self-loss with the primal world-force, creates out of this primal agony a reflection of the same, which is in turn redistanced into a healing, Apollonian representation in tragedy: "When this artistic reflection of primal pain produces out of itself yet a second image, as mock sun, then we have the communal *Dionysian-Apollonian* artwork" (KSA 7:335). Nietzsche declares of this "highest double art": "There is no Dionysian appearance [*Schein*] without an Apollonian reflection [*Wiederschein*]" (KSA 7:335). Note the nature of this "duplicity" or "duality" (*Duplicität* or *Zweiheit*) involved here between the sex drives of art, as Nietzsche identifies them in *The Birth of Tragedy* (KSA 1:25; BT §1, p. 33)—they do not interact from fixed sexual identities; rather, their inseparable yet antagonistic interdependency confuses gender identity. The phallic symbolism of the Dionysian is hence also the realm of the orgiastic female, as in the original Greek festivals,[29] while the Apollonian calm is as applicable to the realm of predominantly male representation as it is to the performance by woman of herself. As Pautrat makes clear, the artwork is born of impure, because bisexual, parentage (*Versions,* pp. 87, 120); Nietzsche's sexual dialectic emphasizes the literally functioning bisexuality of both the Apollonian and the Dionysian.

When the later Nietzsche moves beyond *The Birth of Tragedy*'s Apollonian-Dionysian dialectic of creativity to subsume it within the contradictory nature of Dionysus—whom Pautrat calls "oblique Dionysus" (*Versions,* p. 155), and whose female double is Baubo (Kofman, "Baubô," p. 197)—it is woman who takes over as the Apollonian degree of separation required for Dionysian insight to materialize in the self as artwork. In narcissistically representing herself, she is distant from man and from herself: she becomes and weaves her own garment, or *veil,* which in turn sustains the dialectic of sexual difference. In *The Gay Science* passage entitled "Women and their action at a distance" (*in die Ferne*), Nietzsche is entranced by this veil as it is transformed into the butterflylike white sails of the boat gliding past the writer: "When a man stands in the midst of his own noise, in the midst of his own surf of plans and projects, then he is apt also to see quiet, magical beings gliding past him and to long for their happiness and seclusion: *women.* . . . Yet! Yet! . . . even on the most beautiful sailboat there is a lot of noise, and unfortunately much small and petty noise. The magic and the most powerful effect of women is, in philosophical language, action at a distance, *actio in distans;* but this requires first of all and above all—*distance*" (KSA 3:424–25; GS §60, p. 124). If the Nietzschean artist gets too close to the seemingly still sails he would find his own "noise" to be drowned out, or written over, by the female voice, and so he prefers recovering a philosopher's distance from this woman-vessel; her best effect remains a seductive play of apparent silence, for the dialectic of sexual attraction works by not totally merging the female and male voices, but by an "*actio in distans*" inspiring euphonic composition out of opposition.[30]

The Nietzschean insistence on woman-as-veil has proved problematical for feminist interpretations,[31] the role of the veil being castigated as a separation for woman from her own identity, as well as from that of man as the locus of power; the dilemma here is that the same self-distancing from identity and truth plays a major role in Nietzsche's new self-empowerment, with a creative tension between the masculine and the feminine within oneself. In her *Marine Lover of Friedrich Nietzsche*, Irigaray complains that he does not allow woman "her self" (p. 32). She advocates a return to female beginnings which are not reduced to veils or illusions by Nietzsche's gaze: "I want to disentangle myself from your appearances, unravel again and again the mirages conjured up by your seductiveness, and find where I begin once more" (p. 31)—and yet Irigaray still maintains *other* veillike enigmas of woman (as origins, as marine, and as maternal). Mary Ann Doane, reading through her own veil of Derrida and Irigaray, abhors the naivety with which Nietzsche's woman creates her veil, asserting that this "deprives woman of subjectivity."[32] In particular, Doane indicts Nietzsche's sailboat passage, cited above, as a "*mise-en-scène* of the philosophical hypostatization of Woman" (p. 124)—an understandable reaction, since she does not consider the use of the veil/sail as a barrier between two active/passive forces, only between master and slave. Doane's basic contention with the veil in Nietzsche is the same as her reading of classic cinema: she is uncomfortable with (man's) troping of woman per se (p. 141). Nietzsche, however, is keen to stress the veil's creative function within his male/female dialectic; and orgasmic power is certainly never denied to either sex (KSA 13:240; WP §799, p. 420).

The veil of woman that Nietzsche refers to is the continuation of the Schopenhauerian veil of *maya*, the illusory barrier that serves as an individuating, life-saving force, renewing itself each time it is torn apart by Dionysian orgiastic insight and despair—this process being in fact less of a rape than is the Socratic epistemological desire to remove the veil altogether to get to a knowable truth.[33] For without the veil of separation there would be no desire, nothing would be hidden, absolute nudity would nullify action, and art as life-affirming illusion would cease. Nietzsche urges his readers to reap the benefits that seduction via the veil may bring, to pay heed to life's false separations and sexual oppositions and reinvent new ones, "to stop courageously at the surface, at the fold, the skin, to adore appearance" in the manner of the ancient Greeks (KSA 3:352; GS—P §4, p. 38). Plato's image of the cave is reversed at the sight of—and by—Nietzsche's woman: for the Apollonian spots of light, or woman's false veils of self-representation and self-fulfillment, are a fortunate "mask" to "cure eyes damaged by gruesome night" (KSA 1:65; BT §9, p. 67). "Yes, life is a woman," confirms Nietzsche: we need her as a *vita femina* covered with a "veil interwoven with gold, a veil of beautiful possibilities, sparkling with promise, resistance, bashfulness, mockery, pity, and seduction" (KSA 3:569; GS §339, p. 272); and it is a good thing that "her great art is the lie" in order to disguise the (castrated) *lack* of truth underneath (KSA 5:171; BGaE §232, p. 164).[34] In other words, when the truth-goddess Baubo reveals her "reasons for not letting us see her reasons" (KSA 3:352; GS—P §4, p. 38), the life-artist can overcome castration via self-representation, just as the spectator of tragedy creates out of the experience of self-loss in the Dionysian god and then of self-individuation in the Apollonian "masked figure" of the Dionysian vision (KSA 1:64; BT §8, p. 66). In this "sweeping opposition of styles" (KSA 1:64; BT §8, p. 66), Nietzsche's viewer of tragedy can be said to experience the two forms of stiffness, defined by Freud, at the sight of Medusa's genitals, where phallic truth is lacking—namely, the stonelike immobility of castration anxiety and its reflective image, an erection.[35]

One is but a step away here from woman as false "truth" in *Beyond Good and Evil,* for the will to truth arises from its opposite, namely the will to deception (KSA 5:16; BGaE §2, p. 33), the lesson for free spirits being to learn how to desire difference without adding on antithetical (genderized, fixed) values. Nietzsche sees affirmation not in the attempt to neutralize woman-truth's otherness by seeking her secrets as do the prejudiced metaphysicians (KSA 5:11; BGaE—P, p. 31), but instead in celebrating her Sphinx-like riddle, in maintaining sexual perspectivism in order to rekindle desire for life. He is not prescribing that the will to truth/desire for woman be somehow flattened out and androgynized; rather, the *highest stimulus* for living creatively illuminates the contradiction of longing for the veil of sexual illusion as such. It is possible, according to Derrida's own definition of phallogocentrism as the "truth value" and "its correlative, Femininity," to accuse Nietzsche of failing to adequately separate the male desire for woman from the metaphysicians' yearning for truth;[36] and yet, even though Nietzsche evidently enjoys the chauvinistic setup, he does insist upon the "dare" of alternating the sexual positions as if in a game: "Which of us is Oedipus here? Which of us Sphinx? It is, it seems, a rendezvous [*Stelldichein*] of questions and question-marks" (KSA 5:15; BGaE §1, p. 33). Irigaray, on the other hand, does not consider any way in which woman can play the game of " 'posing as' "—*and win*—because she views it as solely belonging to the "master" player, namely man and Nietzsche (*Marine Lover,* p. 84). But Nietzsche is not willing his readers to escape desire for woman-truth, for he knows this is impossible; what he is advising is an ironic recognition that we all play the game.

My interpretation of Nietzsche's agonistic writing of woman (as bisexual and asymmetric contradiction, as a self-seducing germination of narcissism, as a veil over "truth") has probably already alerted the reader that I do not consider it to be entirely subsumable within Derridean *différance,* because Derrida does not consider Nietzsche's dialectical emphasis on sexual desire.[37] Derrida's famous *Spurs* (1978) sets out not merely to abolish the Hegelian dialectic, it asserts a *stylistic* position for Nietzsche (and by implication, for Derrida himself, for he tends to speak *as* Nietzsche) beyond "not only dialectics, but also any ontological decidability" (p. 111). Derrida's thesis of nontotality in Nietzsche is demonstrated via a radical antiessentialization of woman. The problematic of the dialectic is immediately dissolved in an infinite multiplicity of styles and of sexualities far beyond the number "two"—beyond which Derrida evidently wishes to go in his critique of Heidegger's neutralizing of sexual difference.[38] Derrida states in *Spurs:* "If the form of opposition and the oppositional structure are themselves metaphysical, then the relation of metaphysics to its other can no longer be one of opposition" (pp. 117–19)—and woman must be made to fit this bill. This text rewrites Nietzsche's woman far more effectively for today's reader (because less offensively) than Nietzsche would do, and one is left wondering if it is at all possible, in Derrida's wake, to raise a feminist-postmodernist voice of complaint. The problem, stated above, of (over)dressing the reader-woman reoccurs vividly in Derrida's version of Nietzsche—all in all an unfortunate consequence of the undecidability of Nietzsche's forgotten little grey umbrella. In his threefold articulation of woman's positions in Nietzsche's text (as "castrated," "castrating," and "affirming," respectively [*Spurs,* p. 101]), Derrida implies that the first two belong to that dreadful dialectical format, while the last, the Dionysian affirmer, escapes this castration anxiety. For Derrida, affirming woman is de-oppositionalized and hence de-problematized. As desirable as this is, it is, unfortunately, not Nietzsche whose perfect woman "tears to pieces." Derrida does not wish to see here that Nietzsche always needs to seduce himself first: the drive for Nietzsche's entire creativity is achieved by dancing on the brink of the abyss of castration, by activating and feeding from this sexual dialectic. Nietzsche is indeed "all these women," as Derrida himself states (p. 101), and many more besides; but one would not think it from a reading of *Spurs,* in which one is hardly reading the "polysexual signatures" that Derrida states are so desirable in sexual difference ("Choreographies," p. 76). For one could say that Nietzsche's provocative insistence on the agon of the sexual dialectic is, in the end, less impervious to feminism than is Derrida's friendly canceling out of all oppositions.

When Nietzsche writes woman, then, what is happening is that he is, so to speak, *womanizing himself:* this double aspect drives his entire creativity. Gayatri Chakravorty Spivak has noted the "feminization of philosophizing" in Nietzsche (and in Derrida), but this recognition about Nietzsche has been in print for the last century.[39] Again, it is Lou Andreas-Salomé who, by writing one of the first books on Nietzsche in 1894, *Friedrich Nietzsche in seinen Werken,* effectively set the stage for current critical discourse on the Nietzschean "feminine."[40] Salomé's writing was totally at odds with the subsequent uniquely masculinist ideology on Nietzsche, spawned as the protofascist Nietzsche myth by Elisabeth Förster-Nietzsche. Instead, Salomé's conception of Nietzsche sees the philosopher as inherently bisexual, as an effeminate and hence more creative male (p. 30). Salomé bases her thesis of bisexuality on Nietzsche's definition, in *Beyond Good and Evil,* of the two basic genius types, the male and the female, imperiously impregnating or being impregnated, forming and giving birth, who are forever seeking each other but misunderstanding each other (KSA 5:191; BGaE §248, p. 180). Indeed, Salomé's text borders on just such a vital *misprision,* for she herself assumes the role of male begetter: as a lover of the Nietzschean woman, and as the archetypal piece of critical interpretation of Nietzsche, she follows the path of the genius-impregnator. *Das Weib,* the vilified genus whom Nietzsche had loved, returns to engage in a procreative exchange with the "fertile ground" of his text (p. 30; KSA 2:602; HH—"The Wanderer and His Shadow" §118, p. 338), and provides an affirmative response to his female attractions and stylistic passions.

It is to Salomé's credit that she divines the nature of the a(nta)gonistic dialectic that Nietzsche constantly reinvents in order to philosophize: "Since neither gradual development nor transition brings opposites closer together, their inherent characteristics keeping them apart, an eternally unbridgeable abyss remains. On the one hand is the force of human drives heightened into the terrifying and chaotic; on the other is a false picture, a superficial reflection of life, and to a certain extent a divine mask without an independent inner substance. . . . That which Nietzsche seems to combat most strenuously, is what he fully incorporates into his theories, with extreme consequences and meanings. . . . Indeed, we can assume with certainty that when Nietzsche denigrates and pursues something with special hatred, he harbors it deep in the heart of his own philosophy or in his own life" (pp. 119–20). As Salomé notes, all that Nietzsche suffers and destroys leads him to a tangential rebirth or "palingenesis" (p. 13)—a feminine re-forming or rewriting of the self, but one where unity is no more solid than a veil. Salomé's text literally sets out to feminize the artist in her own gesture of this palingenesis: she notes Nietzsche's love of posture, "his costuming . . . mantle and mask" (p. 10), and she points out his finely formed, effeminate hands and ears (p. 9). In this way, fear of the internal woman, defined by Kofman as "paranoia" in Freud (*Enigma,* p. 15), is a philosophical gift by Salomé to and in Nietzsche. It is, as Nietzsche himself writes in *Ecce Homo,* part of his "Dionysian endowment" to know women, to be their first psychologist (KSA 6:305; EcH p. 75). And Salomé psychologizes Nietzsche in the way he psychologizes woman; moreover, upon hearing of her plans to write on him in this way, he actually wrote to her to approve of her delineating the "characteristics of my self" through his texts.[41]

Nietzsche's contradictions about woman are thus part of his wider contradictoriness between male and female forces within oneself, an open sore or wound of existence that Zarathustra can reabsorb in the *amor fati,* but only to open it again to subsequent transformation: "Whatever I create and however much I love it—soon I have to oppose it and my love: thus will my will have it" (KSA 4:148; TSZ p. 138). In this sense, too, one can situate Dionysus' oblique tribute to Ariadne's suffering, in "Ariadne's Lament": "Must one not first hate each other if one is to love? / *I am your labyrinth*" (KSA 6:401).[42] Palingenesis can occur only at the dual expense of coauthorship: and the benefits are not for man alone simply because Nietzsche's signature wrote the lines. "One is *fruitful* only at the cost of being rich in contradictions," advises Nietzsche regarding his (feminine *and* masculine) " 'enemy within' " (KSA 6:84; T p. 54); for in sex, in the creation of art, or oneself as artwork, the divisions of male and female become unnervingly reversible in action and in memory. For palingenesis to be ongoing, the sexual struggle of shifting positionality must be recalled to consciousness. As Nietzsche writes in "The Greek State," the "horror and the bestiality of sphinx-nature" coexists dialectically with the "virgin body" of artistic cultural life, and this continually and contradictorily reminds the artist-father of the "shameful" manner in which his beautiful artwork-child was conceived (KSA 1:766–67). At the peak of Dionysian power, there is self-/semen-loss in the *Rausch* of orgasm, just as "in every being-born there is a dying" (KSA 10:213). Henry Staten denotes this as the "Dionysian *sparagmos*" or the chiastic "dialectic of paradoxicality."[43] Nietzsche, the conquering Dionysus-creator, thus confesses to having the *pudeurs* of a blushing bride, or of his faking *Weib,* when she "gives herself."

To conclude: the woman question in Nietzsche has the advantage and the disadvantage that it demonstrates only too brutally the Nietzschean premise of the "*inspirational* spirits (or demons and kobolds)" driving humanity to create, act, interpret, make love and philosophy and war (KSA 5:20; BGaE §6, p. 37). The sexual agon is the front player in a whole host of tyrannies that Nietzsche exposes as basic to human existence: "For every drive is tyrannical: and it is as *such* that it tries to philosophize" (KSA 5:20; BGaE §6, p. 37). This is in fact far from being a bad thing as far as life is concerned, at least in the stimulating style in which Nietzsche advises his readers to live it. "When God understood himself, he created himself and his opposite" (KSA 10:154): the contradictions of palingenesis are more enjoyable than one might think. In this way, then, a feminist reworking of Nietzsche is perhaps best served not by seeking a separate sublime but by the dialectical play at stake in his philosophy of creativity which seems so insistently to write woman. Woman writing Nietzsche is an event that Nietzsche already writes and is written by.

Notes

This essay is a revised chapter from my doctoral dissertation, entitled "In Agon with Nietzsche: Studies in Modernist Creativity" (University of Virginia, 1993). I would like to thank Benjamin Bennett, Adrian Del Caro, Sander Gilman, Lorna Martens, and Walter H. Sokel for their insightful comments on earlier versions of this paper.

1. See Harold Bloom, *The Anxiety of Influence: A Theory of Poetry* (New York: Oxford Univ. Press, 1973).

2. Steven E. Aschheim discusses the dilemma that this caused for the German "New Woman" (*The Nietzsche Legacy in Germany, 1890–1990* [Berkeley and Los Angeles: Univ. of California Press, 1992], pp. 85–91).

3. Michel Foucault defines oriental erotic art (*ars erotica*) as truth arising from

sexual pleasure, rather than the other way around (*scientia sexualis*), the view that has dominated Western culture (*The History of Sexuality, Volume One: An Introduction*, trans. Robert Hurley [New York: Random House, 1978], pp. 57–58).

4. Physically, at least, woman would seem to be required merely as a vehicle for the *Übermensch*'s birth. Critical reactions to this kind of biological division by Nietzsche range from the cautious to the ferocious. For example, one has on the one side the overgenerous and oversimplified belief that there is in Nietzsche "nothing explicitly said about the *Übermensch*" that "necessitates that the *Übermensch* must be male," as stated by Robert John Ackermann in his *Nietzsche: A Frenzied Look* (Amherst: Univ. of Massachusetts Press, 1990), p. 130. On the other hand, one encounters a fierce dismissal of Nietzsche's "Virility School of Creativity," as Christine Battersby writes in *Gender and Genius: Towards a Feminist Aesthetics* (Bloomington: Indiana Univ. Press, 1989), p. 123.

5. Richard Rorty, *Contingency, Irony, and Solidarity* (New York: Cambridge Univ. Press, 1989), p. 65.

6. Alice A. Jardine, *Gynesis: Configurations of Woman and Modernity* (Ithaca: Cornell Univ. Press, 1985), p. 37.

7. It has been the predominant case that a uniquely *gender*-based—i.e., societal—debate of woman in Nietzsche quickly reaches a dismissive tone. For example, Judith Butler rejects Nietzsche's writings on woman because she considers only his remarks on gender and excludes those on sex (*Gender Trouble: Feminism and the Subversion of Identity* [New York: Routledge, 1990], p. 25). Likewise, Margaret Whitford favors Luce Irigaray's rewriting of femininity in Nietzsche as a means of correcting his narrowly *patriarchal* woman (*Luce Irigaray: Philosophy in the Feminine* [New York: Routledge, 1991], p. 114). Sabina Lovibond, furthermore, wary of a "certain collective *fantasy* of masculine agency" in postmodernist theory, argues against the pro-difference Nietzsche for viewing societal feminism as a synonym for "emasculated" sameness ("Feminism and Postmodernism," *New Left Review* 178 [1989]: 18–19).

8. O. F. Scheuer (1923) and Martin Havenstein (1922) both interpreted the young Nietzsche's sexuality as resembling a man and a woman in one body, as Carl Pletsch records in his *Young Nietzsche: Becoming a Genius* (New York: Free Press, 1991), p. 67. See also Joachim Köhler's biographical-cum-textual thesis of Nietzsche as a practicing homosexual (*Zarathustras Geheimnis: Friedrich Nietzsche und seine verschlüsselte Botschaft* [Nördlingen: Greno, 1989]).

9. Although the Nietzschean discourse of self-overcoming is based on a male-female agon and would appear to exclude homosexuality, it would be erroneous to assume that the tactics of sexual destabilization that Nietzsche is offering are not, by implication, also applicable to gay and lesbian studies. In this context, Eve Kosofsky Sedgwick proposes an interesting version of Nietzschean gay difference in her *Epistemology of the Closet* (Berkeley and Los Angeles: Univ. of California Press, 1990), pp. 131–81. Köhler, in *Zarathustras Geheimnis*, portrays a disguised homoeroticism being played out in the traumas of Nietzsche's life.

10. Gilles Deleuze, *Nietzsche and Philosophy*, trans. Hugh Tomlinson (New York: Columbia Univ. Press, 1983).

11. Feminist deconstructions of the Hegelian *light-dark*, *masculine-feminine*, *good-evil* (etc.) dialectic form the Deleuzean theses both of Hélène Cixous's "Sorties"

(in Cixous and Catherine Clément, *The Newly Born Woman*, trans. Betsy Wing [Minneapolis: Univ. of Minnesota Press, 1986], pp. 63–132) and of Michèle Le Doeuff's "Long Hair, Short Ideas" (in *The Philosophical Imaginary*, trans. Colin Gordon [London: Athlone, 1989], pp. 100–128).

12. Bernard Pautrat, *Versions du soleil: Figures et systèmes de Nietzsche* (Paris: Seuil, 1971).

13. In *Spurs: Nietzsche's Styles / Eperons: Les Styles de Nietzsche*, trans. Barbara Harlow (Chicago: Univ. of Chicago Press, 1979), Derrida acknowledges his debt of influence to the author of *Versions du soleil* and others who participated in the 1972 Nietzsche seminar at which Derrida first presented his text (p. 37). These were: Sarah Kofman, Philippe Lacoue-Labarthe, Bernard Pautrat, and Jean-Michel Rey (*Spurs*, p. 146).

14. See Martin Heidegger, *Nietzsche*, trans. David Farrell Krell, 4 vols. (New York: Harper, 1981), 1:200–210.

15. Here I disagree with Rudolf E. Künzli's critique of Pautrat. Künzli faults Pautrat for being a neo-Hegelian synthesizer of the dialectic in Nietzsche: "Nietzsche und die Semiologie: Neue Ansätze in der französischen Nietzsche-Interpretation," *Nietzsche-Studien* 5 (1976): 278–81.

16. Adrian Del Caro, "The Pseudoman in Nietzsche, or The Threat of the Neuter," *New German Critique* 50 (1990): 139. Del Caro, in his critique of Derrida's *Spurs* for having stylistically removed the "social issue of [Nietzsche's] woman from the cultural context" (p. 145), analyzes the male-female will-to-antagonism in Nietzsche, not in the contexts of sexuality and creativity, but in the more specifically gender-oriented sphere of woman as a societal force.

17. Gary Shapiro, *Nietzschean Narratives* (Bloomington: Indiana Univ. Press, 1989), p. 151.

18. Compare Baudelaire's defense of artifice in his essay "In Praise of Cosmetics" (in *My Heart Laid Bare and Other Prose Writings*, ed. Peter Quennell [New York: Vanguard, 1951]) with Schopenhauer's diatribe against woman's dissimulation: "On Women" (in Arthur Schopenhauer, *Studies in Pessimism*, ed. and trans. T. Bailey Saunders [New York: Boni & Liveright, n.d.]).

19. Jean Baudrillard, *Seduction*, trans. Brian Singer (New York: St. Martin's, 1990).

20. In a 1988 interview, Baudrillard states that he has been "above all influenced by my study of Nietzsche. . . . My hypothesis is that masculinity does not exist, it is a gigantic story of simulation. My idea is that power is on the side of the feminine and of simulation. . . . I am interested in seduction apart from ideology. Seduction *plays* with sexual difference. It *plays* with desire. It plays with sexual difference, but it does not believe in it. . . . Seduction is mastery of the symbolic world" (*Image and Ideology in Modern/Postmodern Discourse*, ed. David B. Downing and Susan Bazargan [Albany: SUNY Press, 1991], pp. 287, 290).

21. Sigmund Freud, "On Narcissism: An Introduction," in *The Standard Edition of the Complete Psychological Works of Sigmund Freud*, ed. James Strachey, 24 vols. (London: Hogarth, 1957), 14:69–102.

22. Bram Dijkstra's elegant record of fin-de-siècle representations of woman in art cites instances of both the misogynistic view of autoerotic-lesbian woman as danger-

ously independent from men, as well as the more positive view of feminine narcissism as a sign of self-sufficiency (*Idols of Perversity: Fantasies of Feminine Evil in Fin-de-Siècle Culture* [New York: Oxford Univ. Press, 1986], pp. 119–59). Literary examples of the former would include Zola's Nana or Wedekind's Lulu, while Musil's Agathe or Tonka represent the latter.

23. Sarah Kofman, *The Enigma of Woman: Woman in Freud's Writings*, trans. Catherine Porter (Ithaca: Cornell Univ. Press, 1985), p. 56. Kofman suggests that the Nietzschean "affirming" woman disturbs Freud's otherwise patriarchal thesis on narcissism as a female malady (*Enigma*, p. 53). The affirming woman is a category that Kofman receives from Derrida's *Spurs* and expands in her "Baubô: Theological Perversion and Fetishism," in *Nietzsche's New Seas: Explorations in Philosophy, Aesthetics, and Politics*, ed. Michael Allen Gillespie and Tracy B. Strong (Chicago: Univ. of Chicago Press, 1988), pp. 175–202.

24. Lou Andreas-Salomé, "Die in sich ruhende Frau," in *Zur Psychologie der Frau*, ed. Gisela Brinker-Gabler (Frankfurt: Fischer, 1978), pp. 285–311; also in *Die Erotik: Vier Aufsätze*, ed. Ernst Pfeiffer (Munich: Matthes & Seitz, 1979). See Biddy Martin's discussion of Freud's and the later Salomé's theories of narcissism, in *Woman and Modernity: The (Life)Styles of Lou Andreas-Salomé* (Ithaca: Cornell Univ. Press, 1991), pp. 203–23. The Salomé essay (originally entitled "Der Mensch als Weib" [The human being as woman]) is discussed by Martin (pp. 147–66), but Martin does not relate Salomé's concept of narcissism to Nietzsche (p. 116), except to relate (p. 165) Salomé's image of an eternal and self-contained feminine, desired by man, to Nietzsche's notion of "Women and their action at a distance."

25. Nietzsche's medical records, published in 1930 by Erich Podach, contain an entry about an 1866 syphilitic infection (during Nietzsche's residence at Leipzig University). Köhler points out that Nietzsche's syphilis could equally have come from a *male* prostitute (*Zarathustras Geheimnis*, p. xii). See also Sander Gilman's clarifying summary of the history of medical debates surrounding Nietzsche's illness, in "Nietzsche's Writings and Conversations in His Madness: The Other Unravels Himself," in *Inscribing the Other* (Lincoln: Univ. of Nebraska Press, 1991), p. 342.

26. See Angela Livingstone's biography, *Salomé: Her Life and Works* (Mt. Kisco, N.Y.: Moyer Bell, 1984), p. 49.

27. See Gary Shapiro's *Alcyone: Nietzsche on Gifts, Noise, and Women* (Albany: SUNY Press, 1991), in which he demonstrates a series of feminine-halcyonic mythemes, including Nietzsche's self-representation of his writing via a self-contained "hysterical pregnancy" (p. 136).

28. Luce Irigaray, *Marine Lover of Friedrich Nietzsche*, trans. Gillian C. Gill (New York: Columbia Univ. Press, 1991), p. 26.

29. See C. Kerényi, *Dionysus: Archetypal Image of Indestructible Life*, trans. Ralph Manheim (Princeton: Princeton Univ. Press, 1976). Kerényi's criticism of *The Birth of Tragedy* for ignoring the Dionysian *woman* in the mythic orgies (p. 136) is subsequently contradicted by Kerényi himself, in his complaint against Nietzsche for having introduced (and against Nietzsche's friend Erwin Rohde for historically amplifying) the notion of *female* "orgiasm" and "maenadism," called by Kerényi a "dubious contribution" to studies on the Dionysian (p. 138).

30. Cf. Jean Graybeal, *Language and "the Feminine" in Nietzsche and Heidegger*

(Bloomington: Indiana Univ. Press, 1990). Graybeal misses Nietzsche's irony, regarding his fear of losing his voice in female cacophony, in her assertion that the women of this sailboat metaphor are simply a maternally inspirational "ideal object" (p. 36). Graybeal's reading of the feminine in Nietzsche as the Kristevan *mère qui jouit* tends to essentialize and asexualize woman.

31. Feminist readings that reject the Nietzschean veil, such as Stephen Heath's "Joan Riviere and the Masquerade," in *Formations of Fantasy,* ed. Victor Burgin, James McDonald, and Cora Kaplan (New York: Methuen, 1986), pp. 45–61, generally do so on the grounds of identity formation for woman, an approach which gets dangerously close to Socratism. Readings of the veil that do not reject it tend to come from more Nietzsche-intrinsic critics, such as Sarah Kofman, in "Baubô," or Eric Blondel, in "Nietzsche: Life as Metaphor," in *The New Nietzsche: Contemporary Styles of Interpretation,* ed. David B. Allison (Cambridge: MIT Press, 1985), pp. 150–75.

32. Mary Ann Doane, "Veiling Over Desire: Close-ups of the Woman," in *Feminism and Psychoanalysis,* ed. Richard Felstein and Judith Roof (Ithaca: Cornell Univ. Press, 1989), p. 123.

33. See Peter Canning's "How the Fable Becomes a World," in *Looking after Nietzsche,* ed. Laurence A. Rickels (Albany: SUNY Press, 1990), pp. 189–90.

34. Blondel calls the *vita femina* woman's "pure spectacle of becoming," but he desexualizes the operation by isolating seduction in the camp of the idealist philosophers, and he deprives both her and Nietzsche's "philosopher-physician" of any seductive fun ("Nietzsche: Life as Metaphor," p. 159).

35. Sigmund Freud, "Medusa's Head," in *Sexuality and the Psychology of Love,* ed. Philip Rieff (New York: Macmillan, 1963), p. 212. See also Pautrat's "Nietzsche Medused," in *Looking after Nietzsche,* pp. 168–69. Kofman, on the other hand, emphasizes only the (noncreative) "self-castration" that the Socratic-theological perspective brings upon itself in beholding the *aletheia* of woman-truth ("Baubô," p. 193).

36. Jacques Derrida and Christie V. McDonald, "Choreographies," *Diacritics* 12 (1982): 69.

37. Likewise, Adrian Del Caro faults Derrida for erasing *gender* difference in Nietzsche ("Pseudoman," p. 149).

38. Jacques Derrida, "Geschlecht: Sexual Difference, Ontological Difference," *Research in Phenomenology* 13 (1983): 83.

39. Gayatri Chakravorty Spivak, "Displacement and the Discourse of Woman," in *Displacement: Derrida and After,* ed. Mark Krupnick (Bloomington: Indiana Univ. Press, 1983), p. 180.

40. Lou Andreas-Salomé, *Friedrich Nietzsche in seinen Werken,* ed. Ernst Pfeiffer (Frankfurt: Insel, 1983); *Nietzsche,* trans. Siegfried Mandel (Redding Ridge, Conn.: Black Swan, 1988), p. 30. References are to the translation.

41. See *Friedrich Nietzsche, Paul Rée, Lou von Salomé: Die Dokumente ihrer Begegnung,* ed. Ernst Pfeiffer (Frankfurt: Insel, 1970), p. 231.

42. For a reading of Ariadne as a symbol of the Dionysian nihilistic experience, see Adrian Del Caro's "Symbolizing Philosophy: Ariadne and the Labyrinth," *Nietzsche-Studien* 17 (1988): 125–37. Of interest also is Friedrich Kittler's Mallarmé-inspired essay on the mechanization, circa 1900, of Nietzschean discursive practices via the typewriter: Kittler locates the Ariadne-Dionysus warlike relationship of "Ariadne's

Lament" as a riddle of the same, as wholly part of the modern "discourse network" of self-inscriptive, self-torturing "*mnemotechnics*" (*Discourse Networks 1800 / 1900*, trans. Michael Metteer [Stanford: Stanford Univ. Press, 1990], pp. 196–99). *Mnemotechnik* is Nietzsche's own term for the origins of ascetic memory in pain.

43. Henry Staten, *Nietzsche's Voice* (Ithaca: Cornell Univ. Press, 1990), p. 114.

LYNNE TIRRELL

Sexual Dualism and Women's Self-Creation: On the Advantages and Disadvantages of Reading Nietzsche for Feminists

There is much to hate in what Nietzsche says about women, particularly if one follows Nietzsche's own advice and approaches his writings like cold baths—"quickly into them and quickly out again" (KSA 3:634; GS §381, p. 343). When Nietzsche says that a woman's "first and last profession" is "to give birth to strong children" (KSA 5:177; BGE §239, p. 169), for example, he is bound to alienate those who do not think that any person is reducible to one biological function. As awful as some of what Nietzsche has said about women is (and that example is not the worst), this essay is neither a tirade about his inherent misogynism nor an apology for some of his more virulent remarks.[1] It has been well documented that Nietzsche's writings deliver an unhealthy dose of misogyny, but it has not been generally noticed that they also contain the seeds of a deconstruction of that misogyny.

This paper will expose one set of deconstructing elements of Nietzsche's works with respect to his views on women. I shall argue that the wider philosophical context of Nietzsche's thought provides grounds for taking seriously several passages of *The Gay Science* that reveal a more sympathetic understanding of women, since these passages take seriously Nietzsche's antidualism, his perspectivism, and his early existentialist notion of the self. Once we see the destabilizing force of these passages and understand Nietzsche's remarks about women within this philosophical context, we will see that Nietzsche's works promise more insight than many feminists have previously noted. In particular, his attack on dualisms in *Beyond Good and Evil,* the discussions of the power of discourse that run through *The Gay Science* and beyond, the discussions of the importance of power that run through all his texts, are but a few of the issues of shared concern for Nietzsche and for many feminists. As this paper will suggest, a feminist analysis of these issues promises to inform contemporary feminist concerns about the importance of women's articulating our lives.

While considering Nietzsche's ideas about women in light of his broader philosophical positions, particularly his existentialist notion of the self, I shall compare his view to that of Simone de Beauvoir, whose work I shall argue he might have anticipated had he been more concerned with the internal consistency of his work. I will not be arguing the silly thesis that Nietzsche fails us because he was not Beauvoir, but later in the paper I will highlight a few key similarities and differences between them in order to illuminate the potential that lies within Nietzsche's work for feminists. It is significant that both Nietzsche and Beauvoir were concerned with their own need to tell the stories of their lives, working on the borderland between philosophy and literature, and that both tried to recreate the self that was telling in the process of the articulation.[2]

There are two distinct interpretive issues to contend with in coming to terms with Nietzsche's conception of women. First, there is the issue of how Nietzsche takes the question of the nature of and relation between the sexes to be "settled in him" (KSA 5:170; BGE §231, p. 162), and second, there is the issue of what his writings suggest about what the nature of and relation between the sexes is. In Nietzsche's case, the answers to the first question are overtly misogynistic, hostile, and shallow. Nietzsche's most overtly misogynist remarks miss the point of his more general philosophical attack on dualism and ignore his attempt to articulate an existentialist conception of the self. More importantly, the answers to the second question suggest a much more sympathetic conception of woman, which sees her as created by socialization and by her having been defined in contrast to man. Taken together, we see that the two aspects of Nietzsche's thought on women create a tension in his writing that defies any definitive classification of his view.

Nietzsche himself would probably have us focus on his explicit statements about women; as *Ecce Homo* shows, Nietzsche took great pride in his authorial control, and these remarks are, after all, purposefully included in his texts. Most of these statements show little or no respect for women, and some passages argue that this is a view for which he should be held accountable. Consider, for example, *Beyond Good and Evil* 238, where he writes, "to go wrong on the fundamental problem of 'man and woman,' to deny the most abysmal antagonism between them and the necessity of an eternally hostile tension, to dream perhaps of equal rights, equal education, equal claims and obligations—that is a *typical* sign of shallowness, and a thinker who has proved shallow in this dangerous place—shallow in his instinct—may be considered altogether suspicious, even more—betrayed, exposed: probably he will be too 'short' for all fundamental problems of life, of the life yet to come, too, and incapable of attaining *any* depth" (KSA 5:175; BGE §238, pp. 166–67). As Kaufmann has pointed out, it is a good thing for Nietzsche that he is wrong about this, for in this passage Nietzsche displays the very shallowness he so condemns.[3] If we agree with Nietzsche on this, we will dismiss him unfairly as a poor thinker, and we will miss the insights his texts would lend to our own projects.[4]

Nietzsche's works present a complex character who took himself to hold a very negative view of women but who was not philosophically entitled to hold this view. Add to that his remarks about the importance of dissimulation, and it becomes ever more difficult to discern what Nietzsche really thought. Although Nietzsche is preoccupied with the self that he is creating through writing his books, he also is aware that the books may outstrip even the character created there.[5] So, let us take seriously Nietzsche's claim that "one does best to separate an artist from his work, not taking him as seriously as his work" (KSA 5:343; GM—III §4, p. 100), but this still leaves us with the interpretive question about which elements of the work to emphasize. Since the preponderance of work done on Nietzsche's views on women has focused on its misogynist elements, I will develop the other, nonmisogynist, side of Nietzsche's view. I hope to give Nietzsche's texts the most sympathetic reading possible, by showing how what he usually says about women fails to fit some of his deeper philosophical views and by highlighting what he says, but rarely, which *does* fit with these deeper philosophical views. If this sympathetic reading is plausible, then perhaps other of Nietzsche's views will become more accessible to feminist readers.

Nietzsche's condemnations of women tend to fall into two categories. He condemns them sometimes for their *nature* and sometimes for allowing themselves to be slaves to men. The first sort of criticism suggests an essentialist conception of woman's nature. Some passages clearly support this essentialist reading; consider Nietzsche's claim that "woman is *essentially* unpeaceful, like a cat, however well she may have trained herself to seem peaceful" (KSA 5:96; BGE §131, p. 87). Invoking the distinction between nature and nurture, Nietzsche suggests that women, deep down, have an unchangeable nature.[6] Passages such as this notwithstanding, it would be hypocritical for Nietzsche to rely upon an essentialist conception of women's nature, since his philosophy is so thoroughly antiessentialist. Here we must look at Nietzsche's doctrine in *Beyond Good and Evil* and in *The Gay Science* that what a thing is called is immeasurably more important than what it is, a discussion that anticipates the Sapir-Whorf hypothesis and later feminist discussions of the power of naming.[7] Nietzsche's conception of the nature of a thing is existentialist, and understanding this conception will help us to see that these condemnatory remarks of the first kind actually collapse into the second category: Nietzsche reviles women for being slaves to men. Women have not taken enough control of their self-creation. To understand this position, we must look briefly at Nietzsche's discussion of master/slave relations and the creation of the self. In the end we will see that although Nietzsche engages in blaming the victim and does not come anywhere near to developing a positive feminist conception of women's situation, we can nevertheless see that his work anticipated important aspects of Beauvoir's discussion of man as Self and woman as Other and the problems inherent in women's accepting this status.

The first section of this paper offers a sketch of Nietzsche's attack on dualism, using his discussion of the distinction between conscious and unconscious thought as an example. In the second section, I apply Nietzsche's attack on dualism to the dualist opposition between the sexes. These two sections show one aspect of Nietzsche's thought that is worth appropriation (with expansion) by feminists. In the third section I set out Nietzsche's nonmisogynist conception of woman. This conception, bearing the marks of early existentialism, is in many ways a precursor to today's social-constructivist conceptions of the self.[8] It is marked by a sensitivity to the sexual situation of the upper-class women of Nietzsche's day, and it suggests that Nietzsche was aware of and did not condone the injustice of a society that creates such women and such situations. Amazingly, Nietzsche was able to draw the connection between destructive forms of heterosexuality and the silencing of women.

Nietzsche's Attack on Dualism

Nietzsche's first philosophical work was dualist and realist in its conception: *The Birth of Tragedy* is dualist in that Nietzsche maintains a distinction between appearance and reality; it is realist in that he maintains that the (real) world has a character independent of any description of it.[9] Nietzsche goes even further than this, however, for he does not merely echo the traditional claim that appearance is different from underlying reality—Nietzsche claims that appearance is the very contrary of reality. The character of the appearance was developed in direct opposition to the reality underlying it. The cheerfulness of the Greeks was, for example, a reaction to their underlying terror brought on by their deeper understanding of the "primordial contradiction and primordial pain in the heart of the primal unity" (KSA 1:51; BT §6, p. 55). Their extreme rationality was a reaction to nature's extreme irrationality. This early dualist metaphysic in *The Birth of Tragedy* is followed in Nietzsche's later writings by an increasingly powerful attack on dualism per se.

In an early section of a late work, Nietzsche writes that there are two sorts of doubts one should have about varieties of dualism: (1) "whether there are any opposites at all," and (2) whether the values placed on purported opposites are accurate or "merely foreground estimates, only provisional perspectives" (KSA 5:16; BGE §2, p. 10). He suggests that what constitutes the value of what is deemed good is that these things are related to their opposites, and "maybe even one with them in essence" (KSA 5:17; BGE §2, p. 10). Nietzsche is willing to explore this sort of possibility, this "dangerous 'maybe'" when it applies to the more standard philosophical oppositions such as good/evil, mind/body, truth/falsity, conscious/unconscious thought, but when it comes to man/woman, Nietzsche has more difficulty towing his own philosophical line. In this section, we will see what that line is, so that we may see what consistency would require.

Nietzsche's challenge to our belief in the opposition between conscious and unconscious thought begins with the claim that most of conscious thought should still be considered instinctive, even "higher" forms such as philosophical thought (KSA 5:17; BGE §3, p. 11). In section 6 of *Beyond Good and Evil,* he claims that all philosophy to date has been an "unconscious memoir" of its author (KSA 5:19; BGE §6, p. 13), and in section 17 he points out that even our conscious thought, for which we presume to take responsibility, is beyond our control. (He says "a thought comes when 'it' wishes, and not when 'I' wish" [KSA 5:31; BGE §17, p. 24].) This does not mean that all conscious thought can be reduced to instinct. Such a view would make Nietzsche a reductive monist, and Nietzsche is trying to be more radical than this. The reductive monist accepts the legitimacy of the opposition and then reduces one of the two poles to the other. Nietzsche, on the other hand, attacks the very legitimacy of the opposition.[10]

The sort of dualist dogmatism that Nietzsche describes in part 1 of

Beyond Good and Evil seeks to discredit monism by saying that monism would discredit or taint things of the highest value, on the grounds that it would be a discredit for these highly valued things to arise from the same origins as things of lesser value.[11] If we are to continue holding conscious thought, for which we take responsibility, in high esteem, then we must think of it as having an origin different from that of unconscious thought (which even animals have). Unconscious thought, or instinct, has been traditionally associated with the body, while conscious thought has been associated with the soul. (Notice how one duality involves another.) Nietzsche's nonreductive monism leads him to claim that the soul or mind is not a different kind of substance than the body; it is a *refinement* of the same stuff (no commitment to substances intended). Body is not Descartes's "extended substance" any more than mind is "unextended substance." Nietzsche also rejects the association of the unconscious with the body and the conscious with the soul, saying that "consciousness is the last and latest development of the organic" (KSA 3:382; GS §11, p. 84). In taking consciousness to be "the *kernel* of man," we stunt its growth (KSA 3:382; GS §11, p. 85). Conscious thought, Nietzsche writes, still awaits incorporation into the instinctual level.

This very brief sketch of Nietzsche's discussion of the distinction between conscious and unconscious thought reflects a typical Nietzschean strategy. Nietzsche not only suggests that we need not posit two substances to explain the duality of conscious/unconscious thought, but he also inverts the values of these. Traditionally, conscious thought is valued more highly than unconscious (hence its association with the soul), but Nietzsche associates it with error and treats it like the new kid on the block. Eventually, it will be incorporated. Nietzsche's strategy for disarming the dualist is to claim that the distinction in question is not a distinction in *kind*, but only in degree. One value is not the opposite of the other, but its *refinement*. Further, in taking one value to be primary we reveal our perspective, not something about the world as such, and we exercise our will to power, imposing ourselves on the world. We succumb to this "*faith in opposite values*" (KSA 5:16; BGE §2, p. 10) because it simplifies life (KSA 5:41–42; BGE §24, p. 35), and perhaps even more because it provides such a powerful and tidy vehicle for our exercise of the will to power. In exercising our will to power we create the world in our own image.

Dualism and the Sexes

A parallel treatment of the dualist opposition between man and woman would begin with a recognition of a purported duality between them. That duality would then be attacked. Nietzsche's sexual dualism is apparent even late in *Beyond Good and Evil,* where he says that man and woman are *necessarily* in "an eternally hostile tension" (KSA 5:175; BGE §238, p. 166).[12] It is ironic that this claim appears in a work which attempts a general undermining of dualism and which sets out clearly what is at stake for the philosopher who accepts dualistic metaphysics. Two years later Nietzsche still held fast to the idea of a battle of the sexes, for in *Ecce Homo* he writes: "Has my definition of love been heard? It is the only one worthy of a philosopher. Love—in its means, war; at bottom, the deadly hatred of the sexes" (KSA 6:306; EH p. 267).

Nietzsche recognizes the duality but not its purportedness. What is missing from his works is any direct attack on this variety of dualism. Such an attack would rely on the two questions Nietzsche raises generally about dualism: (1) whether there really is a pair in exclusive opposition, and (2) whether the values assigned to those "opposites" are accurate. Raising these questions with respect to the man/woman duality, it is important today to distinguish between sex, which is a biological category, and gender, which is a psychosocial category. Nietzsche did not articulate this more contemporary distinction between sex and gender, but he did recognize the difference between being female and being a woman, taking the latter to be a socially constructed way of being.

Whether we take "man" and "woman" to designate biologically based sexes or socially based genders, the answer to whether the pair forms an exclusive ontological opposition is no. Today we know that strict biological sexual dualism is false. Most humans are born either male or female, but some researchers estimate that perhaps 5 percent of the population are born with ambiguous genitalia, neither male nor female hormonal structures, etc.[13] A more conservative estimate is one in every 200 to 300 live births.[14] These anatomical "abnormalities" rarely pose any medical risk for the child; nevertheless, usually within seventy-two hours of birth, a sex of rearing is determined for babies born with ambiguous genitalia.[15] Doctors and parents rapidly and surgically impose a sex of rearing because we live in a society in which sexual dualism is the *norm,* and they recognize that living outside that norm would have serious and painful social consequences for the child. Biological sexual dualism is a statistical regularity that we work to make a universal fact. The claim that there are only two genders turns out to be normative as well. Much psychological research suggests that when "masculine" and "feminine" are distinctly defined, few of us fit either category.[16] If we use these categories to anchor the poles of a continuum, it turns out that most people are in the middle, displaying a mixture of masculine and feminine traits. So neither biologically based sexes nor socially based genders form an exclusive ontological opposition.[17]

It is clear that Nietzsche did not take sexual dualism to be an unalterable fact about the world. I say this in anticipation of the following discussion of his more positive view of women, and because in his lambasting the feminist efforts of his contemporaries, Nietzsche argues that they are trying to make men out of women.[18] On an essentialist picture of the sexes, this is not a worry because it cannot be done. Nietzsche's fear that it will be done is of a piece with his antiessentialism. Women are created as such by interpretations, and the new interpretations offered by his feminist contemporaries were threatening to undermine a way of life to which Nietzsche saw no satisfying alternative (see KSA 3:610–12; GS §363, pp. 318–20). Nietzsche does not explicitly make the distinction between sex and gender, and most of his claims about women are about females whose gender-identity fits their sex. Put anachronistically, Nietzsche holds "woman" to be a socially constructed category. He sees sexual dualism as normative and usually tries to uphold the value of that norm.

In section 239 of *Beyond Good and Evil,* for example, Nietzsche argues that the women's rights movement in Europe will result in a net *decrease* in women's power. By giving up traditional feminine roles, women give up their (currently) greatest source of power. The mistake of the modern woman, he holds, is to "lose the sense for the ground on which one is most certain of victory; to neglect practice with one's proper weapons" (KSA 5:176; BGE §239, p. 168). He calls this "a crumbling of feminine instincts" and a "defeminization" (KSA 5:177; BGE §239, p. 169). This sounds very essentialist, but keeping in mind Nietzsche's thesis that instincts are that part of our thought and judgment which is no longer scrutinized, I would argue that here he is talking about women as a biological category with a socially established gender identity (in part dependent upon that biology) that gives them power. Compare this to Simone de Beauvoir's position in the introduction to *The Second Sex,* where she says that one reason that women really have not fought for our rights as full autonomous human beings is that the only power we have had is this sort of derivative power we get through accepting femininity.[19] If we give that up, we risk losing everything. What is missing in Nietzsche, but not later in Beauvoir, is a recognition of the significance of the other forms of power—real power—that women could attain if dualistic sex roles were eradicated.[20] So although Nietzsche is aware of the distinction between the biological category "human female" and the social category "woman," he does not think through all the complexities of the power issues associated with the sexual dualism that defines the category "woman."

Nietzsche's first challenge to dualism, then, denies that there is any real or substantial difference between the two categories posited as opposites. Men and women are created as such by social interpretations, which embody and reinforce our norms. Nietzsche's second challenge to dualism concerns the accuracy of the assigned valuation of the pair. Applied to this case, the issue is whether accurate values have been assigned to men and women (or to masculinity and femininity). Before we can say whether the values are accurate, we must determine what they are. Nietzsche's own views on the relative valuation of men and women are contradictory. It is important to note at the outset that Nietzsche is no great respecter of any person qua member of a group.

Nietzsche suggests that women are the more esteemed (estimable?) sex when he writes: "Woman is indescribably more evil than man; also cleverer; good nature is in a woman a form of degeneration. . . . Woman, the more she is a woman, resists rights in general hand and foot: after all, the state of nature, the eternal war between the sexes, gives her by far the first rank" (KSA 6:306; EH pp. 266–67). This picture of woman, as one who is of the first rank because she refuses the rights and privileges of full citizenship and social status, is obviously a troubled one. In contemporary feminist terms, it is a reversal. He may *say* that she is of the first rank, but he says it because she makes sure that it is not so.[21] Nietzsche's principal estimation of woman's value emerges in his claim that "comparing man and woman on the whole, one may say: woman would not have the genius for finery if she did not have an instinct for a *secondary* role" (KSA 5:98; BGE §145, p. 89). Nietzsche holds that human instincts are that part of our thought which we have ceased to scrutinize; they are the lessons we have learned too well. Instinct is not part of our immutable nature but rather something created; so Nietzsche's appeal to woman's (supposed) instinct for being secondary marks that secondary status as socially inculcated.

If there were an argument against sexual dualism that followed the basic antidualist account we have seen, it would go something like this: (1) men have traditionally been more highly esteemed than women; (2) men and women are not really different in kind but in fact share the same essence and origins; (3) men and women are not really opposites but one is the refinement of the other; (4) we (men and women) give in to the oversimplification wrought by dualistic sex roles and differential valuation of the sexes because (a) it simplifies life and (b) it provides a vehicle for the exercise of the will to power.

This argument against sexual dualism is not explicit in Nietzsche's writings, but it is clearly an argument Nietzsche should have made. It is an argument that can be supported using Nietzsche's more general argument against dualism, his analysis of the master/slave relation, plus those of his insights about women which I will present in the next section. My point here is not a simple appropriation of Nietzsche's form of argument, nor is it simply exposure of his more positive view of women; I also want to show that there are grounds for feminists to take Nietzsche's wider philosophical thought seriously. Rather than address each premise of this argument individually, I will now turn to Nietzsche's more sympathetic discussion of women. This discussion illustrates Nietzsche's support for the crucial third and fourth premises of the argument against sexual dualism. In addition, this more sensitive conception of women foreshadows many of Beauvoir's and later feminists' insights precisely because it depends upon a basic existentialist account of the self.

An Early Existentialist View of Women

Book 2 of *The Gay Science* presents an important bridge between Nietzsche's early acceptance of dualism in *The Birth of Tragedy* and his later rejection of dualism in *Beyond Good and Evil*. Here, in the second book, Nietzsche grapples with the question of realism, beginning with a somewhat scattered but surprisingly insightful discussion of women and ending with a discussion of the ontological power of language. I said earlier that although Nietzsche is aware that "woman" is a category created through social interpretation, he does not think through all the complexities of the power issues associated with the sexual dualism that defines that category. (He does, however, seem to react to them.)[22] Let's turn now to Nietzsche's two most sensitive discussions of women's situation, both found in book 2 of *The Gay Science*.

In section 68 of *The Gay Science* Nietzsche offers a parable that is similar in style to his later *Thus Spoke Zarathustra*. In this passage Nietzsche displays a recognition that sex roles are to the advantage of men and the disadvantage of women, a recognition of the invisibility of the coerciveness of sexual dualism, and offers a lament that others seem unable to recognize this situation. I quote it in its entirety:

> *Will and willingness.* —Someone took a youth to a sage and said: "Look, he is being corrupted by women." The sage shook his head and smiled. "It is men," said he, "that corrupt women; and all the failings of women should be atoned by and improved in men. For it is man

> who creates for himself the image of woman, and woman forms herself according to this image."
>
> "You are too kindhearted about women," said one of those present; "you do not know them." The sage replied: "Will is the manner of men; willingness that of women. That is the law of the sexes—truly, a hard law for women. All of humanity is innocent of its existence; but women are doubly innocent. Who could have oil and kindness enough for them?"
>
> "Damn oil! Damn kindness!" someone else shouted out of the crowd; "women need to be educated better!"—"Men need to be educated better," said the sage and beckoned to the youth to follow him. —The youth, however, did not follow him. (KSA 3:427; GS §68, p. 126)

Nietzsche says that man "creates for himself the image of woman, and woman forms herself according to this image." In this one can see the roots of Beauvoir's claim that woman "is defined and differentiated with reference to man and not he with reference to her; she is the incidental, the inessential as opposed to the essential. He is the Subject, he is the Absolute—she is the Other" (*The Second Sex*, p. xix). Both Nietzsche and Beauvoir are claiming that the duality of man/woman is asymmetrical, that man is primary, woman secondary, and that this asymmetry disadvantages women. For Nietzsche, woman's goal is not to be absolute but to be in command of her own perspective; she fails at this in part because "her great art is the lie, her highest concern is mere appearance and beauty" (KSA 5:171; BGE §232, p. 163). Woman's role as Other (to use Beauvoir's term) makes her an actress who depends upon pretense and illusion to survive. Her mistake is to get caught up in her own illusions: she fails to see herself except through the eyes of others. Nietzsche asks: "Seducing one's neighbor to a good opinion and afterwards believing piously in this opinion—who could equal women in this art?" (KSA 5:99; BGE §148, pp. 89–90).[23] Acting is not inherently bad; Nietzsche may even think that it is a necessary part of everyone's life (KSA 3:595–97; GS §356, pp. 302–4). The problem here is that in acting a part that someone else has written, a part which eventually becomes their reality, women do not develop their own perspective.

At bottom, the distinction between Self and Other and the relation between men and women are, in Nietzsche's framework, a matter of differing perspectives and differing values. The relation between Self and Other is typified by Nietzsche's characters of the master and the slave, offered as empirical generalizations, and presented in both *Beyond Good and Evil* and *The Genealogy of Morals* (KSA 5:208–12; BGE §260, pp. 204–8). In *Beyond Good and Evil,* Nietzsche uses the distinction between master morality and slave morality as yet another example of the "opposite values" he condemns. The distinction plays a different role in *The Genealogy of Morals,* where Nietzsche sets out to discuss both the origin and the value of the values we hold. Although most interpreters focus on Nietzsche's discussion of the origins of morality, Nietzsche stressed the question of value, saying "*the value of these values themselves must first be called in question*" (KSA 5:253; GM—P §6, p. 20).[24]

The basic difference between master morality and slave morality is perspective. This difference in perspective is illustrated by how each acquires values. Both take the master as the primary value: master morality looks at the aristocracy and says "Oh we good noble happy ones!" Slave morality looks with resentment and fear at the same aristocracy and calls it evil. Both are focused on the master. Because the master looks to himself for his own values, Nietzsche claims that the master is a creator of values (KSA 5:208–12; BGE §260, pp. 204–8). The slave, on the other hand, seeks values from outside himself or herself. Slave morality is the morality of the powerless. For master morality, "good" is primary and defined by the master's own way of being, while "bad" is secondary and applies to "those other than [lesser than] us." For slave morality, "evil" is primary and defined by the master's own way of being, while "good" is secondary and derivative, and means "other than *them*."

Nietzsche asks what the value of these values is to those who hold them. Let us begin with the masters and say a little more about what their values are. Seeing themselves as powerful, with power over others as well as over themselves, their actions are spontaneous, not reactive. Seeing themselves as the meaning and justification of their society, the masters accept the sacrifice of members of lower social strata for their own sake (the masters') (KSA 5:206–7; BGE §258, p. 202). Nietzsche describes this phenomenon as the "*pathos of distance*": the aristocracy takes itself to be the seat of all value and defines all else as lower (KSA 5:205–6; BGE §257, pp. 201–2; see also KSA 5:258–60; GM—I §2, pp. 25–26). This *pathos* is necessary, he adds, for "the continual 'self-overcoming of man'" (KSA 5:205; BGE §257, p. 201) both on the social and on the individual level, and so Nietzsche claims that "every enhancement of the type 'man' has so far been the work of an aristocratic society—and it will be so again and again" (KSA 5:205; BGE §257, p. 201). The utility of this perspective should be obvious. The master feels free to sacrifice those who are ranked lower than he is—because they are not like him, and so different (or no) rules apply to their interaction (see, for example, KSA 5:219–20; BGE §265, p. 215).

Now there are those who will say, "Men aren't like that; they don't sacrifice women. If anything, men are sacrificed for women." This is a reversal and turns on what counts as sacrificing. Taking the positive self-regarding values of the slave as primary would make such a claim true—if that were a legitimate privileging. Slave morality is essentially relative; because it reacts to master morality, it cannot be considered in itself. (Most of the slave's values are not positive self-regarding values but are simply self-preserving, with a minimalist construal of what the self is and what counts as its preservation.) Nietzsche explicitly calls slave morality "a morality of utility" (KSA 5:211; BGE §260, p. 207); it is the morality of the oppressed. He says that it promotes values that ease the lot of the sufferer, and the list looks like a short list of womanly virtues: pity, humility, kindness, altruism, and the like. In women, these traits provide a kind of psychological protection from the harmful effects of being those who serve.[25]

In the middle of book 5 of *The Gay Science,* Nietzsche explicitly invokes the language of master and slave to talk about heterosexual love. He claims that for woman, love means "total devotion" *to* the loved one; for man, love means total devotion *from* the other. Men who want to be totally devoted to their lovers, Nietzsche says, "simply are—not men" (KSA 3:611; GS §363, p. 319). He captures the constraining normativity of the definition of woman as slave when he says: "A man who loves like a woman becomes a slave; while a woman who loves like a woman becomes *a more perfect woman*" (KSA 3:611; GS §363, p. 319). It sounds as if calling her a slave would be redundant.

It is important that Nietzsche does not trivialize the sacrifices that women make for men. Just three sections after "Will and willingness," Nietzsche addresses the heart of women's objectification and oppression. In "On female chastity," Nietzsche introduces the theme of articulation as he explains the perils of white European upper-class woman's accepting the sexual education dictated by the men of her class. With surprising empathy for women's sexual situation, he writes:

> There is something quite amazing and monstrous about the education of upper-class women. What could be more paradoxical? All the world is agreed that they are to be brought up as ignorant as possible of erotic matters, and that one has to imbue their souls with a profound sense of shame in such matters. . . . here they are supposed to remain ignorant even in their hearts; they are supposed to have neither eyes nor ears nor words nor thoughts for this—their "evil." . . . And then to be hurled, as by a gruesome lightning bolt, into reality and knowledge, by marriage—precisely by the man they love and esteem most! To catch love and shame in a contradiction and to be forced to experience at the

> same time delight, surrender, duty, pity, terror, and who knows what else, in the face of the unexpected neighborliness of god and beast!
>
> Thus a psychic knot has been tied that may have no equal. . . .
>
> Afterward, the same deep silence as before. Often a silence directed at herself, too. She closes her eyes to herself. . . .
>
> In sum, one cannot be too kind about women. (KSA 3:428–29; GS §71, pp. 127–28.)

This passage shows Nietzsche's understanding of the cruelty of a sexual morality that demands of women that they deny their own eroticism, that places a woman's sexuality at odds with her morality, that makes men sexual agents and women sexual objects. By denying her the psychological apparatus to be a sexual agent, man cripples woman's erotic life. Nietzsche recognizes that one's erotic life is central to one's very being; he writes that the "degree and kind of a person's sexuality reach up into the ultimate pinnacle of his spirit" (KSA 5:87; BGE §75, p. 81).[26] In accepting thorough sexual ignorance, a woman loses the potential for a healthy erotic life. The debilitating effects of this sexual system range over much more than the woman's erotic life, however, for as a result the woman "closes her eyes to herself." She loses the power of self-articulation.

The absolute positing of a perspective by the Self is not limited to morality. It infuses all representation, and so all human life. "On female chastity" shows one method by which man creates for himself an image of woman to which women then conform. The desirable woman, the woman he will marry and support, is a virgin in all respects. By defining her virtue (her value) this way, man establishes a norm that a woman rejects at her economic, social, and psychological peril. As is typical of the norms that define femininity, this norm carries with it a double bind: she is damned if she complies, damned if she doesn't. The perils of noncompliance are obvious. The surprise is that Nietzsche saw the perils of compliance.

More generally, man creates woman in the same way he creates his world. Nietzsche says that this is done through the power of naming. He says:

> What things *are called* is incomparably more important than what they are. The reputation, name, and appearance, the usual measure and weight of a thing, what it counts for—originally almost always wrong and arbitrary, thrown over things like a dress and altogether foreign to their nature and even to their skin—all this grows from generation unto generation, merely because people believe in it, until it gradually grows to be part of the thing and turns into its very body. What at first was appearance becomes in the end, almost invariably, the essence and is effective as such. . . . it is enough to create new names and estima-

> tions and probabilities in order to create in the long run new "things." (KSA 3:422; GS §58, pp. 121–22)

Contemporary feminists are working hard to understand the power of language to shape our ways of being in the world, fully aware that the canons of discourse and culture have always been in the control of men.[27] A contemporary feminist using Nietzsche's terms would claim that through the exercise of the power of naming, men exercise their will to power. This power extends not only over women, but also over the "very nature" of the world itself. Beauvoir recognizes this when she says, "Representation of the world, like the world itself, is the work of men; they describe it from their own point of view, which they confuse with absolute truth" (*The Second Sex,* p. 161). Notice that Beauvoir says "absolute truth"; she does not deny that the power of naming yields true stories about the world. She denies that these true stories are unrevisable stories of unchanging reality. The stories are true because they create or help to create the reality they describe.

Nietzsche describes the effect of the power of naming exercised by men on women in a passage of *The Gay Science* that anticipates his discussion of the *pathos of distance* in *Beyond Good and Evil.* He writes:

> When a man stands in the midst of his own noise, in the midst of his own surf of plans and projects, then he is apt also to see quiet, magical beings gliding past him and to long for their happiness and seclusion: *women.* He almost thinks that his better self dwells there among the women, and that in these quiet regions even the loudest surf turns into deathly quiet, and life itself into a dream about life. Yet! Yet! Noble enthusiast, even on the most beautiful sailboat there is a lot of noise, and unfortunately much small and petty noise. The magic and the most powerful effect of women is, in philosophical language, action at a distance, *actio in distans;* but this requires first of all and above all—*distance.* (KSA 3:424–25; GS §60, p. 124)

In taking man's perspective as primary, this passage illustrates the third point in the argument I said Nietzsche should have made against sexual dualism. That point was that men and women are not really opposites but that one is the refinement of the other. Which of these we take to be the refinement shows *our* perspective and not something about the world as such. It is not that women *are* quiet, peaceful, magical beings; it is that men and women have maintained a distance, in part in order to keep the illusion going.

The coerciveness of sexual dualism is achieved because it simplifies life and provides a vehicle for the exercise of the will to power. Consider the particular form of sexual dualism of the stereotypical 1950s white middle class couple, such as depicted by the characters on "The Donna Reed Show" and "Leave It to Beaver." One thing rigid sex roles have going for them is that people can abdicate making decisions as to how to maintain and display their gender-identity. If I accept as a fact that I ought to aspire to be like Donna Stone or June Cleaver (interesting names), this acceptance simplifies my life. I can get on with the business of being a wife-mother-homemaker. In those roles, I will find some avenues for the exercise of my will to power. I may even feel more satisfied than my twin who tries to have a life that does not fit standard sex roles, for she suffers the trials of a trailblazer. Similarly, a man who sets out to be like Dr. Stone or Ward Cleaver will find ready-made avenues for the exercise of his will to power. The important question is whose will to power is exercised by the instantiation of these rigid sex roles in the first place. To answer that we must find out who, by and large, benefits most from the system, by and large. To identify the group by way of but a few of their benefits, that half of the dichotomy held in higher esteem, who control much more than half of the society's resources, who have equal rights under the law, that is whose will to power is exercised by sexual dualism as we know it.

Nietzsche's position in "Will and willingness" is encouraging, for there we see an unexpected sensitivity to the situation of women under sexual dualism. His insights there are important. What is discouraging, however, is the undercurrent of pessimism that imbues the parable. Will and willingness, he says, "is the law of the sexes," and "all of humanity is innocent of its existence." The invocation of law there does not signal essentialism, for Nietzsche is not arguing that the relation between the sexes is immutable. This law is a constitutive law; it defines the created natures of the sexes. What we must wonder about is in what sense humanity is innocent of this. Are we innocent in the sense that we are not responsible? That would make sense of Nietzsche's saying that "women are doubly innocent," but such a general exoneration would undermine the sage's saying that men corrupt women, that men need better education, and that men need to atone. The language of sin is strong here and cannot be overlooked.

The second pessimistic aspect of this parable is that the youth and the others disbelieve the sage. This is not a truth that the masses can accept. This was true in Nietzsche's day, and it is still true, for the most part, today.

Those who do accept the sort of position sketched in these passages face a difficult interpretive issue: Does this position offer any positive guidelines for women? Nietzsche did not see how the situation could be changed. Since heterosexual love seemed to him to be the root of woman's oppression, that is where the change would have to come. But that is where he saw no acceptable way out. He considers the possibility that men should come to love like women, but says that there cannot be an "equal will to renunciation," for "we should then get—I do not know what; perhaps an empty space?" (KSA 3:611; GS §363, p. 319). Here we can see Nietzsche failing to think through the options using his own philosophical positions, for he goes on to say: "Woman gives herself away, man acquires more—I do not see how one can get around this natural opposition by means of social contracts or with the best will in the world to be just, desirable as it may be not to remind oneself constantly how harsh, terrible, enigmatic, and immoral this antagonism is" (KSA 3:611–12; GS §363, p. 319).

In "Will and willingness" the sage locates the problem squarely with men, saying that men need to be better educated. Does this show that Nietzsche takes women to be completely passive? Not necessarily. He surely sees women as severely constrained by a situation in which they are defined by men. He also sees that the situation makes it very hard for women to gain more power. Beauvoir extends this analysis when she claims that women see acceptance of male definition as the best or easiest or surest route to power. Women have little power under patriarchy, and rejecting male-defined ways for women to be makes us lose what little power we already have. This need to cling to power keeps us complicit in our secondary status. The analysis itself suggests avenues for liberation.

Although Nietzsche fails to apply his general philosophical frameworks here, we need not. A feminist application of his discussion of master/slave morality can be of help. Often Nietzsche writes as if slaves cannot help but be slaves, masters cannot help but be masters, and that's that. On the other hand, Nietzsche's discussion of a slave revolt, which begins when resentment "becomes creative and gives birth to values," suggests no such inevitability (KSA 5:270; GM—I §10, p. 36).[28] According to Nietzsche, it is because the common man even seeks his own value from outside that the common man has always *been* just what he is considered to be (KSA 5:212–14; BGE §261, pp. 208–9).[29] Tracy Strong argues that "the *direction* of willing seems to be the key difference" between masters and slaves, for it "is outward and expended in the masters, inward and 'imposing a form upon oneself' in the slaves" (*Politics of Transfiguration,* p. 240). The master exerts his will upon the world, the slave exerts her will upon herself. Pathetically, when enslavement is most successful, the slave makes herself over into what the master takes her to be. At bottom, what matters is taking responsibility for one's own values and taking actions to reshape the world accordingly. Nietzsche condemns the slave's ressentiment, for the slave revolt brings the triumph of "natures that are denied the true reaction, that of deeds, and compensate themselves with imaginary revenge. While every noble morality develops from a triumphant affirmation of itself, slave morality from the outset says No to what is 'outside,' what is 'different,' what is 'not itself'; and this No is its creative deed" (KSA 5:270; GM—I §10, p. 36).

To be a slave, in general, is to be totally accessible to the will of another person, one's master. In discussing the "aura of negativity about [feminist] separatism," Marilyn Frye argues that such negativity is built into the very logic of the situation. She writes, "When we start from a position of total accessibility there *must* be an aspect of no-saying (which is the beginning of control) in *every effective* act and strategy, the effective ones being precisely those which *shift power,* i.e., ones which involve manipulation and control of access" (*The Politics of Reality,* p. 104). Frye points out that once women have more control, the need to say no to what is now a threat will diminish, and our having gained control will result in and be the result of our being "pleasing active beings with momentum of our own, with sufficient shape and structure—with sufficient integrity—to generate friction" (pp. 104–5).

This amalgam of Nietzschean and feminist considerations suggests that the slave may cease to be a slave once she affirms what she is, treating as peripheral both what others are and what they take her to be. Such an affirmation requires deeds in the world and a momentum of her own, not just thoughts and imaginary changes. The positive guidelines that emerge from Nietzsche's more sensitive view of women suggest that we develop our own perspectives and establish our own values through action. We will do this by taking the power of naming into our own hands, and thus we will cease to be silenced by the debilitating effects of the contradictions of sexual dualism.

Remember that in "On female chastity" Nietzsche explains how woman's sexual objectification leads to her silencing. The danger of silencing is the danger of loss of being. A more Nietzschean way to put this might be that it is through articulation that we become who we are, and if we give up our means for developing our own perspective then we give up everything. Silence is born of fear—fear of pain, fear of death—and, Nietzsche suggests, in the case of women silence is born of her fear of man (KSA 5:171; BGE §232, p. 163).

These themes of silencing, articulation, and the need to take control of one's life run through much of today's feminist discourse. In "The Transformation of Silence into Language and Action," Audre Lorde explicitly addresses these very themes. She says that she has "come to believe over and over again that what is most important to me must be spoken, made verbal and shared, even at the risk of having it bruised or misunderstood," and adds that the source of her silence has been fear.[30] Mary Daly clearly identifies the difficulty of breaking silence, saying that "overcoming the silence of women is an extreme act, a sequence of extreme acts. Breaking our silence means living in existential courage."[31] For Lorde, it took facing the very real, very immediate possibility of her own death to show her how deeply regrettable those silences are. Lorde warns women: "My silences had not protected me. Your silence will not protect you" (p. 41). She challenges us: "What are the words you do not yet have? What do you need to say? What are the tyrannies you swallow day by day and attempt to make your own, until you will sicken and die from them, still in silence?" (p. 41). At stake here is self-revelation, self-definition, and creating a world hospitable to the selves women seek to be. Articulating one's experience in one's own voice is an arduous ongoing process, for the development of a perspective involves constant consideration and reconsideration. Despite the difficulty of speaking out, when Lorde did, she found that her words forged connections with other women that were mutually sustaining: "It was the concern and caring of all those women which gave me strength and enabled me to scrutinize the essentials of my living" (p. 41). At this point the feminist no longer keeps company with Nietzsche, for his project of self-creation is not the project of one who seeks or needs the company of others. His self-in-transformation is profoundly lonely and profoundly isolated.[32]

Conclusion

Nietzsche's misogyny is tempered by a surprising understanding of the situation of the (white, European, upper-class) women of his day. That more positive view has several significant features. It laments the impact on women of sexual dualism fueled by male control of the power of definition. It offers a positive framework for change, albeit one toward which Nietzsche has shown some ambivalence. That framework enjoins women, in contemporary feminist terms, to stop being male-defined and to actively engage in creating their own identities. This more positive view, when intermingled as it is with Nietzsche's misogynist claims with which we are all so familiar, radically destabilizes any straightforward attempt to classify his sexual politics.

Given this reading, why do I still call Nietzsche a misogynist? He shows sympathy for women and some understanding of sexual politics on occasion, but he also engages in and even glorifies blaming the victim. He does this in his discussion of slave morality, and he does it in his discussion of women. This is a species of the contempt that Nietzsche showed for anything he deemed "under." Further, Nietzsche's attack on dualisms pushed him in the direction suggested in this paper, yet *Beyond Good and Evil* takes precious little account of the analysis in *The Gay Science* that would advance that argument. He was not willing or perhaps able to take the sort of feminist stance that is nascent here. In addition, his sketch of an early existentialist conception of the self as constructed through perspective and valuation takes his thought directly to the sort of position developed by Beauvoir in *The Second Sex,* yet he did not make this position explicit. And finally, there are still all the apparently insensitive, philosophically and morally unjustified comments about women that are not easily overlooked.

There are two reasons not to brand Nietzsche simply as a misogynist, however. First, his views are mixed. A simple label oversimplifies. There are misogynist elements in his writings, and as we have seen here there are some remarkably nonmisogynist elements as well. (To go so far as calling them feminist would not be accurate.) My goal in highlighting these more positive passages in Nietzsche's works has been to suggest that we do the hard work of reevaluating his views on women and that we see where his philosophical views would take our own thought on the troubling social questions we face. Second, if we use such a simplistic label, then we run the risk of turning feminist scholars away from Nietzsche's texts unnecessarily. There is much in these texts worth studying, and not out of some kind of misguided philosophical hero-worship. The attack on dualisms in *Beyond Good and Evil,* the discussions of the power of discourse that run through *The Gay Science* and beyond, the discussions of the importance of power that run through all his texts, are but a few of the issues of shared concern for Nietzsche and for feminists.

The bottom line is that given the affinities and possibilities sketched in this paper, we should look at what works and what does not work in Nietzsche's metaphysics and epistemology—specifically in his views about what there is and how it came to be what it is, and in his views about the "nature" and politics of knowledge. Like many feminists, Nietzsche rejects many kinds of philosophical dogmatism in his attempts to articulate his conception of these issues. It will be useful to assess his achievements and his failures in light of *our* purposes, all the while recognizing how Nietzsche's purposes helped shape the positions we are examining. As the discussion here suggests, a feminist analysis of Nietzsche's perspectivism and discussion of the power of naming anticipates and can support contemporary feminist concerns about the importance of women's articulating our lives and reshaping our world.

Notes

I would like to thank Peter Burgard, Claudia Card, and Linda J. Nicholson for helpful comments on an earlier draft of this paper. I would also like to thank Diane McKenzie and Stuart Kupfer, M.D., for help researching the medical aspects of sexual dualism. Thanks also to Bijan Parsia for help with documentation.

1. For insightful discussions of the elements of Nietzsche's views that support his being labeled "misogynist," see Ofelia Schutte, *Beyond Nihilism: Nietzsche without Masks* (Chicago: Univ. of Chicago Press, 1984); Carol Diethe, "Nietzsche and the Woman Question," *History of European Ideas* 11 (1989): 865–75; and J. L. Thompson, "Nietzsche on Woman," *International Journal of Moral and Social Studies* 5 (1990): 207–20.

2. For an account of Nietzsche's self-creation through self-articulation through his work, see Alexander Nehamas, *Nietzsche: Life as Literature* (Cambridge: Harvard Univ. Press, 1985). For an account of Beauvoir's project of self-articulation in a broader feminist context, see my "Definition and Power: Toward Authority without Privilege," *Hypatia* 8, no. 4 (1993): 1–34.

3. See Kaufmann's note 31 at BGE §238, p. 167.

4. To guard against oversimple readings of Nietzsche's apparently nasty remarks, see R. Hinton Thomas's complex and compelling reading of the notorious "do not forget your whip" remark in *Thus Spoke Zarathustra* (*Nietzsche in German Politics and Society, 1890–1918* [Manchester: Manchester Univ. Press, 1983], pp. 132–40). Thomas argues that this passage "has no place in any discussion of Nietzsche's views on the treatment of women as such" (p. 140). See also Thomas's chapter "The Feminist Movement and Nietzsche" for some of the ways in which Nietzsche's views were appropriated by some of his feminist contemporaries.

5. This interpretation of Nietzsche is developed by Nehamas in *Nietzsche: Life as Literature.*

6. See also section 239 of *Beyond Good and Evil,* where Nietzsche says: "What inspires respect for woman, and often enough even fear, is her *nature,* which is more 'natural' than man's, the genuine, cunning suppleness of a beast of prey, the tiger's claw under the glove, the naïveté of her egoism, her uneducability and inner wildness, the incomprehensibility, scope, and movement of her desires and virtues" (KSA 5:178; BGE §239, p. 169). Despite the animalistic imagery here, it is important that Nietzsche uses a comparative.

7. See for example KSA 3:422; GS §58, pp. 121–22.

8. It is important to note that there is considerable debate amongst philosophers developing social constructivism as to the nature of the individual and the extent and duration of the social construction across the individual's lifetime. Some argue that

individuals are largely if not completely determined by their social setting, while others leave room for individual self-determination and self-construction within a social context. It would take a paper in itself to explain this debate and where Nietzsche's views would fit in; my point is that there are overlapping issues for these philosophers and for Nietzsche. For an excellent discussion of a feminist social constructivist position, see Marilyn Friedman, "Feminism and Modern Friendship: Dislocating the Community," in *Feminism and Political Theory,* ed. Cass R. Sunstein (Chicago: Univ. of Chicago Press, 1990), pp. 143–58. For a discussion of Nietzsche's conception of the self, see Tracy B. Strong, *Friedrich Nietzsche and the Politics of Transfiguration* (Berkeley and Los Angeles: Univ. of California Press, 1975, 1988).

9. Philosophical realism is not quite the same as literary realism, and it is the philosophical variety that I attribute to Nietzsche here. The philosophical realist holds that there is a world independent of any description or perception of it, that (contrary to the idealist) the "external world" is not a creation of our mind(s). Philosophical realism is a very sensible position which most people—philosophers or not—hold most of the time. Unfortunately, it generates a host of problems concerning the possibility of knowledge (e.g., of the physical world, of other minds) which lead those who think about these issues into a variety of less obviously sensible positions, like idealism, nominalism, pragmatism, and so on. These other positions settle the epistemological issues, but abandon our everyday commonsense version of realism to do it.

10. I owe this understanding of Nietzsche to Alexander Nehamas.

11. This kind of dogmatism is obviously a throwback to Platonism.

12. Sexual dualism is the normative positing of two sex classes that are interdefined, taking one class as primary and the other as secondary. Our current heterosexist patriarchal sex class system is one form of sexual dualism. Sexual dualism is a normative system, but it purports to be descriptive; it is ideology parading as fact. As both Nietzsche and Beauvoir have pointed out, an effective system of norms has significant descriptive consequences. When a society embraces a norm that says that women ought to live in certain ways, and women accept the norm and do live in those ways, then those practices that constitute the way of living can and do shape who those women are and who they can be. For example, a norm that dictates that the education of men is a necessity and that the education of women is a luxury has tremendous impact on the kinds of people women become within the societies that embrace that norm. We must be careful to understand that even well-entrenched descriptions that arise from such a normative base have the potential to be overturned.

13. This figure is reported by Marilyn Frye and attributed to Eileen Van Tassell; see Frye's "Sexism," in *The Politics of Reality: Essays in Feminist Theory* (Freedom, Calif.: Crossing Press, 1983), pp. 17–40. The actual incidence of sexual ambiguities is very hard to ascertain, because there are so many types of ambiguities and there is no general compilation of the data; see *Practice of Pediatrics,* ed. Vincent C. Kelley, 11 vols. (Hagerstown, Md.: Harper, 1984–), 7:chaps. 60–61.

14. This is the estimate of Stuart Kupfer, M.D., a pediatric endocrinologist at the University of North Carolina School of Medicine in Chapel Hill.

15. *Schaffer's Diseases of the Newborn,* 5th ed., ed. Mary Ellen Avery and H. William Taeusch, Jr. (Philadelphia: W. B. Saunders, 1984), pp. 511–12. As soon as it is medically feasible, these children are made into one sex or the other through surgery and medical treatment. In cases of ambiguous genitalia, genetic structure may be

used to determine the child's future sex of rearing. Usually, the determination depends upon what the urologist, the endocrinologist, and the surgeon can do with the child's anatomy.

16. Interestingly, those who do fit these extreme categories also tend to be psychologically or socially dysfunctional. See, for example, Sandra L. Bem, "The Measurement of Psychological Androgyny," *Journal of Consulting and Clinical Psychology* 42 (1974): 155–62, and Sandra L. Bem and Daryl J. Bem, "Training the Woman to Know Her Place: The Power of a Nonconscious Ideology," in *Roles Women Play: Readings toward Women's Liberation*, ed. Michele Hoffnung Garskof (Belmont, Calif.: Brooks/Cole, 1971), pp. 84–96.

17. Nietzsche, I think, is more concerned with the psychosocial aspects of people and so would be more interested in the application to gender than in the application to sex.

18. Consider for example: "When a woman has scholarly inclinations there is usually something wrong with her sexually. Sterility itself disposes one toward a certain masculinity of taste; for man is, if I may say so, 'the sterile animal' " (KSA 5:98; BGE §144, p. 89; see also KSA 5:175–78; BGE §239, pp. 167–70).

19. Simone de Beauvoir, *The Second Sex,* trans. H. M. Parshley (New York: Vintage, 1974). See also Sarah L. Hoagland's "Femininity, Resistance, and Sabotage," in *Women and Values: Readings in Recent Feminist Philosophy,* 2d ed., ed. Marilyn Pearsall (Belmont, Calif.: Wadsworth, 1993), pp. 90–97, and chapters 1 and 2 of her *Lesbian Ethics: Toward New Value* (Palo Alto, Calif.: Institute of Lesbian Studies, 1988) for discussions that highlight some of the ways in which women have sought to resist male domination while apparently not giving up the limited but important privileges of femininity.

20. I say "eradicated" here because I think radical feminists and socialist feminists have shown that it is not enough for one woman (or several) to reject social sex-role stereotyping and live that rejection. Such heroism may be necessary to the liberation of all women, but it does not constitute that liberation.

21. Nietzsche is sensitive to the irony of romantic love for women; see, for example, KSA 3:511; GS §227, p. 211.

22. Ofelia Schutte writes that "there is a highly anti-critical streak in Nietzsche's *entire* theory of the 'order of rank' and the practical applications derived from it" (*Beyond Nihilism,* p. 182). Although I agree with Schutte on this, my point is the weaker claim that Nietzsche is uncritical here.

23. For an excellent contemporary discussion of the problem of feminine narcissism, see Sandra Lee Bartky's "Narcissism, Femininity, and Alienation," in *Femininity and Domination: Studies in the Phenomenology of Oppression* (New York: Routledge, 1990), pp. 33–44.

24. Similarly, feminists may care to learn about the origins of our current sex class system, but I would argue that the pressing question is the value of that system. It is only by undermining those values we reject and finding alternative ways to embody those we accept that we will be able to change the system (eradicate patriarchy). Nietzsche poses the question: What if morality is precisely what keeps us down, keeps us low and base, prevents us from attaining the "*highest power and splendor* actually possible to the type man?" (KSA 5:253; GM—P §6, p. 20). Good question for women too.

25. While many men will say that they do not see themselves in the description of the masters, for they do not see themselves (individually) as the meaning and justification of their society, when they are pressed to name such a normative base, often the answer will concern the work and goals of men. The service of women can be seen in much of our paid and unpaid labor, and it is underscored by the fact that in our society nearly all domestic labor is done by women. Whatever their class status, as long as they do not have paid daily domestic help, it is common for the man in a cohabitating heterosexual couple to accept that the woman will stay up late after a hard day at work to finish cleaning the house, tending the needs of the children (if any), preparing food, doing laundry, and so on. Or, if she does not work outside the home, he will consider it a luxury that she "gets to stay home all day" and "not work," but just cleans the house, feeds and clothes and teaches the children, and so on. It is important to remember that often men's work generates recognition and rewards that women's work, traditionally construed, does not. She works in support of him, and although she may share in his rewards, the rewards are ultimately his. This is one sort of sacrifice, of self and interests, of economic, social, and psychological reward, that justifies the analogy developed here; see Arlie Hochschild, *The Second Shift: Working Parents and the Revolution at Home* (New York: Viking, 1989), for an intriguing discussion of how even among couples with explicit ideological commitments to shared domestic labor, the women still do more than half.

26. The German is more generic than the English in this case: "Grad und Art der Geschlechtlichkeit eines Menschen reicht bis in den letzten Gipfel seines Geistes hinauf."

27. This issue has been a concern of Mary Daly's at least since the time of *Beyond God the Father* (Boston: Beacon, 1973), where she says that "women have had the power of *naming* stolen from us" (p. 8). See also Maria Lugones, "Playfulness, 'World'-Travelling, and Loving Perception," in *Lesbian Philosophies and Cultures,* ed. Jeffner Allen (Albany: SUNY Press, 1990), pp. 159–80; Lugones and Elizabeth V. Spelman, "Have We Got a Theory for You! Feminist Theory, Cultural Imperialism, and the Demand for 'The Woman's Voice,'" *Hypatia: A Special Issue of Women's Studies International Forum* 6 (1983): 573–81; Alice Walker, "In Search of Our Mothers' Gardens," in *In Search of Our Mothers' Gardens: Womanist Prose* (San Diego: Harvest/HBJ, 1983), pp. 231–43; and Carolyn G. Heilbrun, *Writing a Woman's Life* (New York: Ballantine, 1988). For a helpful discussion of these issues with respect to philosophy of law, see Martha Minow, *Making All the Difference: Inclusion, Exclusion, and American Law* (Ithaca: Cornell Univ. Press, 1990).

28. Slave morality is essentially "No-saying," for it says no to the world of the master, which it perceives as hostile. Nietzsche says that slave morality needs the hostile world created by master morality (which really directs no hostility toward the slaves). If it is to exist, it exists by inverting "the value-positing eye" (KSA 5:271; GM—I §10, p. 36). The analogies and disanalogies between this case and the case of the sexes should be obvious.

29. Compare with the following from Beauvoir's introduction: "As George Bernard Shaw puts it, in substance, 'The American white relegates the black to the rank of shoeshine boy; and he concludes from this that the black is good for nothing but shining shoes.' This vicious circle is met with in all analogous circumstances; when an individual (or a group of individuals) is kept in a situation of inferiority, the fact

is that he *is* inferior. But the significance of the verb *to be* must be rightly understood here; it is in bad faith to give it a static value when it really has the dynamic Hegelian sense of 'to have become.' Yes, women on the whole *are* today inferior to men; that is, their situation affords them fewer possibilities. The question is: should that state of affairs continue?" (Beauvoir, *The Second Sex,* p. xxviii).

30. Audre Lorde, "The Transformation of Silence into Language and Action," in *Sister / Outsider: Essays and Speeches* (Freedom, Calif.: Crossing Press, 1984), p. 40.

31. Mary Daly, *Gyn/Ecology: The Metaethics of Radical Feminism* (Boston: Beacon, 1978, 1990), p. 21.

32. For a discussion of the importance of community to the project of self-articulation, see my "Definition and Power."

PART FOUR

Feminist Philosophy

DAVID FARRELL KRELL

To the Orange Grove at the Edge of the Sea: Remarks on Luce Irigaray's *Amante marine*

Is it too late to touch you, Dear?
We this moment knew—
Love Marine and Love terrene—
Love celestial too—

—Emily Dickinson

In what follows I shall try to read Luce Irigaray's *Amante marine: De Friedrich Nietzsche* ("Nietzsche's She-lover, Sea-lover") against the backdrop of questions I raised some years ago in a book entitled *Postponements: Woman, Sensuality, and Death in Nietzsche.*[1] Irigaray resists the figure of woman that often dominates Nietzsche's texts, the funereal figure that incarnates sensual love as tragic death. She also resists the figure of woman as Maenad, the frenzied lover of Dionysus. Both are figures in which sensuousness and demise converge. The strategies and styles of Irigaray's resistance will be my focus—along with the hopes she invests in the she-lover and sea-lover who rises in waves against the Nietzschean mountain.

Yet one does not merely "focus" on strategies and styles of resistance: one resists them or joins forces with them, or sometimes resists and sometimes joins forces. In either case, one finds oneself caught up in the ἀγών and πόλεμος of "Nietzsche and the feminine." Further, the very style of one's thinking and writing shifts insensibly in such a confrontation. Inasmuch as Irigaray thinks and writes in fragments—they are sometimes extended fragments, but they are always nonetheless nodes of fragmentary writing—it is difficult for a reading of *Amante marine* to submit to the discipline and rigor of an "essay" or "commentary." Hence the fragmentary character of these "Remarks" of mine.

I shall begin with the filiation of Irigaray's "aerial" interpretation of Nietzsche and Gaston Bachelard's "ascensionalist" reading. I shall then take up the three successive parts of *Amante marine:* "Speaking of Immemorial Waters," "Veiled Lips," and "When Gods Are Born." Finally, I will allow my own resistance to many of Irigaray's suspicions concerning the master of suspicion to dissolve—in a way that I hope would intrigue the two philosophers, though not altogether allay their suspicions.

Almost fifty years ago Gaston Bachelard published *L'Air et les songes: Essai sur l'imagination du mouvement.*[2] He was pursuing his project of a "physiology of the imagination" based on the four elements, fire, earth, air, and water. Because the element of air rendered very little to the "material imagination," Bachelard proposed to append to the latter a phenomenology or psychoanalysis of "dynamic imagination" (pp. 15–16), that is to say, the imagination of *movement.* Movement through the air he defined as essentially *ascensional,* on the vertical axis that organizes human valorization as such. "All valorization is verticalization," Bachelard declared, emphasizing that "*of all metaphors, those of height, elevation, depth, abasement, and fall are the axiomatic metaphors* par excellence" (p. 18). Inquiry into the material imagination of air, as a study of dynamic imagination, would more than any other study expose the *valuative* basis of human psychology. The confrontation with Nietzsche was therefore inevitable.

The fifth of Bachelard's twelve chapters offers a detailed study of "Nietzsche and the Ascensional Psychism" (pp. 146–85). Here it cannot be a matter of surveying Bachelard's methods and hypotheses, even though they are instructive with regard to Irigaray's *Amante marine.* Bachelard examines Nietzsche's poetic works, especially *Thus Spoke Zarathustra,* seeking evidence of the poet and thinker who is "the very type of *vertical poet,* the *poet of summits,* the *ascensional poet*" (p. 147). Bachelard, and Irigaray after him, deny that Nietzsche is a poet of the earth, even if the cry by which all remember him is "Be faithful to the earth!" (KSA

4:15; cf. Z—P §3, p. 125). For earth is a mixture of soil and water, its texture is "spongy," and Nietzsche is not one of the lovers of the porous, muddy earth, lovers whom Bachelard describes as follows: "Only a passionate lover [*amant*] of the earth, only a terrestrian affected by a touch of the aquatic, can escape from the *automatically pejorative* character of the metaphor of the *spongy*" (p. 148). If the *mucal* or *mucous* may be associated with the spongy and slimy organs and orifices of the body, then the filiation of Irigaray and Bachelard at once becomes clear. It is a filiation Irigaray has never wished to deny or conceal.

Why is Nietzsche not a lover of the earth? Because he works against its moist receptivity, accepting it only as a platform for action, an action that he alone initiates. Even if Bachelard distorts Nietzsche's relationship to the burrowing mole (*talpa europea*) by characterizing Nietzsche's attitude toward it as a "redoubled contempt," even if he misses the genial fraternity of the groping genealogist and the subterranean mole, Bachelard's account of the essentially aerial Nietzsche is challenging.[3]

Nietzsche insists that the musical air be clear and well articulated, an air for dancing rather than drowning. His polemics against Wagner (and Heidegger joins him in these polemics, thus betraying his own ascensional tendencies), his opposition to the metaphorics of the musical flood, of waves, of the infinite sea of sound (Bachelard, p. 152), clearly expose Nietzsche's aerial, Mozartian preference. Further, Nietzschean air is as bright and cold as Boreas, or Hyperboreas—a piercing arrow forged in solar fire and tempered in polar ice. Bachelard characterizes the joys of the four elements as follows: "*Terrestrial* joy is bounty and weight—*aquatic* joy is mollification and repose—*igneous* joy is love and desire—and *aerial* joy is freedom" (p. 156). Nietzsche's is clearly the joy of the air, the liberty of a soaring eagle, the brisk wind across the mountain crag. His is the joy of the predator. "Air is the *infinite substance* that one traverses in a line, with a freedom on the offensive, triumphant as lightning, the eagle, the arrow, the imperious and sovereign gaze. In the air one carries off one's victim in the clear light of day—there is no place to hide" (p. 157). The bracing air, chill and empty, utterly pure, is the *tonic* of Nietzsche's aerial soul, which is desperate to leave all odors and memories behind and below.

"Chill, silence, height—three roots for the same substance. Cut one root and you destroy Nietzsche's life" (p. 161).

If Zarathustra's enemy is the spirit of gravity, Nietzsche's war is fought to gain the high ground. To go *over man* in order to fulfill the earth's promise. To rob the temples, to flee and fly, to evaluate: *voler, voler, évaluer.* Nietzsche's is thus not a reversal of Platonism in any sense, but remains a Platonism of the *will* (p. 167). The Nietzschean hierarchy is thus less Heraclitean than Platonic (and once again Heidegger would concur with Bachelard): "The earth over water, fire over earth, air over fire—such is the utterly *vertical* hierarchy of Nietzschean poetics" (p. 173).

~

One might well resist the force of Bachelard's psychopoetics of Nietzsche's ostensible ascensionalism. One might insist instead on a kind of "descensional reflection," where the word *descensional* is chosen to counter Bachelard.[4] One would be emphasizing the obvious, to wit, that Nietzsche's mountain heights remain on the earth, and that the old mole of genealogy needs the ethereal affirmation of eternal return precisely in order to sustain him or her in an underground no-saying and no-acting. While unable to deny the powerful metaphorics of ascension in Nietzschean poetics, it seems important to stress the terrestrial base—the point from which all flights depart and to which they return, without any hope of limitless soaring. When we accuse Nietzsche of a traditional form of ascensionalism, say, that of anamnesic ascent to the divine banquet in Plato's *Phaedrus,* I wonder whether we are simply failing to take the measure of what Nietzsche had to oppose, ignoring the earthbound labors of the subversive mole.

~

At the very end of his chapter on Nietzsche, Bachelard alters his thesis slightly. He suggests that Nietzsche's "aerial life" is less a flight from the earth than "an *offensive* against the sky" (p. 178). He intimates what Albert Camus was soon to argue strongly for in *L'Homme révolté,* namely, that Nietzsche is forever in rebellion against the agents of the heavens. Nietzsche's voluntarism is his only flight plan: *vouloir* and *voler* revert to the same *volo* (p. 180). And yet, Bachelard now concedes, "there is no eternal climb, there is no definitive elevation" (p. 181). For Nietzsche, as for Heraclitus, the way up is the way down, and not for nothing is *Thus Spoke Zarathustra* dominated by the rhythm of ascents and descents. Not for nothing does it begin and end with descent rather than ascent. In the end, Bachelard concedes, "Nietzsche is not an alpinist." "His poems were often composed *on climbing back down* from the heights, returning to the valleys where human beings dwell" (p. 184). The "double perspective" of height and depth results in something both more and less than a traditional ascensionalism: alongside the *élan* of Nietzsche's aerial offensive we find a *volonté de richesse*, an affirmation of the bounty of the *earth*. Exposure to Nietzsche's text, to Nietzsche's poetics, thus in some way tempers the Bachelardian judgment so confidently pronounced at the outset.

From Bachelard's *L'Air et les songes* one retains many impressions, many questions. For example: If Nietzsche's ascensionalism tempers its aerial quality with an affirmation of the bounteous earth, is the bounteous *sea* anywhere to be found on Nietzsche's earth? Yet one also retains a haunting sense of the inadequacy of all one-sided judgments here, the inappropriateness of all polemic. Indeed, Bachelard's own visions and revisions raise a suspicion: Does not the desire to shoot arrows—whether *in* Nietzsche or *at* Nietzsche—reflect an essentially aerial, rather than an aquatic, imagination?

Irigaray's *Amante marine*, to repeat, consists of three parts. The first, "Speaking of Immemorial Waters," responds to Nietzsche's *Thus Spoke Zarathustra*. Here the she-sea-lover addresses the man-in-the-mountain, inviting him to return to the sea. The second part, "Veiled Lips," is a meditation on the central Nietzschean theme of *sich geben als, se donner pour*, the self-giving of truth and woman that is always at the same time *dissimulation*. The third, "When Gods Are Born," muses on the birth and destiny of Dionysus, Apollo, and the Christ. There can be no question of doing justice to Irigaray's text in any one of its three parts. The worst injustice would be to try to encapsulate her text in "arguments" or "theses." However, my own scattered remarks here should not be taken as signs of *Irigaray's* incoherence: the rhythm of her fragmentary writing works as waves on the shore, for while her thoughts are never predictable, they show a remarkable regularity and insistence. They constitute a plea as well as a case, and neither case nor plea should be ignored. I will have to leave to other voices a more coherent account of her challenge to Nietzsche and a more sensitive appreciation of her plea on his behalf.

Irigaray counterposes midnight to midday. The ugliest man alone thinks eternal recurrence as an affirmative thought, and he thinks it as the midnight thought, behind Zarathustra's back, as it were. Nietzsche's affirmative thought cannot be a thought of gold, possession, the sun, or the same. Nor will it be a lunar reflection of solar light. It will be dark. Even as the hollow fold or pocket in a delicate membrane. Beyond the master's reach. However, the affirmative thought is precisely for that reason the heaviest burden. "For hollows mean only the abyss to you. . . . The membrane was not yours to have. We formed it together. And if you want it for yourself, you make a hole in it just because I lack any part. And don't you make God out of that absence?" (pp. 13–14; p. 7).

Why the suspicion against volume, possession, and divinely solar gold? Because they always seem to serve as compensation for something feared and despised. "Isn't your sun-worship still a kind of ressentiment? Don't you measure your ecstasy against the yardstick of envy? And isn't your circle made of the will to live this irradiation—there will be no other but me?" (p. 21; p. 15). One is reminded of the helio-basileo-patro-theology of *Phaedrus,* as analyzed in Derrida's *Pharmacy.*[5] The legacy will always be passed from father to scion, from sun to son. Even though Pharmacia herself is anything but one of the two.

~

Irigaray repeats Gaston Bachelard's complaint, albeit in a remarkably different voice:

> You teach the overman: the meaning of the earth. But do you come from earth or sea to announce the news? Is it fluid depths or solid volume that engendered you?
>
> Are you fish or eagle, swimmer or dancer, when you announce the decline of man? Do you want to flow or climb? Overflow or fly? And in your entire will for the sea are you so very afraid that you must always stay up so high?
>
> Perched on every mountain peak, hermit, tightrope-walker, or bird, you never dwell in the great depths. And as companion you never choose a sea creature. Camel, snake, lion, eagle, and doves, monkey and ass, and . . . Yes. But no to anything that moves in the water. Why this persistent wish for legs or wings? And never gills?
>
> And when you say that overman is the sea in whom your contempt is lost, that's fine. That is a will wider than man's own. But you never say: overman has lived in the sea. That is how he survives.
>
> It is always hot, dry, and hard in your world. And to excel for you always requires a bridge.
>
> Are you truly afraid of falling back into man? Or into the sea? (pp. 18–19; pp. 12–13)

~

When in Plato's *Phaedrus* Socrates is displeased by the words that have at that moment rolled off his tongue, he compares the bitter taste they leave in his mouth to the taste of brine, and says that he will wash his mouth out with sweet water. Later, in the course of his *second* speech, his panegyric on the winged steeds of the aerial soul, he compares the soul of mortals to an oyster imprisoned in the shell of the body. Why doesn't Socrates like oysters? Why does he identify the salt sea as bitter? Why does Plato's Socrates prefer pegasus to pearls? And, in the end, is Nietzsche simply one more victim of the Socratism he otherwise so deftly portrays?

As a boy Nietzsche was afraid of the water. When he finally learned to swim it changed his life. Nothing made him happier, not even riding. He describes it in letters and journals—giving his body over to buoyancy. The year at Sorrento with Malwida von Meysenbug and Paul Rée, swimming in the bay below the orange grove—after that, he wanted to divide his whole life seasonally between the sea and the mountains, between salt air and pine breeze. The most agonizing day his mother had with him after he was released from the Jena Institute for the Care and Cure of the Insane was the day they closed the swimming pool for repairs. He raged. He ran off and discovered another place to swim. A policeman found him.

What Irigaray pleads for is a certain fidelity of memory. For example, the memory of water in the mouth, as Sartre's Roquentin recalls it in *La nausée*. Yet here, in Irigaray, with a notable difference in taste:

> So remember the liquid ground. And taste the saliva in your mouth also—notice her familiar presence during your silence, how she is forgotten when you speak. Or again: how you stop speaking when you drink. And how necessary all of that is for you!
>
> These fluids softly mark the time. And there is no need to tap, just listen, in order to hear the music. With very small ears! (p. 43; p. 37)

Not that it can ever be a question of Nietzsche "becoming woman," or even "writing with the hand of woman." Bad politics joins bad writing in such a presumption, no doubt.[6] It is rather a question of not ignoring the resources in and of the *other*. "Why are we not, the one for the other, a resource of life and air?" (p. 37; p. 31). It is a question of finding the courage for pleasure beyond the death principle. "But you will never have pleasure [*jouir*] in woman if you insist on being woman. If you insist on making her a stage in your process. There is nothing like unto women. They go beyond all simulation. And when they are copied, the abyss remains. Well on this side of your measurements, the women, the abandoned ones, take place" (pp. 45–46; p. 39).

Yet Nietzsche wants eternity alone for his wedded wife, desires eternity alone to be the mother of his children. Irigaray suspects that the cost of such nuptials is extravagant: "And for your only wife you want eternity. For in her, finally, you can give yourself up wholly. Though dead" (p. 49; p. 43). It is as though in the thought of recurrence Nietzsche wants to give birth to himself, to mother himself through all eternity, to take his birth into his own hands—*s'enfanter à nouveau,* as Pierre Klossowski puts it.[7] Yet that thought is madness, a mere parody of eternal recurrence:

> Forever you lose hold of the place where you take body. And to repeat your own birth is simply impossible. And by wishing for it, you choose to die. Finding again that dark home where you began to be once upon a time. Once and for all.
>
> That event does not happen twice. That necessity and that chance, horrendous and wonderful as they are in the blind term of their meeting.
>
> And, as you enter into the eternity of your recurrence, you cut yourself off from that unique occasion when you received life. All powerful, perhaps, for a fleeting moment; until the thread breaks that connected you to the earth. Then begins the decline. (p. 63; p. 57)

It is as Ursula, in *One Hundred Years of Solitude,* knows: only one century, one saeculum, is granted to mortals: "Because lineages condemned to one hundred years of solitude had no second chance on the earth."[8] Eternal return must engage that realization each time it is thought. It must be thought in the way Heidegger insisted—as *downgoing.* As anything but ascensional. Thus it is a matter of overcoming our anguish—"The danger of immersion in primary matter endlessly feeds your anguish, your forgetfulness, and your death" (p. 73; p. 66)—by means of whatever resources of life and air the other affords us. Resources of life and air *immersed* in fluid matter.

Thus the thinking of recurrence abolishes the thought of *the same.* Nietzsche knows that: the notebook in which he first elaborates the thought of return (KSA 9:441–575) contains his most trenchant critique of the metaphysics of the same, *des Gleichen*. Indeed, the thinking of recurrence must get along without recurrence itself, so that Nietzsche would affirm *with* Irigaray, "Become other, and without recurrence" (p. 75; p. 69).

~

If there is a "final judgment" expressed in the first part of *Amante marine,* it is something like this: one expects to find in Nietzsche an encounter with radical otherness, but, at least in terms of the other that is *woman,* the expectation is disappointed. At the very end of her book Irigaray reiterates: "Nietzsche—perhaps—has experienced and shown what is the result of infinite distance reabsorbed into the same [*le même*], has shown the difference that remains without a face or countenance" (p. 200; p. 187). If his "thought of thoughts" or his "Idea" is eternal recurrence of the same, his resistance to the same does not rescue him from the thought itself. "The sacrifice he makes to the Idea is inscribed in this—that he preferred the Idea to an ever provisional openness to a female other [*l'ouverture, toujours temporisante, à une autre*]" (p. 200; p. 187). The other is (in) the feminine. Such temporization, which is more than merely "provisional," I would now define less as a being in *postponement* than as the need to persist *on the verge*. In a sense, Nietzsche was too impatient, was too anxious to absorb the other into his own experience. Irigaray's complaint: "That he refused to break the mirror of the same [*du même*], and over and over again demanded that the other be his double. To the point of willing to become that female other. Despite all physiology, all incarnation. Hermit, tightrope-walker, or bird, forgetful of the one who bore him, accompanied him, nourished him; in a solitary leap he leaves everything below him or in him; the chasm becomes bottomless" (p. 201; pp. 187–88).

What then is missing? "Rhythm and measure of a female other [*une autre*] that endlessly undoes the autological circle of discourse, thwarts the eternal return of the same, opens up every horizon through the affirmation of another point of view whose fulfillment can never be predicted. Always at risk? A gay science of the incarnation?" (p. 201; p. 188).

Yet the very demands of the gay science of incarnation prevent one from closing the Nietzsche case too hastily. Indeed, one must respond to Nietzsche as a lover, not petulantly, but importunately.

~

Like Klossowski and many others, Irigaray (pp. 79–80; pp. 72–73) appears to accept the view that Nietzsche's rejection by Lou was the fatal source of his ressentiment against woman. A look at the letters confirms that Nietzsche would never be the same after this *nonconfrontation* with the other, although it is the way in which "Naumburg" (that is to say, his sister and his mother) became implicated in the Rée-Lou fiasco to which the letters most eloquently attest. Perhaps it is inevitable that the biographical *argumentum ad hominem/foeminam* be trotted out against Nietzsche: that the one who inveighed against the human, all-too-human should all-too-humanly fall in love, and that his love should be spurned—who can suppress a rancorous chuckle, a poke in the ribs, a knowing wink? Yet what does one gain by such not very subtle aggression? An ephemeral sensation of power, Nietzsche would have said; a brief victory over one who otherwise always carries the day. Winning the lover's quarrel, losing the lover's war.

A final suspicion. Is it entirely certain that the sea and the sea-lover constitute the ultimate and unequivocal challenge to Nietzsche's thought? Entirely certain that the sea—the shroud of the sea that rolls on as it rolled five thousand years ago—is altogether without metaphysical consolations, devoid of romanza, liberated from illusions? Or might the sea be the very milieu of eternal recurrence of the same in its most consolatory guise? Might the sea—the wine-dark, life-giving sea—be the counterelement of transiency; might it be the symbol of the eternity sought for all things? Recall Nietzsche's note from the winter of 1887–88, which identifies the sea as a source of consolation (*Trost*): "Ought one to pour the costliest unguents and wines into the sea? —My consolation is that all that was is eternal: —the sea spews it forth again" (KSA 13:43; WP §1065, p. 548). The sea: shroud or cornucopia, white shark or coral reef? And what if the pretension to *gills* were the very pretense of birthing oneself anew, birthing oneself as the (always selfsame) "other"?

Part 2 of *Amante marine,* "Veiled Lips," offers a devastating reading of *The Eumenides,* with Pallas Athena sprouting from the head of Zeus and testifying in the courtroom in such a way as to fulfill all her Father's wishes. "The cunning of the father, of the God? Rape/rob the female one so that the other can indefinitely produce doubles for him" (p. 114; p. 106). Part 2 also offers telling responses to those famous passages of Nietzsche's *The Gay Science* (KSA 3:422–25; GS §§59–60, pp. 122–24) on women and "naturalness" as well as their "action at a distance." The response to section 59 of *The Gay Science* is particularly powerful, and I shall reproduce some passages from Nietzsche's text, followed by Irigaray's reply.

> *We Artificers!* —When we love a woman we may well fly into a rage against nature, thinking of all the repulsive naturalnesses [*Natürlichkeiten*] to which every woman is exposed. . . . Here one stops one's ears against all physiology and secretly decrees for oneself: "I want to hear nothing about human beings' consisting of anything more than *soul and form!*" The human being "under the skin" is for all lovers a horror and an abomination, a blasphemy against God and against Love. . . . It is enough for us to love, hate, desire, sense anything at all—*immediately* the spirit and force of the dream comes over us and we climb the most hazardous winding ways, open-eyed, coolly confronting every danger, up to the rooftops and turrets of fantasy, without a hint of vertigo, as though we were born to clamber—we somnambulists of the day! We artificers! We concealers of naturalness! Moonsick, Godsick! Relentless wanderers, still as death, along heights we perceive not as heights but as our level plains, our securities! (KSA 3:422–24; cf. GS §59, pp. 122–23)

In this passage the "we" is captivating. It oscillates somewhere between an outwardly directed analysis of the moonsick artist-artificer and the most painful sort of recoil, recoil back onto the genealogist of unnaturalness himself. Or herself. Irigaray replies less acerbically than one might have expected, perhaps in appreciation of the recoil already at work in Nietzsche's text.

> Nature can be loved only if she is concealed: as if in a dream. No sooner do they sense nature than the men of yesterday and today climb high onto the roofs and towers of fantasy. They are born to climb—to rise up. And they feel not the slightest giddiness, provided their climb is concealed from them. These night-walkers by day, these God-struck ones, these moonstruck men with eyes open, see nothing in it but art.
>
> Their dream: to cover the natural with veils. To climb ever higher, get farther and farther off, turn away from nature toward certainties that they can no longer see, as an escape onto dangerous heights—their plains, their plans. As a way to rid their thoughts of the disgusting things to which nature subjects every woman (?). (p. 115; p. 108)

It is difficult, if not impossible, to separate out Nietzsche's own contribution to Irigaray's reply, that is to say, to delineate the ways in which that reply remains indebted to the Nietzschean analysis: it cannot be a matter of mere mockery here, no matter how severe the recoil on "Nietzsche" "himself" may be. Lack of generosity would also be a lack of perspicacity. Nietzsche's greatest gift/*Gift* is his ability to *enable* his genealogical analyses to recoil, in this way helping his readers to their own responses. If Nietzsche did not have the *φάρμακον* that makes of him a *φαρμακός*, no one would bother to reply to him—or to love him. Yet can one learn such recoil and such generosity from Nietzsche? Can one presume to love him?

In this second section of *Amante marine* Irigaray presents the romanza of Demeter and Kore, rather too predictable in its contours: "The mother's daughter, and the nearness they shared. . . . The end of the young girl, torn from her mother's arms, carried off into death" (p. 121; p. 113). When *Postponements* first appeared, I asked a psychoanalyst friend whether Nietzsche's misogyny troubled her. Her reply silenced me. "It doesn't trouble me at all," she said. "Whenever Nietzsche uses the word *woman* I substitute the words *my mother,* and then I have no difficulty accepting what he says." Sometimes Kore prefers life in hell.

Once again in these pages Irigaray reproduces her rhapsody of the lips, the one and the other in absolute intimacy, the lips of woman touching each other in perfect self-embrace (p. 91; p. 85). Of course, she senses the danger of such a claim, a familiar danger, a danger she wants to avert: "And she does not oppose a feminine truth to the masculine truth. Because this would once again amount to playing the—man's—game of castration" (p. 92; p. 86). There follows the by now familiar gothic horror tale of these lips generously and altogether gratuitously setting aside their self-sufficiency in order to embrace "him":

> But because, through the reembrace of her lips—both passive and active, experienced without ressentiment—she still remains familiar to the other, she is disposed to receive him again and yet again into her. She does not take him *into* her. The other is not, here or there, taken into the whole of herself. She "wills" herself only with the other. She takes endless pleasure in ensnaring [*d'enlacer*] the other. Always moving inside and outside at the same time, passing between the edges, thriving in the depth and thickness of the flesh, as though outside the universe, more or less removed from it. She goes and comes, in herself and outside herself, ceaselessly. According to at least four dimensions:

> from left to right, from right to left, from before after, from after before, the threshold of the inside to the outside of the body.
>
> Thus is ceaselessly engendered the expansion of her "world," which does not develop within any square or circle or anything else, and which remains without limit or boundary. Anything occurring in that world is wedded in movement, if it remains an other that self-embraces. Passive and active, feeling without feeling ressentiment. (p. 123; p. 115)

Activity and passivity, self-embrace, generosity without need, sheer altruism and pure spontaneity: the Demiurge redivivus, without a demisemiquaver of either desire or need, except perhaps the desire to find hands outstretched to receive the proffered honey. Irigaray's is more Zarathustra's solar desire, more a yearning for the aerial realm "which remains without limit or boundary," than the receptive generosity and nocturnal languor of Schelling's desirous God, who is on the verge of discovering that He is a woman.

Without feeling ressentiment. That is the key. While the arrow of ressentiment is deflected back again and again upon Nietzsche, which is precisely where the genealogist himself or herself always needs to have it deflected, Irigaray expresses the truth or the desire-of-the-truth to have been utterly devoid of ressentiment. The interiorized cruelty that Nietzsche identifies as the energizing force of ascetic ideals should have, must have, can have, nothing to do with woman. No ascetic priestesses, not ever. Yet when the arrow is deflected back at Nietzsche one must wonder whether it isn't the same aerial arrow that Nietzsche shot from *his* bow. Indeed, deflection and return would not be the action of the sea; it would not suit the sea to shoot or deflect arrows and accusations. After writing of ressentiment as though it were a sentiment quite beneath or altogether outside of woman, perfectly phallically foreign, Irigaray writes the concluding words of "Veiled Lips":

> And if the latest fashion is to will that she be phallic, she will prove to you that she is phallic, that you are right to believe it. Piling it on, until the phallus, and all the rest, go to their ruin.
>
> Since, of course, all the perspectives that have already been fixed, all the shapes already outlined, all the boundaries already laid down, appear to her as merely a set in a game. That will entertain her—perhaps? But only for a moment. For as long as it takes to feel the limit, and start her operation again.

> Unless she has been dead since birth. An immortal virgin, because never a little girl. A flower hypostasized into truth, appearance, semblance. . . . According to your [*votre*] will, the necessities of your power, the historical moments. Everything at the same time, every woman at the same time, in order to please you.
>
> Stop, dead stop, without end [*Arrêt, et de mort, sans fin*]. (p. 127; p. 119)

Without ressentiment, yet with all the accusatory pathos of one who has received the death sentence; piling it on, in the desperate gamesmanship of Death Row, giving itself (out) as (if) without ressentiment. *Se donner pour, sich geben als. . . .*

Part 3, "Where Gods Are Born," offers a remarkable reading of the birth and (shared) character of Dionysus, Apollo, and the Christ. Surprisingly, the readings become more generous as they proceed, so much so that one discerns a shadow of Mariology hovering over the final pages of Irigaray's book. The response to Nietzsche's analysis of the hypersensitivity of the Redeemer type (in *The Antichrist*) and the outspoken preference for a secular Jesus is more generous to the Crucified than to Dionysus. For in the case of Christianity, it is putatively a mere matter of betrayal by a "tradition":

> Was he like that? Or has tradition made him like that? The place of his loves is rendered virgin, or childlike, or adolescent. Must the Christic redemption mean that the advent of the divine has never taken place in the incarnation of an amorous relationship with the other? Must this messenger of life neglect or refuse the most elementary realities? Must he be a timid or morbid adolescent, too paralyzed to realize his desires, always attentive to his Father's edicts, executing the Father's wishes even to the point of accepting the passion and the Father's desertion. . . .
>
> Who interpreted him in this way? Who abominated the body so much that he glorified the son of man for being abstinent or castrated? (p. 189; p. 177)

The generosity here is that of *The Last Temptation of Christ* or of the Dutch theologians—in distant memory of and nostalgia for Vatican II. "Search for traces of the divine in anything that does not preach, does not command, but enacts the work of the incarnation" (p. 182; p. 170).

Most ironic and intriguing in Irigaray's treatment of the Christ is her reflection on the lance wound in the side of the Crucified. As though in reply to Augustine, who argues that the Glorified Body of every deceased Christian woman must be outfitted with a Christic phallus before it can be assumed into heaven, or with a bow to Leo Steinberg's remarkable *The Sexuality of Christ in Renaissance Art and in Modern Oblivion,* Irigaray calls this wound a *vagina* (p. 177; p. 166).[9] She does not speculate that it may be the very sheathe from which the rib of Adam was removed.

~

In general, Irigaray's treatment of Apollo equates the Delphic god with what Nietzsche calls *Socratism*—the death of the tragic thought. There is no discussion of the meeting and mating of Apollo and Dionysus, the impossible yet intermittent coupling that produces the miracle of tragedy, no discussion of Apollo's "removing the weapon" from the hand of the Lydian god (KSA 1:32; cf. BT §2, p. 39), no discussion of their productive difference(s). Irigaray focuses instead on the ostensibly identical genealogy of these male gods:

> Apollo does not exclude Dionysus. They complete each other in Zeus, but never reproduce his unity. Apollo hands down the celestial patrimony of the mantic, the light, measured restraint, justice, the organization of the city. Dionysus inherits his father's thunderous excesses, the gift of seducing women in drunkenness and ecstasy, the attraction for water, the possessive and devastating passion of night.
>
> The two—couple of false twins?—must coexist as incarnations of the power of Zeus. Even if one surpasses the other in power, the division of possessions, here, cannot be closed. The whole will no longer belong to any one. It is up to the brother-men, without resorting to bloody warfare, to divide up the Father's attributes. Including those he has stolen from the ancestress or the mother. (pp. 170–71; p. 159)

One can understand the desire to abnegate whatever the sons of Zeus have touched. Including Ariadne, who is here surrendered to Gilles Deleuze's interpretation: "Ariadne—double of the male" (p. 125; p. 117).[10] However, if Dionysus is, as Irigaray writes, the god of excess, the one who seduces women (but how? what kettle logic will explain it, or explain it away?), the god who displays "an attraction for water," which is something the sea-lover should know about, and "the possessive and devastating passion of the night," which is at least not altogether solar—then one might expect a rather different response to Dionysus. As Zagreus. Without ressentiment.

Even if one remains within the confines of Olympian genealogy, the sons of Zeus have at least something to do with the *downfall* of the Father. What else is Aeschylus concerned with, especially in his *Prometheus Bound,* than the inevitable demise of Zeus? If the bloody passage of power from Ouranos to Kronos to Zeus is something that tragedy is well aware of, then perhaps the *birth* of tragedy in the (impossible, intermittent, intromissive) mating of Apollo and Dionysus has something to do with the collapse of the Deus? That Nietzsche—amid the ruins of fallen gods and the toppled statue of Pan—sought out the ways of the *mothers* in his first major work, that he sought out the ancestress or the mother from whom the Father stole "his" attributes, suggests that a reading of *The Birth of Tragedy* ought to have lain at the heart of *Amante marine,* "When Gods Are Born." It does not.

Both Hölderlin and Nietzsche were convinced that the very essence of tragedy involved the figure(s) of woman and sensuous love. Even though tragic poetry could never be confused with sentimental poetry, Panthea and Delia (originally *Rhea*) are present in Hölderlin's *The Death of Empedocles.* Nietzsche's own plans for an Empedoclean drama locate the sensuous love of man and woman at the very center of the action. To the extent that these *Empedocles* plans dovetail with later plans for *Thus Spoke Zarathustra,* we can say that they reveal something very near the core (or ecstatic center) of Nietzsche's concerns. Now, the figure of Empedocles is at the heart of Irigaray's own response to Heidegger—in *L'Oubli de l'air.*[11] One might therefore have hoped to follow the thread of Irigaray's response to the Dionysian in the direction not of the genealogy of the (false) twin gods but of Love and Strife in the Empedoclean sphere—the tragic sphere. Yet Irigaray everywhere resists the Dionysian and the Maenadic. The enthusiasm of the Maenads is too violent, too destructive (p. 132; p. 124). Irigaray thus accepts in a straightforward way Heraclitus' identification of Dionysus and Hades. Her suspicion of the god who has down on his cheeks is this: "In calling us once again to desire, does he not destroy the body?" (p. 137; p. 129). That is the very accusation brought against this foreign god by Pentheus. Ironically, Irigaray's suspicion of the Maenad throng reduplicates that of the Theban King. However, no messenger comes to reassure her about the women:

> Starting out from the mountains, the women are worshippers of the phallus. Leaving their sea clan far behind, they are caught up and carried out of themselves by their eternal betrothals to the god who is coming. And their desire becomes a chorus of suppliant women in exile, the convulsive rites and dances of women in a trance. And the throbbing music of the summons to a wedding that is forever deferred pours out of them, like a fluid that the women still breathe out but is already bent to the rhythm of the man-god and therefore no longer flows in them. Or between them. The whole thing is driven by the very cult of the phallic effigy.
>
> Their madness is still visible. And their pain. The violence of their passions. Exasperated to the point of destroying life. Still wild, but a kind of wildness already inspired by the beyond. A wildness in which the women become impassioned, lose their wits, their energies, move out of their natal element. In the grip of movements too swift to last. Between rhythms, finding no passage, losing the harmony. And they collapse onto the ground from weariness at the conclusion of their intoxication [*ivresse*]. (p. 149; p. 140)

Each complaint finds its parallel in the complaint of the King, and each is contradicted by the shepherd messenger who has actually seen the women at their revels. Irigaray's nightmare vision mirrors that of Pentheus: convulsive rites of women entranced, women poisoned, women intoxicated and betrayed by promises of a wedding that will never take place; madness, pain, and violence mar their passions, which are passions destructive of life; women without wits, women driven out of their element, women deprived of the fluidity that is their birthright, like fish out of water; women whose rhythms now lack harmony, whose convulsions won't last, whose frenetic movements will gain them no sure eternity; women worshippers who ignominiously collapse to the ground in weariness and exhaustion.

Oddly, Irigaray adopts a position close to that of *one* of the Nietzsches, namely, the medi-cynical Nietzsche who fears and derides the Maenads. "I know these lovable Maenads. . . . Ah, what dangerous, insidious, subterranean little predators! And so pleasant all the while!" (KSA 6:306; cf. EH p. 266). Yet there is another Nietzsche, one who is closer to the Maenadic throng, and whom Irigaray herself resists. This other Nietzsche embraces the message of the one who has seen the women, rather than the fantasies of the solar-aerial King who fears them: in one of the unpublished essays surrounding *The Birth of Tragedy* Nietzsche tells us that the women unite in their midday dream extreme sensitivity and passionate suffering with "the most luminous contemplativeness and perspicacity" (KSA 1:591; cf. KSA 1:31, 555–56, and 583). The only life they will destroy is that of Pentheus, who resists and oppresses them. Pentheus is of course the first cousin of the god—for their mothers are sisters—and is himself the next reincarnation of Dionysus. The god is always doubled, masked, and remarked, and always from his mortal mother's side. True, it is the mourning (*πένθ[ε]ος*) that Irigaray objects to, the sense of loss that surrounds the god from the moment of his violent birth: "But the primitive whole is already destroyed. And Dionysus shows more signs of sadness confronting that disappearance than of rejoicing in a new harmony" (p. 139; p. 131). And it is his mourning, she says, that drives the women to distraction: "From him to whom they give life, they receive death. If he is son of the God. For now the women kill the little children of simple mortals, in their madness" (p. 151; p. 142). To repeat, however, the only child the women kill is Pentheus, "mourning," and Irigaray's opposition to the Maenads is startlingly close to that of the proud, doomed patriarch.

By what were the Maenads seduced away from the sea? By the mountain wine—away from the wine-dark sea? By the flowers and herbs inland? By the statue of Pan, not yet toppled? By the thyrsos, wound in ribbons and ivy? By the phallus? Thus commences the kettle logic of seduction—a seduction that is both impossible and inevitable. What can never have interrupted the intrinsic self-embrace of the lips except by sheer extrinsic violence now becomes *seductive,* invading from the *inside,* as it were, and thus contaminating the perfection of the female inside/outside. Whence the fifth-column phallus? It is carved from driftwood, which is wood of the sea, supposedly. Whence the potency of the phallus, whence its power to seduce creatures who are perfect without it? Its potency too is from the sea, presumably, the sea that long ago left its calcareous mark on the alluvial mountain.

> Since he is not yet a god, Dionysus shows the way. And one of his favored masks is the phallus. Carved out of hard wood, supposedly taken from the sea.
>
> Mask of birthing [*génération*]? Supernatural birthing? Of desire? One already modeled by the law of the Father of the gods? Effigy of love among the living (men) [*vivants*]? Interdict of happy relations with mortal women? Petrified potency fished out [*repêchée*] of the great depths after the mother's murder?
>
> Power that still shows its ambiguity. Phallic Dionysus grants drunkenness [*ivresse*] and ecstasy. Calls beyond. Sets absence within and

> between bodies. Desire becomes an exodus toward death, sign of its approach. Erection commemorating its fulfillment. A monument to crime in its cadaveric stiffness, fascination of a ghost [*revenant*] that is/is not in the depths, evanescent rising of one who survives only in the anxiety of disappearing, in the terror of vengeance. The mask covers the whole thing over—in a format larger than life. (pp. 141–42; p. 133)

Each word resounds with ambivalence, even where massive univocity seems to prevail: the proscription of the phallus, which always and everywhere is ruinous of "happy relations with mortal women," *all* mortal women, differences in preference or taste or individuality notwithstanding; ostracism of the Maenads, who are revoltingly drunk with the god's juice, besotted, beside themselves; erection, with its deadly entelechy, its fulfillment in inevitable demise. The erect penis, itself insecure and anxious, donning the brave phallic mask, is declared outlaw, criminal, and cadaverous—in view of its very rigor, not to say vigor. The sea-lover finds the driftwood dry, and pours contumely upon it:

> In wetness the seed of the living (men) [*la semence des vivants*] finds its fecundation. Not in phallic erection, its mask. Frozen parodic appropriation. Where one believes the seed resides, although it does not. Always under every surface, in the fluid depths. Short of any form that is already visible. Short of or beyond all erection. Sterile.
>
> Except for the seduction in drunkenness [*la séduction dans l'ivresse*]. Involving ecstasy—outside the body. Summoning dance and music. Recalling and forgetting the flesh as it remains in the movement of its becoming. The rhythm is too fast and goes beyond the natural beat [*la mesure naturelle*]. Exaltation that tears away from the roots. Attracts one out of the self, upward. Finding a place high up, on the very peak. Coming to it by moving away from it. Having no element but the one that exaltation opens up at the peak of its elevation. Always ecstatic. Always beyond one's own body. Always in exile from one's own completeness. (pp. 145–46; p. 137)

Why contumely, when wetness is desired? Why the arid, scathing sarcasm of "frozen parodic appropriation"? To what does the isolated word *sterile* refer? What will keep that word in its place? The phallus dependably impotent and without possible effect. A sort of dildo, the "woman's best companion," advertised in the back pages of magazines. Risible. "Except for the seduction in drunkenness." Why this exception? Why the biblical anathematization of drunkenness? "Summoning music and dance," as though to Geneva, for trial. The messenger, however, says that the women are not drunk, not in their cups, not sloppy, not witless, as the King imagines them to be. Why the insistence that Maenadic ecstasy is *outside* the body? Uprooted from their native soil—a soil, to be sure, that belongs to the sea only in catachresis? Why the presumption that every woman's body, once it is infected by wine or by the phantasm or fluid of the phallus, once it tastes exaltation, can be denigrated in this prescriptive way? Who says there is no Socrates among the women, the imbibing yet serene Socrates portrayed by Alcibiades? Who dictates the rhythm of becoming? Who possesses the measure of the "natural beat"? Whose is the Mariological wisdom that will appropriate all nature and propound the measure? Who will prohibit ecstasy or restrict it within bounds, the oneiric bounds of "one's own completeness"?

Nothing is less certain, according to contemporary archaeologists and classicists generally, than the intoxication and frenzy imputed to the Maenads. Nothing is less certain than the effects of the phallus on the women worshipers of Dionysus. It is therefore not surprising to find at least one contemporary classicist who goes even farther than Euripides' shepherd messenger in shattering the assumption that the Bacchants have been driven out of their minds and morals: "Maenads are inviolable . . . as chaste as they are sober." Furthermore, there is "no symmetry of masculine and feminine around Dionysus: it seems that when a woman is associated with the *phallos,* she is not Dionysiac, and when she is Dionysiac, she is not associated with the *phallos.*"[12]

If one thinks through the disconcerting association of Irigaray with Pentheus—both of whom challenge Dionysus because of his putative reduction of woman to an alienated plaything of (masculine) desire, outside herself, a fish out of water, gasping on the strand—one arrives at the doublings, duplicities, and double binds of what one might call *Pentheic projection.* Can one utter *anything* about the god and "his" effects on "the women" without holding up the mirror of Dionysus to oneself—to one's own fragmented, distorted, and distorting self? Would not one be less likely than ever to shoot arrows, or throw boomerangs, at such projected images?

"One's own completeness"? Whose completeness, in the mirror play of whose dreams? Always the claim of perfection, plenitude, self-embrace. Always the concomitant condemnation of ecstasy. Always insistence on the *interiority* of one's own womanly body, sufficient unto itself, untouchable and impenetrable, as inconcussible as the truth of the cogito. Always the return to the allegorical island-fortress of metaphysics. Always the accusation of crime committed by the (readily identifiable, always selfsame) other and the victimization of oneself. And the cry, Pity me, Pity me who nevertheless am invincible, except when I am drunk or doing kettle logic. Pity me—and feel the piercing of my arrows. Shot without ressentiment.

Always the arrows—arrows such as these, these very arrows here, in these very words of mine now—shot back in anger and frustration and anxiety. As though refutation could touch erotic difference(s).

Who owns the phallus? Need it always be desiccated? Need it always be surface elevation, without depth? Why does Irigaray never mention the niches carved into the wood, niches containing figurines, niches that certainly would have fascinated all the Nietzsches? Doesn't contumely aggravate the desiccation that creates the brave mask, the hated phallic scepter and dildonic verge? Is it not possible, or even quite likely, that the tumescent organ of the man is the creation of woman, born of the wet, maintained—insofar as it ever can be maintained—by the wet? Does not that organ too bespeak the brine, stammer of the salt sea? Never an architectonic erection, never the phallic edifice, never a mask that is not a molding of multiple hands and mouths. Perhaps Lacan is right when he says that the cock of the walk is a woman. It isn't always easy to make clear-cut gender divisions in matters of eggs and lips, buttons and stems, depths and surfaces, and liquids that smack of the sea. Only the bird's-eye view, only the aerial view, would ever try to distinguish what the sea is happy to commingle.

They say that when Nietzsche celebrated his fiftieth birthday in 1894 Paul Deussen came to visit. He brought chrysanthemums and chocolates, and Nietzsche's mother lit the candles on the cake. Nietzsche himself had trouble concentrating. At the word *birthday* he could only think of three things: one of the final sets of page proofs he had corrected, proofs of a text he had begun to write on his forty-fourth birthday, the last birthday he could really remember, mixed up with memories of a much earlier time when he felt very close to Jesus, realizing that Jesus was in some sense the credulous son of a prison warden, and, finally, mixed up with phantasms of what he called "birthing." It was all muddled in his head. Proofs. Jesus. Birthing. Mums. He would have wanted to jot it all down in his fictional autobiography. Proofs and mums and chocolates. He remembered too a woman who used to visit him in secret many years before, somewhere in Italy, somewhere near the sea where he bathed and the smell of oranges. It was now the fifth year of his insanity, everything was higgledy-piggledy and yet oddly, intensely, unbearably focused, everything in uncanny repose. Sometimes you have to get that muddled before you can think clearly about the sea-lover.

happy birthday to me pouring over page proofs. my way of birthing. i wrote very beautiful things once upon a time mama i kept working on them until they were printed and even while they were being printed because i loved the smell of paper and ink intoxicating mama. it was like birthing. read me some of them dont be shy i know that secretly when no one is watching you admire them. open one of them mama and read to me in the night when no one is there to interrupt us birthing. it can happen more than once mama birthing and it can happen backwards in reverse. getting your tongue around the words. corinna calina i dont remember very well the stiffening stiffens my memory. i was writing it was evening no not yet evening i remember the late afternoon sun slanting in through the window on my left i was writing about what i dont remember wait a prison and the warden that was my father mama and the son thats what i was writing with great joy smoothly easily even though calina corinna i dont remember was there all that afternoon in ree myself. she was no longer singing not even humming softly as she always did just sitting quietly i didnt even notice her mama giving birth parturing me and what i was writing making me her own son not the wardens son i dont know how she did it i cant remember i can only see the oblique rays redorange lighting laving her skin it was all she wore mama sitting on a hardwood straight-backed chair pressed up against the whitewashed wall. nice? no. rapallo? no. portofino? i dont know. fino molto fino italia somewhere in ree. sitting slouching ever so slightly mama her head turned hard to the right away from the sun her gaze relentless on the floor. rose marble. that place near naples with ree in ree malwida and brenner consumption all consuming in the orange grove yes that was it the smell of ink and oranges not nice at all not rapallo not portofino not torino it will come back to me in a moment mama. her inky hair in careless tresses hanging the uneven tips of it brushing the swollen indolent brown nipples near naples yes chocolates mamas huge puffy bittersweet setting suns burning in the late afternoon sun. she paid me no mind i was writing she was birthing me and my writing it came so smoothly so easily the warden and his only begotten son no not capri not ligure not levanto i cant remember i see only corinna calina her slouch her gaze fixed averted her hands lopped lazily over her raised knees opening like the wings of a butterfly in the warm rees of the afternoon sun. her heels poised on the very edge of that straightbacked hardwood chair her feet wide apart each foot pointing down and away the long delicate toes the second toe much longer than the big toe beside it botticelli feet corinna calina i cant for the stiffening neck the throbbing head mama cant remember anything now not mesopotamia not messina not sicily not acragas empedocles agrigentum not herculaneum ashes cast in plaster i looked up from my writing just as the wardens son was suffering the jeers of the prisoners disbelief looked up and over to her she was absent to me to herself hands draped hands so beautifully busy before mama now like the folded wings of a swan vain and languorous the bubs of swollen unmistakable for anything else flesh and below the cupped weight and swagger of breasts her belly folding in the slouch and sloth of bellybutton omphalos center of the earth the great cleft beneath tartaros the burning black bush where moses put down his rosen steel tip pen replaced the rubber stopper in the inkbottle pushed back the cane chair it creaked and scraped the floor she never moved her head mama hardright the tendon at the base of her throat distended taut an animal would have seized her there what am i mama im not an animal am i but without moving her head without hinting she might have heard the creak and scrape heard my noiseless tread felt it through the floor of roses and slowly infinitely slowly lowered her hands between her knees her thighs and joined thumb to thumb and index to index forming a diamond windowframe about her smiling notmouth her notclosed lips her ragged gaping vertical smile no thorns no agave mother do you know it only colors more colors in the redorange burntsienna light no not sienna than ever were in the white incandescence of noon the purple veins almost jetblack. sparkle of sequins dans la saison des fleurs. i was on my knees now mama i was as close as birthing mama not yet praying not yet whispering no longer writing only seeing rapt observant inquisitive beholding the infinitesimal porphyry veins of the rose wall wet with the underground spring the font of castalia corinna calina kali phosphoricum trimethylamin all the walls watery wet with lambent mother of pearl opal of seawash breath of brine and orangeblossom birthing it was the same flow as writing mama descrying where the setting sun could penetrate no longer she was sinking now in the ponient waters nothing there in that noplace was dark not even at the crease where the light glistened but could not penetrate no dark beneath the scrub i would have thought there was dark there mama but there was no dark until i closed my eyes and my head went into the gesture of reception like the boys and girls at the communion rail in the italian churches mama tasting god and for a very long time i was not afraid i was not anything or anywhere to be seen my face in a world that gave way but never budged withdrew but never retreated surrendered but never capitulated a face that never denied or abnegated never affirmed or asserted anything but only sighed hissed yes yes yes yes. birthing. happy birthing. i slake no horses. i can remember nothing mama not rimini not deiva marina not serendipity not papi not sorella read to me o please mama what i wrote birthing read me remind me because i am on the very verge of remembering without being able in the end to remember calina corinna whatever became of you sorella how can you not be here when i am there now again yes here and now in mind and mouth of you in not even surrender sorrento yes sorrento of course it was sorrento the orange grove outside the house above the bay perfume of oranges rising off the page on the haze of evening overpowering even the fragrance of the sea the grotto the cavern where — — — sorrento dido the orange fire smoldering into purple night and i was lost at sea the wardens son no more i was an other that orangeblossom evening pledging endless inky promises yes yes yes yes sorella sorrento.

Notes

I would like to thank Ashley Carr for her help in preparing the manuscript.

1. David Farrell Krell, *Postponements: Woman, Sensuality, and Death in Nietzsche* (Bloomington: Indiana Univ. Press, 1986). I came to know of Luce Irigaray's book (through the kindness of Gary Shapiro) only when my own book was in print—time enough only to extract an epigraph (*Postponements*, p. 71). In the remarks that follow I will refer to both the French and English versions of her remarkable book—*Amante marine: De Friedrich Nietzsche* (Paris: Minuit, 1980); *Marine Lover of Friedrich Nietzsche*, trans. Gillian C. Gill (New York: Columbia Univ. Press, 1991). I will quote from the published translation, with some modifications; citations will be by page number without any further designation, first the French, then the English.

2. Gaston Bachelard, *L'Air et les songes: Essai sur l'imagination du mouvement* (Paris: José Corti, 1943).

3. On Nietzsche and the mole, see my "Der Maulwurf: Die philosophische Wühlarbeit bei Kant, Hegel und Nietzsche," in *Why Nietzsche Now?* ed. Daniel T. O'Hara (Bloomington: Indiana Univ. Press, 1985), pp. 155–85.

4. See my "Descensional Reflection," in *Philosophy and Archaic Experience: Essays in Honor of Edward G. Ballard,* ed. John Sallis (Pittsburgh: Duquesne Univ. Press, 1982), pp. 3–12; see also my "Heidegger, Nietzsche, Hegel: An Essay in Descensional Reflection," in *Nietzsche-Studien* 5 (1976): 255–62.

5. See Jacques Derrida, "La pharmacie de Platon," in *Dissémination* (Paris: Seuil, 1972), especially sections 2 and 3. I have discussed this heliocentrism in chapter 4 of my *Of Memory, Reminscence, and Writing: On the Verge* (Bloomington: Indiana Univ. Press, 1990), especially pp. 187–204.

6. See the response to *Postponements* by Kelly Oliver in *International Studies in Philosophy* 22, no. 1 (1990): 118–19.

7. Pierre Klossowski, *Nietzsche et le cercle vicieux* (Paris: Mercure de France, 1969), p. 260. Birthing himself anew, taking his life into his own hands: such would be the obsessive reading of an obsessional phrase in *Ecce Homo:* "I now have it in hand, I have the hand for it. . . . I took myself in hand" (KSA 6:266; cf. EH pp. 223–24).

8. Gabriel García Márquez, *One Hundred Years of Solitude,* trans. Gregory Rabassa (London: Jonathan Cape, 1970), p. 422.

9. Leo Steinberg, *The Sexuality of Christ in Renaissance Art and in Modern Oblivion* (New York: Pantheon/October Books, 1983).

10. See Gilles Deleuze, *Nietzsche et la philosophie* (Paris: Presses Universitaires de France, 1962), pp. 16–24, 199, 213–22; see also his more recent reflections on Ariadne, summarized in his "Mystère d'Ariane," *Magazine littéraire* 298 (April 1992): 21–24. As far as I can see, these more recent reflections dissolve none of the dilemmas I discussed in *Postponements,* pp. 28–31.

11. Luce Irigaray, *L'Oubli de l'air, chez Martin Heidegger* (Paris: Minuit, 1983). I have discussed this remarkable text in chapter 9 of my *Daimon Life: Heidegger and Life-Philosophy* (Bloomington: Indiana Univ. Press, 1992). On the Empedoclean dramas of Nietzsche and Hölderlin, see my "Nietzsche Hölderlin Empedocles," *Graduate Faculty Philosophy Journal* 15, no. 2 (1991): 31–48, and "Stuff—Thread—Point—Fire: Hölderlin's Memory of Tragic Dissolution in the Theoretical Writings of 1795–1800," forthcoming in my *Lunar Voices: Of Tragedy, Poetry, Fiction, and Thought.*

12. François Lissarrague, "The Sexual Life of Satyrs," in *Before Sexuality: The Construction of Erotic Experience in the Ancient Greek World,* ed. David M. Halperin, John J. Winkler, and Froma I. Zeitlin (Princeton: Princeton Univ. Press, 1990), pp. 63, 65–66. In this same collection, see the excellent article by Anne Carson, "Putting Her in Her Place: Woman, Dirt, and Desire," pp. 135–69.

ALAN D. SCHRIFT

On the Gynecology of Morals: Nietzsche and Cixous on the Logic of the Gift

A gift-giving virtue is the highest virtue.

—Nietzsche, *Thus Spoke Zarathustra*

Desire knows nothing of exchange, *it knows only theft and gift.*

—Deleuze and Guattari, *Anti-Oedipus*

Who could ever think of the gift as a gift-that-takes? Who else but man, precisely the one who would like to take everything?

—Cixous, "The Laugh of the Medusa"

Gynecology, the *logia* of the *gynaeco,* can mean either the science of women or the discourse of women. It is the latter sense, with its double genitive uncertainty, that I wish to recall in the title of this paper, although the punning on the title of one of Nietzsche's most important texts is not meant only to suggest that women speak differently about morals than do men.[1] This point has been at the center of the feminist challenges to the traditional discourses of ethics since the appearance of Carol Gilligan's *In a Different Voice* if not before.[2] Rather than focus on morals, I want instead to address an issue raised in the works of Hélène Cixous, among others, namely, that women speak and think differently about economies (libidinal, textual, political) than do men. In addressing this issue, whose scope and importance far exceeds what can be discussed adequately in a short paper, I will focus on several points concerning exchange and appropriation in an effort to show how Cixous develops certain insights that exist in germinal form in Nietzsche's works.

I should say at the outset that in the following remarks, I do not intend to discuss Nietzsche's various comments about women, "woman" or the "feminine." Whether or not Nietzsche's comments are themselves misogynistic is not an issue I will address, although I will confess that many of his remarks on women and his frequent use of "feminine" as a defamatory qualifier are, to say the least, disturbing. That one can paint a picture of Nietzsche as a misogynist is clear. And it is equally clear that one can construct an interpretation that explains, or explains away, many of the most offensive of Nietzsche's remarks about women.[3] In the present discussion, I am interested neither in condemning Nietzsche's misogyny nor apologizing for it. Such efforts, when done well, can be useful and important. My interest in "Nietzsche and the feminine" lies elsewhere. It has long been recognized that Nietzsche, whose perspectives can at times be those of the worst of nineteenth-century prejudices, is also able to give voice to insights that now a century later are still at the forefront of critical reflection. Rather than look at Nietzsche's remarks on women, I want instead to explore a theme in Nietzsche's works to which insufficient attention has been paid. This theme pertains to a possible distinction between what one might call a masculine and a feminine economy, and the locus of this distinction is centered around different ways to understand property, appropriation, generosity, exchange—what I am here calling the logic of the gift. Although not specifically connected to gender in Nietzsche's texts, setting Nietzsche's discussion of gifts and giftgiving alongside Cixous's will highlight what one might want to regard as an unacknowledged feminine side of Nietzsche's economic discourse. By examining the exchange model and the definition of subjectivity in terms of the acquisition of property that accompanies this model, and experimenting with another model based on an economy of generosity that in different ways is suggested by both Nietzsche and Cixous, we will be addressing issues whose importance extends far beyond the margins of these particular authors' texts. It is in part toward proceeding with this thought-experiment, imagining what intersubjective relations might look like if grounded on practices of generosity rather than reciprocal exchange, that the present paper seeks to put Nietzsche and Cixous into dialogue.

"The great book of modern ethnology," Deleuze and Guattari write in *Anti-Oedipus*, "is not so much Mauss's *The Gift* as Nietzsche's *On the Genealogy of Morals*."[4] In the second essay of the *Genealogy*, Nietzsche turns to the origins of guilt and bad conscience and, in so doing, he offers his own "myth" of human beings' departure from the "state of nature." "The oldest and most primitive personal relationship," Nietzsche writes, is "that between buyer and seller, creditor and debtor" (KSA 5:305–6;

GM—II §8, p. 70). The moral concept "guilt," conceived as a debt that is essentially unredeemable, has its origin in the economic-legal notion of a debt as something that can and should be repaid. We can see this in the origin of punishment, which as retribution emerges from the inability to repay the debt. Because " 'everything has its price [and] *all* things can be paid for' " (KSA 5:306; GM—II §8, p. 70), the debtors, having made a promise to repay and now being unable to make that payment directly, are obligated to offer a substitute payment of something they possess: their body, their spouse, their freedom, even their life. *Schuld,* debt/guilt, thus operates within a strange logic of compensation which seeks to establish equivalences between the creditor and the debtor.

Like guilt, obligation, and punishment, Nietzsche also sees the origin of justice residing in the relationship between creditor and debtor. This primitive contractual relationship made possible the comparative evaluation of relative worth, and the focus on the perspective of measured value allowed primitive society to arrive at "the oldest and naïvest moral canon of *justice* [*Gerechtigkeit*], the beginning of all 'good-naturedness,' all 'fairness,' all 'good will,' all 'objectivity' on earth" (KSA 5:306; GM—II §8, p. 70)—the *jus talionis:* "an eye for an eye." In the preface to the *Genealogy,* Nietzsche refers us to several passages in his earlier works where he treats subjects to which he here returns. One of these, entitled "*The Origin of Justice* [*Ursprung der Gerechtigkeit*]," offers a succinct summary of Nietzsche's view of the egoistic and economic origin of justice:

> Justice (fairness) originates between parties of approximately *equal power*. . . : where there is no clearly recognizable superiority of force and a contest would result in mutual injury producing no decisive outcome the idea arises of coming to an understanding and negotiating over one another's demands: the characteristic of *exchange* is the original characteristic of justice. Each satisfies the other, inasmuch as each acquires what he values more than the other does. One gives to the other what he wants to have, to be henceforth his own, and in return receives what one oneself desires. Justice is thus requital and exchange under the presupposition of an approximately equal power position: revenge therefore belongs originally within the domain of justice, it is an exchange. Gratitude likewise. (KSA 2:89; HH §92, p. 49)

This initial canon of justice, based on economic principles of universal exchange and equivalency, gave rise to communities that operated on the assumption that equal settlements between individuals were always possible and morally obligatory.

The evolution of society saw the creditor-debtor relationship extended from a moral guideline among individuals to the standard that dictated the relationship between individuals and the community itself. The community stands in relation to its members as a creditor to its debtors (KSA 5:307; GM—II §9, p. 71), and to break the laws of the community will entail a future payment of that debt (punishment understood as "a debt paid to society"). In primitive, insecure, and unstable societies, Nietzsche claims, debts had to be repaid in accordance with the primitive canon of justice, the *jus talionis*. But as a community gained in strength, he sees emerging a new notion of justice. The creditor, now confident of its wealth/strength, might measure its wealth precisely in terms of how much injury it could endure without suffering and feeling the compulsion to respond. The self-overcoming of the old model of justice that demanded equal payment for debts incurred has "given itself a beautiful name—*mercy* [*Gnade*]": "It is not unthinkable that a society might attain such a *consciousness of power* that it could allow itself the noblest luxury possible to it—letting those who harm it go *unpunished*. 'What are my parasites to me?' it might say. 'May they live and prosper: I am strong enough for that!' The justice which began with 'everything is dischargeable, everything must be discharged,' ends by winking and letting those incapable of discharging their debt go free; it ends, as does every good thing on earth, by *overcoming itself*" (KSA 5:309; GM—II §10, pp. 72–73).

This image of strength as the ability to actively forget and forgive the debts one is owed, to endure petty injury without reacting, to withhold punishment, is a recurring image in Nietzsche's texts. Earlier in the *Genealogy*, it is offered as a fundamental contrast to ressentiment. The men of ressentiment react negatively to external conditions, but lacking the strength to act, they are forced to take refuge in the imagination. Unable to act, and unable to forget the "harm" done to them by the outside, ressentiment festers in the weak and poisons their thinking. When they are finally prompted to create, these men of ressentiment can only create a system of diseased values that reflects their decadent desires. On the other hand, when ressentiment does appear in noble and strong individuals, and it does on rare occasions, its harmfulness is mitigated by their ability to act directly. But what is more likely the case with noble individuals is that ressentiment does not appear at all because they have the strength to actively forget what displeases them: "To be incapable of taking one's enemies, one's accidents, even one's misdeeds seriously for very long—that is the sign of strong, full natures in whom there is an excess of power to form, to mold, to recuperate, and to forget" (KSA 5:273; GM—I §10, p. 39).

This strength to forget will promote the "deliverance from revenge" which Zarathustra teaches is "the bridge to the highest hope" (KSA 4:128;

Z p. 211). Where the preachers of equality proclaim the necessity of revenge, Zarathustra teaches that "to *me,* justice speaks thus: 'Men are not equal.' Nor shall they become equal! What would my love of the *Übermensch* be if I spoke otherwise?" (KSA 4:130; Z p. 213). In *Daybreak,* Nietzsche envisions a time when revenge and the law of equal return will no longer be the principle of justice to which society appeals: "At present, to be sure, he who has been injured, irrespective of how this injury is to be made good, will still desire his *revenge* and will turn for it to the courts—and for the time being the courts continue to maintain our detestable criminal codes with their shopkeeper's scales and the *desire to counterbalance guilt with punishment:* but can we not get beyond this?" (KSA 3:177; D §202, p. 121). To overcome the old instinct for revenge, and with it to get rid of the concepts of sin and punishment, will be for Nietzsche a sign of the health of a community. A healthy community will be characterized not by revenge but by generosity, which will be evaluated "according to how many parasites it can endure" (KSA 3:178; D §202, p. 122).[5]

To summarize the preceding discussion, we find Nietzsche isolating two types of economy that give rise to two types of justice. The lower, baser, slave economy is grounded on the law of equal returns: justice demands that all debts be paid in kind; the creditor is not capable of forgetting the debt, and the debtor is obliged to return some equivalent form of payment. This notion of justice, exhibited in the *jus talionis,* operates in those societies whose economies depend on rules of exchange. Nietzsche's theorizing, in fact, is supported by the account provided by Marcel Mauss's *Essai sur le don:* a "genuine," "free," "unencumbered" gift is not possible.[6] Instead, gifts are given in a social setting whose "rules" obligate the receiver to return the gift in kind, that is, to offer in return a countergift of equivalent value. This does not conflate giftgiving with barter, however, for the former has an essential diachronic dimension (the passage of some determinate amount of time) which the latter lacks. Nevertheless, the principle of equivalent exchange underlies and makes possible the transactions in either a barter or a giftgiving relationship.

The higher, nobler economy that Nietzsche sketches is based on a fundamentally different principle, one closer to what Bataille called a "general economy" of "expenditure" than to a simple, restricted exchange economy.[7] Nietzsche's higher economy is one grounded in excess strength sufficient to squander its resources if it so chooses. In the foreground of this noble economy "is the feeling of fullness, of power that seeks to overflow, the happiness of high tension, the consciousness of wealth that would give [*schenken*] and bestow [*abgeben*]: the noble human being, too, helps the unfortunate, but not, or almost not, from pity, but prompted more by an urge begotten by excess of power [*Überfluss von Macht*]" (KSA 5:209–10; BGE §260, p. 205). In this economy, gifts can be given without expectation of return and debts can be forgiven without penalty or shame.[8] Justice here can but need not demand repayment; tempered with mercy, it is empowered to forgive and forget what it is due. We see this higher justice and "general economy" most clearly at two points in Nietzsche's texts: in the relationships between Zarathustra and those to whom he offers his teachings and in the relationship between Nietzsche and the readers to whom he offers his texts.

When Zarathustra first goes down from his cave to rejoin humanity, like the bee that has gathered too much honey or the cup that wants to overflow, he is overfull and needs to locate those to whom he can bring the gift of his teaching (see Z—Prologue §§1–3). Initially, as the hermit who meets him along the way predicted, Zarathustra encounters only those who are suspicious of the gifts he brings. Soon enough the situation changes, however. Zarathustra quickly comes to stand in relation to his followers as a giver of gifts, and his followers are only too eager to receive his teachings as gifts from on high. But unlike his followers, Zarathustra knows the dangers involved in giftgiving, for the receivers of gifts often feel beholden to the one who gave to them. Zarathustra thus cautions:

> Great indebtedness does not make men grateful, but vengeful; and if a little charity is not forgotten, it turns into a gnawing worm.
>
> "Be reserved in accepting! Distinguish by accepting!" Thus I advise those who have nothing to give.
>
> But I am a giver of gifts: I like to give, as a friend to friends. Strangers, however, and the poor may themselves pluck the fruit from my tree: that will cause them less shame. (KSA 4:114; Z p. 201)

To be able to give gifts rightly is an "*art* [*Kunst*]" (see KSA 4:333–37; Z pp. 380–84), and great care and skill are required in order to prevent feelings of indebtedness in the receivers. One repays one's teacher badly if one remains only a student, Zarathustra tells his followers in his speech "On the Gift-Giving Virtue" at the end of part 1, as he urges them to lose him and find themselves (KSA 4:101; Z p. 186). To remain a student is to return the teacher's gifts in kind, either by simple obedience to the teacher's lessons or by presenting the teacher with a comparable gift in return. Neither response takes the gift freely and with forgetfulness of its origin, neither receives the gift with mercy (*Erbarmen*). For Zarathustra, overfull with wisdom, giving is a necessity (*Nothdurft*) (see KSA 4:279; Z

p. 335), and while his followers will return eternally to the words of their teacher, the return on Zarathustra's gifts will not return to him. "I do not know the happiness of those who receive. . . . This is my poverty, that my hand never rests from giving" (KSA 4:136; Z p. 218). His gift, to be sure, is an investment, but an investment in a future that he will not share and from which he will not derive profit.

We see a similar relationship exhibited with respect to the "presents" Nietzsche gives to his readers in the form of his texts. With *Thus Spoke Zarathustra,* Nietzsche "has given humanity the greatest present [*das grösste Geschenk*] that has ever been made to it so far" (KSA 6:259; EH—P §4, p. 219*). In the preface to *Ecce Homo,* Nietzsche refers to his texts of the last quarter of 1888 (*The Antichrist, Twilight of the Idols, Dionysus Dithyrambs*) as "presents" (*Geschenke*), and *Ecce Homo* itself is a present Nietzsche makes to himself on the occasion of his forty-fourth birthday. What is to be done with these presents? Are they to be returned to their author in the same condition that he delivered them? Or are they to be made use of, not to be returned but to be put to use in the production of other gifts? For Nietzsche, the goal of the writer is to stimulate, not to be consumed: "We honor the great artists of the past less through that unfruitful awe which allows every word, every note, to lie where it has been put than we do through active endeavors to help them to come repeatedly to life again" (KSA 2:431–32; HH—"Assorted Opinions and Maxims" §126, p. 242). Good philosophical writing should inspire one to action and, Nietzsche writes, "I consider every word behind which there does not stand such a challenge to action to have been written in vain" (KSA 1:413; UM p. 184). Nietzsche does not so much want to be understood as to incite. His writings are incendiary devices: he speaks "no longer with words but with lightning bolts" (KSA 6:320; EH p. 281). He seeks readers who will not be mere consumers of his texts but experimenters (*Versucher*), "monster[s] of courage and curiosity; moreover, supple, cunning, cautious; born adventurer[s] and discoverer[s]" (KSA 6:303; EH p. 264). He seeks, in other words, to free his readers from the constraints of a textual economy that demands that they occupy a place as passive beneficiary/consumer of the text rather than its active coproducer. Which is to say, he seeks to write within a textual economy that does not guarantee the author any return on his or her gift as it is disseminated through an intertextual field.[9]

To write, and live, within a textual/libidinal/political economy freed from the constraints of the law of return is part of Hélène Cixous's vision of a postpatriarchal future, and Cixous's comments bring to the fore a "feminine" side of Nietzsche's economic reflections.[10] Cixous suggests we distinguish between two kinds of economies, two kinds of writing, two kinds of spending, two kinds of giving. One, grounded on the law of return, finds its philosophical justification in Locke's definition of property in chapter five of the *Second Treatise of Government:* one possesses and has a right to as one's private property whatever "he removes out of the state that nature hath provided and left it in [and] he hath mixed his labor with." This account of property and the practices which it underwrites find themselves instantiated throughout what has counted as "History." The other set of practices, only recently voiced, also has a long history, but one that has until recently not been acknowledged "publicly" because it only concerned "women." To be sure, Nietzsche does not acknowledge the practices of this other economy as feminine. In fact, on those few occasions when he does engender his economic reflections, more often than not and in the most traditional of ways, he associates giving with the feminine and possession with the masculine, as for example when he writes that man has a "lust for possession" and man's "love consists of wanting to *have* and not of renunciation and giving away," while "woman gives herself away" and "wants to be taken and accepted as a possession" (KSA 3:611–12; GS §363, pp. 319–20). Nevertheless, Cixous does obliquely connect her remarks to Nietzsche's through the mediating effect of Jacques Derrida. In "The Laugh of the Medusa," upon introducing "the whole deceptive problematic of the gift," she suggests in a footnote that the reader "re-read Derrida's text, 'Le Style de la femme.' "[11] Of particular significance to Cixous is Derrida's identifying the gift, in Nietzsche, as "the essential predicate of woman,"[12] and she, like several other feminists who have written "on" Derrida, brings to our attention gifts and giftgiving as a central and recurrent Derridean theme from *Spurs: Nietzsche's Styles,*[13] where the gift is linked specifically to "woman," to *The Post Card,* in which Derrida addresses issues surrounding giving and the gift in terms of *envois* and their failure to arrive at their destinations, the giving and return of the *fort/da* in Freud, the giving/theft of the letter in Poe, and the *es gibt* of *Sein* and *Ereignis* in Heidegger.[14]

According to Cixous, current economic realities operate within what she calls "*L'Empire du Propre,*" the "Empire of the Selfsame/Proper."[15] She identifies the philosophical underpinnings of this empire with Hegel, who in the *Phenomenology of Spirit* framed the fundamental relationship between self and other in terms of the acquisition of property: the subject goes "out into the other *in order to come back* to itself."[16] The phallocentric desire that animates the Hegelian dialectic of self and other is a desire for appropriation: one confronts the other as different and unequal and one seeks to make the other one's own. The desire to possess, to receive a return on one's investments, animates an economy that Cixous suggests we call "masculine," in part because it "is erected from a fear that, in fact, is typically masculine"—the fear of castration—"the fear of expropriation, of separation, of losing the attribute" (*NBW*, p. 80). Cixous summarizes her point succinctly in the following remark:

> Etymologically, the "proper" is "property," that which is not separable from me. Property is proximity, nearness: we must love our neighbors, those close to us, as ourselves: we must draw close to the other so that we may love him/her, because we love ourselves most of all. The realm of the proper, culture, functions by the appropriation articulated, set into play, by man's classic fear of seeing himself expropriated, seeing himself deprived . . . by his refusal to be deprived, in a state of separation, by his fear of losing the prerogative, fear whose response is all of History. Everything must return to the masculine. "Return": the economy is founded on a system of returns. If a man spends and is spent, it's on condition that his power returns. If a man should go out to the other, it's always done according to the Hegelian model, the model of the master-slave dialectic.[17]

Economies of the *propre,* proper economies, economies based on the possession of private property, are structured around the fear of loss, the fear of losing what is already possessed. The fear of expropriation thus drives the desire for appropriation which Cixous designates with the qualifier "masculine." This designation, she quickly adds, does not name the biological male, and to speak of "masculine" or "feminine" economies is not to fall into essentialism. "Words like 'masculine' and 'feminine' that circulate everywhere and that are completely distorted in everyday usage,—words which refer, of course, to a classical vision of sexual opposition between men and women—are our burden, that is what burdens us. As I often said, my work in fact aims at getting rid of words like 'feminine' and 'masculine,' 'femininity' and 'masculinity,' even 'man' and 'woman,' which designate that which cannot be classified inside of a signifier except by force and violence and which goes beyond it in any case."[18] She is sometimes led to speak of "the *so-called feminine economy*" in order to indicate that women do not necessarily operate according to this type of economy. In fact, "one can find these two economies in no matter which individual."[19] For this reason Cixous herself prefers the language of bisexuality, "that is to say, the location within oneself of the presence of both sexes, evident and insistent in different ways according to the individual, the nonexclusion of difference or of a sex" (*NBW*, p. 85).

Although she prefers the language of bisexuality and she frequently cautions against the dangers of resorting to the classical binaries of feminine/masculine or femininity/masculinity, she continues nevertheless to use the qualifiers "masculine" and "feminine" in reference to economies because "the (political) economy of the masculine and the feminine is organized by different demands and constraints, which, as they become socialized and metaphorized, produce signs, relations of power, relationships of production and reproduction, a whole huge system of cultural inscription that is legible as masculine or feminine" (*NBW*, pp. 80–81). Guided by the prime directive to appropriate, what a masculine economy is not truly capable of is giving. Inscribed under the law of return, the masculine gift expects, nay demands a return, as Mauss's *Essai sur le don* demonstrated.[20] Rephrasing the insights of Mauss and Nietzsche in terms of a gendered unconscious, Cixous notes the lack of ease with which a masculine economy confronts generosity: "Giving: there you have a basic problem, which is that masculinity is always associated—in the unconscious, which is after all what makes the whole economy function—with debt" ("CD," p. 48). Freud showed the effects that this debt has on the child, who must confront the obligation to repay his parents for their gift of his life. If you are a man, nothing is more dangerous than to be obligated to another's generosity: "For the moment you receive something you are effectively 'open' to the other, and if you are a man you have only one wish": to return the gift as quickly as possible ("CD," p. 48).

Escaping from the openness to the other has driven masculine exchange practices which, grounded on opposition, hierarchy, and a Hegelian struggle for mastery, "can end only in at least one death (one master—one slave, or two nonmasters = two dead)" ("Laugh," p. 893*). Although these practices arose in a time "governed by phallocentric values," Cixous argues that another system of exchange is possible. The fact that the period of phallocentric values "extends into the present doesn't prevent woman from starting the history of life somewhere else. Elsewhere, she gives. She doesn't 'know' what she's giving, she doesn't measure it; she gives, though, neither a counterfeit impression nor something she hasn't got. She gives more, with no assurance that she'll get back even some unexpected profit from what she puts out. She gives that there may be life, thought, transformation. This is an 'economy' that can no longer be put in economic terms" ("Laugh," p. 893). A "feminine" "economy," one no longer understandable in classical "exchangist" economic terms, allows for the possibility of giving without expectation of return, for giving that is truly generous: it gives without trying to "recover its expenses. . . . If there is a *propre* to woman, paradoxically it is her capacity to de-propriate herself without self-interest" (*NBW*, p. 87*). Although brought up in a social space framed by debt, "one can ask oneself about the possibility of a real gift, a pure gift, a gift that would not be annulled by what one could call a countergift."[21] Cixous is quick to point out, however, that "there is no 'free' gift. You never give something for nothing. But all the difference lies in the why and how of the gift, in the values that the gesture of giving affirms, causes to circulate; in the type of profit the giver draws from the gift and the use to which he or she puts it" (*NBW*, p. 87). Where masculine economies can make only quid pro quo exchanges by means of which a direct profit is to be recouped, feminine economies transact their business differently. They are not constrained to giving as a means of deferred exchange in order to obligate a countergift in return, but encourage giving as an affirmation of generosity. A feminine libidinal economy, she writes, "is an economy which has a more supple relation to property, which can stand separation and detachment, which signifies that it can also stand freedom—for instance, the other's freedom."[22] It is an economy, in other words, in which direct profit can be deferred, perhaps infinitely, in exchange for the continued circulation of giving.

To put this another way, we can perhaps use a distinction drawn by C. A. Gregory and say that whereas a feminine economy is an economy based on the exchange of gifts, a masculine economy is an economy based on the exchange of commodities. Gregory distinguishes between the two types of exchange in the following way: "Commodity exchange establishes objective quantitative relationships between the objects transacted, while gift exchange establishes personal qualitative relationships between the subjects transacting."[23] Where commodity exchange is focused on a transfer in which objects of equivalent exchange-value are reciprocally transacted, gift exchange seeks to establish a relationship between subjects in which the actual objects transferred are incidental to the value of the relationship established. Commodity exchange thus exhibits the values which, for example, Gilligan associates with an ethic of rights based on abstract principles of reciprocity, while gift exchange exhibits the forming of and focus on relationships which she associates with an ethic of care based on interpersonal needs and responsibilities, an ethic which speaks in a voice different from the one which has heretofore dominated the moral tradition.

Because of its "more supple relation to property," Cixous also emphasizes the difference between feminine and masculine economies insofar as the former promote the establishing of relationships through the giving of gifts. In particular, she draws our attention to maternal gifts as ones which escape the logic of appropriation that structures the commodity economy she labels masculine. Mother and child do not stand in a relationship of self/other, opposing parties with competing interests, and the gift to the child of a mother's love or a mother's breast is not comprehensible in terms of quantifiable exchange-values or the law of return that governs an economy based on the exchange of commodities. Nor are these maternal gifts understandable in terms of the fear of expropriation, for the mother is willing to expend these gifts without reserve or expectation of return. In fact, like Nietzsche, Cixous emphasizes and affirms the positive value of plenitude: insofar as the mother can supply as much love or as much milk as the child might demand, Cixous articulates a set of economic principles that refuse to accept the modern assumption of the givenness of conditions of scarcity. Cixous encourages us to understand this ability to give that animates feminine (libidinal) economy in terms of maternity and the specificity of women's bodies: insofar as women have the potential to give birth/life to another, they have an anatomically grounded relationship that makes possible their experiencing "the not-me within me" (*NBW*, p. 90). While Cixous tethers this relationship to pregnancy, lactation, and childbearing, at the same time she wants to link it to the possibility of writing. "Woman is body more than man is. . . . More body, hence more writing" (*NBW*, p. 95).

> It is not only a question of the feminine body's extra resource, this specific power to produce some thing living of which her flesh is the locus, not only a question of a transformation of rhythms, exchanges, of relationship to space, of the whole perceptive system, but also of the irreplaceable experience of those moments of stress, of the body's crises, of that work that goes on peacefully for a long time only to burst out in that surpassing moment, the time of childbirth. In which she lives as if she were larger or stronger than herself. It is also the experience of a "bond" with the other, all that comes through in the metaphor of bringing into the world. How could the woman, who has experienced the not-me within me, not have a particular relationship to the written? To writing as giving itself away (cutting itself off) from the source? (*NBW*, p. 90)

Elsewhere, she articulates women's writing more specifically in terms of generosity:

> The question a woman's text asks is the question of giving—"What does this writing give?" "How does it give?" And talking about non-origin and beginnings, you might say it "gives a send-off" [*donne le départ*]. Let's take the expression "giving a send-off" in a metaphorical

> sense: giving a send-off is generally giving the *signal* to depart. I think it's more than giving the departure signal, it's really giving, making a *gift* of, departure, allowing departure, allowing breaks, "parts," partings, separations . . . from this we break with the return-to-self, with the specular relations ruling the coherence, the identification, of the individual. ("CD," p. 53)

To put the issue this way comes dangerously close to the sort of "essentialist ideological interpretation" that Cixous acknowledges is "a story made to order for male privilege" (*NBW*, p. 81).[24] Yet she willingly runs this risk, as she frequently appeals to maternal and anatomical images and metaphors in expressing the implications of feminine economies and *écriture féminine*. Whether or not Cixous herself sometimes falls victim to essentialist thinking when she focuses on the anatomical specificity of women's bodies in terms of the possibilities of pregnancy and childbirth, one could, perhaps less problematically, ground the practices of feminine economies and writing sociohistorically rather than anatomically. To do so would perhaps focus attention on those maternal practices discussed by Cixous as *exemplary* of different intersubjective relations that warrant further generalization and application while avoiding becoming entangled in the problems raised by either the culturally constraining aspects of maternity or the appeal to anatomical specificity. Cixous herself appears to make this move when she replaces "*écriture féminine*" ("feminine writing") with "*écriture dite féminine*" ("writing said to be feminine"): "It is not anatomical sex that determines anything here. It is, on the contrary, history from which one never escapes, individual and collective history, the cultural schema and the way the individual negotiates with these schema, with these data, adapts to them and reproduces them, or else gets round them, overcomes them, goes beyond them, gets through them" ("EF," p. 18). To speak of a feminine economy, Cixous writes, "does not refer to women, but perhaps to a trait that comes back to women more often."[25] Insofar as women have been prohibited throughout history from possessing things for themselves, they have come to understand and appreciate property differently in terms of an economy based not on the law of return but on generosity. Likewise, insofar as women have at times been positioned socioeconomically *as* gifts, it is not at all surprising, nor should it be taken as a function of anatomy or biology, that women's perspectives on gifts and giving might differ from men's.[26] By virtue of certain social necessities, Cixous writes in "The Laugh of the Medusa," women constitute themselves as " 'person[s]' capable of losing a part of [themselves] without losing [their] integrity" ("Laugh," p. 888). They are able to exist in a "relationship to the other in which the gift doesn't calculate its influence" (*NBW*, p. 92). And they can negotiate within an economy "that tolerates the movements of the other."[27] They have learned, to use a distinction made by Pierre Bourdieu in his critique of Lévi-Strauss's analysis of gift exchange, to distinguish "giving" from "swapping" or "lending." This distinction is central to Bourdieu's critique of objectivist anthropological accounts of gift exchange. By reducing the exchange of gift and countergift to a straightforward transfer of commodities of relatively equal worth, the objectivist account conflates gift exchange with "*swapping*, which . . . telescopes gift and counter-gift into the same instant, and . . . *lending*, in which the return of the loan is explicitly guaranteed by a juridical act and contract capable of ensuring that the acts it prescribes are predictable and calculable."[28] According to Bourdieu, the reality of the gift exchange presupposes both the necessity of a deferred and different countergift *and* the "(individual and collective) misrecognition (*méconnaissance*) of the reality of the objective 'mechanism' of the exchange."[29]

Unlike Bourdieu, Cixous is not content with describing current gift-giving practices in terms of a misrecognition of what is in reality reciprocal exchange. Instead, she wants to retrieve giftgiving from the economic necessities imposed upon it within an exchangist economy and to reframe the practices of giving in an account that does not imprison transactions within private proprietary relationships in which loans and loans paid back masquerade as the bestowal of gifts. In so doing, certain heretofore unrealized opportunities emerge. In Cixous's idiom, women have learned how to exceed the limits of themselves and enter into the between of self and other without losing themselves in the process. Escaping the proprietary constraints on subjectivity is what makes possible *écriture féminine:* "Writing is working; being worked; questioning (in) the between (letting oneself be questioned) of same *and* of other without which nothing lives; undoing death's work by willing the togetherness of one-another, infinitely charged with a ceaseless exchange of one with another—not knowing one another and beginning again only from what is most distant, from self, from other, from the other within. A course that multiplies transformations by the thousands" (*NBW*, p. 86). To be sure, men too know how to question/be questioned in the between of self and other, and Cixous readily admits that some men (she names, among others, Kleist, Shakespeare, Genet, Kafka) have written *écriture féminine*. Similarly, because most women "have been subjected to the obligations of masculinization in order to hoist themselves on to the scene of socio-political legitimation, . . . most of the texts by women up to our own time have been terribly marked by the 'masculine' economy" ("EF," p. 25). To recognize these gender correlations is not to fall victim to some tired old essentialism, and Cixous cautions against so interpreting such "facts" of literary history, for what counts as "man" or "woman" is a historical-cultural construct: "There is 'destiny' no more than there is 'nature' or 'essence' as such. . . . Men and women are caught up in a web of age-old cultural determinations that are almost unanalyzable in their complexity. One can no more speak of 'woman' than of 'man' without being trapped within an ideological theater . . . [which] invalidate[s] in advance any conceptualization" (*NBW*, p. 83). Which is to say that radical transformations of gender relations and identities, accompanied by transformations in libidinal economies, are possible: "Then 'femininity' and 'masculinity' would inscribe quite differently their effects of difference, their economy, their relationship to expenditure, to lack, to the gift. What today appears to be 'feminine' or 'masculine' would no longer amount to the same thing. No longer would the common logic of difference be organized with the opposition that remains dominant. Difference would be a bunch of new differences" (*NBW*, p. 83).

"We are forgetting how to give presents," Adorno wrote in *Minima Moralia*.[30] Cixous seeks a place "where it was not impossible or pathetic to be generous" (*NBW*, p. 72). Nietzsche envisions a society with a level of power sufficient to allow it to be merciful, that is, sufficient for it to allow its debts to go unpaid. To be sure, Nietzsche does not identify this society with the feminine, nor does he associate the generosity of overfullness with the feminine. In fact, the reverse is more nearly the case: the degree of strength necessary for such generosity is almost always put forward in masculine images of mastery, virility, productivity, and activity. But need this have been the case? I think not. By setting Nietzsche's discussion of plenitude and generosity together with Cixous's discussion of feminine libidinal economies and the giving of gifts, I have tried to show some of the affinities between their respective accounts. Perhaps we might look upon Cixous as the sort of reader Nietzsche was seeking, one who would pay him back not by repeating his text, but by taking that text and making it her own, putting it to use as she sees fit. Perhaps this is what Cixous calls *voler, theft/flight,* an other/the other side of giving: "To fly/steal [*voler*] is woman's gesture, to steal into language to make it fly. We have all learned flight/theft, the art with many techniques, for all the centuries we have only had access to having by stealing/flying; we have lived in a flight/theft, stealing/flying, finding the close, concealed ways-through of desire. It's not just luck if the word 'voler' volleys between the 'vol' of theft and the 'vol' of flight, pleasuring in each and routing the sense police" (*NBW*, p. 96). Is this not what Cixous is doing when she provides an account of generosity that does not require *übermenschliche* strength to enact as she replaces the masterly indifference affirmed by Nietzsche with maternal compassion? By recasting the economic insights of Nietzsche and Mauss in terms of sexual difference, and by making it possible to see the gendered dimension of giftgiving which Nietzsche too quickly discarded, Cixous articulates an alternative logic of the gift, one with several advantages over more classical exchangist logics. As anthropologists, sociologists, psychologists, and historians have shown, we find more women than men engaged in cultural practices that can be construed as generous. Cixous gives voice to this empirical finding while showing that generosity has always been an option of which, for complex social and historical reasons, men have not sufficiently availed themselves.

If an economy or ethic of generosity is deemed worth pursuing and cultivating, as I have tried to suggest in terms of the ideas of Nietzsche and Cixous, then we must take care to develop economic and ethical practices that draw on the lived experiences of women without, as perhaps Cixous and Nietzsche each in their own way have done, "reifying women's social identities under stereotypes of femininity, on the one hand, [or] dissolving them into sheer nullity and oblivion, on the other."[31] And we must take care also to insure that the practices of generosity are generalized and become the behavioral norms throughout the social matrix. For if they do not, if the practices of giving are enacted only by some, these practices will continue to be exploitative of those who give without return, as they have heretofore always been. Avoiding this eventuality calls for another dimension of the logic of the gift, one which neither Nietzsche nor Cixous sufficiently attend to, namely, the dimension of social action and activism. Attention to this dimension is the task that now confronts us.

Notes

This paper has benefited from the careful reading and thoughtful suggestions of several people, including Caroline Gebhard, Paula Smith, Johanna Meehan, Jill Schrift, Aletta Biersack, Debra Bergoffen, and Marcia Stephenson. Although most of these readers no doubt still have questions concerning my approach to the issues raised in this paper, I thank them for the generous gift of their time and their criticisms, which made this a better paper than it would otherwise have been. Research for this article was supported by the Harris Faculty Fellowship of Grinnell College, and an undisturbed setting for its writing was provided by the University of Oregon Humanities Center.

1. This pun was, in fact, suggested to me by Avital Ronell's reference to a "gynecologist of morals" in her "Namely, Eckermann," in *Looking after Nietzsche,* ed. Laurence A. Rickels (Albany: SUNY Press, 1990), p. 236.

2. Carol Gilligan, *In a Different Voice: Psychological Theory and Women's Development* (Cambridge: Harvard Univ. Press, 1982).

3. In addition to several of the essays in this collection, the reader interested in discussions of Nietzsche as or as not a misogynist is referred to Luce Irigaray, *Amante marine: De Friedrich Nietzsche* (Paris: Minuit, 1980); Sarah Kofman, *Nietzsche et la scène philosophique* (Paris: Union générale d'éditions, 1979), especially chapter 8: "Baubô: Perversion théologique et Fétichisme," pp. 263–304 (a translation of this chapter by Tracy B. Strong appears in *Nietzsche's New Seas: Explorations in Philosophy, Aesthetics, and Politics,* ed. Tracy B. Strong and Michael Allen Gillespie [Chicago: Univ. of Chicago Press, 1988], pp. 175–202); Elizabeth Berg, "The Third Woman," *Diacritics* 12 (Summer 1982): 11–20; Christine Allen, "Nietzsche's Ambivalence about Women," in *The Sexism of Social and Political Theory: Women and Reproduction from Plato to Nietzsche,* ed. Lorenne M. G. Clark and Lynda Lange (Toronto: Univ. of Toronto Press, 1979), pp. 117–33; Jacques Derrida, *Spurs: Nietzsche's Styles / Eperons: Les Styles de Nietzsche,* trans. Barbara Harlow (Chicago: Univ. of Chicago Press, 1979) and "Choreographies," trans. Christie V. McDonald, *Diacritics* 12: *Cherchez La Femme: Feminist Critique / Feminine Text* (Summer 1982): 66–76; David Farrell Krell, *Postponements: Woman, Sensuality, and Death in Nietzsche* (Bloomington: Indiana Univ. Press, 1986); R. Hinton Thomas, "Nietzsche, Women, and the Whip," *German Life and Letters* 34 (1980): 117–25; Gayle L. Ormiston, "Traces of Derrida: Nietzsche's Image of Women," *Philosophy Today* 28 (1984): 178–88; Debra B. Bergoffen, "On the Advantage and Disadvantage of Nietzsche for Women," in *The Question of the Other: Essays in Contemporary Continental Philosophy,* ed. Arleen B. Dallery and Charles E. Scott (Albany: SUNY Press, 1989), pp. 77–88.

4. Gilles Deleuze and Félix Guattari, *Anti-Oedipus: Capitalism and Schizophrenia,* trans. Robert Hurley, Mark Seem, and Helen R. Lane (Minneapolis: Univ. of Minnesota Press, 1983), p. 190.

5. The connection between Nietzsche's idea that a community shows its strength in terms of its capacity for generosity and the ideal of the welfare state is worth noting. I thank Johanna Meehan for first bringing this connection to my attention.

6. Marcel Mauss, *Essai sur le don: Forme et raison de l'échange dans les sociétés archaïques,* in *Année sociologique,* 1923–24, pp. 30–186; *The Gift: Forms and Functions of Exchange in Archaic Societies,* trans. Ian Cunnison (New York: Norton, 1967).

7. See Georges Bataille, *The Accursed Share: An Essay on General Economy, Volume I: Consumption,* trans. Robert Hurley (New York: Zone, 1988), part 1. For an earlier discussion of his concept of "expenditure," see "The Notion of Expenditure," trans. and ed. Allan Stoekl, in Georges Bataille, *Visions of Excess: Selected Writings, 1927–1939* (Minneapolis: Univ. of Minnesota Press, 1985), pp. 116–29. In this account, which at many places reminds one of Nietzsche, Bataille offers an economic account based on excess and loss to counter the utilitarian assumptions that all expenditures must be productive and compensated.

8. Although Nietzsche was quite hostile to what he understood to be the goals of socialism, the position that I am characterizing here as a noble economy is not far from the ideal expressed by Marx in *Critique of the Gotha Program* when he writes that on the banner of the higher phase of communist society will be inscribed: "From each according to his ability, to each according to his needs!"

9. Nietzsche's prefiguration of Derridean dissemination should here be noted.

10. In the following discussion of Cixous, I will for the most part refrain from qualifying "economy" with either of the adjectives "textual," "libidinal," or "political." As I read Cixous, she sees these three economies working in terms of the same principles and what is true of one will be true of the others. If I do choose to use one of these adjectives, it will be to emphasize that particular economy in the context of what I am discussing at that moment, but should not be understood to isolate that economy from the others.

11. Hélène Cixous, "The Laugh of the Medusa," trans. Keith Cohen and Paula Cohen, *Signs: Journal of Women in Culture and Society* 1 (1976): 888. Subsequent references will be cited parenthetically as "Laugh" followed by page number. The essay to which Cixous refers appeared as "La Question du style," in *Nietzsche aujourd'hui,* 2 vols. (Paris: Union générale d'éditions, 1973), 1:235–87. Derrida later revised and republished this text, which in English translation is *Spurs: Nietzsche's Styles* (see note 3); for his discussion of the gift, see pp. 109–23.

12. Derrida, *Spurs,* p. 123.

13. I can here only note the appearance of a "sexual difference" among Derrida's "commentators" concerning whether or not they regard the thematics of the gift in Derrida's work as a topic worthy of comment. Compare, in this regard, the work of Peggy Kamuf, Christie McDonald, or Alice Jardine with that of Jonathan Culler, Rodolphe Gasché, Christopher Norris, or Gregory Ulmer.

14. Since this essay was first written, Derrida has published another work—*Donner le temps: 1. La fausse monnaie* (Paris: Galilée, 1991); *Given Time: I. Counterfeit Money,* trans. Peggy Kamuf (Chicago: Univ. of Chicago Press, 1992)—in which he focuses his attention explicitly upon giving, exchange, and the possibility of the gift in Mauss, Heidegger, Benveniste, and Baudelaire. In the present context, it is worth noting the following from a footnote to the foreword of this work, where Derrida remarks that the problematic of the gift has been at work in his texts "wherever it is a question of the *proper* (appropriation, expropriation, exappropriation), economy, the trace, the name, and especially the *rest,* of course, which is to say more or less constantly" (p. ix).

15. That Cixous's discussion of the "*Empire du Propre*" is, in part, a rejoinder to Jacques Derrida's raising the "*question du propre*" with respect to the questions of style/woman in Nietzsche can only be suggested here. I discuss Derrida's "*question du propre*" in some detail in my *Nietzsche and the Question of Interpretation: Between Hermeneutics and Deconstruction* (New York: Routledge, 1990), pp. 104–6, 117.

16. Hélène Cixous and Catherine Clément, *The Newly Born Woman,* trans. Betsy Wing (Minneapolis: Univ. of Minnesota Press, 1986), p. 78. Subsequent references to this text will be cited parenthetically as *NBW* followed by page number.

17. Hélène Cixous, "Castration or Decapitation?" trans. Annette Kuhn, *Signs: Journal of Women in Culture and Society* 7 (1981): 50. Subsequent references will be cited parenthetically as CD followed by page number.

18. Hélène Cixous, "An exchange with Hélène Cixous," trans. Verena Andermatt Conley and published as an appendix to Conley's *Hélène Cixous: Writing the Feminine* (Lincoln: Univ. of Nebraska Press, 1984), p. 129.

19. Hélène Cixous, "Extreme Fidelity," trans. Ann Liddle and Susan Sellers, in *Writing Differences: Readings from the Seminar of Hélène Cixous,* ed. Susan Sellers (New York: St. Martin's, 1988), p. 15. Subsequent references will be cited parenthetically as EF followed by page number.

20. In this paper, I will only be able to touch the surface of the divergent logics of giftgiving. Although I am not able to do so here, a full treatment of these divergent logics is worth pursuing. In fact, this inquiry has been ongoing within the domain of anthropology since, as Gayle Rubin has put it, Lévi-Strauss, in *The Elementary Structures of Kinship* (Boston: Beacon, 1969, chapter 5), added "to the theory of primitive reciprocity the idea that marriages are a most basic form of gift exchange, in which it is women who are the most precious of gifts" (Gayle Rubin, "The Traffic in Women," in *Toward an Anthropology of Women,* ed. Rayna R. Reiter [New York and London: Monthly Review Press, 1975], p. 173). Any serious analysis of giftgiving would, at the very least, have to consult and address the work of a wide range of recent feminist and feminist-inspired reappraisals of the effects of gender on exchange relations including, among others: Daryl K. Feil, *Ways of Exchange: The Enga 'tee' of Papua New Guinea* (St. Lucia: Univ. of Queensland Press, 1984); Renée Hirschon, ed., *Women and Property, Women as Property* (London: Croom Helm, 1984); Lisette Josephides, *The Production of Inequality: Gender and Exchange among the Kewa* (London: Tavistock, 1985); Marilyn Strathern, *The Gender of the Gift: Problems with Women and Problems with Society in Melanesia* (Berkeley and Los Angeles: Univ. of California Press, 1988); J. van Baal, *Reciprocity and the Position of Women* (Amsterdam: Van Gorcum, 1975); Annette B. Weiner, *Women of Value, Men of Renown: New Perspectives on Trobriand Exchange* (Austin: Univ. of Texas Press, 1976) and *Inalienable Possessions: The Paradox of Keeping-While-Giving* (Berkeley and Los Angeles: Univ. of California Press, 1992).

21. Cixous, in Conley, p. 158.

22. Cixous, in Conley, p. 137.

23. C. A. Gregory, *Gifts and Commodities* (London: Academic Press, 1982), p. 41.

24. The appeal to maternity, maternal language, and maternal images in French feminist writing is frequently an object of criticism by other, especially American, feminists; see, for example, Domna Stanton, "Difference on Trial: A Critique of the Maternal Metaphor in Cixous, Irigaray, and Kristeva," in *The Thinking Muse: Feminism and Modern French Philosophy,* ed. Jeffner Allen and Iris Marion Young (Bloomington: Indiana Univ. Press, 1989), pp. 156–79.

25. Hélène Cixous, *Reading with Clarice Lispector,* ed. and trans. Verena Andermatt Conley (Minneapolis: Univ. of Minnesota Press, 1990), p. 156.

26. I am grateful to Paula Smith for first suggesting this point to me.

27. Cixous, in Conley, p. 137.

28. Pierre Bourdieu, *Outline of a Theory of Practice,* trans. Richard Nice (Cambridge: Cambridge Univ. Press, 1972), p. 5.

29. Bourdieu, *Outline,* pp. 5–6; cf. p. 171. Bourdieu also recognizes two different economies which are distinguished along gender lines: "The opposition between the

two 'economies' is so marked that the expression *err arrtal,* also used to express the taking of revenge, means the *returning of a gift,* an exchange, in the men's speech, whereas it means 'giving back a loan' when used by the women" (p. 62). He goes on to note that "loan conduct" is more common among women than is gift exchange, which he takes to indicate that although less socially prestigious, "economic truth . . . is closer to the surface in female exchanges" (p. 63).

30. Theodor Adorno, *Minima Moralia,* trans. E. F. N. Jephcott (London: NLB, 1974), p. 42.

31. Nancy Fraser, "The Uses and Abuses of French Discourse Theories for Feminist Politics," *Boundary 2* 17, no. 2 (1990): 101.

ARKADY PLOTNITSKY

The Medusa's Ears: The Question of Nietzsche, the Question of Gender, and Transformations of Theory

A woman's countenance, with serpent-locks,
Gazing in death on Heaven from those wet rocks.

—Shelley, *On the Medusa of Leonardo da Vinci*

"To be popular one must be a mediocrity." "Not with women," said the Duchess, shaking her head; "and women rule the world. I assure you we can't bear mediocrities. We women, as someone says, love with our ears, just as you men love with your eyes, if you love at all."

—Oscar Wilde, *The Picture of Dorian Gray*

You'll pass the *Buci Market,* where Picasso bought his sausages, and le Bonaparte café, where Sartre pitched existentialism to Simone de Beauvoir.

—Richard Saul Wurtman's Ultimate Guide, Paris Access

Nietzsche's presence on the scene of modern and postmodern theory has been pervasive. His name is now customarily joined to those of Marx and Freud in defining modern intellectual history. More significantly, several major transformations of twentieth-century theoretical thinking, culminating in poststructuralist theory, have taken place in conjunction with readings and rereadings of Nietzsche. In the case of poststructuralist theory, these rereadings have often proceeded specifically against Heidegger's reading of Nietzsche. It is conceivable that, whatever radical transformation of the theoretical field in the humanities and the social sciences emerges (as must occur sooner or later) in the wake of poststructuralist theory, a reading or rereading of Nietzsche will play a prominent role in it. Such a transformation is, of course, likely to generate a new reading of Nietzsche regardless of the role of his ideas in this transformation itself. Such a rereading may proceed against readings of Nietzsche by Bataille, Deleuze, Foucault, Derrida, and others whose work defines the poststructuralist landscape and for whom Nietzsche's thinking was decisive.

All these developments—from Marxism to poststructuralism and beyond, via Nietzsche—have played a crucial role in modern feminist theory. Nietzsche's thought has been the subject of direct engagements by several major feminist thinkers, particularly in France, as in the works of Hélène Cixous, Luce Irigaray, and Sarah Kofman. Feminist theory has, however, in turn profoundly affected the landscape of modernity and postmodernity, including the history of reading Nietzsche. This influence can be detected already in Gilles Deleuze's *Nietzsche and Philosophy* (1962), which comes *after The Second Sex* (1949). *The Second Sex,* of course, itself comes *after* Nietzsche, who comes *after,* but, especially given Heidegger's discourse, also *before* philosophy.

The question of philosophical discourse is inescapable here. It arises, first, in view of Nietzsche's great confrontation with philosophy, on the one hand, and Beauvoir's relationships to philosophy, including Husserl's, Heidegger's, and, of course, Sartre's, on the other. Secondly, and more generally, according to Derrida a certain philosophical closure delimits the classical and even deconstructive theoretical fields in any discipline, whether linguistics, anthropology, psychoanalysis, or literary criticism and theory. The closure (*clôture*) of philosophy in Derrida designates our dependence on the language and concepts developed throughout the history of philosophy, but operative elsewhere as well. This dependence extends far beyond the text and institution of philosophy, compelling one to speak of the *closure* of philosophy and to engage deconstruction in other fields. This dependence and this closure are, for Derrida, fundamental and irreducible, even, and in particular, in the practice of deconstruction. The latter must not only critically engage philosophy, which is obviously necessary if one wants to deconstruct it, but must also, Derrida argues, borrow from the resources of, and depend on, what it deconstructs.

The field of the present essay is defined by this triple conjunction of the question of Nietzsche, the question of gender, and the question of transformations of theory—in the aftermath of philosophy and its closure—in the fields of the human and social sciences, such as literary or critical theory. My concern, thus, is not so much the question of gender itself but how the problematics of gender may affect the constitution and transformations of the historico-theoretical field defined by the "event" and the *after*math of Nietzsche, which themselves take place *after* the history of philosophy. I shall proceed by considering and interrelating three key figures or metaphorical economies in Nietzsche and feminist theory: the ear, the Medusa, and the Dionysian. I shall begin by connecting the figures of the ear and the Medusa in Nietzsche and in feminist discourse. Then I shall discuss the question of the feminine in Nietzsche and relate it to the question of the Dionysian. Finally, I shall address the question of transformations of the theoretical field, in the wake of feminist and gender theory, that can be seen as simultaneously postphilosophical and post-Nietzschean.

The Ear and the Medusa

While invoking, in an extraordinary way, the figure of the Medusa, Hélène Cixous's "The Laugh of the Medusa" does not, at least overtly, invoke the figure or pose the question of the ear, specifically "the ear of the other"—one of Nietzsche's grand questions.[1] The questions Who listens, or who may or may not listen? and To whose ears does one speak? are, however, continuously, incessantly posed by the essay; and in view of the history of the question of woman, they may indeed be inevitable. In his reading of Guido Crepax's *The Story of O,* Roland Barthes brilliantly observes:

> The order which O's partners continually give her and to which the book's erotic provocation confines itself, the ideal form of the phantasmatic interlocution, is this: *that the other be nullified except as he listens and obeys*. Represented, placed before our eyes, under our noses, O's erotic organ is most certainly not her sex (or her breast or her buttocks), it is—a bizarre thing to say—*her ear*. And Crepax has understood just that: he has drawn (in many different ways, it is true, none of which is auricular) only one ear: O is depicted, in a great number of positions and through many parts of her body, only as she listens. Listens to what she hears.[2]

Barthes's conclusion may in fact be more inevitable than bizarre. The economy described here has shaped the interactions among the other, the feminine, and the ear throughout a very long history. This economy and the locutions—they are seldom, if ever, *inter*locutions—that it implies are always more than sexual and erotic. For example, they are often, and in a certain sense always, political.

It is not surprising, therefore, that the figure of the ear plays a key role in Cixous, Irigaray (who often invokes it directly), and other feminist authors. According to Irigaray, "One would have to listen with another ear, as if hearing *an 'other meaning' always in the process of weaving itself, of embracing itself with words, but also of getting rid of words in order not to become fixed, congealed in them*. For if 'she' says something, it is not, it is already no longer, identical with what she means. What she says is never identical with anything, moreover; rather, it is contiguous. *It touches* (*upon*)."[3] Irigaray is possibly alluding to Nietzsche's remarks on listening "with another ear." Her *Marine Lover* opens with "another gaze"—and the gaze of the other—to move swiftly to "the ear," even becoming an ear—"I am your resonance. . . . I hear you. And I don't hear you. I am your hearing"—echoing and responding to Nietzsche, who, gazing at and listening to the sea, writes on "women and their action at a distance" in *The Gay Science* (KSA 3:424–25; GS §60, pp. 123–24).[4] The passage cited above from *This Sex Which Is Not One* also refers to Derrida's *différance* and *writing*. In effect, it alludes to the Medusa as well. For the Medusa—or the fear of the Medusa—fixes, congeals one in words, making one and one's language and figures forever identical to themselves. The figure of the Medusa has obvious metonymic connections to (the figure of) the sea, as does the figure of the ear, by virtue of its seashell-like architecture. One can read *Marine Lover* by combining the figures (each always more than one) of Nietzsche, the feminine, and Irigaray herself with the figures of the marine landscape—the sea, the ear, the seashell, and the Medusa. The last two are mostly hidden inside Nietzsche's and Irigaray's sealike texts, but are sometimes brought to the surface or to the shore by their waves—uncontrollable, even by these texts themselves—just as seashells and jellyfish (the sea's eyes and ears, as it were) are brought to the surface and to the shore by the waves of the sea. The seashell is shaped and is often figured as the ear, to which one can also listen—like to Nietzsche, or Irigaray—and hear the sea. The sea, as Irigaray says, can also be heard—or read, or written—as woman and as text, or as woman's text, or as woman-text, which "shines with a myriad eyes. And none is given any privilege" (*Marine Lover*, p. 47). "Out of the sea the overman is reborn," not unlike Botticelli's Venus—who may be another metamorphosed Medusa—standing on a giant seashell. But, unlike Venus or the Medusa, "still he fears to sink under the waters even as he aspires to their vastness" (*Marine Lover*, p. 52*).

The Medusa's eyes or, again, the fear of her eyes, is deadly. The Medusa's ears are never seen, hidden in the snakes, perhaps in turn imagined, of her elaborate coiffure. Leonardo's *The Head of the Medusa* survives only in a copy, very likely by Rubens, so that it cannot stand as the strongest possible evidence. In Leonardo's studies for the head of Leda (Royal Library, Windsor Castle), however, the suggestion of the Medusa's snakes in Leda's hair is clearly no accident. In the *Study for a Kneeling Leda* (Devonshire Collection, Chatworth), the swan seems to be reaching for Leda's ear, hidden in the "snakes" of her hair. The Medusa's "snakes" may have been intimated in the hair of Botticelli's Venus as well. One is also reminded of Milton's famous description of the "wanton ringlets" of Eve's hair in book 4 of *Paradise Lost*—"Shee as a veil down to the slender waist / Her unadorned golden tresses wore / Dishevell'd, but in wanton ringlets wav'd / As the Vine curls her tendrils"—followed by a parallel description of the coiling Serpent: "the Serpent sly / Insinuating [i.e., coiling], wove with Gordian twine / His braided train." Satan is then discovered in the Garden, next to sleeping Eve, "close at the ear of *Eve* / Assaying by his Devilish art to reach / The Organs of her Fancy" (*Paradise Lost,* 4.304–7, 347–49, 800). In book 2 Sin is "Serpent arm'd" and is called "the Snaky Sorceress" (2.652, 724). The "tresses" of woman's hair accompany one of the great enigmatic exchanges of *Zarathustra,* between life and Zarathustra:

> "O Zarathustra, I know it, of how you want to leave me soon."
> "Yes," I answered hesitantly, "but I also know"—and I whispered something into her ear, right through her tangled yellow foolish tresses. "You *know that, O Zarathustra?* Nobody knows that."
> And we looked at each other and gazed on the green meadow over which the cool evening was running just then, and we wept together. But then life was dearer to me than all my wisdom [*Weisheit*] ever was.
> Thus spoke Zarathustra. (KSA 4:285; Z p. 339)

It is not inconceivable that Milton's imagery was known to Nietzsche (the serpent, we recall, is one of Zarathustra's animals). The network of possible sources and connections is huge, however. The history of the image of the Medusa extends throughout (and before) the history of Western philosophy or literature. In particular, the Medusa episode of canto 9 of Dante's *Inferno* was familiar to all figures invoked here—Leonardo, Milton, Shelley, Nietzsche, Irigaray, and Cixous.[5]

The Medusa is only one among many possible pertinent mythologemes, many of which are engaged, for example, by Irigaray in *Marine Lover.* As Cixous's essay shows, however, it profoundly relates to the history of the feminine; and it is worth recalling that in mythology the Medusa had no power against women. Cixous's essay has had a major impact in contemporary feminist and gender theory. This theory also happens to be, perhaps inevitably, a theory of reading Nietzsche: the theory of how he can and cannot be read, or listened to, or even made to listen, or, of course, looked at. *Seen* classically, Nietzsche's text is one of the most Medusa-like ever—a direct confrontation with it converts classical theories into stone monuments, perhaps beautiful, but no longer alive. It is conceivable that Nietzsche allegorized his text in this way, as, according to John Freccero, Dante did. This theory of reading Nietzsche also entails a theory of reading in general. Such a theory may no longer allow one to dispense with the necessity of reading woman and gender, but may also demand that we read both differently from any reading offered hitherto, including those by Nietzsche and possibly even previous feminist readings.

The Externally Feminine

Nietzsche's text cannot, I think, be "saved" on the question of woman and gender—in spite of interesting and often productive efforts in this direction, including those in Derrida and deconstruction, and in some recent feminist studies.[6] I refer here specifically to the theoretical problems of Nietzsche's understanding—or lack of understanding—of the economy of gender, rather than to the more or less pronounced antifeminism of Nietzsche's text. One cannot, of course, discount any antifeminism, whatever its reasons—psychological, historical, or political—and however untheoretical these reasons may be or may appear to be. Nor can one unequivocally or unconditionally separate the theoretical field from its untheoretical complements or what are conventionally so seen. By the same token, however, one cannot suspend determinations that may and sometimes must, however provisionally, be seen as theoretical; and at certain points such theoretical determinations become decisive.

"May I here venture the surmise that I *know* women [*dass ich die Weiblein kenne*]? That is part of my Dionysian dowry. Who knows [*Wer weiss*]? Perhaps I am the first psychologist of the eternally feminine"—Nietzsche writes in *Ecce Homo* (KSA 6:305; EH p. 266). Perhaps; more likely, however, it is "the eternally feminine" that is the problem, no less in Nietzsche than in Goethe, who is Nietzsche's main source here, even leaving aside that, as Irigaray reminds us, woman "is not to be reduced to mere femininity. . . . The femininity of woman, that would be her other, which amounts to the same. . . . Femininity—the father's indispensable intermediary in putting his law into force" (*Marine Lover*, pp. 77, 80, 95). May not "the eternally feminine," no matter *how* it is inscribed or reinscribed, be a remnant, one of very few in Nietzsche, of metaphysics as ontotheology? Here it takes the form of the ontotheology of the feminine, or ontophallotheology, as it may be called, by analogy and in conjunction with phallogocentrism. Such ontotheologies of the feminine may or may not be conceived via the eternally feminine. But they always relate to and manifest, in a relatively trivial form, what may be called the externally feminine; and this exteriority and this (non)femininity may not, finally, be accessible to any ontotheological economy of exteriority. Ontotheology is the tradition—from, let us say, Anaximander to Heidegger—in which Nietzsche destroys so much, "*philosophizing* with a hammer," a rather antiphilosophical weapon and instrument. It is also a musical instrument—"tympani"—which, as shall be seen, is another key figure of the Nietzschean theoretical economy.

The eternally feminine would remain a problem even if one were to suspend the accompanying—and still more problematic—antifeminist propositions in *Ecce Homo* and elsewhere. Nietzsche, it is true, does admit that such things as the "emancipation of women" and "feminism," or rather what makes them possible—"At bottom, the emancipated are *anarchists* in the world of the 'eternally feminine,' the underprivileged whose most fundamental instinct is revenge"—are by no means absent in man. "One whole species of the most malignant 'idealism'—which, incidentally, is also encountered among men; for example, in Henrik Ibsen, this typical old virgin—aims to *poison* the good conscience, what is natural in sexual love" (KSA 6:306–7; EH p. 267*). Can one speak, however, of the 'natural' in sexual love? Has not Nietzsche questioned, more radically than anybody else, the possibility of all these concepts—natural morality, natural mentality, natural nature, certainly natural man, although perhaps not quite natural woman? Nietzsche precedes his attack with comments on what is, according to him, natural to women, or to the best women, "these charming maenads" (KSA 6:306; EH p. 266)—the women of Dionysus. This "naturalness" of woman's nature would remain problematic, however much positive value—some of which is very traditional—is assigned to it by Nietzsche and however much certain forms of feminism, "also in men," represent the species of the reactive (ressentiment) psychology.

"Every human 'feminism' too, also in men—is a closing of the gate [*ein Thorschluss*] for me; it prevents entrance into this [Nietzschean] *labyrinth* of audacious insights" (KSA 6:303; EH p. 264*). One no longer needs Ariadne's thread in this labyrinth where, as Bataille says, "NIETZSCHE'S DOCTRINE CANNOT BE ENSLAVED. It can only be followed."[7] As Nietzsche writes:

> One must never have spared oneself, one must acquire *hardness* as a habit to be cheerful and in good spirits in the midst of nothing but hard truths. When I imagine a perfect reader, he always turns into a monster of courage and curiosity; moreover, supple, cunning, cautious; a born adventurer and discoverer. In the end, I could not say it better to whom alone I am speaking at bottom than Zarathustra said it: to *whom* alone will he relate his riddle? "To you, the bold searchers, researchers, and whoever embarks with cunning sails on terrible seas—to you, drunk with riddles, glad of the twilight, whose soul flutes lure astray to every whirlpool, because you do not want to grope along a thread with cowardly hand; and where you can *guess,* you hate to *deduce.*" (KSA 6:303–4; EH p. 264*)[8]

One needs much courage on these "terrible seas" and in this labyrinth, the courage of Perseus and Theseus, and, perhaps against Nietzsche, even more courage, and of a different kind—to look at the monster's face, the Medusa's face, for example, or to speak to (the labyrinth of) the Medusa's ear—the ear of the other. And it may indeed be that, as Irigaray says, "[woman] is [Nietzsche's] labyrinth, [Nietzsche] hers" (*Marine Lover,* p. 73).

It is important to keep in mind that some forms of feminism are also found among men and that in many ways women are, for Nietzsche, better than some, indeed most men. Nor can one ignore Nietzsche's frequent identification with women—*along certain lines.* This aspect of Nietzsche's thought has been crucial for deconstructive readings of Nietzsche, specifically by Derrida and Irigaray, and it may enable one to save (some) Nietzsche on women. As the same section of *Ecce Homo* (KSA 6:305–7; EH pp. 266–67) and his other statements would demonstrate, Nietzsche's attack against equal rights for women is part of his general critique of the metaphysics of rights. Insofar as the question of woman is concerned, however, Nietzsche's "reevaluation of all values" produces propositions and values that are problematic, even if one accepts the effectiveness of this critique elsewhere.

The question of woman and women is largely excluded in the first essay, "'Good and Evil,' 'Good and Bad,'" of *On the Genealogy of Morals,* an exclusion that may compel one to re*write* the genealogy of morals, in whatever sense of the term *writing,* including Derrida's.[9] This question does, however, reenter the text and writing of the many genealogies at issue in the book. In the third essay, "What Is the Meaning of Ascetic Ideals?," it acquires a considerable prominence. It appears first as the question of wisdom-woman—joyful wisdom, *fröhliche Wissenschaft* (or *Weisheit*), Sophia, a kind of reversal of the Medusa, in the epigraph from *Zarathustra:* "Unconcerned, mocking, violent—thus wisdom wants *us:* she is a woman and always loves only a warrior" (KSA 5:339; GM—III p. 97). Then it is used against Kant's aesthetics of the disinterested, via the story of Pygmalion (KSA 5:347; GM—III §6, p. 104). Finally, woman—"the sick woman"—becomes an example of the most extreme form of ressentiment:

> Nor is there lacking among them ["men of good will"] that most disgusting species of the vain, the mendacious failures whose aim is to appear as "beautiful souls" and who bring to market their deformed sensuality, wrapped up in verses and other swaddling clothes, as "purity of heart": the species of moral masturbators and "self-gratifiers." The will of the weak to represent *some* form of superiority, their instinct for devious paths to tyranny over the healthy—where can it not be discovered, this will to power of the weakest!
>
> The sick woman especially: no one can excel her in the wiles to dominate, oppress, and tyrannize. The sick woman spares nothing, living or dead; she will dig up the most deeply buried things (the Bogos say: "woman is a hyena"). (KSA 5:369–70; GM—III §14, p. 123)

While in this case, too, one cannot ignore that all reactive or ressentiment forms of the will to power are attacked by Nietzsche, neither can one ignore that it is "the sick *woman*" that represents this limit. Or is such the case by virtue of the fact that women are put—by other wills to power, active or reactive—into this position? Perhaps; but Nietzsche, at least, does not say so. Nor does he provide any other justification for positioning woman as such a limit; and the book contains some of Nietzsche's most vehemently antifeminist statements. Even if such were the case, then, this part of the genealogy of morals may have to be rewritten—*against* Nietzsche.

The Question Marks of the Dionysian

The Nietzschean woman, if she is a "healthy woman," may then be much better than some men, indeed, it appears, better than most men. But is she better than or equal to the best men—the *Übermensch* or Zarathustra? Zarathustra or the *Übermensch* as a woman may be the greatest question mark posed by Nietzsche's text at the juncture of feminism and theory. This question mark is also the question mark of—or perhaps after—the Dionysian, the highest new value in Nietzsche's revaluation of all values. The Dionysian, it is true, is figured in Nietzsche as a kind of force and, thus, strictly speaking, is not defined by gender, not even the gender of Dionysus himself, surrounded by his "charming maenads," in whom, as we have seen, Nietzsche may have seen a higher value and perhaps even the true nature of the feminine. Nietzsche, however, never speaks of the Dionysian woman, while he does speak of the Dionysian man, and of the Dionysian philosopher—himself, for example.

The Dionysian woman may be the laughing Medusa of Cixous's essay. Cixous's "woman is obviously not that woman Nietzsche dreamed of who gives only in order to receive" ("Laugh," p. 259). I shall not consider Cixous's economy of the feminine itself or her understanding of the Nietzschean woman, which appears to displace Nietzsche's view somewhat. Woman may be none of these "figures"—neither Nietzsche's, nor Derrida's, nor Cixous's, nor Irigaray's. We must keep in mind that they all warn us against attempting to figure "woman" or figure woman out. All these thinkers "define" woman as that which defies figuration or definition, however multitropological or deconstructive such a definition may be. Even if the woman "Nietzsche dreamed of" is not quite the one Cixous thinks she is, woman may indeed not be "that woman Nietzsche dreamed of." That is not to say, of course, that there *is* such a thing as woman, especially *the* woman, in the sense of classical ontology, as Nietzsche, Derrida, Cixous, and Irigaray warn us; what is in question is a different inscription—writing and reading—of woman and gender. The question of the Dionysian and the question of the Dionysian woman have, however, great significance throughout Cixous's work, beginning with her work on Joyce—another Medusa-like, unconfrontable text.

The economy of woman and the feminine is often processed by Cixous through a Derridean matrix. Derrida's meditation on Medusa in *Glas* proceeds via Freud, situated between Hegel and Genet—the column of Freud raised alongside the columns of Hegel and Genet.[10] In the architecture of *Glas,* one could expect the Medusa's appearance at any point in the text. The giants are turned into stone, as it were; they are *erected* as columns, perhaps by the Medusa's eyes—imaginary or symbolic, or real, also in the sense of Lacan's registers. Lacan is one of the columns, open or hidden, supporting the architecture of *Glas.* Derrida points out that Freud, in his analysis of *das Medusenhaupt,* correlates with erection the turning to stone in the sight, and the gaze, of the Medusa. "The Medusa provides for no off-scene [*hors-scène*]. She sees, shows only stony columns."[11] Much of *Glas* can be reinscribed through a certain Medusan economy, beginning with its opening lines, "What, after all, of the remain(s), for us, here, now, of a Hegel? . . . magisterial coldness and imperturbable seriousness, the eagle caught in ice and frost, glass and gel" (*Glas,* p. 1a), as Derrida places the column of Hegel's text next to the column of Genet's text. Both, as

Glas itself, can be allegorized as Medusa-like texts, even the texts that are Medusas to themselves. "Let the emblanched [*emblémi*] philosopher be so congealed" (*Glas,* p. 1a), and—along with Genet, or inside the Genet column of *Glas*—congealed "as a stone" under the Medusa's gaze:

> as a stone, a firestone, a silex, verily an uncuttable [*inentamable*] diamond. Let that fall [*ça tombe*] to dust, but as funerary slab, so natural that it would reconstitute itself in the earth itself, and always harder. He is Medusa [*se méduse*] to himself. How can one be Medusa to oneself? He has to understand that *he* is not *himself* before being Medusa to himself.
>
> He occurs to himself since the Medusa. To be oneself is to-be-Medusa'd, and from then on the Medusa'd-being constitutes itself, that is, defends itself, bands itself erect, and elaborates itself only in being Medusa'd by oneself, in eating-Medusa'ing oneself, in making oneself a bit [*mors*] that gives oneself/itself up as lost [*fait son deuil*]. Dead sure of self. No *logic* is more powerful than this apotropic. No absolutely general economy, no exposition or pure expenditure: a strict-ure more or less strong.
>
> His [*Sa*] Medusa('s), always. (*Glas,* p. 202b)

Perhaps through a certain general economy as opposed to restricted—ontotheological and ontophallotheological—economies (Derrida clearly refers here to the notion of general economy as developed by Bataille), one can think of the Medusa as the other—the Dionysian other, or the other beyond the Dionysian.

In *Nietzsche et la scène philosophique* Sarah Kofman invokes the Medusa in her reading of *The Birth of Tragedy,* the Apollonian Medusa, or the (non)space—*différance*—between the Apollonian Medusa and the Dionysian Medusa: "The veiled Medusa versus a Medusa stripped of all veil; blinding by the light versus blinding by the Night, such are the remedy-poisons [*pharmakon*] of Apollo; it is a case of the homeopathic medication of a cathartic type."[12] Nietzsche has many a *pharmakon,* no less than Plato or Socrates, although these are very different economies of remedy or poison; and the relation "the remedy-poison—*pharmakon*—of Apollo" to "the [Aristotelian] homeopathic medication of a cathartic type," may be more complex than Kofman suggests.[13]

Nietzsche never speaks of the Apollonian woman, either; and at one point of *The Birth of Tragedy* it is the Medusa's head that guards, for a while, the Greek culture, as the Apollonian culture, against the invasion or the return of the Dionysian: "For some time, however, the Greeks were apparently perfectly insulated and guarded against the feverish excitements of these festivals, though knowledge of them must have come to Greece on all the routes of land and sea; for the figure of Apollo, rising full of pride, held out the Gorgon's head [*Medusenhaupt*] to this grotesquely uncouth Dionysian power—and really could not have countered any more dangerous force" (KSA 1:32; BT §2, p. 39). However, particularly in the later Nietzsche, where the Dionysian becomes a very general matrix, the question of Nietzsche's woman must be posed in relation to the question of the Dionysian—Nietzsche's great question. Dionysus' female surrounding is important to this symbolism. "I know no higher symbolism than this *Greek* symbolism of the Dionysian festivals," Nietzsche says (KSA 6:159; TI p. 562*). This aspect of the Dionysian symbolism is a substratum of the Nietzschean economy of the feminine; and, as the chapter "When the Gods Are Born" of Irigaray's *Marine Lover* suggests, it can also be seen or *written* as a kind of *différance* of the female surrounding and the genealogy of the Apollonian symbolism, or the Christian (or anti-Christian) symbolism, in Nietzsche (*Marine Lover,* pp. 121–90). Although hardly a unique example (and Achilles would be another relevant case, as it is for Cixous in "Sorties"), Dionysus, perhaps more than any other mythological figure, appears at times as a woman, or disguised as a woman. That metamorphosis or disguise, obviously familiar to Nietzsche, may have been among the forces in the economy of Nietzsche's identifications and metaphorical exchanges with women and the feminine. Neither these Dionysian elements nor this economy itself, however, would suspend the problematic character of the Nietzschean economy of the feminine. But these women of Dionysus are, I think, different from the *Dionysian* woman—the laughing Dionysian Medusa. These women would still belong to Dionysus, although not *properly* or authentically (*eigentlich*) or as *property.* Nothing can properly—authentically or as property—belong to anything within the economy of the Dionysian. It is possible that by so suspending or refiguring the economy of the proper a certain congruence between Nietzsche and feminism can emerge, as Derrida's and related feminist readings of Nietzsche appear to suggest. It is also conceivable, however, and perhaps more likely that the very symbolism of the Dionysian, even the laughing, Dionysian Medusa, might have to be given up.

Nietzsche does speak of Ariadne and Dionysus in his critique (with Kant clearly in mind) of the concept and the judgment of the beautiful in *Twilight of the Idols:* " 'O Dionysus, divine one, why do you pull me by my ears?' Ariadne once asked her philosophic lover during one of those famous dialogues on Naxos. 'I find a kind of humor in your ears, Ariadne: why are they not even longer?' " (KSA 6:123–24; TI p. 526). The questions to which this scene is a reply proceed by way of a whisper into the skeptic's *ear:* "At bottom, man mirrors himself in things; he considers everything beautiful that reflects his own image: the judgment 'the beautiful' is the *vanity of his species.* For a little suspicion may whisper this question into the skeptic's ear: Is the world really beautified by the fact that man thinks it beautiful? He has *humanized* it, that is all. But nothing, absolutely nothing, guarantees that man should be the model of beauty. Who knows what he looks like in the eyes of a higher judge of beauty? Daring perhaps? Perhaps even amusing? Perhaps a little arbitrary?" (KSA 6:123; TI pp. 525–26).

Long ears can even be beautiful—in a woman—and particularly for Dionysus. Nietzsche, however, also speaks of his own ears in *Ecce Homo:* "All of us know, some even know from experience, which animal has long ears. Well then, I dare assert that I have the smallest ears. This is of no small interest to women—it seems to me that they may feel I understand them better. —I am the *anti-ass par excellence* and thus a world-historical monster—I am, in Greek, and not only in Greek, the *Antichrist*" (KSA 6:302; EH p. 263). Nietzsche may feel not only that he understands women better but also that women understand him better, better even than men. That may have been true, indeed it may still be true; women may well understand Nietzsche better; and they may also understand him better where his understanding becomes a problem unperceived by Nietzsche himself. Certainly, when it comes to the ear of the other, such as Ariadne's ear, a certain asymmetrical—or *ass* symmetrical—relation enters Nietzsche's "revaluation of all values."

Nietzsche's economy of the feminine may, therefore, be related to the economy of the ear and of "the ear of the other," including the economy of his relationships with women or women's relationships with him, from Lou Salomé to Luce Irigaray. Here one should perhaps also consider his letters to women, written in the style of writing no longer "originarily subordinate to the logos and to truth" (*Of Grammatology,* p. 19).[14] This text, or case, would demand a long analysis that cannot be undertaken here. It may be suggested, however, that even though in Nietzsche all value is differentiated—perspectivized—his discourse assigns *woman* and women positions that, while not the same, are *structurally* analogous to classical hierarchies.[15] The highest values always manifest themselves in men—Zarathustra, the *Übermensch,* or Nietzsche himself, who has the smallest ears, the ears "to listen to hear the music" (*Marine Lover,* p. 37).

There remain great insights, especially on the concept of *truth*-woman —more so, I think, on *truth*-woman than on truth-*woman*—that lead to powerful deconstructions of truth, metaphysics, philosophy, the authentic, and the proper (*le propre, eigentlich*). As I have indicated, particularly on the question of property—theoretical, political, or economic—Nietzsche offers great critical resources to feminism.[16] Also, at certain points, these are women, as against men, to whom Nietzsche attributes a more profound—and often his own—understanding of things, specifically the supplementary—"adornmentlike"—character of truth. According to Nietzsche, truth is woman's last concern, although, as shall be seen presently, this view can also be placed within an antifeminist economy. This ambivalence characterizes Nietzsche's economy of woman and the feminine throughout. This economy, then, may be played out so as to relate woman to Nietzsche's many Dionysianisms and thus help to puncture the ears of philosophy with Nietzsche's tympani, which Derrida invokes in "Tympan":[17] "To philosophize with a hammer. Zarathustra begins by asking himself if he will have to puncture them, batter their ears (*Muss man ihnen erst die Ohren zerschlagen*), with the sound of cymbals or tympani, the instruments, always, of some Dionysianism. In order to teach them 'to hear with their eyes' too."[18]

"The Ear of the Other" is the title of one of Derrida's essays on Nietzsche, a text that inscribes a complex economy of the ear.[19] *Ecce Homo* is "above all the book on music," and thus on the ear ("Eisenman," p. 99). These Nietzschean themes are invoked by Derrida in the context of architecture. The ear may indeed be the most architectural human organ, and the metaphor was explored by Derrida, alongside Nietzsche's musical instruments, in "Tympan." The ear has both tympani and labyrinths, music and architecture. Are the ears of philosophers too delicate for the music of Nietzsche's hammers—also the carpenter's instrument, the tool through which architecture fulfills its ambitions—or for his architecture? Or, in their musical sensibility and in their architecture, are they not delicate enough? Or are they both at once? For one must move "beyond that which is inscribed on the internal vestibule of his [Hegel's] ear. This implies a vestibule in a delicate, differentiated structure whose orifices remain undefinable, and whose entry and exit remain barely passable" ("Tympan," p. xi).

Nietzsche's style demands different ears, "ears related to ours." Nietzsche, too, speaks of such ears by way of the architectural metaphor of the entrance into the labyrinth: "All the nobler spirits and tastes select their audience when they wish to communicate; and choosing that, one at the same time erects barriers against 'the others.' All the more subtle laws of any style have their origin at this point: they at the same time keep away, create a distance, forbid 'entrance,' understanding, as said above—while they open the ears of those who are related to us by way of ears [*während sie Denen die Ohren aufmachen, die uns mit den Ohren verwandt sind*]" (KSA 3:634; GS §381, p. 343*).[20] This style is, thus, also Medusa-like, for, just as (or as) the woman, the Medusa, too, keeps away, creates distance, forbids "entrance." These are all, according to Nietzsche's persistent invocations, attributes of woman, who acts at and seduces from a distance. The pathways of the style between "those whose ears are similar to ours" and "the others" involve many detours, perhaps inevitably via letters—for example, those addressed to the eyes and the ears of women, who, as Irigaray says, are Nietzsche's "resonances" and "hearing."[21]

It is not that women would necessarily want to identify with Nietzsche or Nietzsche's Dionysianisms, their music or architecture. "What does woman want?" is, of course, Freud's question, not Nietzsche's. In the opening of section 232 in *Beyond Good and Evil,* which is one of his most antifeminist elaborations (KSA 5:170–72; BGE §232, pp. 162–64), Nietzsche says, however: "Woman wants to become self-reliant—and for that reason she is beginning to enlighten men about 'woman as such' [*Weib an sich*]: *this* is one the worst developments of the general *uglification* of Europe" (KSA 5:170; BGE §232, p. 162). Nietzsche's general critique of anything "as such" and of superficial forms of enlightenment and scientificity which he invokes here are, of course, important, as are his accompanying elaborations in this and surrounding sections. These elaborations continuously play the economy of proximity-distance between Nietzsche and woman without, however, ever erasing the problematic aspect of Nietzsche's economy of the feminine. Thus, Nietzsche qualifies that in wanting "enlightenment about herself" a woman may only

> seek a new adornment for herself that way—I do think adorning herself is part of the Eternal-Feminine?—she surely wants to inspire fear of herself—perhaps she seeks mastery. But she does not *want* truth: what is truth to woman? From the beginning, nothing has been more alien, repugnant, and hostile to woman than truth—her great art is the lie, her highest concern is mere appearance and beauty. Let us men confess it: we who have a hard time and for our relief like to associate with beings under whose hands, eyes, and tender follies our seriousness, our gravity and profundity almost appear to us like folly. (KSA 5:171; BGE §232, p. 163)

A bit later Nietzsche refers, jointly, to Dante and Goethe, in the context of the eternally feminine and the gaze, and thus again, by implication, of the Medusa (KSA 5:173; BGE §236, p. 165). One must also keep in mind Nietzsche's earlier qualification: "I shall perhaps be permitted . . . to state a few truths about 'women as such'—assuming that it is now known from the outset how very much these are after all only—*my* truths" (KSA 5:170; BGE §231, p. 162). It is, however, *Nietzsche's* truths or perspectives on women that are in question, particularly insofar as who is entitled to know and to speak about women, even if, and indeed because, the ontotheology and ontophallotheology of truth becomes no longer possible. This part of *Beyond Good and Evil* is remarkable for its oscillations between Nietzsche's critique of all ontotheology and his antifeminism. Section 232 ends at a juncture of Nietzsche and Napoleon, on the one hand, and women and politics, on the other: "And I think it is a real friend of women that counsels them today: *mulier taceat de muliere*"—woman should be silent about woman, as, according to Napoleon, speaking to Madame de Staël, she must be silent about politics (KSA 5:172; BGE §232, p. 164).

It is possible that, as understood by Nietzsche, "All 'feminism,' too, also in men—closes the door; it will never permit entrance into this labyrinth of audacious insights" (KSA 6:303; EH p. 264). The question may well be, however, whether on the question of woman these insights are audacious enough, or Dionysian enough, or whether the Dionysian itself is audacious enough. In the latter case, the question would be whether women even want or can afford to be on the opposite, Dionysian end of the Nietzschean spectrum. Whether the theorists of the feminine want or can afford to be Dionysian philosophers, such as Nietzsche himself. Indeed whether women and theorists of the feminine want or can afford to be positioned anywhere along this spectrum. Or whether an altogether different optics becomes necessary, all the deconstructive and affirmative power of Nietzsche's discourse notwithstanding. Women may want and need to use this power whenever necessary. But do women really feel that Nietzsche understands them better? Nietzsche may well have understood women better than some of his contemporaries—men. But women? Does Nietzsche *know* women, whether in the sense of *kennen* or *wissen? Who* knows? A double question about Nietzsche and about women. A double question mark. In a section of *The Gay Science,* entitled "Our Question Mark," Nietzsche asks: "But you do not understand this? Indeed people will have trouble understanding us. We are looking for *words;* perhaps we are also looking for *ears*. Who are we anyway?" (KSA 3:579; GS §346, pp. 285–86; emphasis added). This too is at least a double question, and unquestionably the question of woman and gender, which, as Nietzsche may in fact have been first to realize, is also the question of the irreducible doubling of all sameness.

Is Nietzsche looking for Ariadne's ears, too? Ariadne, Irigaray suggests, "faithfully reproduc[es] the perspective suggested to her." She may even be "the double of the male," which is very different from doubling, splitting the sameness of the male and, by implication (or by definition), any single order (*Marine Lover,* p. 117). Even if one talks to (the ears of) the Medusa—who is no Ariadne—one might still manage to avoid looking into her eyes, never knowing whether she is laughing or not, unless one can also laugh with one's ears. The Medusa's eyes and ears may be those of a very different form of the externally feminine, an entirely different other—the other of philosophy and, perhaps, of the Dionysian as well.

Of the Medusa's eyes much has been said. The Medusa's ears remain an open—or thus far closed—question. Nobody thinks about speaking to the Medusa, or writing (to) her perhaps, in a style "no longer originarily subordinate to the logos and to truth." A postcard, detoured through that famous route from Socrates to Freud and beyond, via Nietzsche? But can one assume that either economy—that of the voice and conversation (dialogue or dialectics) of philosophy or that of the postal (mail or male?) deconstructive detours and delayed ("purloined") letters of writing—or any circulation between them can handle such a communication? A phone call, possibly, like the one Derrida mentions in *The Post Card* (p. 21), from (by that point dead) Martin Heidegger or Martine Heidegger? Still the same traffic? Music, then, or dance? For, if, according to Nietzsche, tragedy is born out of the spirit of music, music is born out of the spirit of dance—the maenads' dance, or Salome's. Lou Andreas-Salomé is a very important proper name for Friedrich Nietzsche and in the case history designated by the name "Nietzsche."[22]

The Ends of the Closure

The main theoretical question suggested by the preceding discussion is, then, to what extent one can succeed in approaching the questions of woman and gender from within the Nietzschean matrix, effective as this matrix is as a critique of philosophy, morality, religion, and theology—in short, of all ontotheology. Or, instead, it may be that in order to approach these questions, one needs to replace or least to transform fundamentally the whole Nietzschean or post-Nietzschean strategic-theoretical field. "Must not these [Nietzsche's] *apparently feminist* propositions [*writing* being a woman, if style were a man] be reconciled with the overwhelming *corpus* of Nietzsche's venomous anti-feminism?"—Derrida asks in *Spurs* (pp. 56/57). As Derrida suggests in response to this question, "Their congruence (a notion which I oppose by convention to that of coherence) is very enigmatic, but rigorously necessary"

(*Spurs*, pp. 56/57*). This "congruence" may thus be opposed to subtracting "the overwhelming corpus of Nietzsche's venomous anti-feminism" from Nietzsche's *writing* as "no longer originarily subordinate to the logos and to truth." If so, however, then the whole Nietzschean matrix may be in question. The congruence suggested by Derrida in *Spurs* and "Choreographies" and (following Derrida's analysis) by others *produces* a "Nietzsche" that is more or less equivalent or very close to (Derrida's) deconstruction. Elsewhere Derrida suggests a potential difference, at least at certain points, between Nietzsche's and his own projects.[23] It is possible that deconstruction and the deconstructively refigured Nietzsche form a more effective overall matrix for feminist theory. It is also possible, however, that such a matrix is insufficient, in part, paradoxically by virtue of not being Nietzschean enough. One would need, that is, to stratify Nietzsche's text differently, and not only in relation to Nietzsche's inscription of the feminine and gender. Then one would have to use Nietzsche—or certain strata of Nietzsche's text—against (Derridean) deconstruction, on the one hand, and use gender theory—including possibly some (post)deconstructive gender theories—against Nietzsche, on the other. In particular, it may be argued that, while the economy of (anti)truth-woman developed by Derrida's analysis in *Spurs* may well precomprehend the economy of *truth*-woman in the text of philosophy, a very different economy of the feminine and gender may be produced from within alternative gender theories, even if the latter cannot position themselves fully outside philosophy and its closure.

From this perspective, it may be suggested that a double or triple move—first with or by way of Nietzsche against philosophy, possibly even against deconstruction, and then against Nietzsche, via the question of gender—may lead to a more effective theory of gender and, as a result, to a transformation of a much broader theoretical field. By a radical break with philosophy I mean here a break with ontotheology or the metaphysics of presence. Nietzsche, Derrida, and others demonstrate, however, that there has been no other philosophy in institutional and textual terms (with the possible exception of some post-Heideggerian developments, including Derrida's work, insofar as the denomination philosophy can apply in these cases).[24] Furthermore, one can speak of the possibility of a radical break not only from philosophy itself but from a broader field defined by Derrida as the closure of philosophy. An interminable investigation ("interminable analysis") of this closure might be seen as characterizing Derrida's deconstruction as a theoretical economy on the *margins* of philosophy.

The question of gender, however, may entail a still more radical transformation of the theoretical field, insofar as the Nietzschean or post-Nietzschean field itself becomes radically refigured or perhaps even abandoned. This latter possibility also implies that, while Nietzsche's antifeminism need not be seen as emerging from within his theoretical matrix and cannot be seen only in these terms, it is quite possible that an effective gender theory cannot be developed from within this matrix, even though it may need to utilize some of its aspects, just as it may need to utilize philosophy or deconstruction.

Can a break from Nietzsche, specifically via the question of gender, lead to a return to some "old" philosophy or a move to some new modern or postmodern form of philosophy—*after* Nietzsche and *after* deconstruction? Or, conversely, will such a move lead to a more radical departure from philosophy than has hitherto been the case? And will it lead to a break from the conceptual and historical closure of philosophy in Derrida's sense? According to Derrida, "The efficacity of the thematic of *différance* may very well, indeed must, one day be superseded, lending itself if not to its own replacement, at least to enmeshing itself in a chain that in truth it never will have governed" (*Margins,* p. 7). If such is the case, what role will the *thematics of gender* play in this process? That question may well relate to a *different* reading of Nietzsche, different specifically from Derrida's and related readings, including feminists'. Indeed the thematics of gender may no longer be comprehended under the rubric of gender difference or gender *différance*. Derrida brilliantly locates the question of *writing* as the persistent blind spot of philosophy. On the one hand, writing is a great *sign* of philosophy's interminable neurosis; and on the other, it is suggestive of a much more effective and productive matrix. Woman is unquestionably no less of a problem for philosophy, and it is not impossible that the question of woman and the question of gender cannot be precomprehended by the thematics of writing, however productive the relationships between the economy of gender and the economy of writing may be. To return to Cixous's terms: speaking, and not necessarily whispering, into the Medusa's ears, along with looking into her laughing eyes, and listening to her, certainly cannot be a return to philosophy's speech, voice, or gaze as the presence, above all the conscious presence, of thought, meaning, or concept.[25] But such an exchange would demand a voice different both from the voice of philosophy and from the *writing* of deconstruction, indefinitely suspended within the closure of philosophy and its voice. As Freccero notes, "In ancient mythology [the Medusa] was also said to be a kind of siren" ("Medusa," p. 127). The only way to survive a siren's song, at least up till now, appears to have been to tie oneself to a mast—a kind of phallus—like Odysseus, who was worried, in book 11 of the *Odyssey*, that the Gorgon would prevent his departure from the underworld ("Medusa," p. 127).

A different economy of gender does not exclude philosophy—the philosophy of language, the philosophy of history, the philosophy of literature and art, or any other philosophy—at least not simply, not quite, and not yet. The *theoretical* effectiveness of philosophy, however, may well be the greatest question mark posed by Nietzsche, including to Heidegger, who comes *after* Nietzsche. One can reread the whole Heideggerian enterprise as an attempt to save philosophy in the wake of Nietzsche's "philosophizing with a hammer"—"philosophizing" in order to destroy philosophy, with Zarathustra finally dancing outside its house. This dancing outside the house is different from operating on the margins of philosophy by way of interminable analysis, as Derrida appears to suggest in "The Ends of Man" (*Margins*, pp. 135–36). Derrida's interminable questioning does transform the field as well, while remaining, in part by design, within the closure of philosophy, and "what is held within the delimited closure may continue indefinitely."[26]

What is at issue is thus also the difference, or *différance*, or perhaps no longer either difference or *différance*, between these two modes of transformation—Nietzsche's radical break from and Derrida's interminable (re)engagement with philosophy. When Cixous says in "The Laugh of the Medusa," "Break out of the circles; don't remain within the psychoanalytic closure. Take a look around, then cut through" (p. 263), this gesture is much more Nietzschean than Derridean. It is true that she invokes here psychoanalytic, Freudian and Lacanian, closure. We can extend this Nietzschean operation, however, to the closure of philosophy as demarcated by Derrida.[27] Such moves—cutting through or breaking away—do not come from nowhere. They depend on other histories and conceptual chains or developments. One can dance outside the house (*oikos*) and the household (economy, *oikonomia*) of philosophy. But one also needs a body to dance. The body is something that has always already been outside philosophy, imprisoned—"disciplined and punished"—in the household of philosophy by all sorts of debts. Nor is the outside of this house a desert—other buildings and materials may be available, and other things are and have always been going on. Philosophy owns property in many places. But it cannot own everything. Momentous transformations—revolutions—are at stake, changing ownerships and abolishing and rewriting laws.

The return of the repressed? Reinstating philosophy and ontotheology, even in its most naive form, by forgetting or abandoning it, as Derrida warns? Such a reinstatement is, of course, possible, but it is not inevitable; and the interminable engagement with philosophy is no guarantee of anything. The most "faithful" adherence to Derrida's warnings and strategies may lead and has led to uncritical reinstatements of what deconstruction warns against or prohibits.

Can there be a *philosophy*—old or new—of gender? What would feminist philosophy as *new* philosophy be? Although it cannot be "old" in historical context, it goes back much further than it is sometimes thought, to Mary Wollstonecraft or even earlier. To be sure, there can be and there are philosophies—ontotheologies of gender—and, at least for now, most feminist theory must, perhaps, proceed within the closure of philosophy in Derrida's sense. But can such ontotheologies or theories within the closure of philosophy, such as deconstructive feminism, be effective enough? Or could something else emerge as a result of these transformations of the theoretical field, conditioned by and conditioning the economy of gender?

Nietzsche, then, could prove to be very important for feminism, first by offering the strategies for a radical break, along with a critique of much that feminism must destroy. Equally importantly, one could learn and benefit more from seeing Nietzsche as a problem, rather than from trying to save him. One would not want to suggest that the *question* of Nietzsche, in whatever form, is irreducible with respect to the question of gender. No question is irreducible, including the question of gender, which itself can be (re)figured in different ways. The exploration of the *problem* of gender in Nietzsche against the power of Nietzsche's insights elsewhere can, however, yield extraordinary theoretical results. They might lead to so radical a transformation of theory that, as a result, the whole Nietzschean or post-Nietzschean theoretical field itself becomes, if not quite abandoned, radically refigured. Among many other deaths, the death of God in Nietzsche is the death of philosophy, at least as hitherto understood. *The Second Sex* may have been the first sign of the second death of philosophy. But then, what needs to die twice may continue to live forever elsewhere.

This brings me back to my epigraph and to Simone de Beauvoir and Sartre. The love affair between feminism and philosophy is possible, it may even be very long, but it may never come to marriage. It does become necessary, however, to refigure the politico-theoretical economy of all these terms and relations—"philosophy," "woman," "feminism," "love affair," and "marriage." Indeed, it may be necessary to refigure everything—*after* feminism that comes *after* Nietzsche.

Notes

1. Hélène Cixous, "Le rire de la méduse," *L'Arc* 61 (1975): 39–54; "The Laugh of the Medusa," in *New French Feminisms: An Anthology*, ed. Elaine Marks and Isabelle de Courtivron (New York: Schocken, 1981), pp. 245–64.

2. Roland Barthes, "I Hear and I Obey . . . ," in *On Signs*, ed. Marshall Blonsky (Baltimore: Johns Hopkins Univ. Press, 1985), p. 55; emphasis added. I am grateful to Silke M. Weineck for pointing out this text to me.

3. Luce Irigaray, *Ce sexe qui n'en est pas un* (Paris: Minuit), p. 28; *This Sex Which Is Not One*, trans. Catherine Porter with Carolyn Burke (Ithaca: Cornell Univ. Press, 1985), p. 29.

4. Luce Irigaray, *Amante marine: De Friedrich Nietzsche* (Paris: Minuit, 1991); *Marine Lover of Friedrich Nietzsche*, trans. Gillian C. Gill (New York: Columbia Univ. Press, 1991), pp. 3, 104–5.

5. See John Freccero's "Medusa: The Letter and the Spirit," in *Dante: The Poetics of Conversion* (Cambridge: Harvard Univ. Press, 1986), pp. 119–35, which also explores the thematics of the feminine.

6. I am not suggesting that these readings are blind to Nietzsche's antifeminism; hence the profound ambivalence toward Nietzsche in Irigaray, Cixous, and other feminist writers. Derrida's *Spurs* (*Eperons: Les Styles de Nietzsche*, [Paris: Flammarion, 1976]; *Spurs: Nietzsche's Styles / Eperons: Les Styles de Nietzsche*, trans. Barbara Harlow [Chicago: Univ. of Chicago Press, 1979]) and "Choreographies" (*Diacritics* 12 [1982]: 66–76), however, never sufficiently problematize Nietzsche's text in this respect. By contrast, in exposing, via Derrida, the "solidarity between logocentrism and phallocentrism," Cixous, in "Sorties," sees a certain complicity between Nietzsche and Hegel, Plato, and the history of philosophy in the process of "repression, repudiation, distancing of woman" (Cixous and Catherine Clément, *The Newly Born Woman*, trans. Betsy Wing [Minneapolis: Univ. of Minnesota Press, 1986], pp. 65, 130 n.1).

7. Georges Bataille, "Nietzsche and the Fascists," in *Visions of Excess: Selected Writings, 1927–1939*, ed. Allan Stoekl (Minneapolis: Univ. of Minnesota Press, 1985), 184; "Nietzsche and les fascistes," in *Oeuvres complètes* (Paris: Gallimard, 1970–), 1:450.

8. In invoking this passage in "Why Peter Eisenman Writes Such Good Books," in *Restructuring Architectural Theory*, ed. Marco Diani and Catherine Ingraham (Evanston: Northwestern Univ. Press, 1989), pp. 99–100 and passim, Derrida truncates Nietzsche's reference to "feminism" from his quotation. This omission may be understandable in the context of an essay on architecture. This section of the book, however, contains some of Nietzsche's most pronounced antifeminist statements.

9. See Derrida's remark on rewriting the "genealogy of morals" in his analysis of Lévi-Strauss in *Of Grammatology*, trans. Gayatri C. Spivak (Baltimore: Johns Hopkins Univ. Press, 1974), p. 140. The question of woman plays a key role in this analysis.

10. See also Derrida's elaborations in his recent *Mémoires d'aveugle: L'Autoportrait et autres ruines* (Paris: Editions de la réunion des musées nationaux, 1990), pp. 84–88.

11. Jacques Derrida, *Glas*, trans. John P. Leavy and Richard Rand (Lincoln: Univ. of Nebraska Press, 1986), p. 46a; *Glas* (Paris: Galilée, 1974), p. 65a.

12. Sarah Kofman, *Nietzsche et la scène philosophique* (Paris: Union générale d'éditions, 1979), pp. 76–77.

13. See Andrzej Warminski's discussion in *Readings in Interpretation: Hölderlin, Hegel, Heidegger* (Minneapolis: Univ. of Minnesota Press, 1987), pp. xxxv–lxi. On *pharmakon*, see Derrida's "Plato's Pharmacy," in *Dissemination*, trans. Barbara Johnson (Chicago: Univ. of Chicago Press, 1981).

14. Derrida opens his analysis in *Spurs* with Nietzsche's letter to a woman, Malwida von Meysenbug (1872, the year of *The Birth of Tragedy*), where "the visit as such, *der Besuch an sich*," is that of "Wagner *mit Frau*, Wagner with wife" (*Spurs*, pp. 34/35). Derrida's "*Envois*," in *The Post Card: From Socrates to Freud and Beyond*, trans. Alan Bass (Chicago: Univ. of Chicago Press, 1987), are also love letters in and about a plural style, but, I think, a style different from Nietzsche's.

15. Nietzsche's early (1871) elaborations on the Greek woman (KSA 7:170–75, 349) are of considerable interest in this respect, and they would confirm the point at issue.

16. Again, see Cixous's essay ("Laugh," p. 259). The economy of the proper is crucial to Derrida's analysis throughout his work, especially in *Spurs*.

17. See in particular Nietzsche's comment on "old women" who are "more skeptical in their most secret heart of hearts than any man" (KSA 3:426; GS §64, p. 125). Feminism as understood by Nietzsche may also be seen as a desire for truth, relating, if not identifying, feminists with scientific man. To identify these completely in Nietzsche would be hasty, and the stratifications of the positive and negative aspects of being scientific, on one hand, and being a feminist, on the other, are complex. Cf., however, Derrida's analysis in *Spurs*, pp. 62/63–66/67.

18. Jacques Derrida, "Tympan," in *Margins of Philosophy*, trans. Alan Bass (Chicago: Univ. of Chicago Press, 1980), pp. xii–xiii; *Marges de la philosophie* (Paris: Minuit, 1972), p. iv.

19. Jacques Derrida, *The Ear of the Other*, ed. Christie V. McDonald (New York: Schocken, 1985). Cf. "Heidegger's Ear: Philopolemology (Geschlecht IV)," in *Commemorations: Reading Heidegger*, ed. John Sallis (Bloomington: Indiana Univ. Press, 1992).

20. See, however, Philippe Lacoue-Labarthe's "The Echo of the Subject," in *Typography: Mimesis, Philosophy, Politics*, ed. Christopher Fynsk (Cambridge: Harvard Univ. Press, 1989) for a discussion of "seeing" and "hearing" in the context of Nietzsche and psychoanalysis.

21. One may refer to the economy of the letter and letters, including the letters to women considered in Lacan's "Seminar of 'The Purloined Letter'" and then in Derrida's reading of Lacan and "*Envois*" in *The Post Card*.

22. Here a reference to Oscar Wilde is due, by this somewhat but perhaps not altogether fortuitous association of proper names. Wilde's *Salome* and his other plays, often centered around the question of women, and his prose and critical essays offer, I think, productive possibilities to feminist theory. One would not want to give too much significance to the statement in my epigraph: "We women, as someone says, love with our ears, just as you men love with your eyes" (*The Picture of Dorian Gray* [Harmonds-

worth: Penguin, 1985], p. 233). It is interesting, however, that Wilde attributes it to a woman, and "a very clever woman" (p. 210).

23. See "Tympan," xiii, and "Living On: Border Lines," in Harold Bloom et al., *Deconstruction and Criticism* (New York: Continuum, 1979), pp. 124–25 ("Border Lines").

24. See Philippe Lacoue-Labarthe's opening discussion in *La Fiction du politique: Heidegger, l'art et la politique* (Paris: Christian Bourgois, 1987); *Heidegger, Art and Politics: The Fiction of the Political,* trans. Chris Turner (Oxford: Basil Blackwell, 1990). See also Jean-Luc Nancy's Introduction, in *Who Comes after the Subject?* ed. Eduardo Cadava, Peter Connor, and Jean-Luc Nancy (New York: Routledge, 1991).

25. See especially Cixous's comments in "Sorties," p. 94.

26. Jacques Derrida, *Positions,* trans. Alan Bass (Chicago: Univ. of Chicago Press, 1981), p. 13*; *Positions* (Paris: Minuit, 1972), p. 23. I have considered this issue in *Reconfigurations: Critical Theory and General Economy* (Gainesville: Univ. Press of Florida, 1993), pp. 194–211.

27. Derrida's work may be seen as a kind of juncture of the Heideggerian incessant questioning and Freud, leading to an interminable treatment of the finally incurable neuroses of philosophy. In *The Post Card* he speaks of the "picture" of "two thinkers whose *glances* never crossed and who, without ever receiving a word from one another, say the same. They are *turned* [*tournés*] to the same side" (*The Post Card,* p. 191). Perhaps both are also turned away from the Medusa's eyes and ears.

PART FIVE

"Digression"

LAURENCE A. RICKELS

Insurance for and against Women: From Nietzsche to Psychotherapy

> Freud was aware that in its practical application analysis must undergo dilution. This is but the natural fate of every great ideology: it loses its noblest characteristic, its splendid isolation, and acquires practical value only in its dilution, alteration, adaptation. This is necessarily the destiny too of analysis because as an empirical science it serves practical ends wherein the immediate result must be of permanent value. Thus of the genius-given gift of Freud humanity will acquire its fullest social value only when it becomes by this dilution a common property, even indeed divorced from the name of its creator.
>
> —Helene Deutsch, "Freud and His Pupils: A Footnote to the History of the Psychoanalytic Movement"

In Love and War

During the formulation of Freud's second system, the number of claims made on psychoanalysis in Nietzsche's name were, on all sides, on the rise. Will to Power and *amor fati* went along for the death drive while the model of the psyche was changing into id and superego inside Superman's booth. Nietzsche's inside view of life as self-affirming joy or as suffering that says yes scored Big Time inside the second system's alternation of takes on female sexuality, group psychology, and the death and destruction drive (the sadomasochistic distribution of pleasure). Like Nietzsche, like Freud: it's the experience of women that constitutes the group-psychological moment.

The same pull tugging inside and between Nietzsche and Freud (which collapses group-psychological concerns onto a question of woman raised together with that life-and-death issue which comes complete as drive) can be found stretching and marking the reception of the Nietzsche-to-Freud connection. Women caught the connection and were admitted into the theoretical discourse that turned on sexual difference: it was the first discourse (some call it misogynist) to give gender politics shelter.

The wish to equalize in theory what was pressing for equal rights in practice (a shift in register from politics to thinking which Freud diagnosed as psychosis-compatible) counted in such followers as Adler and Jung while counting them out of psychoanalysis.[1] The couplification of repression around the bisexuality thesis—the opposition or the equalization of sexual difference—brought us the grand opening of the psychotherapies which, already by 1914, flourished in the afterglow of their breakup with psychoanalysis. The breakaway Adlerian and Jungian movements were, by 1933 at the latest, much more popular than psychoanalysis. It was at the time he was reinscribing the traumatic origin of identification within the psychopolitical contexts introduced by World War I that Freud issued the warning that his science must not be confused with the new and improved therapies and theories.[2] But psychoanalysis too was making the headlines with its interventionism in the military complex. That's why the reunification of the German therapies and theories in 1933 could not count psychoanalysis out. "When I knew Professor Freud in Vienna in 1922, he was aged 65 and more or less at the height of his career. Soon after 1910 the solitary obscurity which had surrounded him and his work for something like 20 years had begun to lessen, while the war neuroses in Europe had generated, both in the medical profession and in the general public, an interest in the psychological approach to such disorders."[3]

The triad of group psychology, female sexuality, and the death-and-destruction drive was admitted into the second system via the serial dreams of traumatized war and accident victims. The traumatized dreamers' compulsion to repeat rather than remember had shot up through the shock's penetration beyond pleasure or before defense: it "was there" at the starting point of all absorption, preparedness, or first-line defense. With catastrophe you start all over again from the first scratch of the breach of defense: but once you have the catastrophe where you want it (down inside identification), it leaves you there, in a state of catastrophe-preparedness that's *über alles*.

Pre–World War I Freud was still figuring out the death-wish fulfillment at the vampiric heart of identification. As though there were such a thing as symptomatic synchronicity, the pre–World War era was at the same time the danger zone of the first departures from or improvements on psychoanalysis. Led by her autoanalytic and endopsychic insights into the groupified position of female sexuality, Sabina Spielrein didn't so much split psychoanalysis as give the advance preview of Freud's second system. The "psychotic Hysteric," as she was diagnosed, started out as Jung's bedside discovery: their transference–love affair gave her the cure.[4] Which is why she became a Freudian analyst. But Spielrein was still riding out the countertransferential current of Freud's resistance when she decided to be Freud's disciple but Jung's best friend. That's why even though she was indeed giving him a bad case of ct's, Freud had no choice but to defend his underworld exploration of delusional systems against Spielrein's premature acceleration of death wishes into death drive.

In 1912 Freud could write Jung that he found Spielrein's destruction drive not to his liking because it was "personally conditioned": "She seems abnormally ambivalent."[5] It was too much ambivalence—too soon. (What's more, she was hooked on biology.)[6] But by the time he admitted the death drive into his system, Freud was also admitting a measure (beyond pleasure) of personal conditioning and ambivalence overload, indeed, a strong dose of biological (or biographical) dependence: it was the time of his daughter Sophie's death. It was only at this point that Freud admitted life insurance (i.e. the death drive) into the system: it was a group protection plan that granted female sexuality equal coverage. It was then that Freud took in Spielrein's inspired or dictated anticipation of the death drive—at the time, then, of Nietzsche's increasing claim on psychoanalysis. And it was time for psychotherapy to grow an influence that in the name of the precursor was already in World War I outflanking psychoanalysis. Thus in 1917 Jung interrupts his all-out attack on Freud to give Spielrein some sound advice: "You must read Adler or Nietzsche."[7] Women were getting the reading lists about pathologies they modeled. It was the contribution of these women that exhumed the pre-Oedipal mother. Spielrein's transvestization—Norman-Bates style—of psycho Nietzsche first marked the spot of her haunting return. Spielrein's 1912 *Destruction as the Cause of Becoming* dropped inside its preview of Freud's second system a case study of Nietzsche as matricentric schizo.

Spielrein had, then, already in 1912, diagnosed Nietzsche. His lifelong solitude (especially when it came to libido) was too much for the poet: he created along the group-psychological trajectory the imaginary friend Zarathustra (with whom he identified). "The yearning for a love object brought about that Nietzsche became in himself man and woman and both of these in the shape of Zarathustra."[8] The celebration by Nietzsche/Zarathustra of a natural sensurround of mergers (for example between the sun and the sea) strikes up an internal depth inhabited ultimately by mother: "If the mother is his own depth, then the union with the mother must also be seen as autoerotic, as union with himself" (p. 31). What goes around comes around: in the series of Nietzsche's displaced mergers, the finale transforms Nietzsche into "the engendering, creating, becoming mother" (p. 31). In the feminine position of identification with the mother who penetrates him, the dementia praecox patient living in autoerotic isolation tends to pack a homosexual component.

This maternal bond scores an almost perfect regression on a scale of identification. But, says Spielrein, it's just the radical feminine mode of destruction and self-destruction control: the internalized distribution of desire between the sexes puts man in the position of subject loving the object projected into the outside and woman in a position to love herself as his object (p. 32). According to Spielrein's family outing, both woman and child hang out with "homosexuality" and "autoerotism": "the child must imagine how she is loved and accordingly put herself in the role of her parents" (p. 33).

"But if, through identification with the loved individual, the object representations grow in intensity, then the love reserved for oneself leads to self-destruction" (p. 34). That's why even the act of procreation follows the beat of self-destruction (the other fact of life, which Nietzsche's imaginary friend calls "self-overcoming"). The destruction drive may make you come *and* go but it also has you covered: the eternal returns on identification keep even schizo Nietzsche in business.

According to the coverage Spielrein gives the psyche, you get what you ask for: one's relation to one's ancestors (*Ahnen*) embodies a resemblance or likeness (*Ähnlichkeit*) that, whether downing identification or doing sex, one likes—to be like. That's why reproduction is a merger with one's ancestors through the lover that looks like you. The death that follows on the Oedipal heels of incest is not just punishment and prohibition; incest realizes, one, one's desired restoration to the engenderer and, two, the dissolution in him (p. 39).

This ancestral likability bond pervades all experience—which can never be in the present tense. "Every content of conscious thought is a product of differentiation from other, psychologically more ancient contents" (p. 40). By making the content fit the present moment we personalize it and give it the character of an ego connection. But when we share the fantasy (with the other), that is, when we start talking, then we dedifferentiate and depersonalize back to the generic which goes for the species. This move travels the second opposing tendency in us, the beaten track to assimilation and dissolution. "I" no longer speaks for a unity that has been transformed into a larger unit for which "We" is the spokesperson or talkshow host. This is how art, dream, and the pathological symbolicity of dementia praecox form an alignment on parallel tracks. The creation/dissolution of the ego connection goes with the upsurge of pleasure or unpleasure. Whenever the personal experience has been transformed into a generic one we relate to it as members of the audience to a staged event in which we participate only if we get into it. That's our role when we're unconscious: dreams are our time shares in the complete conglomerate or complex called dementia praecox.

Ambivalence is along for the generic drive (the one that's out to preserve the species): this is where each positive component releases a negative counterpart and vice versa. The ego drive is the static one that tries to defend the egoic or individual status quo against foreign influence. The differentiation tendency is along for the drive to preserve oneself. The drive to sustain the species is a reproductive drive that goes the way (down) of dissolution and assimilation. But here another differentiation of the primal material comes up: it's the one called love. Dissolution of the ego in one's lover is at the same time the strongest self-affirmation; it means a new life lease or policy for the ego in the person of the lover. Without love, the change that comes over the psychic and physical individual from the outside (as in sex) gets represented as death and destruction. That's why resistance to life is *the* neurotic symptom (there is no other symptom).

In the case of Nietzsche, the schizo solo course of libido alone contains eternally the same tension between the sexes. Drawing current from the interchange or charge between annihilation phantasms and autoerotic satisfaction loaded into her Nietzsche diagnosis, Spielrein plugs in the ultimate connection—all the way into the future—between groupie psychology and war neurosis. To read between the dreams (in which girls see themselves knifed) she activates the psychoanalytic decoder: dreams contain no negation and thus no negation of life.

> In accordance with the fact that the woman gets penetrated in the sex act, the girl sees herself, as does the woman, as the victim in the dream of a sadistically colored sexual act. That's why the events of warfare are so suited for the outbreak of neurosis, which at bottom has its source in the disturbances of the sex life. It is war that goes along with ideas of destruction. Now, since one idea calls up other related ones, so the ideas of destruction in war excite ideas associated with the destructive components of the reproductive instinct. These latter ideas can ruin existence as something outright transitory and pointless even for normal people and especially for the neurotic, in whose thoughts

> the ideas of destruction outweigh those of becoming and who thus only has to wait for appropriate symbols for the representation of these destruction fantasies. (pp. 26–27)

Spielrein goes on (down) to interrogate in these contexts the teen girl fantasies of lying in graves. These open onto womb fantasies right down to the interchangeability of gravedigging and penetration (and birth). For the neurotic this is the same as the live burials and aftershocks brought to us by shell blast: "For a normal girl the idea of being buried gives rise to ecstasy as soon as she thinks of dissolution in her lover. A young girl told Binswanger, 'the greatest happiness for her would be to be held inside the body of her lover' " (pp. 28–29). In Spielrein's reading (as would also be the case, on the other side of World War I, in Freud's "The 'Uncanny' ") the womb covers all the test sites of repetition compulsion—in particular the dream series in which many eternal returns of the traumatic incident must be watched by the war neurotic. The womb is the bottom-line guarantee that the war bond of neurosis (the bonding of group identification which scored an origin in trauma) can be converted back to the treatable effects of a sexual disturbance that made the one predisposed to neurotic outbreak always on the lookout for destruction symbols: what already had the stranglehold (on the inside) on sex or reproduction reaches the outside and gets the upper hand in war neurosis.

In her analysis of Nietzsche, Spielrein thought she was doing Jung and Freud. In Geneva when she was doing Piaget she thought she was doing Jung and Freud too (two). (Yes, Spielrein analyzed Piaget and conducted her research on children with him.) She was the first psychotherapist. Her eclecticism was born of the spirits of psychotic or unresolved transference (the one that crushes love into adoration). In short, she was the loyal type. Which means every thinker she followed she stabbed in the back. The eclecticism or reunification of the collected psychotherapies that had split off from psychoanalysis (and which included psychoanalysis as one more therapy to borrow from in treatment) was already part of the *Destruction* manual Spielrein shared with analysis in 1912. Already part of the primal preview we find parallel treatments of war neurotics and homosexuals, of girls and schizos, against a backdrop of their interchangeable theorization in group format. This group protection (projection) plan was negotiated in Nietzsche's case and name. And it's no accident that the psychotherapeutic eclecticism thus introduced or anticipated was bent on (or was it already based on?) insurance coverage.

Jung Hitler

The way Jung back in 1912 suddenly turned to mythology gave Freud advance signs of their break coming soon. Spielrein was already a Jungian when she cut too quickly to an interpretation based on manifest rather than latent contents. The distinction Freud made re mythology between psychoanalytic rereading and Jung's (and Spielrein's) receptivity also goes for their different takes on psychotic delusions, the occult, technology—on all the contexts, in short, of Freud's discovery and delegation of the unconscious. "Consequently I hold that surface versions of myths cannot be used uncritically for comparison with our psychoanalytical findings. We must find our way back to their latent, original forms by a comparative method that eliminates the distortions they have undergone in the course of their history."[9]

Jung's 1936 current-events essay "Wotan" met latent latest standards when it still met, in all its alleged ambiguity, with Nazi approval.[10] Wotan is the divine trendsetter for German youth movements which in 1933 followed Hitler's beat and thus signaled that "Wotan the wanderer was on the move" (p. 180). On this forward march everyone's a stand-in for some precursor: "The German youths . . . were not the first to hear a rustling in the primeval forest of the unconscious. They were anticipated by Nietzsche" (p. 181). Wotan thus is "an elemental Dionysus breaking into the Apollonian order" (p. 187). Breaking in with Wotan into Nietzsche's opening of the origin of the community spirit brought to us by music, Jung brings Nietzsche up to date: "The maenads were a species of female stormtroopers, and, according to mythical reports, were dangerous enough. Wotan confined himself to the berserkers, who found their vocation as the Blackshirts of mythical kings" (p. 185).

In "After the Catastrophe," Jung claimed (in 1945) to be picking up where he left off in 1936.[11] This time around he developed a diagnosis of the German modeled after Nietzsche's case:

> Inferiority feelings are usually a sign of inferior feeling—which is not just a play on words. All the intellectual and technological achievements in the world cannot make up for inferiority in the matter of feeling. . . . This spectacle recalls the figure of what Nietzsche so aptly calls the "pale criminal," who in reality shows all the signs of hysteria. . . . A feeling of inferiority . . . can easily lead to an hysterical dissociation of the personality, which consists essentially in one hand not knowing what the other is doing . . . and in looking for everything dark, inferior, and culpable *in others*. . . . Therefore all hysterical

> people are compelled to torment others, because they are unwilling to hurt themselves by admitting their own inferiority.
>
> . . . . .
>
> Nietzsche was German to the marrow of his bones, even to the abstruse symbolism of his madness. It was the psychopath's weakness that prompted him to play with the "blond beast" and the "Superman." . . . The weakness of the German character, like Nietzsche's, proved to be fertile soil for hysterical fantasies. (pp. 202–3, 212)

But Jung admits that in 1933 or 1934 the "information" he was receiving, had it stopped short then, could have called for a different judgment: back then it was, after all, a "refreshing wind" (p. 205). But the show of dementia praecox was nonetheless in place. Jung is not reviewing only Hitler's maenadlike "shrill, grating womanish tones" which cheerled "the power fantasies of an adolescent" (p. 204). He's interested in the fantasies that were shared (and which conform to the course Spielrein charted for the likability principle which comes on strong when love isn't at the top): "The nation of eighty millions crowded into the circus to witness its own destruction" (p. 204). However, when Jung concludes that the Germans in their "hysterical twilight-state" followed their "mediumistic Führer . . . with a sleep-walker's assurance" (p. 208), he is repeating (without the more open, even upbeat, conclusion) remarks he made re German events on Radio Berlin in 1933.

Jung's 1945 diagnosis of German hysteria as the exciting cause or first run of what must issue in collective guilt takes the diagnoses of women made by Nietzsche, Freud, and Jung and contains them in this one-sided reception of Nietzsche as the German time capsule. Between the (at best) ambiguous reception of the Nazi libidinal upsurge that had led a new Teen Age and the postwar thesis of collective guilt (which, before everyone else gets body-counted as innocent bystander, counts in Nietzsche as one of the in-group of hysterics teleguiding the emergence of the Nazi symptom), there was a continuity that was there. From 1933 to 1940 Jung was the international leader of Nazi psychotherapy, the president of the "International General Medical Society for Psychotherapy." This international organization was the cover for the local psychotherapy outfit renamed in 1933 "German General Medical Society for Psychotherapy." Between 1934 and 1936 many articles by Jungians were special featured in the central organ of Nazi psychotherapy (*Zentralblatt für Psychotherapie*), while its second issue (after the 1933 takeover) was totally devoted to Jung's analytical psychology. In his introduction to the December 1933 issue of the new *Zentralblatt* (which had just been reanimated and renamed for the new era) Jung concluded: "The difference between Germanic and Jewish psychology, which has already been long recognized by genuinely solid and insightful people, will no longer be blurred, which can only be of benefit to research."[12]

The society reunified all the psychological interventionisms, in the first place the ones that had split off from Freud's science (in pursuit of the human being as a totality, something Freud was not into), but also including, just the same, psychoanalysis itself. The head of the new total organization was Göring's cousin Göring (who was trained as an Adlerian therapist). Adler had all along championed in the name of Nietzsche a holistic socialization approach against Freud's insatiable working of sex and transference. He coupled his therapy with left-wing politics and was thereby able (between the wars) to introduce his real-time counseling into schools and other institutions of the everyday. While the Nazi socialists had to strike out against the completely external and recognizable labels of political groups that had competed with them (just as they had to strike out against anyone Jewish) the assignment was considered complete with the shutdown of left-wing–sponsored programs in Vienna and Berlin (and with the forgetting of Adler's name). But individual psychology remained real popular in Nazi Germany where its Nietzschean and Vaihingerian therapeutic attitude—the "as if," the testing rapport with risk—was fixed upon. As in: what if psychoanalysis had been invented by Nietzsche, which, in a sense, was Adler's question all along. That the head of Nazi psychotherapy was Adlerian is not extraneous to what was all along part of the Adlerian challenge to Freud; it's the same difference that is getting displaced here too. Although Adler made the move to the United States, which is where the "Jewish" psychotherapies went with their names, centers, testing grounds, and sense of where one had to make it to be considered successful at large, Adler's eclecticism (which is the other side of reunification) continued to rule the Göring institute in Berlin.

In 1934 Nazi psychotherapist Leonhard Seif (another Adlerian) turned to Nietzsche and Clausewitz as the two authors of the notion of a psychologically conceived community feeling that was congruent with the war effort. Politics would continue to provide the institutional frame of community; but pedagogy and psychotherapy would lube the tracks guiding each child to his or her life tasks within the national community. As Seif put it in 1940: "Education or psychotherapy is the task of forming a vital community, a 'we' relationship."[13] (Spielrein's psycho-generic-pronoun empire strikes back.)

In 1945 Jung's conception of "collective guilt" extended the coverage he had given himself in 1933 when he tried to run down Freud on those unresolved transference tracks that happened to traverse certain externalizable or political effects (the ones Jung in 1945 still chose to disown). He extended coverage to fellow collaborators by sharing the blame for the special effects with everyone (else). "They should realize that the German catastrophe was only one crisis in the general European sickness" ("After the Catastrophe," p. 214); Germany remains, after all, "the nerve-center of Europe" (p. 213). Didn't it all already start with Maenad-like Nietzsche and his shrill, womanish invitation to the Superman to replace the dead God, Jung asks. "It is an immutable psychological law that when a projection has come to an end it always returns to its origin. So when somebody hits on the singular idea that God is dead, or does not exist at all, the psychic God-image, which is a dynamic part of the psyche's structure, finds its way back into the subject and produces a condition of 'God-Almightiness,' that is to say all those qualities which are peculiar to . . . madmen and therefore lead to catastrophe" (pp. 214–15).

With Jung's charge of projection there's also a double or group projection, that is, an all-out group protection. "If collective guilt could only be understood and accepted, a great step forward would have been taken" (p. 217). "Psychological collective guilt is a *tragic fate*. It hits everybody, just and unjust alike" (p. 197).

Jung nevertheless turns in industrialization and massification as the other collective guilt that's ultimately the guilty party. It's his party—so he can try to make a break if he wants to. It's the line of argument or defense that the reunified psychotherapists and psychoanalysts used during the Third Reich to "save" their line of work and their otherwise Aryan but just the same neurotic clientele. Different time, same station: public intelligence and morality are automatically undermined by the devastating "psychic effects of living together in huge masses" (p. 200). How could it be any other way, even today, and even in another setting: "We, who have so many traitors and political psychopaths in our midst?" (p. 200). The condition of this "state of degradation" "is the accumulation of urban, industrialized masses—of people torn from the soil, engaged in one-sided employment, and lacking every healthy instinct, even that of self-preservation" (p. 200). The loss of this instinct is a liability covered by overdependence on the State. "Dependence on the State means that everybody relies on everybody else (= State) instead of on himself. Every man hangs on to the next and enjoys a false feeling of security, for one is still hanging in the air even when hanging in the company of ten thousand other people. The only difference is that one is no longer aware of one's own insecurity" (p. 201). Hanging with Jung, then, on the air waves, we've got the insurance coverage of collective guilt. Cut off from the self-preservation drive, man, in Jung's words, "becomes the shuttlecock of every wind that blows." At that point of sickness (Jung was there) "nothing short of catastrophe can bring him back to health" (p. 201), nothing, that is, short of insurance.

1932

In *German Ideology* Marx and Engels locate in the German social theory under their attack a propaganda or war-readiness trend that turns on a pretending or testing rapport with risk. Marx and Engels already covered this rapport on the social-scientific side: "Whenever, through the development of industry and commerce, new forms of intercourse have been evolved, (e.g., insurance companies, etc.) the law has always been compelled to admit them among the modes of acquiring property."[14] But the preemptive—pretending and testing—mode of risk and (same difference) grief management that insurance sells cannot be bought back as the time share of socioeconomic causes. Already on the side of propaganda, insurance cannot switch back from social science's other side. The new-founded rapport with risk, with a self/other bond always at risk (and that's the bond), shoots up the psychology of group protection or projection which is no longer enrollable in Marx's classes. By 1932 (the year of the complete *German Ideology*'s publication) the testing rapport with risk had assumed a propagandistic or psychological agenda irreducible to its scientific status or social origin.

It proves possible, maybe necessary, to read the ingredients of the debate between Adorno and Benjamin (same time, same station) off the back of the 1932 release of *The German Ideology*. In the three corners of their match or mismatch: Marx, Freud, and Mickey Mouse. Benjamin's double take on Marxism and Freudian group psychology followed his upbeat reception of Mickey Mouse as *the* group mascot. It's the antidotal shock inoculation that mass culture, with Mickey Mouse at the front of the line, administers. The shots of catastrophe-preparedness control-release the psychotic breakdown our ongoing technologization or massification otherwise telecommands. But, Adorno complains, with Mickey Mouse "things are far more complicated, and the serious question arises as to whether the reproduction of every person really constitutes that *a priori* of the film which you claim it to be, or whether instead this reproduction belongs precisely to that 'naive realism' whose bourgeois nature we so thoroughly agreed upon."[15] Which is to say, the theory of mass ego or mass identification that reproduces the inoculating shock or shot of catastrophe packs its own case of repression. Adorno argues that catastrophes (which appear to go down as prehistory) represent and repress only the recent past; the repression of the scientific or objective inside view brought to us by Freudian psychoanalysis and Marxian social theory adds another layer of primalization to what just went past. Benjamin's mass ego or collective consciousness, like Jung's less conscious conception, is "open to criticism," Adorno writes, "on both sides; from the vantage point of the social process, in that it hypostasizes archaic images where dialectical images are in fact generated by the commodity character, not in an archaic collective ego, but in alienated bourgeois individuals; and from the vantage point of psychology in that . . . a mass ego exists only in earthquakes and catastrophes, while otherwise objective surplus value prevails precisely through individual subjects and against them. The notion of collective consciousness" serves thus only, Adorno concludes, "to divert attention from true objectivity and its correlate, alienated subjectivity" (p. 113). That's why Adorno wants to get Benjamin back to the social science test: Benjamin's notion of testing as the ready-made mass rapport with technologization not only exchanges an old taboo for a new improved one but also misdirects Benjamin's own larger-scale rapport with Marxism away from mediation through the total social process toward the metaphorical, the concrete, the mere as-if. But as Adorno would go on to prove in his own Mickey Mouse essays on jazz and the fetish character of mass music, the metaphorical-concrete-as-if doesn't go away with social conditioning. Indeed, as Benjamin saw it, the trigger-happiness of gadgets, the push-button origin of the test, injects into whatever gets technoreproduced, right down to the moment, a "posthumous shock."[16] "The phantoms of their brains"[17] that Marx and Engels had diagnosed in a social theory that does not see (Nazi) a difference between the reality of war and its anticipation or make-believe had nonetheless encrypted themselves deep down and for keeps inside the test, risk and grief management, the propagandistic bond with warfare or catastrophe, and the psychologization, the merger, of Marxian and Freudian sciences.[18]

Bouncing across the range of symptoms produced by the discursivity merger, Mickey Mouse scored Big Time in a veritable Rorschach Blitz. Nazi Film journals reported in 1936 on Mickey Mouse's premier in the Soviet Union: Moscow critics recognized Disney as a genius and his achievement as consummate social criticism.[19] With Disney the public opinion that went around, came around (even in Nazi Germany): as late as 1940 Nazi socialist ideologues celebrated Disney as injecting the socius with magical antidotes to sociology (p. 103). Early local criticisms of Mickey Mouse in Nazi Germany (for example, as the manic measure or rat race of Western degeneracy) were premature articulations still in line with pre-Nazi diagnoses based on the forensic psychiatry of, say, Kraepelin and Weygandt. The 1931 issue of *Der Querschnitt,* for example, records the psychiatric consensus: "The chronic film image of Mickey Mouse exhibits unmistakable symptoms of his creator's paranoid mental state. . . . But even in the vast majority of the audience we can observe an abnormal state similar to that of Mickey Mouse" (p. 62).

But the spontaneous syndication of psychiatric assessment by the Nazi locals was not followed by the leader. Goebbels records in his diary on December 20, 1937: "I'm giving the Führer for Christmas 30 class films of the last 4 years and 18 Mickey Mouse films. He's already quite excited and very happy. This treasure will hopefully grant him much pleasure and relaxation" (p. 11). Here we watch sitcom-style the upwardly mobile advance that psychotherapy was able to make (in or even in Nazi Germany) toward establishing itself alongside, and that means also against, the interests of psychiatry. The contest prize was equal but separate insurance coverage.

Nazi adoration of Disney (who was rumored to be in fact Walter Distler, native German through and through) supported the years of tortured indecision, renegotiation, ambivalence occasioned by the German release (coming soon even at that late date) of *Snow White.* The movie would in fact never be shown in Nazi German theaters. Hitler, who requested a copy on February 5, 1938 for his private cinema, simply loved it. But it was not enough that Disney was the one (and only) director to receive Leni Riefenstahl on her 1938 visit to Hollywood. That alone could not offset the hurt caused by the anti-Nazi activities (from petition signing to the production of anti-Nazi films) supported by the rest of the industry. Even inside his own studio, Disney told Riefenstahl as he was receiving her, he could not screen the copy of *Olympia* she had brought along since everyone else in his organization right down to the projectionist was dead set against the Nazi cause.

But back in Nazi Germany it did remain possible to apply to the Reichs Film Archive for private screenings of *Snow White* and, after 1941, of Mickey Mouse films. In 1944 one reason recorded for a Nazi minister needing to view *Snow White* was: "to obtain information on animation technique in connection with the planned production by the Reichsministry for Armament and War Production of technical-instructional films" (p. 137).

The Limit

Only under Nazi reunification did psychotherapy and with it psychoanalysis qualify for the Eternal Return of insurance coverage. The psychological warfare that the Nazis were out to total contains a limit that insurance observes. It's the limit that American post–World War II "Psy Warriors" deliberately promoted as the lesson they had learned from the Nazis' biggest mistake: not knowing when to stop winning. Perpetual war (just ask Napoleon) joins the losing streak of war waged to end all war.

H. D. Lasswell, the first American sociologist between the wars not only to take note of the psychological effects of military propaganda but even the first to mount an openly psychoanalytic social theory, defined psychological warfare for the post–World War II phase of conflict: "The best success in war is achieved by the destruction of the enemy's will to resist, and with a minimum annihilation of fighting capacity. The political aim is limited destruction. . . . We are looking at the conduct of war in the perspective of psychology when we are seeking to widen the gap between the physical destruction of capabilities on both sides and the magnitude of the impact upon the enemy's intention to resist."[20] The discovery of the limit alongside a savings in expenditure of destructiveness in the course of war sets a limit to victory and thus to warfare. It creates the conditions for a media war that, as total or totaled war's last stand or auto-overcoming, would no longer be interchangeable with wars said to be in history.

In California at the start of World War I, Josiah Royce proposed international mutual insurance coverage among nations as the limit to total war. (Royce conceived the plan as an extension of workers' compensation, which was Germany's contribution to the history of insurance.)[21] "Modern wars may, as we now know, become more widespread, more democratic in spirit, more ideally self-righteous, than ever they were before" (p. 10). But first things first: there are "positive virtues" backing the militant spirit that cannot be reduced to a hatred exclusive. War's appeal is its appeal to nonimmediate, noncouplified others or authorities. The relation to immediate neighbors is covered by hate. But the relation to honor, to one's own country, but also ultimately to mankind, is what puts war on the side of "fearless faith in life" (p. 19). In a sense, then, war practices a form of violence control. The danger grows in immediate relations, in the one-on-one: "*A pair of men is what I may call an essentially dangerous community*" (p. 30). When one neighbor says to another (out of love for his fellow man *and* for his own voice), "Listen! Don't interrupt. I've got something to say to you," that's the start of war. "A certain social tension is therefore a perfectly natural accompaniment of any concrete social relation between two people" (p. 31).

> We hate not merely because we remember injuries. Many of our sources of antipathy seem to be, in the single case, much more petty than is a desire for revenge; but are actually deeper in their meaning than is such a desire. Very often we tend to hate simply because there are so many of us, and because we are so different one from the other; and so because, when we are taken in pairs, we thus appear in each pair as interrupters and intruders, each member of the pair annoying his fellow even while trying to express whatever love he chances to possess for the other, and each emphasizing his own hatred when he feels it, by dwelling on these dual or bilateral contrasts. (p. 38)

Family ties and other bonds of solidarity or loyalty (such as the ones recycled in war) are readily available alternatives to the violence of the couple. "Love, when it is a merely dyadic relation between a pair of lovers, is essentially unstable and inconstant. For the two tend in the long run to interrupt, to bore, or collide each with the other" (p. 35). "In those communities which are mere pairs, time is the consumer of love but the nourisher of hate" (p. 41). To counter couplified conflict Royce introduces the third person (excluded from the couple via its ongoing groupification, its invasion by the group's one-on-one of mutual identification). There are a few social and commercial institutions around that promote triadic relations. But insurance, which tends to take the form of mutual insurance, promotes formation or coverage of larger social units: "It tends, in the long run, to carry us beyond the era of the agent and of the broker into the coming social order of the insurer" (p. 64). This new world order of insurance will keep wars "progressively less destructive and less willful" (p. 66).

The danger uncovered by insurance lies alongside its saving power; it's the democratic one of making no difference. The agency ultimately of democratization (workers' compensation outdated or psychologized the notion of class warfare), insurance packs a danger of unlimited sameness. It's the danger that tends to get symptomatized in psychoanalysis-compatible theory as the charge of homosexuality. In "Freudian Theory and the Pattern of Fascist Propaganda," Adorno quotes Freud: "Homosexual love is far more compatible with group ties, even when it takes the shape of uninhibited sexual tendencies." Adorno comments: "This was certainly borne out under German Fascism where the borderline between overt and repressed homosexuality, just as that between overt and repressed sadism, was much more fluent than in liberal middle-class society."[22]

It's the danger that neo-Freudian therapies and theories (the ones that won their biggest victory—against psychiatry—when they attained insurance coverage under the Nazis) inadvertently release inside psychoanalysis. By revoking the otherwise therapeutically unresolvable differentiation that Freud packed into his notion of the ego, neopsychoanalysis and with it psychoanalysis must go either way, toward regression or control. That the logic of psychoanalysis could never think the ego as at once a piece of drive and something other, shuts down the difference between the sexes. Having staked this claim, Adorno releases his symptom: "Psychoanalysis appears in its flattening out of all it calls unconscious and thus of everything human to succumb to a mechanism of the homosexual type: not seeing what is different. Homosexuals evince a kind of color blindness in experience, the inability to recognize what is individualized: for them all women are in the double sense 'the same.' "[23] This homosexual inability to love shares its coldness, Adorno concludes, with Freudian analysis, which puts on rigor to cover its aggressive control tendencies.

One can't help but wonder if this is yet another text Adorno dictated to wife Gretel. Beginning with the case of Nietzsche, the measured inroads women were invited to make into all-male monopolies were blazed inside heterosexual couples under the cover that comes with the charge that homosexuals are the ones who can't love women. That's why Nazi psychotherapy was given three party-line research assignments covering different aspects of the military-sexual complex: war trauma, infertility in women, and homosexuality. When it came to these sex problems, psychological factors were openly admitted (in theory and therapy) into the German body and soul.

Top of the list was the SS requirement that the artist or genius "transcend his homosexuality" rather than end up "self-impaled."[24] Himmler's "concern ranged from musings on the possible correlation of lefthandedness and homosexuality to his thoughts that it was a perversion related to espionage, sabotage, and evasion of military service."[25] Indeed Himmler's inside view was corroborated by Nazi psychiatrist L. Fritzsching, whose diagnosis of desertion was included in the 1941 Survey and Bibliography *German Psychological Warfare,* through which the American military sought to catch up with Nazi psychological research, which was suddenly recognized on all sides to be state of the art. Fritzsching views a soldier's individual decision to surrender as "reversal of the military conscience" and thus, clinically, as inversion and perversion.[26] Prewar training that would expose soldiers to heavy doses of "subconscious elements leading up to surrender" is, Fritzsching concludes, a must. But Fritzsching thus remained within the military complex the Freudians first uncovered through their treatment of war trauma. Karl Abraham, for example, shifted from fear of death and the shocks of actual combat to what was really at issue: unresolved homosexuality.[27] The commitment to psychotherapeutic interventions in and understandings of homosexuality grew as strong as the prohibition against homosexual activity: the racially pure could not be biologically degenerate. There had to be a safety zone somewhere from (for) Nazi all-out racist hypercriticism of the other. Psychological correction had to replace in the first place biological exclusion. In an institute survey conducted by Felix Boehm in 1938 it was reported that since 1923 510 homosexual patients had been treated and 341 cured. In 1940 Boehm cited the institute's recovery statistics in a critical review of a psychiatric study claiming homosexuality as a congenital disposition. In a 1944 update I. H. Schultz issued a counterclaim (in a similar dispute, this time with the military) that by 1938 500 homosexuals had been straightened out thanks to the institute's interventions. Indeed, the adolescents who were referred to the Göring institute by supervisors of Hitler Youth and League of German Girls for homosexual behavior were often considered (and even welcomed) as candidates for long-term psychoanalysis. This was the claim filed by Kalan von Hofe, who was especially active at the Göring Institute in the treatment of these cases. (It turns out that there were a good number of high-ranking Nazi neurotics with sex problems.)[28]

According to Adorno, the psychotic delusions that were everyone's collective share in the Third Reich kept many individuals from going, one by one, psychotic.[29] Adorno modeled his view of the split-level distribution of the psychopathology continuum on Ernst Simmel's work on war traumatization. That the relationship between war neurosis and war psychosis is one of *Sicherung* pulls up a continuum or continuity between war and "insurance" (or "safeguard," "security," "safety catch") which fits squarely within the psychologization of warfare. War readiness was Adler's favorite "analogy" (in other words: model) for the constitution of neurosis; *Sicherung* was Adler's key term for *the* pathogenic fantasy, desire, and repressive mechanism from neurosis to psychosis. Simmel: "The war neuroses are in essence switched-on *Sicherungen* which aim to protect the soldier against psychosis. Whoever has mustered such a large patient population for a year and a half with analytic focus, must come to the realization that the relatively small number of war psychoses is only to be explained through the relatively large number of war neuroses."[30]

Hands-on influence on this distribution between neurotic and psychotic levels of the Nazi fantasy was a job for psychotherapist Erika Hantel, who while stationed in Berchtesgaden gave regular treatment to Nazi functionaries after another one of Hitler's late-night or early-morning Jonestown-style monologues.

Between the Wars

> Nearly all of our neurotic patients come to us in the "stadium of virtue," after having experienced a defeat.
>
> The liberation of the sadism from the neurotic predisposition, and in the sense of Freud, from the unconscious and from repression, is to be likened to a carrying back of the neurosis to an earlier stadium, to a time before defeat.
>
> —Adler, *The Neurotic Constitution*

Adler too made neurosis psychosis's distributor: "The neurotic tendency toward security . . . is always the effective cause of the psychotic construction."[31] Indeed it is often enough a "buried feeling of humiliation" that demands "over-compensation in the psychosis" (p. 422). Thus what Adler calls "insurance" covers the progression from normal, conscious use of a fiction (a "useful safety-device"), through neurotic attempts to realize the fiction, all the way to the psychotic's conviction that his fiction is a reality (p. 169).

The psychotic, at the nonnegotiable extreme of the insurance phantasm, Adler counsels, "acts under the most intense urgency. . . . In a similar manner he simultaneously feels himself to be woman and Superman" (pp. 170–71). Adler recycles Nietzsche through the psychotic's endopsychic perception and replaces Freud's theory of anxiety with Nietzsche's philosophy of power (and of war between the sexes). Where there's war there's also equal coverage.

> It is only to this fixity of the uncertainty that Nietzsche's assertion is applicable, namely that every one carries within him a portrait of womankind which he has derived from his mother, and which makes him honor women or despise her or entertain a total indifference toward her.

. . . . . .

> That along with this the mother serves in a certain sense as a model for the boy has long been known and has been mentioned by Nietzsche. . . . [The child] even goes so far as to entertain sexual wishes in regard to the mother, a proof of how boundless is the Will to Power. (pp. 79, 114)

Inferiority, compensation, guiding fiction, insurance: these are the terms of a constitution of neurosis that trades in pleasure for securities. Thus Adler was empowered to look beyond Freud's "imperfect and one-sided theory of dreams": "The dream . . . always drives towards security" (p. 399). Adler holds equally displaced views of sexual etiology and transference, both of which can be explained (away) by putting repression back in its place as "byproduct" of "the striving towards a fictitious goal" (p. 6). The "neurotic desires to insure himself" by clinging to what appears "to him to be useful for his security" (p. 150). Thus a "guiding principle" requires "an insuring anxiety" (p. 181) and related "security devices" (p. 192). One can also obtain "security through neurotic anxiety" (p. 272) or even cop the "security of the feeling of self-accusation" (p. 273). The stress is on "when a renunciation without adjustment is demanded" (p. 155).

Nietzsche's Will to Power models Adler's notion of the guiding principle (which marshals "the insuring anxieties," with Nietzsche's Eternal Return of the Same at the front of the line). With Vaihinger's "philosophy of as if" Adler can expand on Nietzsche's "will to seem" and underscore the fictitiousness of the guiding goal (Will to Power) (p. 30). This intertextual complex is contained in Adler's notion of masculine protest and thus given a one-way or phallic sense: the tendency to gain security is the same one that's out to conquer woman and at its strongest takes out the insurance policy of homosexuality (p. 249).

"The sexual feature of the psychology of the neuroses which Freud looks upon as a cardinal point is in this wise explained as the effect of a fiction" (p. 62). Instead, following Vaihinger and Nietzsche, Adler sees neurosis, including neurotic sexual conduct, as craving for and pursuit of security or insurance. "I have discussed the reasons for the marked prominence of the sexual guiding principle in neurotics, first, because it, like all other guiding principles is considerably accentuated in the neurotic, and so to speak, felt as real instead of what it was intended for—namely, as a protective guiding line—and second because it (the sexual guiding principle) leads in the direction of the masculine protest" (pp. 158–59). Thus

Freud's libido theory is just another fiction, one of the "bad sort" (p. 69).

There is, then, a certain symptomatic correspondence between neurotic thinking and Freud's theory: "It is no wonder that in the psychoanalysis of these cases with the male-female manner of apperception which belongs to the foundation of the neurotic psyche, one hits only upon sexual relations" (p. 293). But in Adler's view, "every perversion and inversion," indeed "all sexual relations in the neurosis are only a simile," "a symbol" (pp. 368 n. 2, 303). They reflect the guiding fiction's eternal negotiations for security, insurance, compensation, masculine protest, preparedness: "Repressed or conscious perverse tendencies . . . are . . . detours . . . symbols of an imaginary plan of life whose purpose is self-assurance" (p. 63).

"The 'recurrence of the same' (Nietzsche) is nowhere so well illustrated as in the neurotic" (p. 17*). Even when the neurosis is in open competition with the influence of situations or events, Nietzsche leads Adler to see through the current event to the larger pattern of guiding fiction, compensation, and insurance. This is the way Freud marked Nietzsche's entry into his second system: return of the same doubled as that uncanny return of the repressed that does not acknowledge outside influence. It's an instance of boundary blending (it takes two) within a constitution that aims to declare independence. "The 'return of the same' (Nietzsche) leads to the belief that the patient must have had her part in the play since both times she helped herself out of the situation by a neurotic arrangement so as to break off at the same moment" (p. 397*).

That's why the break in the place of a boundary concerns transference. When Freud worked the transferences of his ex- or neofollowers (in "The History of the Psycho-Analytic Movement"), he called Adler on circuitously saying (or admitting) no more than: resistance is resistance. For example: "Freud's hypothesis of transference . . . is nothing more than an expedient of the patient who seeks to rob the physician of superiority" (p. 225). It's true that intimate contact or anticipated contact is a catalyst, but what it releases is a "heightened tendency to gain reassurance" that "causes the outbreak of that which is ordinarily termed a neurosis or psychosis" (p. 252). Thus the onset of a neurosis can also be "such symptoms as fear . . . of a test" (p. 254) or of "danger of death" (p. 28). And the neurosis then "continues in its construction of assurances" (p. 258).

"The neurotic carries his feeling of inferiority constantly with him. . . . his fear of the new, of decisions and tests, which is usually present, originates from lack of analogy for these new conditions" (p. 18). But the neurotic is also always just testing: "The insatiableness with which the neurotic tests his partner is an indication . . . of his lack of self-esteem"

(p. 380). "In the relation of the sexes there arises nearly always an obstinate and selfish feature, a tendency to put to test" (p. 215). Thus "a premeditation and testing of difficulties carried on in accordance with the patient's own peculiar scheme" provides "a protective way for the ego-consciousness out of a situation which threatens a defeat" (p. 148).

One of the ways to "seek security" is to make "preparations for security" (p. 235). Adler unpacks a mode of catastrophe-preparedness organizing one neurotic's "insurance" policy. "Whenever he used an automobile, the thought that a collision might take place came to his mind. . . . Yes, even when he used the tram cars for an extended trip, the thought occurred to him, upon reaching the point where the cheap fare terminated and the more expensive one began, that a collision might take place, or that the bridge which had to be crossed might collapse, so that he would always pay the cheaper fare, save a few pennies and cover the rest of the distance on foot" (pp. 145–46).

What's along for the ride in the ego-driven reading of the taxi meter of accident protection and compensation is the superegoric editing that is always getting ready to go to war and already belongs in the movies.

> The gaze of the neurotic . . . is directed far into the future. All present existence is to him only a preparation.
>
> . . . . .
>
> But with neurotic strivings of "anticipatory thinking," attention approaches problems and arranges them in accordance with the neurotic's antithetical mode of apperception, which values a defeat as death, as inferiority, as effeminacy, and victory as immortality, higher values, masculine triumph, while the hundreds of other possibilities of life are annihilated by withdrawing them from attention. In the same manner the way is entered upon to the anticipation of future triumph and terror as well as an hallucinatory reinforcement for the sake of security.
>
> . . . . .
>
> In our sort of neuropsychology one always gains the impression that the visible neurotic conduct is directed straight to the Final Purpose, to the fictitious goal, as if one were examining one of the intermediary pictures in a cinematographic film. (pp. 21, 389, 232)

The ready position of "neurotic preparedness" (p. 29), "neurotic preparedness to attacks" (p. 361), or "anxiety preparedness" (pp. 233–34), requires (for lack of any other analogy) an all-out mobilization of defense, "somewhat like our modern states conducting war preparations without even knowing the future enemy" (p. 134). (As Freud put it, Adler only wanted to secure for his own theory and therapy "a place in the sun.")[32]

> The already existing preparedness for the symptom becomes embodied in the web and woof of memory as an insuring agent against the fear of being under-estimated or neglected. . . . The whole army of neurotic symptoms . . . may well be traced to these ready-for-use psychic attitudes.
>
> . . . . .
>
> A certain manifestation which one frequently observes in the neurosis was likewise present here, and in an especially accentuated form, namely, the strong emphasis of a pedantic character trait, which, not unlike the "crack regiment" in war time, took over the task of coming in touch with the enemy. The enemy was first of all the mother. (pp. 213, 194)

Epilogue

In 1939 Göring went public with his commitment to equal coverage in an article entitled "The Significance of Neurosis in Social Insurance."[33] Göring had already appointed psychoanalyst Gerhart Scheunert as head of the outpatient clinic because of the view they both shared that short-term therapy was most effective, particularly in solving the time-is-money problems that kept psychotherapy outside the state health insurance system. The neurotic tends to live in the futural mode of preparedness only; he must be confronted with the quick results of short-term therapy that lock him into a short attention span as though he thus inhabited the present. Also in this context, Schultz, the real popular, real nice psychotherapist at the Göring Institute (who favored, in the short run, autogenic training and yoga therapy) gave his support to the outpatient clinic: "The outpatient clinic is our weapons forge. That sometimes there are metal fragments and sometimes hammers clash may be somewhat disturbing to you . . . but it is necessary. We desperately need that. You are perhaps not entirely clear about how threatened even today your whole existence as psychotherapists is."[34]

In 1935 Charles Baudouin's contribution to the journal of Nazi psychotherapy was an analysis of risk which psychologized calculations that began with Pascal. Baudouin opens by conjugating risk through Jung, Adler, Freud, and Rank as follows (and respectively): introversion, inferiority, castration, birth trauma. The risk of mutilation was controlled through the invention of consensual mutilation (in other words: sacrifice). Thus the risk with which, Baudouin argues, every action comes complete must be managed over and again: a veritable "action drive" is matched on the other side by a sacrifice drive (which permits or controls the risks you end up wanting to take). This drives the notions of risk and security into interchangeable places. A couple is formed (that of risk and security) which leaves us with the one alternative to alternation "between loss of will power and the frenetic course headed towards catastrophes."[35]

In theory insurance covers funeral arrangements; in practice its coverage extends via catastrophes and wartime mobilization.

When Pascal was commissioned around 1654 to figure out the chances of a certain number recurring at roulette he at the same time introduced the notion of calculable risk, which became the basis of modern insurance (and of the new and improved self-other bond or group psychology that insurance also covers). Thus it was gambling, the first of the modern causes or explanations of out-of-control group behavior, that promoted, in its calculation as risk, the modern mass formations of catastrophe-preparedness. Wherever Freud's second system can be located, the first one isn't far behind. One of the first applications of Pascal's symptomatic or side-effect discovery was the calculation of life expectancy (in 1671, for example, Johan De Wit applied the theory of probability to the value of a life annuity). Indeed, primally speaking, life insurance began with the Burial Clubs of Rome, into which the members paid down payments and fixed monthly fees to guarantee the funding for their proper funerals. "That club members did not always intend these entire funds to be used for burial purposes is clearly evidenced by Roman rulings which forbade men from joining more than one burial society at a time."[36]

But with risk calculation insurance shifted from speculation on down payments to coverage of risk in the mass format of catastrophe-survival. By the end of the seventeenth century, marine underwriting and fire insurance were available. In 1683 the "Friendly Society" was the world's first *mutual* fire insurance association. By the end of the nineteenth century (with railway passenger insurance and workers' compensation already in place), the insured bond with the other via risk had grown a group psychology that displaced class interests. But Bismarck's pioneering welfare legislation in the 1880's (his package deal of sickness insurance, accident insurance, old age and disability insurance) had everyone's best interests in mind.

The move in the United States to set up compulsory health insurance, which began revving up in 1912, lost its momentum when it extended into World War I, all the way into the U.S. war effort. At that point Germany had to be targeted as psychologically programming the world to accept its *Kultur* through the spread of its insurance system. The reception of societywide insurance (in other words: the German brand of group psychology) was staggered within the shifting takes on propaganda and war psychology, in which now the Allies, now the Germans, took the lead.[37]

The projective identification via the feminine (which goes back and forth between Nietzsche or Freud and Spielrein, Anna O., or Dora) creates an antagonist who observes pathology while exercising a transparent Will to Power over that pathology in the name of a born-again truth, the one called true love. But this adoration, which must find maxiprotection against the ambivalence that created it, collapses (down unresolved or psychotic transferences) onto the death drive. The group-formatted ambivalence of female sexuality (in other words: Spielrein's transference-love affair or her theorization of the failures and betrayals that get downed with loyalty-or-identification transferences) redeveloped the death wish and paved the way for death drive. It was no accident that Spielrein packed a case of Nietzsche into this introduction and thus at the same time contained him (the mascot of her preemptive scoop of Freud's second system) in observable scenes of therapeutic interventionism. The Eternal Return of insurance is the matricenter of group protection or projection. The insurance system promotes the rise (so what if it's, at first at least, only the equal opportunity) of women's involvement in observing. Mother is transformed into the (uncanny) measure of correct observation and intervention. In a letter to Freud dated March 15, 1916, Lou Andreas-Salomé fixes the focus on the camera inside a paranoid delusion analyzed by Freud: "Also in the case of the supposed camera, I am reminded of the mother's *eye,* which like God's eye 'sees everything,' which has always seen the child all alone, naked and stripped." Margaret Mahler's subsequent view of mothering as the unconscious of relations would fold out a military espionage network (the psychological warfare aspect of modern mass psychology) that comes complete with refueling stops at home base.[38]

But first psychoanalysis had to be diversified and reunified. Lay analysis covered the interests of mother and the group which were acted out between the reunited psychotherapies and psychiatry over the prize of insurance coverage and, on the winning side, in Nietzsche's name. Adjunct or lay psychotherapists were able to overcome global resistance to their inclusion at the Berlin institute of psychotherapy. With their admission an overall affirmative action balance between men and women throughout the institute was created.

The preponderance of women therapists in the Adlerian and Jungian groups was established already by the twenties. Notwithstanding the overt bias of the "masculine protest," Adler set himself up as defender of women's equal rights against Freud's unfair practice. (Freud had already argued, however, that the way Adler had lined it up, masculine protest could be successfully realized or overcome only by women.)[39] The neurotic giveaway on Adler's checklist or questionnaire was the estimation of the opposite sex (i.e., of women): "It will become apparent that every stronger denial of the equality of the sexes, every detraction or overvaluation of the opposite sex is invariably connected with a neurotic disposition and neurotic traits. They are all dependent on the neurotic tendency to obtain security" (*The Neurotic Constitution,* p. 263).

In essays scattered across the extent of his independent career, Adler came out Big Time on the side of equal rights for women. The other side of the same agenda was his cure-all for homosexuality, which he also promoted. "In times when women step more vigorously into the foreground of public life, a large number of men prefer to increase the distance from the female sex and resort among other safeguards also to homosexuality."[40] Indeed: "Every sexual deviation is the expression of an increased psychological distance between man and woman" (*Cooperation between the Sexes,* p. 159). That's the way it was in ancient Greece, says Adler. Women, who were on the rise, deprivileged and insecurized men who had two optional coverages to choose from: either depreciation or idealization of women. The homosexual trend was set. But even if Greek pedophilia prepared the boy for the package deal of heterosexuality-plus-comradeship, still Adler found this approach as incorrect as the one masturbation represents (pp. 157–58). (That's right: Adler's community spirit didn't approve of the for him related diversions of homosexuality and masturbation. As Freud saw it, it was because Adler was so freaked by sexuality that he promoted aggression over love.)[41] Thus Adler baits the master as pro-homosexual. "Why must people take an actually hostile attitude toward homosexuality," Adler rhetorico-strategically asks: "Freud and his followers are satisfied with the answer: because they have repressed their own homosexuality or have sublimated it." But Adler then counters: "This explanation is not only improbable, it also can certainly not be verified. It is derived not from facts but from psychoanalytic theory" (pp. 149–150). Adler's position is psychotherapeutically correct:

> We expect from the future first of all a more correct attitude toward this problem, a voluntary decision of the offender to be treated.
>
> . . . . .
>
> Cure and improvement are possible through psychotherapy.

. . . . . .

> As for many other ailments, so also for the neurosis of homosexuality, treatment should be mandatory. (pp. 150, 167, 170)

Adler doesn't want to criminalize homosexuals, he just wants to reintroduce them into the community through a consensual treatment, which is a laying down of neurotic arms and the canceling of neurotic insurances but not the laying down of arms or the cancellation of coverage. It's still lay analysis. The ex-homosexual, who had come under Adler's treatment and was to date an impotent heterosexual, talks to Adler about the current war: "He had at once registered as a volunteer. But the closer the date of his call approached, the greater his fear became and the desire to get out of it. From this attitude, I could easily guess the present phase of his sexual development" (p. 230). The extraneousness or curability of homosexuality is the camouflage its centrality to the military-insurance complex assumes, a complex that outdoes the Oedipus one in universality, in coextensivity with everything else. In the policy fine print to *The Neurotic Constitution* it was already granted that militarization participated in the kind of acceleration of norms that characterizes neurosis (with homosexuality, the paragon of neurotic insurance right down to the safeguards against women, at the front of the line): "For the benefit of psychologists of a keener insight, I note here the prevalence of examples which have been taken from military life have been chosen by me with an especial object in view. In military training the starting point and fictive purpose are brought into closer relation, can be more readily noted, and every movement of the training soldier becomes a dexterity which has for its purpose the transformation of a primary feeling of weakness into a feeling of superiority" (*The Neurotic Constitution,* p. 77 n. 6).

In *The Problem of Homosexuality* Adler drops into the ditch of a footnote a connection that ultimately confirms that homosexuality is to neurosis what espionage is to psychological warfare and what desertion or flight is to war. "In the first edition of this study, which appeared during the World War, I noted at this point that the increasing understanding of war neurosis had strikingly shown the validity of the Individual Psychology view."[42] In this applied-Nietzschean or psychotherapeutic view, equality of (or, same difference, war between) the sexes is the policy of group protection; it shifts the couple outside the personalizable policies of neurotic insurance into the global zones of war and diplomacy. The danger of sameness (and thus of bilateral violence or suicide), which a vote for the community at the same time brings into closer range, is embodied (in this context of emancipation) as homosexuality. So that the mobilization of defenses can proceed along the lines of equal coverage, homosexuality must be not so much defended against as "transcended" (as the SS prescribed for the *Wehrmacht*). When it comes to group psychology or psychological warfare (as the Nazis knew best) the homosexual must be *geheilt:* at once cured and hailed.

Murnau, who was commissioned through the German embassy in Switzerland during World War I to make propaganda films for the German war effort, fits right in here. Kafka's case, too, opens and shuts within the terms and liabilities of insurance, technofeminism, and denial rights for inversion. Everything we knew about Kafka and Felice Bauer, or Kafka and media technology, or Kafka and his dead brothers has not yet been reviewed in terms of his overtime commitment to the daytime program of his official work (and writing). Employed at the local headquarters of workers' comp, he wrote propaganda for increased safety at various work sites (including those on the homefront of World War I), or (in 1916) for the funding and construction of institutions to care for war neurotics.

> The world war, which contains the accumulation of all human misery, is also a war of nerves, more a war of nerves than any earlier war ever was. Too many have already fallen victim to this nerve war. Just as in peacetime over the last decades the intensive activity of machines has endangered, disturbed, and sickened the nerves of workers, so the increased machinic aspect of current war operations has introduced the most severe dangers for and afflictions of the nerves of the combatants. . . . The nervous trembler and jumper in the streets of our cities is just a relatively harmless delegate of a monstrous mass of sufferers.[43]

Kafka "was there" when insurance became the ultimate forum of all interests (and returns), and when the group psychology of risk calculation introduced the new woman, gadget love, and homo espionage. (Turing and Wittgenstein fit right in here.) Everything we thought we knew about modernism and beyond-modernism must be reenrolled in the policies of insurance coverage, psychological warfare, and technofeminism (which psychotherapy originally took out in Nietzsche's name).

Notes

1. For Freud's remarks re transfer of the democratic principle "from politics to science," see Peter Gay, *Freud: A Life for Our Time* (New York: Norton, 1988), pp. 566–68.

2. Sigmund Freud, "On the History of the Psycho-Analytic Movement," in *The*

Standard Edition of the Complete Psychological Works of Sigmund Freud, ed. James Strachey, 24 vols. (London: Hogarth, 1957), 14:7–66.

3. Joan Riviere, "An Intimate Impression" (1939), in *Freud as We Knew Him,* ed. Hendrik M. Ruitenbeck (Detroit: Wayne State Univ. Press, 1973), p. 128.

4. This is Jung's diagnosis first published in 1907, cited in *Tagebuch einer heimlichen Symmetrie: Sabina Spielrein zwischen Jung und Freud,* ed. Aldo Carotenuto (Freiburg: Kore, Verlag Traute Hensch, 1986), p. 250.

5. Freud to Jung, 21 March 1912.

6. Freud to Jung, 30 November 1911.

7. Entry of 30 November 1917, in *Tagebuch einer heimlichen Symmetrie,* p. 215.

8. Sabina Spielrein, *Die Destruktion als Ursache des Werdens,* ed. Gerd Kimmerle (Tübingen: Diskord, 1986), p. 30. Further references are given in the text.

9. Freud to Jung, 17 December 1911.

10. C. G. Jung, "Wotan," in *Civilization in Transition,* trans. R. F. C. Hull (New York: Pantheon, 1964), pp. 179–93. References are given in the text.

11. C. G. Jung, "After the Catastrophe," in *Civilization in Transition,* pp. 194–217. References are given in the text.

12. C. G. Jung, "Geleitwort," *Zentralblatt für Psychotherapie und ihre Grenzgebiete einschliesslich der medizinischen Psychologie und psychischen Hygiene: Organ der internationalen allgemeinen ärztlichen Gesellschaft für Psychotherapie* 6 (1933): 139.

13. Cited in Geoffrey Cocks, *Psychotherapy in the Third Reich: The Göring Institute* (New York: Oxford Univ. Press, 1985), p. 59.

14. Karl Marx and Friedrich Engels, *The German Ideology,* parts 1 and 3, ed. R. Pascal (New York: International Publishers, 1947), pp. 61–62.

15. *Aesthetics and Politics,* ed. Ronald Taylor (London: NLB, 1977), p. 124. References to the Adorno-Benjamin correspondence are given in the text.

16. Walter Benjamin, "Über einige Motive bei Baudelaire," in *Gesammelte Schriften,* vol. 1, part 2, ed. Rolf Tiedemann and Hermann Schweppenhäuser (Frankfurt: Suhrkamp, 1974), p. 630.

17. *The German Ideology,* p. 1.

18. See Laurence Rickels, "Mickey Marx," *Lusitania* 1, no. 4 (1993): 205–15.

19. *Im Reiche der Micky Maus: Walt Disney in Deutschland 1927–1945: Eine Dokumentation zur Ausstellung im Filmmuseum Potsdam* (Berlin: Henschel, 1991), p. 90. References to Mickey Mouse's Nazi reception are to this catalogue and are given in the text.

20. Harold D. Lasswell, "Political and Psychological Warfare," in *A Psychological Warfare Casebook,* ed. William E. Daugherty and Morris Janowitz (Baltimore: Johns Hopkins Univ. Press, 1958), p. 22.

21. Josiah Royce, *War and Insurance* (New York: Macmillan, 1914), p. xli. Further references are given in the text.

22. Theodor W. Adorno, *Gesammelte Schriften,* ed. Rolf Tiedemann (Frankfurt: Suhrkamp, 1972), 8:413 n. 7.

23. Theodor W. Adorno, "Zum Verhältnis von Soziologie und Psychologie," in *Gesammelte Schriften,* 8:84.

24. Cited in Cocks, p. 206.

25. Cocks, p. 208.

26. Cited in *German Psychological Warfare: Survey and Bibliography,* ed. Ladislas Farago (New York: Committee for National Morale, 1941), p. 43.

27. Karl Abraham, "Zur Psychoanalyse der Kriegsneurosen," in *Gesammelte Schriften in zwei Bänden,* ed. Johannes Cremerius (Frankfurt: Fischer, 1982), 1:69–77.

28. See Cocks, pp. 209–10.

29. Theodor W. Adorno, "Bemerkungen über Politik und Neurose," in *Gesammelte Schriften,* 8:439.

30. Ernst Simmel, "Zweites Korreferat," in *Zur Psychoanalyse der Kriegsneurosen,* Internationale Psychoanalytische Bibliothek Nr. 1 (Leipzig/Wien: Internationaler Psychoanalytischer Verlag, 1919), p. 45.

31. Alfred Adler, *The Neurotic Constitution: Outline of a Comparative Individualistic Psychology and Psychotherapy,* trans. Bernard Glueck and John Lind (New York: Moffat, Yard, 1917), p. 241. Further references are given in the text.

32. Freud, "On the History of the Psycho-Analytic Movement," 14:51.

33. Matthias Göring, "Die Bedeutung der Neurose in der Sozialversicherung," *Zentralblatt für Psychotherapie* 11 (1939): 36–56.

34. Cited in Cocks, p. 182.

35. Charles Baudouin, "Esquisse d'une pathologie du risque," *Zentralblatt für Psychotherapie* 8, no. 3 (1935): 113.

36. G. A. Maclean, *Insurance Up through the Ages* (Louisville: Dunne, 1938), p. 5.

37. See Ronald L. Numbers, *Almost Persuaded: American Physicians and Compulsory Health Insurance, 1912–1920* (Baltimore: Johns Hopkins Univ. Press, 1978).

38. See, for example, Margaret S. Mahler, Fred Pine, and Anni Bergman, *The Psychological Birth of the Human Infant: Symbiosis and Individuation* (New York: Basic Books, 1975), p. 69. Credit for these terms is awarded a certain Furer via "personal communication."

39. Sigmund Freud, "'A Child Is Being Beaten,'" in *The Standard Edition,* 17:203.

40. Alfred Adler, *Cooperation between the Sexes: Writings on Women, Love and Marriage, Sexuality and Its Disorders,* ed. and trans. Heinz L. Ansbacher and Rowena R. Ansbacher (Garden City, N.Y.: Anchor, 1978), p. 155. Further references are given in the text.

41. Freud, "On the History of the Psycho-Analytic Movement," 14:58.

42. Alfred Adler, *The Problem of Homosexuality,* excerpted in *Cooperation between the Sexes,* p. 161 n. 11.

43. Franz Kafka, *Amtliche Schriften* (Berlin: Akademie, 1984), p. 295.

PART SIX

Supplements

BENJAMIN BENNETT

Bridge: Against Nothing

Elles affirment triomphant que tout geste est renversement.

—Monique Wittig, *Les Guérillères*

I

Revolutionaries are people who go out on a limb, but in such a way as to raise the question of whether their limb is not after all a bridge, the bridge to an Elsewhere that is substantially different from what we suppose ourselves able to recognize immediately as the shape of our own social or political or economic or sensory or linguistic existence. The claim to have found such a bridge—along with the absence of any basis whatever for adjudicating it—is what makes the revolutionary in thought, and makes its daring, its untenability, its vulnerable or in fact doomed situation, out on a limb. There is no need for revolutionary thought, no impetus, except where a positive value accrues to the degree of sheer differentness of its Elsewhere, which in turn, however, is exactly the degree to which the existence of a usable bridge becomes improbable, hence the degree to which that Elsewhere, in the judgment of reasonable people, stands revealed as a Nowhere, a utopia.

That revolutionary thought—or at least a revolutionary appetite in thought—persists nonetheless, in all its unreasonableness, has to do with the belief that revolutions *have happened* in history, and so might conceivably happen again. But the trouble with revolutions that are supposed actually to have happened is that we see them the wrong way round, from the wrong end of the bridge. The arrival of the bridge at its destination is visible to us. But the moment that really matters—if we are interested in learning how to recognize or validate or promote revolutionary thought here and now—the moment of the bridge's becoming, the moment at which revolution makes the leap from untenable fantasy into the historically actual, is still obscured. Precisely to the extent that we insist on the radicality of a particular revolutionary process in past history, our attempt to reconstruct that process involves us in difficulties similar to those that bedevil any attempt to eradicate the teleological component in our description of natural processes. The undeniable *existence* of the bridge obscures the quality of thought strictly out on a limb.

This consideration, I think, goes a long way toward explaining the interest aroused among nonscientists by the discussion of "scientific revolutions." Here, at least, we expect that the record—in the form of texts written with a view to maximum exactness, plus repeatable experiments—may be clear enough to support a convincing reconstruction. But what Kuhn (for instance) gives us, though it is interesting as history, is of little use for the understanding of revolution. It is a cartography of "shifts" whose very complexity—whose *lack,* therefore, of the quality of simple bridges—leaves us with a vision of gradualness that obscures the revolutionary from another direction. Even Feyerabend's more engaged and engaging argument "against method" does not escape being infected by the inherent complacency of the retrospective view. It is symptomatic that Feyerabend concludes his book with an account of the growth of its thought, a story of excited intellectual voyaging that often reads distressingly like an alumni-reunion speech.

II

It is true that I have not attempted—and will not attempt—to state exactly what I mean by "the revolutionary," or especially "the revolutionary moment." And it is true that there are good reasons for doubting whether it is possible to give this notion flesh by reference to particular cases from history. Perhaps the best existing attempt to evoke a revolutionary moment from the past is Trotsky's *History of the Russian Revolution.* But if so, then only because Trotsky himself strenuously *denies* that his own thought or Lenin's was ever actually out on a limb to begin with, a denial which paradoxically complements the recognition, for all his book's enormous factual detail, that his thought is in truth still out on a limb, still as revolutionary (and unfulfilled) as ever.

My reason for raising the question of the revolutionary here, however, has to do with a case in the present, a revolution in the making, the case of feminism. For feminist thought is either revolutionary in the fullest sense, or pointless. This follows—to the extent that a proposition that involves the category of the unreasonable can "follow"—from feminists' own ever-better understanding of what they are up against, of the depth at which women's subjugation, their occupancy of the position of "other," their function as property or medium of exchange, or as the vessel of an either perfected or monstrous "nature," is involved in the structure of especially Western culture and language. In fact, if we accept Lacan's suggestion that the unconscious "itself" is never strictly distinguishable from the historical details of its discovery and discussion, then a developing grasp of the phallic or patriarchal bias in Freud, as well as in Lacan, confronts feminists with a task that can be described, without much exaggeration, as *the renewal of the human psyche*—the psyche, not merely "consciousness," and certainly not consciousness in the sense that we can imagine its being "raised."

The difficulty of setting limits to the feminist project produces a tendency toward theoretical leapfrogging, the repeated undermining of theoretical positions by a showing of their complicity with what the thought as a whole is up against. But not leapfrogging in a direct line, as if toward a goal. Even a disagreement as apparently straightforward as Kelly Oliver's response to David Farrell Krell's *Postponements* has unexpected twists. Oliver competently exposes the posturing in Krell's argument. But her attempt, in the process, to sweep aside all of Nietzsche, ends by mirroring itself in the shopworn metaphor of needing to "open a space for women to articulate themselves."[1] As if, in order to meet the problem of colonizing, the whole notion of a "space" for articulation did not require radical rethinking, a rethinking, in fact, of exactly the type that Krell's idea of "postponed" articulation, for all its difficulties, shows is integral in precisely Nietzsche's philosophical project.

Or to take another instance that has to do with the space or position of speaking, Shoshana Felman's "Women and Madness" is nothing if not revolutionary: "If, in our culture, the woman is by definition associated with madness, her problem is how to break out of this (cultural) imposition of madness *without* taking up the critical and therapeutic position of reason: how to avoid speaking both as *mad* and as *not mad.* The challenge facing the woman today is nothing less than to 're-invent' language, to *re-learn how to speak:* to speak not only against, but outside of the specular phallogocentric structure, to establish a discourse the status of which would no longer be defined by the phallacy of masculine meaning."[2] But the essay is also a critical response to Luce Irigaray's *Speculum:*

> If, as Luce Irigaray suggests, the woman's silence, or the repression of her capacity to speak, are constitutive of philosophy and of theoretical discourse as such, from what theoretical locus is Luce Irigaray herself speaking in order to develop her own theoretical discourse about the woman's exclusion? Is she speaking the language of men or the silence of women? Is she speaking *as* a woman, or *in place of* the (silent) woman, *for* the woman, *in the name of* the woman? . . . What, in a general manner, does "speech in the name of" mean? Is it not a precise repetition of the oppressive gesture of *representation,* by means of which, throughout the history of logos, man has reduced the woman to the status of a silent and subordinate object, to something inherently *spoken for?* To "speak in the name of," to "speak *for,*" could thus mean, once again, to appropriate and to silence. This important theoretical question about the status of its own discourse and its own "representation" of women, with which any feminist thought has to cope, is not thought out by Luce Irigaray. . . . Although the otherness of the woman is here fully assumed as the subject of the statement, it is not certain whether that otherness can be taken for granted as positively occupying the un-thought-out problematical locus *from which* the statement is being *uttered.* (pp. 3–4)

What exactly is the force of this criticism?

Only a slight shift of focus is needed in order to read Felman's apparent attack as an expression of *perplexity* at Irigaray's (non)stance. If Irigaray followed Felman's advice and "thought out" her position, would this not simply embed her discourse *more* firmly in the history of theory? Does Felman really want a discourse about whose position one can be "certain"? Is Irigaray's "un-thought-out" position not perhaps the adumbration of a nonposition, of precisely the avoidance of both "mad" and "not mad" that Felman herself hopes for? This situation is typical of the dynamics of revolutionary thought. Irigaray and Felman each force the other out onto a limb. And it turns out to be the same limb they are both out on.

III

But the idea of revolutionary thought in progress brings with it the question of how we can possibly *recognize* such thought. To return to my opening metaphor, if we can see the whole bridge, then it turns out not to be the kind of bridge we are interested in. Or in Felman's terms, if our task is to "establish a discourse," how shall we keep it from becoming a part, precisely, of "established" discourse? Obviously this problem cannot be solved; but it becomes at least approachable if we turn it around and ask: How can the revolutionary quality of a text, its participation in a revolution in progress, be integrated into its communicative structure? How can a text *identify or present itself* as revolutionary?

Let us take two instances, as it were from opposite ends of the spectrum. Of pivotal importance in Monique Wittig's *Les Guérillères,* first, is the repeated phrase "elles disent," which establishes two incompatible perspectives upon the material being recounted. A distanced perspective, "our" pre- or indeed nonrevolutionary perspective: since what "they say" is after all only what "they say," in a saying that merges with the visionary saying of the text as a whole and cannot claim to determine what "we" say or know or think; and since, after all, there is no unequivocal way of distinguishing the force of the "elles disent" from that of the reactionary "ils disent" in the passage where the women claim to reject in toto the language that had enslaved them.[3] But at the same time a perspective in the midst of the revolutionized female society: since the provisional "they say" reflects the women's own resistance to any entrapment in doctrine or ideology (p. 80); and since there is after all (in French) a difference between "elles disent" and "ils disent," which is perhaps one of those accidental "intervals" in language (p. 164) that the appropriative operation of meaning cannot fill up.

Thus—as also by other devices, like negation, statements about what the women do *not* say or do—the text manages to occupy both ends of its visionary bridge without pretending actually to have built it, without compromising its situation out on a limb. I do not mean that *Les Guérillères* is therefore somehow a successful revolutionary text, or somehow more revolutionary than others that lack its rhetorical subtlety. The question is simply: How, without losing control of the problems in the very idea of the revolutionary, can the revolutionary appetite be integrated into a text's rhetorical and communicative structure? How can a text at least sketch the claim to be revolutionary (not merely shocking or angry or radically critical or bewildering) without benefit of hindsight?

The other example I have in mind is an apparently very tame essay by Nancy K. Miller, "Changing the Subject: Authorship, Writing, and the Reader."[4] Miller begins by setting forth the problematic situation of feminist thought in a theoretical atmosphere conditioned by Barthes's "Death of the Author." What status has the question of women's writing or reading if "it matters not *who* writes" or "who reads" (pp. 104–5)? Precisely the "enabling move" of "destabilization of the paternal (patriarchal, really) authority of authorship" (p. 105) contributes to a situation where, for feminists, "it is difficult to know where and how to move" (p. 115). And Miller, in the face of this difficulty, avoids high theory altogether by choosing to anchor her thought firmly on this end of any conceivable revolutionary bridge, with the question: "What does it mean to read and write as a woman within the institution that authorizes and regulates most reading and writing?" (p. 112). But a revolutionary vista is opened after all by the answer she suggests to this question: "Irony . . . a trope that by its status as the marker of a certain distance to the truth, suits the rhetorical strategies of the feminist critic" (p. 114). What does *irony* mean here? Does it distinguish feminism from the larger practice of poststructuralism, which surely, at the very least, maintains its own "distance from the truth"? Is irony a matter of hairsplitting, of making "distinctions," like Lucy Snowe in *Villette,* a matter of accepting the "relation" to an inhospitable theoretical environment while still somehow escaping "the system of institutional authorization in which [the] relation is inscribed" (p. 113)—as if this were possible? Does irony mean simply keeping silent, immobilized by "an anxiety about claiming theoretically what we [women] know experientially" (p. 115)? Can one, above all, advocate irony without being ironic in one's advocacy? What *is* "an ironic manipulation of the semiotics of performance and production" (p. 116), if not a radical disruption of the semiotic as such, opening onto a space where nothing whatever is signified?

In this suggestion, I think the other end of the bridge, the revolutionary Elsewhere, is glimpsed. The theoretical environment—Miller says "Terry Eagleton *et al.*" (p. 115) and quotes Gayatri Spivak[5]—insists on the question of an appropriate feminist "move," a move that would therefore sacrifice in advance its specifically feminist force by responding to the wrong type of question. And the logic of the concept of irony, in this context, suggests the idea of making *no* move, having *no* "rhetorical strategy," an idea that may be theoretically questionable (is the making of no move not itself a move?) but is not simply dismissible, since the feminist *position* evinces a mode of existence that is categorically different from that of any strictly theoretical position. That we cannot say exactly how the feminist position is constituted—Miller concludes by worrying about the question of "becoming women" or "becoming feminists" (p. 117)—does not change matters. The difference alone (from the type of theoretical position that does not exist *as* a position except by authorizing specific moves) makes room for a revolutionary reading of the notion of irony.

Again, as with Wittig, I do not claim to explain what Miller "means" by irony, and I am not setting up her text as a model. My aim, for the moment, is only to call attention to certain typical rhetorical phenomena that appear when we look at feminist texts by way of the problematics of the revolutionary.

IV

But is anything *accomplished,* either by these rhetorical subtleties or by the nonlimitable cross-questioning of texts like Felman's and Irigaray's? Is there any *basis,* outside feminist thought itself, for the assertion that that thought is revolutionary in character? Or more specifically, is there any place "within the institution that authorizes and regulates most reading and writing," any place on this end of the bridge, that provides *leverage* for feminist thought considered as revolutionary?

This is the question that brings us to Nietzsche. For in Western literary tradition, Nietzsche's writings are the locus—as far as I know, the unique locus—of *free revolutionary thought,* thought that is revolutionary in its structure and problems, but despite its fondness for the metaphors of bridge and tightrope, is tied to no revolutionary project whatever—assuming we agree, for example, that "the word *Übermensch*" (KSA 4:248; cf. Z p. 310) names not a project but an antiproject, the absence of any project. The *Übermensch* is located Elsewhere, at the far end of a bridge; but it is a bridge that, for our purposes, has no near end, no beginning, no approach, a bridge that takes shape not in our knowledge or belief or desire but in our mere existence, a bridge (or tightrope) that we *are* (see, e.g., KSA 4:16, 248; Z pp. 126, 310). The difference between Nietzsche and other revolutionary thinkers, in this regard, is not difficult to recognize in particular cases. Artaud, for instance, whom we often situate not far from Nietzsche in the discussion of the unfolding and supersedure of modernism, is much more project-focused. No less rigorously critical a mind than Derrida comes close to thinking in terms of a conceivable realization of Artaud's vision, whereas even without the actual fascist experiments to learn from, it would be clear that the whole notion of realization, or application, misses the point in Nietzsche.

I will attempt to support this characterization of Nietzsche's writings in the next section. But if we assume for a moment that it is valid, then the importance of Nietzsche for feminist thinking follows quickly. Nietzsche's writing, in which the revolutionary moment is an operative force, yet is also denied any form of realization, in which therefore the revolutionary moment is not even speculatively subject to being obscured by hindsight, would become something like a study in revolutionary method, a model for revolutions in progress, the touchstone by which to know and sustain a revolutionary focus in thought, despite the absence of reasonable criteria for distinguishing such a focus from mere eccentricity, from the condition of being out on a limb. And feminism, which *is* out on a limb, exposed to any number of reductive or co-optive moves, is eminently in need of such a method or touchstone.

That there is also a more specific and more complex relation between Nietzsche and feminist thought, is strongly suggested, if not established, by Derrida in *Spurs*. There are, however, problems in Derrida's presentation, which appear less obviously in his own text than in projects, like Krell's, that use that text for support and, in the end, tend to confuse feminist issues rather than develop them. Indeed, it is not certain that the term *phallogocentrism,* in itself, is not a co-optive move with respect to feminist thought, an exhortation to the wild variety of feminist initiatives that it come in from out on its limb, or limbs, and organize itself as a form of deconstruction. (If there is a besetting fault in feminist writing, it is the facile use of the verb "deconstruct.") Even as consistent and painstaking an advocate as Gayatri Spivak, in her essay "Displacement and the Discourse of Woman," raises important questions about the ability of deconstruction to operate "as a 'feminist' practice."[6]

My own view of the specific usefulness of Nietzsche for feminist thinkers is much simpler than Derrida's. I will argue that in all of Nietzsche, the question of the reader's historical situation is crucial, and the question of the reader's *use* of the text in history. In later Nietzsche, however, this question becomes unanswerable. Precisely the situation of being a qualified reader, a reader addressed by the text and in a position to understand it, *denies* one the possibility of making any reasonable historical use of one's understanding. The text therefore becomes useless, except perhaps, paradoxically, from the point of view of the *disqualified* reader, the reader who is excluded from the text's projected community of understanding, the reader whom the text never speaks *to,* but only *about,* which means the (or a) woman. Thus the relation of women to the Nietzschean text occurs at exactly that point where the text develops what I call its free revolutionary leverage, the point of divorce or disjunction between the text's *use* and its understanding, or more precisely, between use and *meaning*.

For meaning—by whatever theoretical path we approach the idea—names the implacably conservative aspect of discourse. Meaning awakens only in the bosom of meaning, of what we are eventually reduced to speaking of as "accepted" or "established" meanings, and cannot participate in the kind of discontinuity that is required by the idea of the revolutionary moment. (Again, perspective is crucial here. From the far end of the bridge, with the revolutionary moment safely past, no discontinuity is to be seen, and the revolutionary text simply means its historical destiny after all.) But in Nietzsche, the normal contiguity of use and meaning—our sense that it is wrong to use a text except in some relation (however negative) to its meaning—is utterly disrupted. Of course it is possible to "use" any text in any wildly eccentric way we can imagine. But my point is that Nietzsche's texts are set up so as to *enforce,* without limiting, such eccentricity. Spivak suggests that the task of women as readers may be "to produce useful and scrupulous fake readings" ("Displacement," p. 186). I contend that Nietzsche writes in a manner that may justify even that otherwise uncomfortable and practically contradictory adjective "scrupulous."

But if the divorce between use and meaning can be deduced from Nietzsche's texts, is it not therefore itself a type of meaning? I will leave this question open for the time being, in the hope that it will be answered by my detailed argument. The other question that is likely to arise at this point—whether I have not gotten into the business of defining or essentializing the feminine, of putting woman in her place, or of enlisting Nietzsche to do it for me—is more easily dealt with. My point about later Nietzsche is that the text forms a kind of vortex. The qualified (male) reader, by the mere act of understanding, finds himself irrevocably in a situation offering no possibility whatever of useful historical action or vision. This vortex, this ever inwardly self-gathering structure, is the only "place" defined by the texts. And the place of women (the unlimited room for women's fake but scrupulous use of the text as leverage for being or aiming Elsewhere) is simply everywhere or anywhere "else," everywhere outside of that self-centralizing readerly location.

It follows that no valid general statements can be made about feminist uses of Nietzsche—at least no statements sufficiently positive to provide a useful orientation for feminist thought. The argument is therefore vacuous except to the extent that it can adduce actual particular instances of such use. The instance I will discuss, without claiming that it is in any sense definitive, is Irigaray's *Amante marine.*

V

Nietzsche's early work, through the *Thoughts Out of Season,* is concerned primarily with history, as an attempt not to describe or to understand, but to *make history,* by suggesting a novel and complex relation between the text and its reader. The starting point, the point from which *The Birth of Tragedy* sets out, is the idea, insisted upon by Kant, of the history-making operancy of philosophical *systematics*.

For *The Birth of Tragedy* is constructed upon a thoroughly organized and entirely decipherable systematic basis, a basis that in fact approaches being a *summary* of Western philosophical systems. The metaphysics of "das Ur-Eine," the primordially self-separating Original One, strongly recalls Hermetic or emanative philosophy. Kant's *Critiques* are credited with the systematic turning of the method of "Wissenschaft" (science, or systematic knowledge) against precisely the delusion that had made possible the development of that method; Nietzsche speaks here of "Dionysian wisdom in the form of concepts" (KSA 1:128; cf. BT §19, p. 121), which implies that his own present thought is amenable to systematic closure. The idea of a historical process driven by dialectical opposition is Hegelian, while the derivation of the dialectic from a single ever self-realizing dualism is borrowed from the system of Schiller's letters *On Aesthetic Education*—a book that Hegel himself studied while preparing the *Phenomenology.* And Nietzsche's insistence on contradiction, on dissonance, on originary dismemberment, together with the omission of Schiller's reconciling "play-drive," adds up very nearly to the positing of *difference* as a strictly primitive notion. The Apollonian and the Dionysian, at their point of full philosophical intensity as marked by the form of tragedy, *are* nothing but their difference, which in turn is the difference *of* difference, the difference by which difference itself (the Apollonian domain) is instituted. Thus any number of semiotically based systematic possibilities are suggested, theories of human being as nothing but the vessel of difference. "If we could imagine," says Nietzsche, "musical dissonance as such in the form of a human being—and what else," he continues, "*is* a human being?" (KSA 1:155; cf. BT §25, p. 143).

The possibility of systematic closure is therefore constantly present in the discourse, a closure that would presumably complete the work of Kant and Schopenhauer by explaining and discrediting the whole Socratic world view. But Nietzsche does not carry out in detail the system his own thought suggests. "We will have gained much for aesthetic science [*die aesthetische Wissenschaft*] when we have arrived not merely at the logical insight, but at an unmediated certainty of apprehension, that the development of art . . ." (KSA 1:25; cf. BT §1, p. 33). This, the book's first sentence, is disturbing, to say the least. How can "aesthetic *science*" discredit Socratism? And what, for a professed admirer of Kant, does science have to do with "unmediated certainty of apprehension," "unmittelbare

Sicherheit der Anschauung"? Still it is possible to explain why Nietzsche talks this way. For one of precisely the systematic consequences of his thought is that human culture *constitutes* the world in which it occurs, that the particular illusion by which we deal with the otherwise insupportable knowledge of the void *is* the very fabric of our existence, whence it follows that since our age is inescapably characterized by Socratic culture, we would merely delude ourselves if we claimed to occupy the point of view implied by a system that reduces Socratic culture to a finished object. Hence the actual method of *The Birth of Tragedy,* which is Socratic in a relatively uncomplicated way, in its implied claim to achieve knowledge concerning art by way of the critical questioning of accepted prejudices (e.g., the idea of Hellenic "serenity" or "naïveté").[7] The Socratic quality of the text, its anchoring on *this* end of the bridge to a new cultural age that its system (once perfected) would build, is thrown strongly into relief by the idea that German music and German philosophy are evidence of an "awakening of the Dionysian spirit" in contemporary Germany (KSA 1:127–28; BT §19, pp. 119–20). Nietzsche in fact goes so far as to assert: "Where Dionysian forces make themselves felt as tempestuously as in our experience today, there also Apollo, wrapped in a cloud, must already have descended among us; surely the next few generations will behold his most opulently beautiful effects" (KSA 1:155; cf. BT §25, pp. 143–44). But if the Apollonian is "already" (*bereits*) in process of realization among us, why write a *treatise* on this historical state of affairs? Is Nietzsche not here being a Socrates in advance with respect to the impending neo-Apollonian age? Is the understanding of Apollonian illusion, even the strictly correct understanding, not also a spoiling of that illusion? Again, Nietzsche *must* write in the Socratic manner. Yet in doing so, he appears to destroy the bridge to his own envisioned Elsewhere, and so writes himself out onto a limb.

But what of the reader? If *we* recognize the possibility of a bridge in *The Birth of Tragedy,* the possibility of a complete systematic closure that will supersede the Socratic, then it would be nonsense to suggest that "the reader" is not meant to recognize it. We, therefore, the readers, are invited to *pretend* to be naïve Socratic believers in the innocence of understanding, in our ability to understand our historical situation without thereby altering it. But on the other hand, the systematic aspect of the work (on which the bridge, the whole vision of a new artistic age, is founded) is *also* unquestionably Socratic in character, is indeed the ultimate in Socratic arrogance, an assertion of the dominion of an objectively valid reason over the very idea of such dominion. (We think of the preface to *The Cri-*

tique of Pure Reason, the idea of subjecting reason [*Vernunft*] itself to the method of science [*Wissenschaft*].) We the readers, precisely in *pretending* to operate within the Socratic delusion, thus also occupy a systematic perspective which *is* Socratic. The reader is literally of two minds. He (I say "he" advisedly) at once both *is* and *pretends to be* a Socratic thinker. And this combination in turn fulfills exactly the central vision of *The Birth of Tragedy,* the idea of the transformation of Socratism itself into a form of art. We cannot overcome or overthrow our Socratic cultural situation; but we can overcome our *subjection* to it by learning to manipulate it affirmatively, by making of it an object of *pretending,* thus making it the art it in truth is. We can, in Schiller's terminology, transform our "condition" into our "act." We can *pretend* willingly to be what we still inescapably *are*. The reader is thus as it were one step ahead of the text, which he looks back on and understands only by grasping what he himself is already doing as a reader. He contributes the work's meaning as much as he receives it. The real bridge (as opposed to the delusive bridge of systematic certainty) is not *there;* but it is *there to be built* by the reader, and is so exactly to the extent that the text finds itself *actually* out on a limb.

This is the kind of case one can make for speaking of Nietzsche as a revolutionary writer—although not yet a *free* revolutionary writer (since the project, the Elsewhere, is still focused upon), thus, for Nietzsche, not yet revolutionary enough. *The Birth of Tragedy* still imposes a specific role on the reader, and so compromises its own revolutionary force by erecting a kind of bridge (in the reader's response) after all. Hence the developed procedure of the *Thoughts Out of Season,* especially the essay "On the Use and Abuse of History," which pins its revolutionary hopes on a group of *non*readers, the German "youth" of its time (KSA 1:324–34; UM pp. 116–23). For the essay is itself inescapably a form of the "history" it rails against—perhaps a radical form of what it calls "critical history" (KSA 1:269–70; UM pp. 75–77), directed against the very practice it exemplifies, but history nonetheless, part of what must be kept from cluttering the minds of a youthful generation of cultural pioneers.

And yet, even here the bow is not strung to its tightest. Even the young nonreading history-makers are imposed upon, and so in a sense made readers after all, by being assigned a specific role in the text's vision. (What *is* a "reader," except someone who enacts a role with respect to a text?) In fact, at the conclusion of the essay, Nietzsche suggests that those coming generations may get around to reading him after all, when a state of cultural health is achieved and it again becomes possible to use history, including "critical" history, in the service of life (KSA 1:332; UM pp. 121–

22). The limbs onto which Nietzsche's revolutionary ambition drives him are thus not yet long enough to exceed the reach of his own rhetorical and visionary ingenuity. But it is still the ambition that drives him, not the ingenuity.

VI

I will not attempt to cover Nietzsche's whole development. But his early works illuminate the tensions that lead to what I call the divorce between meaning and use in his later work. To the extent that meaning and use overlap—or indeed practically coincide, as in *The Birth of Tragedy*—the bridge to a radically new *kind* of text-using becomes unnecessary and the text's revolutionary force is compromised. And conversely, the admission of a link between meaning and usefulness encourages the insinuation of the (normally conservative) manner in which the text happens *actually* to be used into our sense of what the text means. In fact, in the last aphorism of *Beyond Good and Evil,* Nietzsche suggests that the mere *writing* of the text is already a form of use that interferes with the text's revolutionary effectiveness (KSA 5:239–40; BGE §296, pp. 236–37). And then, in his farewell to the aphoristic mode, he "supplements" *Beyond Good and Evil* with a "polemic" for its "clarification," *The Genealogy of Morals.*[8] For *Beyond Good and Evil,* like the other aphoristic works, is a book that is too joyful and affirmative for its own good. The reader is constantly tempted to assume that the spirited and skillful and daring leaps he must make as a reader, from mountain peak to mountain peak, are in the end *getting him somewhere,* or getting him Elsewhere, perhaps even eventually to a place of reward where his daring (and with it, his joy) is no longer required. And this assumption must be countered. The reader, so to speak, may jump however he pleases, only not to the conclusion that there is any place worth jumping to.

Or to put it differently, a text that is at once both perfectly joyful (treating its leaps like bridges) and perfectly useless (positively *denying* an Elsewhere at the other end, with "a pessimism *bonae voluntatis* that not only says no and wills no but—horrible thought! *does* no" [KSA 5:137; cf. BGE §208, p. 129]) would be a free revolutionary text, a model of revolutionary method. And the import of *The Genealogy of Morals* is to show *Beyond Good and Evil* as (or make it into) such a text. Especially the last section of the *Genealogy,* "What Do Ascetic Ideals Signify?," draws an ever-tightening ring about the reader. The ascetic ideal, the insidious violence of life against life itself, characterizes not only religion but also the self-distancing of science from religion, not only the pretended objectivity of science but also the philosophical critique of that pretense, and even the resolutely atheistic critique of that critique. Can the reader imagine that his own point of view somehow escapes this deadly chain? The ascetic ideal arises with the recognition of human existence as a *problem.* "Wozu leiden?" (KSA 5:411; cf. GM—III §28, p. 162), "Why do we suffer?" And once this problem is responded to in an ascetic manner—which means simply, once it is responded to at all, once we accept it as a problem—a vicious circle is established. For the response, the justification of suffering, being itself a form of self-injury on the part of life, increases our suffering (not to mention our perplexity at its needlessness), thus makes the problem more acute, thus provokes a subtler and more devious response, and so on, until we arrive at "our problem"—as Nietzsche says to the "*unknown* friends" among his readers—until we arrive at the recognition "that in us even the will to truth [the drive to explain or justify anything whatever] has become conscious of itself *as a problem*" (KSA 5:410; cf. GM—III §27, p. 161). Nor is it insignificant that Nietzsche refers directly, if cryptically, to his reader here. For if the question "Why do we suffer?" is such that any answer to it turns out to be a wrong answer, is this not also true of the question "Wozu *lesen?*"—"Why do we read?"

The question Why do we read?—if it asks after the conceivable use in history of a particular text—is normally answered by a kind of story. In reading *The Theater and Its Double,* my eyes are opened to the narrowness of the European dramatic tradition in which writing is the dominant element, and to the relation of this tradition to certain structures of political dominance. And it is conceivable that a revolution in the theater itself (other traditions, after all, are available) would contribute to a further opening of eyes, perhaps eventually to a revolutionizing of society. What matters here is not whether the text's cultural and political argument is well founded but whether the reader's story is plausible, whether a reasonable reader can leave the text with a sense that something is to be done. Even in the case of *Les Guérillères,* the reader is not forced into a corner. The fantastic elements in the narrative, especially the women's weapons, plus the points of strong contact with existing Western myth and symbolism, make it possible to read the text as the sign of a state of mind buried in our actual social conditions, whereupon it becomes reasonable to inquire into the future of that state of mind and its historical effects.

But in the case of *Beyond Good and Evil* and *The Genealogy of Morals,* the only available story for the reader is the story of the ascetic ideal itself. The reader cannot reasonably ignore the connection between his own activity in reading, his role in relation to the text, and the "will to truth," however firm his grasp of the "problem" of that will. It is true that possibilities of living outside the ascetic mechanism are suggested. The pride and good taste of "coming philosophers," we are told, will be offended by the idea that *their* truth should be "a truth for everyone" (KSA 5:60; cf. BGE §43, p. 53). But the articulation of this possibility only throws into relief the hopeless situation of the reader; for it is a possibility which, *by* being a reader, I have *already* left behind. How can I boast of *my* truth in the very process of insinuating myself into someone else's, adjusting my thought with respect to the text? How can I claim any relation whatever to the quality of being "vornehm" (distinguished, of high rank) when the action of reading this text actually discloses only my "need" of this quality (KSA 5:232–33; BGE §287, pp. 227–28)? I can employ the text in the historical direction it itself suggests only by *not* reading it, having no need of it. We talk a good deal these days about reading texts "against the grain"; and this talk, I think, is an index of precisely the discomfort at being a reader that Nietzsche, more than anyone else, provokes. But it is only talk. If I perform, say, a psychoanalytic reading of text X "against its grain," then the text I am really reading, really trying to use in history, is not X at all, but Freud or Lacan or whoever.

Even the perhaps honest and courageous conclusion, on the reader's part, that there is no escape from history as shaped by the ascetic ideal, accomplishes nothing; for the whole tenor of the book makes this conclusion—valid as it may be—strictly unacceptable. On the level of meaning, *Beyond Good and Evil* and *The Genealogy of Morals* do nothing but thoroughly and repeatedly *demolish* ascetic ideals—in a manner, for example, in which the Socratic world view is *not* demolished in *The Birth of Tragedy,* where precisely the artistic affirmation of Socratism is offered the reader as his historical task. The reader of the later books is left not out on a limb but at a simple historical dead end, without even the vision (as in the *Thoughts Out of Season*) of a youthful generation of nonreaders, to whose historical mission he might contribute by way of a reform of educational institutions. The "coming" philosophers are perhaps really on their way; there are perhaps still individuals with "an *instinct for rank*" (KSA 5:217; BGE §263, p. 212), for whom history is not hopeless. But these groups stand in *no relation whatever* to the reader of Nietzsche's text.

The meaning of *Beyond Good and Evil* and *The Genealogy* is dense, varied, complex, inexhaustible. But the intersection of the text's meaning with its usefulness in the historical situation that it itself reflects is empty. The meaning of the text, with respect to the idea of its usefulness in history, is entirely contained in the statement: the text is useless. But it does not follow that this is a true statement, that the text *is* useless. What follows, as I have suggested, is that *if* the text is useful, then it is so only for those people who are positively disqualified as understanding readers. The situation is a curious one. (Conceivably a person utterly unqualified in music might find in the printed score of a Bach fugue the secret of socially equitable city planning.) But given that Nietzsche's text is revolutionary in spirit (*Beyond Good and Evil* is subtitled "Prelude to a Philosophy of the Future"), given that its vision of history requires that something radical be done by somebody, then it is just that curious situation that arises with respect to it—without (again) being part of its meaning.

VII

And the positively disqualified reader of *Beyond Good and Evil,* again, is above all the reader who is a woman. The well-known sexist aphorisms in this book (KSA 5:170–78; BGE §§231–39, pp. 162–70), more than those in other books, concentrate precisely on the inadvisability of educating women, of giving them intellectual status, of qualifying them as readers. Not that this quality of the aphorisms justifies my argument as an *interpretation* of the book. On the contrary, Kelly Oliver's outright dismissal of any attempt to read Nietzsche from a feminist perspective, even if her psychoanalysis is oversimple, comes much closer to what might reasonably be called the *meaning,* with respect to women of, say, *Beyond Good and Evil*—meaning, again, in the sense that it is available to a qualified (male) reader. But the special historical situation of women with respect to this text obtains nonetheless, and can perhaps be opened by the discussion of two actual readings of Nietzsche, a feminist text written by a man and a book with no feminist component written by a woman, Derrida's *Spurs* and Susan Sontag's *Against Interpretation.*

I have mentioned Spivak's doubts, which I think are well founded, about the effectiveness and legitimacy of *Spurs* as a feminist initiative. But it is certain that Derrida associates "the question of woman" with the revolutionary quality of Nietzsche's writing, with its attempt to escape from an inherently conservative tradition of meaning, from the "hermeneutic project which postulates a true sense of the text."[9] It is also certain that Derrida reads Nietzsche as what I have called *free* revolutionary writing, as a text to which no project or proper (meaning-related) use can be assigned, a text that, "in some monstrous way, might well be of the type 'I have forgotten my umbrella'" (pp. 132/133). And it is then at least rhetorically consistent—if not logically necessary, and certainly not demonstrable as a self-interpretation—that Derrida now feels entitled to suggest that his own text follows Nietzsche in this respect, that it may be a text of the same "monstrous" type (pp. 134/135). After all, one cannot talk hermeneutic sense about the escape from the hermeneutic.

But there is one place where Derrida cannot follow Nietzsche, although he is honest enough to quote him: where Nietzsche, in *Beyond Good and Evil,* introduces his "truths" about women by saying, "provided one knows from the outset how completely they are only—*my* truths" (KSA 5 : 170; cf. BGE §231, p. 162). Derrida's commentary on this passage, which touches on "ontology" (pp. 102/103) in its relation to "biographical desire" (pp. 104/105), can never get back to the simple exclusionary force (excluding precisely the reader, as I have said) of Nietzsche's "my." Derrida says: "The very fact that 'meine Wahrheiten' ['*my* truths'] is so underlined, that they are multiple, variegated, contradictory even, can only imply that these are not *truths*. Indeed there is no such thing as truth in itself. But only a surfeit of it. Even if it should be for me, about me, truth is plural" (pp. 102/103). This statement is perhaps defensible as an *interpretation* of Nietzsche's words. But the word *me* (*moi*) as Derrida uses it—here, and also where he is talking about his own text (pp. 136/137)—belongs to a universe entirely different from Nietzsche's. It means "me, whoever I might be," or "me for instance." It means in effect "one" (*on,* or in German, *man*), and completely lacks the exclusionary force of Nietzsche's "my," which, whatever it may "imply," still *asserts* that its "truths" are after all truths—truths (to repeat) that are not hermeneutically reducible to meanings. And this exclusionary force is crucial for the possibility of feminist discourse. Derrida scorns any "essentializing" discourse about "woman" (pp. 54/55), and suggests that such essentializing is finally put aside by "the epochal regime of quotation marks" (pp. 106/107), which surrounds all "decidable" concepts with a sphere of critical or indeed skeptical distance. But one word, in this regime, must be free of quotation marks, must simply mean what it says, the word *I* or *me* or *my.* For "I" in quotation marks—meaning "whoever I might be," referring only to a *position* with respect to some concept or truth—implies that its position is in principle available to anyone, hence that its truth can become "a truth for everyone" (KSA 5 : 60; cf. BGE §43, p. 53), or an essence, an "in itself" (*en soi, an sich*) after all. And how, also, shall *free* revolutionary writing operate without a strictly exclusionary "me," a word that says: whatever my revolutionary vision might be, it is not available to "you" or "us" as a project?

The question of the "subject," or of "subjectivity," does not arise here. Or if "you" raise that broad conceptual question anyway, then this questioning is a symptom of precisely "your" exclusion from the simple narrow particularity of my (or Nietzsche's) "I." And here is where Sontag's *Against Interpretation* comes in. For Sontag, even in accepting Nietzsche's authority in many crucial areas of cultural history, also manages to follow Nietzsche in the exclusionary use of the (expressed or implied) "I."[10] But she achieves this only by failing utterly to be "scrupulous" (we recall Spivak's use of this word) in her reading of Nietzsche. "Against" interpretation? On the basis of the inseparability of hermeneutics from metaphysics, of the "hermeneutic project" from a "truth of being" (*Spurs*, pp. 106/107), Derrida uses Nietzsche to make nonsense of the very idea of "against" as Sontag uses it: "If the form of opposition and the oppositional structure are themselves metaphysical, then the relation of metaphysics [hence also hermeneutics] to its other can no longer be one of opposition" (*Spurs*, pp. 116/117–118/119). And Sontag herself calls attention to this objection, quoting Nietzsche: "Of course, I don't mean interpretation in the broadest sense, the sense in which Nietzsche (rightly) says, 'There are no facts, only interpretations.' By interpretation, I mean here a conscious act of the mind which illustrates a certain code, certain 'rules' of interpretation."[11] As if the whole critical force of Nietzsche's statement did not depend on its meaning "interpretation" in a sense that does *not* exclude what Sontag attacks here.

It would be reasonable to say simply that Sontag gets Nietzsche wrong. She reads him to mean, in a vague general sense, "everything is subjective," a statement he in fact derides in the same aphorism (KSA 12:315; WP §481, p. 267). But on the other hand, it follows from the divorce between meaning and use that if Sontag's text can be considered a somehow valid use of Nietzsche, then the question of meaning, of getting Nietzsche right, does not arise. Of course the mere fact that I get Nietzsche wrong does not qualify me as a valid or fruitful user of Nietzsche. But Sontag is also a revolutionary, in something like an early Nietzschean sense. She insists on the hopeless idea of an art strictly beyond the reach of interpretation. And in a wildly paradoxical move, she embeds her text by quotation in a far-flung *literary* culture (at one point [p. 298] she says, "the writings of Nietzsche, Wittgenstein, Antonin Artaud, C. S. Sherrington, Buckminster Fuller, Marshall McLuhan, John Cage, André Breton, Roland Barthes, Claude Lévi-Strauss, Sigfried Giedion, Norman O. Brown, and Gyorgy Kepes") that makes her project plausible by way of the concealed supposition that art *is* what it is interpreted as being. Assuming, therefore, that we do not simply dismiss Sontag altogether—which we can always reasonably do with a revolutionary text—might we not recognize her egregious misreading of Nietzsche (and not only Nietzsche) as the focus of precisely a Nietzschean exclusionary "I," an "I" in which we are prevented from participating precisely by our understanding of Nietzsche?

Sontag's text, with respect to Nietzsche, is what Derrida's text wishes it could be, a text made of outright exclusionary lies. "Je peux mentir," "I could be lying" (*Spurs,* p. 136/137), says Derrida. But he is *not* lying, not for a minute; the conceptual structure of his writing, despite the "Distances" (pp. 36/37) covered by its metaphorical, etymological, orthographic leaps, is much too tight and scrupulous. He reads (others and himself) too well. And conversely, Derrida's text is what Sontag's wishes it could be. For how shall we move past "literature" to a grasp of "the new sensibility" (Sontag, pp. 298–99) without first getting literature right, without reading it (and ourselves) to the point where it is compelled to tie up its own nagging loose ends by whatever improbable leaps?

Not that Derrida's procedure and Sontag's could ever in any sense be combined. Rather, they each play gropingly into the other's hand, like the defenders in a game of bridge, in hopes of finding the one extra trick that will at last "set" Nietzsche the Declarer, position him, fix his shape, establish him, make him at last useful and usable.

VIII

I use the metaphor of a game of bridge with a view especially to the role of the dummy, which in French happens to be "le mort," the dead man. A hand in auction bridge opens with the "bidding," which establishes the trump suit for the hand and the number of tricks needed for either side to win. The player who first bids the eventual trump suit becomes "declarer"; the cards of the declarer's partner, whose hand is now the "dummy," are turned face up for all to see after the opening lead; and in the ensuing play, the declarer plays both his or her own concealed hand and, in turn, the cards of the dummy. The player whose hand is dummy at this point becomes a pure spectator, may as well not exist.

This structure, to my mind, suggests a preter-interpretive or metahermeneutic ideal. If only we could avoid playing our part in the interpretive process—our part, our activity as interpreters, which inevitably distorts what we claim to be looking for. If only we could somehow simply lay down our cards and let the text itself play (or play with) them. This is not to desire mere passivity. The cards are still *our* cards; the object of play (the contract) is still the product of a tentative cryptic communication with the interpretand, the text that declares. If we could at that point simply stop and think about something quite different (perhaps the umbrella we have forgotten), the result would be an unprecedented type of interpretive *act,* an act perhaps at last able to come to grips even with the strictly uninterpretable, even with a text characterized by the absolute divorce between meaning and use.

I think it is possible that with respect to Nietzsche—but also, indispensably, with respect to Derrida and Sontag, or at least with respect to the positions I have assigned them—Irigaray's *Amante marine: De Friedrich Nietzsche* shadows forth such an act. At least this claim is suggested by her title, which means: "the marine lover (or betrothed), a book on (de) Friedrich Nietzsche"; or "a book about (or by, or in the person of) the marine lover of (de) Friedrich Nietzsche"; or "marine lover, a book by (de) Friedrich Nietzsche." And the complexities of the title are then sustained, in the first long section, "Dire d'eaux immémoriales" ("Speaking of Immemorial Waters"), by complexities in the use of the first person, the "je" or "I." In a context dominated by the figure of Nietzsche, namely, the "I" gains exclusionary force from the mere fact of its being spoken *by a woman*—a fact which, even without grammatical indications, as in the clause "il ne fallait pas que je sois trouée" ("I should not have been holed"), we cannot deny our knowledge of.[12] For Irigaray not only *is* a woman, but is known to us (unlike Sontag) as one who speaks *as* a woman. Derrida strives to reproduce Nietzsche's exclusionary "I," and in striving necessarily fails; the *second* "I" (Derrida's) places us inescapably "among ourselves"—meaning, inescapably, "among men"—"unter sich" (KSA 5:171; BGE §232, p. 163; quoted in *Spurs,* pp. 64/65). But Irigaray's "I" can claim to imitate Nietzsche's—and can actually imitate, say, the marine fantasy in no. 60 of *The Joyful Science* (KSA 3:424–25; GS §60, pp. 123–24)—while still retaining the force that excludes precisely Nietzsche's (male) reader.

Nor does it follow that Irigaray's first person is an instance of that speaking "in the name of woman" that Felman criticizes. For in the first place, it is Nietzsche himself (his exclusionary "I") who is made to speak here, to speak as he in effect had always spoken, with the voice of the Outside or Elsewhere that had automatically arisen relative to the vortex of his late texts: "But isn't that your game: that the Outside be ceaselessly drawn back inside? And that there be no Outside that you yourself had not thrown forth? My cry would thus be [note the conditional] only the sign of your calling back" (*Am,* p. 18). And in the second place, it is also the impossible, disallowed female reader of Nietzsche who is speaking here, and who therefore requires a new *kind* of reading, a reading that produces no "unter sich," even "among women," since any such community of understanding-Nietzsche is necessarily male. "For I love Division where you [Nietzsche] wish to preserve the Whole" (*Am*, p. 17). In order to be "spoken for" by this "I," even a woman must "aimer le partage," insist on Division, *decline* to be spoken for: "But woman? Is not reducible to femininity. Or to lying or appearance or beauty. Except by 'remaining among themselves' ['unter sich'] and projecting 'at a distance' that other of themselves to which truth, from the origin, is hostile" (*Am*, p. 83). And the condition of being "unter sich," which reduces women to femininity, is precisely what is denied to female readers of Nietzsche. The "I," here, is spoken by *a* woman, not by "whichever woman I happen to be."

We must be clear, however, about the status of this argument. By its own showing, it is *not* an interpretation of either Nietzsche or *Amante marine*. Neither the argument itself, nor the bridge it erects between Nietzsche's text and Irigaray's, could occur except in relation to *the question of the "I"*; and a main point of the argument is that this question *does not arise* in late Nietzsche. Nietzsche's "I," as soon as it becomes an object of questioning, as it does in Derrida, *loses* precisely that radically simple exclusionary quality that makes it interesting in Nietzsche, and becomes merely an instance of "the subject." The same point, for the same reasons, applies to Irigaray, where the exclusionary force of the "I," the impossibility of a communicative network (an *unter sich*), is created by a radically simple (because simply "real") gender difference. (Derrida says that "there is no truth in itself of the sexual difference in itself, of either man or woman in itself" [*Spurs*, pp. 102/103]. And it is in the space left open by that "in itself" (*en soi*), the space of utter untheorizable particularity, that Irigaray's "I" asserts its difference.)

But on the other hand, the *relation* between late Nietzsche and *Amante marine*, hence the whole of the present argument, presupposes precisely a raising of the question of the "I," presupposes therefore something like the "defense" against Nietzsche that I claim emerges from the (however "unwittingly") interacting initiatives of Sontag and Derrida. The subject matter of the argument, consequently, the object of interpretation, is neither Nietzsche's text nor Irigaray's, but is the whole structure of response, the game of bridge, in which those texts are involved. And this structure in turn, which in a sense originates with Nietzsche, but cannot be considered an interpretation of his meaning, opens at least the possibility of a historically significant use of Nietzsche's text.

There is still a paradox here. The exclusionary force of Irigaray's "I," like that of Nietzsche's, must be prior to any raising of the question of the "I." But at the same time, it is constituted by a gender difference which implies (and requires, so to speak, for leverage) a specific difference *from Nietzsche*—from the *unter sich* as such, which specifically in Nietzsche is revealed as a male discourse-vortex—hence presupposes the relation with Nietzsche and the question of the "I" after all. That this is a paradox, not merely a confusion, has to do with Irigaray's speaking as a *dis*qualified reader of Nietzsche—not merely as an *un*qualified reader, which is how we might characterize Sontag's position. The negative force of disqualification, from Nietzsche, operates directly in Irigaray's discourse ("But isn't that your game . . . ?") as it does not in Sontag's, and collapses the "relation" Nietzsche-Irigaray, as far as the "I" is concerned, into something more like an identity. Nietzsche "himself" in a strong sense inhabits Irigaray's discourse at the point of utter untheorizable particularity marked by her "I." And this paradox—which is itself a form or aspect of exactly the exclusionary force, the escape of Irigaray's "I" from any reasonable theoretical resolution, that it expounds—this situation of Irigaray across the table from Nietzsche, yet also in Nietzsche's "own" position, is what I am trying to capture in the image of declarer and dummy.

IX

But is Nietzsche *really* playing the cards in *Amante marine?* This question is meaningless except in relation to the other two texts (or text-types) I have mentioned, Derrida's and Sontag's, which are each, and both, a kind of defense against Nietzsche. And in this relation, I think the answer is yes. In the second main section of Irigaray's book, "Lèvres voilées" ("Veiled Lips"), the "je" of the first section is largely supplanted by "la femme" and "elle," "woman" and "she," and we have what appears to be a psychoanalytic-mythological-feminist essay more or less in the manner of *Speculum.* But the constantly recurring theme of this section is no. 361 of *The Joyful Science*—which also figures centrally in *Spurs* (pp. 68/69)—on women's "giving themselves out as" even when they "give themselves" (KSA 3:609; GS §361, p. 317). And Irigaray *accepts* this formulation. She plays with it and develops it; she does not dispute it. Which has obvious consequences for our sense of the structure of her own writing. By talking about "woman," she in a sense "gives herself," exposes herself to co-option by the essentializing male discourse that puts "woman" in her place. But by surrendering herself to the one specific fragment of male discourse (Nietzsche's) that she focuses on, she also calls attention to the impossibility of distinguishing her surrender from a "giving herself out as," so that her exclusionary "I" is enabled to survive beneath the surface after all (she etymologizes, "sub-sister" [meaning roughly "survive," *Am,* pp. 119, 122, 126]—with a play on English "sister"?).

And this structure, in "Veiled Lips," also draws Nietzsche into itself, makes him the player of the cards. For it is exactly Nietzsche's game ("giving herself [out as]") that Irigaray is playing here, even down to the detail of herself actually being a woman. It is exclusively Nietzsche's game—as Derrida's inevitably interpretive game, or Sontag's arbitrary defiance of the rules, cannot be. Which raises the possibility of the game's doubling back on itself, the possibility that it is here Nietzsche himself who—in a sense that is difficult to specify, but also difficult to set limits to—"gives himself out as" a woman: "Ariane—double du mâle. Ne reproduit que du masculin. Que celui-ci se veuille, aussi, du féminin, redouble peut-être la mise. Ne change pas le jeu" (*Am,* p. 125) (Ariadne—double of the male. Reproduces only the masculine. That the latter, also, might want itself [involved in or partaking of the] feminine, perhaps doubles the stakes. Does not change the game). The game is unchanged, is still Nietzsche's own game ("de Friedrich Nietzsche"), even in being played through the open, proffered, upturned hand of the *Amante marine.*

But this part of the argument must be qualified in the same way as that of the preceding section. For it is also not an interpretation. It leans too heavily on an assertion concerning reality, as opposed to meaning, on the idea of the *real* openness of Irigaray's text to co-option by an established antifeminist discourse; otherwise the idea of Nietzsche's presence in that text (a strictly antifeminist presence on the level of meaning), the idea of Nietzsche's playing the cards, would be idle.

The corresponding interpretive argument (or the present argument, considered as an interpretation of *Amante marine*) would describe an ironic textual "strategy" by which Irigaray "undermines" the inevitably essentializing or colonizing tendency of any discourse focused upon the idea (however subtly shaded in terminology) of "woman." Irigaray—the argument would run—plays with that discourse on woman by borrowing from Nietzsche's version of it the paradox of genuineness and dissimulation (the idea of woman's "giving herself out as" in the very act of "giving herself"), which now supposedly disorients the reader by making it impossible for him (or even her) to decide whether the present discourse on woman (Irigaray's, in "Veiled Lips") is not itself a complicated dissimulation, disguising a subversive feminist intent. And this disorientation, in turn—the argument would conclude—itself already "subverts" established male discourse by introducing an element of undecidability, of uncertainty, at its core.

The trouble with this argument is that it would be an instance of precisely the co-optive move to which Irigaray's text is vulnerable. "Disorientation" and "subversion," in the sense of an argument of this type, are nothing but typical moves *in* the established discourse that is supposedly called into question, nothing but the construction of an internal tension to which the discourse may then respond, typically, with its culminating move of triumphant self-reflexive closure. In the particular case, this closure is interpretive, the successful reduction of Irigaray's text to a smoothly operating interaction of meanings. Our insistence that those meanings are "subversive" or "disruptive" changes nothing; for these ideas (precisely in the course of interpreting) have themselves been fitted into the hermeneutic order. And it follows, since the interpretation is itself a co-option, that the feminist countermove (which it itself postulates) must lie entirely beyond its scope, so that a new interpretation is required, and so on.

There is no way out of this bind except by changing the terms of the argument altogether. We must recognize that we are not, in a strict sense, talking about Irigaray's text, that we are not merely bringing Nietzsche to bear (or Sontag or Derrida) upon an *understanding* of that text. On the contrary, if we are talking about anything at all—which, in the case of an argument out on a limb, is admittedly open to question—then we are talking about a situation that is too simply and strictly *real* to be hermeneutically accessible, a situation in which terms like *co-option* and *subversion* would have to name implacable historical turnings not subject to hermeneutic reconsideration. But a situation, nevertheless, that is made up of texts and relations among texts—certainly more than just the four examples I have used to sketch a kind of cross-section—texts in which the hermeneutically impossible problem posed by Nietzsche, the divorce of use from meaning, straining against the rock of gender difference, may provide paradoxically, for those texts, a form of leverage upon the hermeneutically inconceivable task of revolution, relative to the very discourse that grounds them.

X

These ideas could be supported and developed by further references to *Amante marine*. By the idea of Nietzsche's still uncompleted *birth* (*Am*, pp. 40, 51, 71–72); or the idea of Nietzsche's fated "announcing what can only take place after you [Nietzsche], and without you" (*Am,* p. 47), which means the divorce between meaning and use. And we have not even begun on the last section of the book, "Quand naissent les dieux" ("When the Gods Are Born").

But detailed textual exegesis would only bring us back repeatedly to the unreasonable idea of discourse revolution, and only compel us to disavow, yet again, the entirely reasonable interpretation of our own procedure as an interpretive one. What is important, I hope, is the structure of relations among texts, the game of bridge, that I have sketched, and the recognition that this structure, considered as a response to Nietzsche, is characterized by *radical multiplicity.* There is no debate, no possibility of debate, between Sontag and Derrida; there is only a gulf, into which both texts can perhaps be imagined as groping. There is hardly even a basis for comparison between Sontag and Irigaray as readers of Nietzsche. And although Irigaray's text is constantly aware of Derrida—from the first page, with the image of the "Tympan" (*Am,* p. 9)—it is not as if she took issue with Derrida's reading of Nietzsche. She simply admits Derrida—takes him, so to speak, as read—and remains irreducibly separated from him, nonetheless, by the gender difference that disqualifies her reading.

That precisely these texts form a single structure that is coherent in Nietzschean terms—assuming I have shown this to be the case—is therefore a point of some significance. And it seems to me that the notion of the revolutionary, difficult as it may be to pin down, suggests at least one way in which that structure may make sense historically.

But I am not suggesting that the texts I have looked at, or any others that may stand in similar relations to them, either achieve or even foreshadow a usefully organized feminist discourse. Precisely the radical multiplicity of those texts, or of their specific discursive initiatives, is crucial. For the solitary reader of Nietzsche—male or female, feminist or otherwise—is inevitably confronted with a kind of historical Nothingness, with the perfect uselessness of his or her endeavor. It is as if one's reading, by failing to get anywhere at all, were somehow not really happening. Only the multiple game of readings can conceivably liberate the revolutionary energies in Nietzsche, the revolutionary moment, the step out onto the limb or the bridge, which is Nietzsche's own but can take place only (as Irigaray says) "without" him. And the more strictly without him (hence the more completely his own) for being revolutionary in a feminist sense.

Notes

1. Kelly Oliver, "Nietzsche's Woman: The Poststructuralist Attempt to Do Away with Women," *Radical Philosophy* 48 (Spring 1988): 29. The sentence in which these words occur is obviously faulty; a line of print appears to be missing. But the meaning is clear. Oliver is discussing David Farrell Krell, *Postponements: Woman, Sensuality, and Death in Nietzsche* (Bloomington: Indiana Univ. Press, 1986).

2. Shoshana Felman, "Women and Madness: The Critical Phallacy," *Diacritics* 5, no. 4 (1975): 2–10, here p. 10.

3. Monique Wittig, *Les Guérillères* (Paris: Minuit, 1969), pp. 162–64.

4. Nancy K. Miller, "Changing the Subject: Authorship, Writing, and the Reader," in *Feminist Studies: Critical Studies,* ed. Teresa de Lauretis (Bloomington: Indiana Univ. Press, 1986), pp. 102–20.

5. Gayatri Chakravorty Spivak, "The Politics of Interpretations," *Critical Inquiry* 9 (1982–83): 259–78. Miller quotes pp. 276–77 where Spivak is responding to Terry Eagleton, *Walter Benjamin: Or, Towards a Revolutionary Criticism* (London: Verso, 1981). Needless to say, I do not accept Eagleton's notion of the "revolutionary."

6. Gayatri Chakravorty Spivak, "Displacement and the Discourse of Woman," in *Displacement: Derrida and After,* ed. Mark Krupnick (Bloomington: Indiana Univ. Press, 1983), pp. 169–95. The present quote is on p. 184. In a footnote, incidentally, Spivak says, "Given the tradition of academic radicalism in France, and our experience with the old New Left, 'feminist' should not be taken as a subset of 'revolutionary' " (p. 195). I hope it is clear that this remark and its context do not affect the use of the term *revolutionary* in my argument, where its conceptual identity is not such as to admit the relation of set to subset in the first place. It follows from the discussion of historical perspectives with which we began that thought or action, in any particular case, is "revolutionary" only by being so in (precisely) a strictly revolutionary manner, and that the comparison of different cases (hence the construction of "subsets") automatically brackets the whole idea of revolution. Again, I do not claim that this idea of revolution is conceptually sound. I claim only that it names a relatively common intuitive perception concerning the utter unaccountability of history. Maybe it is a misperception; maybe there are no revolutions in the sense I mean. But feminists, given the radicality with which the problems confronting their endeavor have been stated, can be reasonable, can dispense with the idea of revolution, only at the cost of being content with unsatisfactorily limited (and probably, for just that reason, unachievable) goals. Feminist discourse, I think, has gone too far to compromise.

7. See my "Nietzsche's Idea of Myth: The Birth of Tragedy from the Spirit of Eighteenth-Century Aesthetics," *PMLA* 94 (1979): 420–33, especially p. 430, on Nietzsche's *affirmation* of the development of Socratic culture. That article still suffers, however, from an unclear view of the place of the idea of system in *The Birth of Tragedy.*

8. "A Polemic" ("Eine Streitschrift") is the subtitle of *The Genealogy of Morals;* and in the first edition of 1887 (not to mention a large number of modern editions), the reverse of the title page bears the note: "Dem letztveröffentlichten 'Jenseits von Gut und Böse' zur Ergänzung und Verdeutlichung beigegeben" (Appended to the just-published *Beyond Good and Evil* as a supplement and clarification). Colli and Montinari, however, include this note neither in the KSA, nor even in their larger "Kritische

Gesamtausgabe," part 6, vol. 2 (Berlin: de Gruyter, 1968). There may be a reason for this omission, but as far as I can see, Colli and Montinari do not explain it.

9. Jacques Derrida, *Spurs: Nietzsche's Styles / Eperons: Les Styles de Nietzsche,* trans. Barbara Harlow (Chicago: Univ. of Chicago Press, 1979), pp. 106/107.

10. Susan Sontag, *Against Interpretation and Other Essays* (New York: Farrar, Straus & Giroux, 1966). See especially pp. 49–50, 54, 88, 98, 132–33, 249–55, 260–62, 299, not to mention the whole essay "On Style," pp. 15–36.

11. Sontag, p. 5. She is quoting Nietzsche's posthumous aphorism "against positivism" (KSA 12:315). She might also have used section 22 of *Beyond Good and Evil* (KSA 5:37), if the latter passage had not insisted uncomfortably on anti-interpretation as itself an interpretive act.

12. Luce Irigaray, *Amante marine: De Friedrich Nietzsche* (Paris: Minuit, 1980), p. 9. References in the text by *Am* plus page.

LUCE IRIGARAY

Ecce Mulier? Fragments

Qui me lit, respire. J'en ai fait plusieurs fois l'expérience. Devant moi, qui abordait un de mes écrits se mettait à inspirer. A ses côtés, j'étouffais à demi. J'aurais pu expirer et prendre le rythme. Mais le mélange des souffles avec qui je n'ai pas choisi me déplaît. Avec un arbre, d'accord. Je suis quasi certaine d'en recevoir de l'oxygène. Mais un humain?

Ce n'est pas que j'apprécie d'être au-dessus de. C'est plutôt que l'air pur me convient. Il m'est idéal. Pas besoin d'idoles. Une bouffée d'air frais, et le monde change de consistance. Toujours matériel, il se subtilise, se transsubstantialise. L'idéal, pour moi, est fait d'air pur. Chacun de ses inspirs vous porte la vérité. Le moindre véhicule à moteur par contre y est une sorte de faute originelle, ou le rappel d'une décadence sans merci.

Dire que j'ai fait à l'humanité "le plus grand cadeau" me déplairait. Comparer n'est-ce déjà confondre? Et un cadeau n'est jamais qu'un cadeau. Je préfère lui avoir dévoilé un horizon. Ni plus haut ni plus bas, mais caché dans la réalité du quotidien. Peut-être lui ai-je un peu ouvert les yeux? Ou les oreilles? Ou autres sens? Peut-être ai-je rendu un peu chacun(e) à sa vie, à la vie? Je souhaite lui avoir enseigné à renoncer à être ceci ou cela, plus ou moins que, plus haut ou plus bas. . . .

LUCE IRIGARAY

Ecce Mulier? Fragments

Whoever reads me, breathes. I have experienced it several times. Before my eyes, someone who was starting to read one of my works was beginning to *in-spire*. Next to him, I was almost suffocating. I could have *ex-pired* and kept pace. But it irks me to mix breaths with someone I haven't chosen. With a tree, all right. I'm almost certain to receive oxygen. But a human?

It is not that I relish being above. It is rather that pure air agrees with me. It is ideal for me. No need for idols. A breath of fresh air, and the world changes substance. Still material, it is subtilized, transubstantiated. For me, the ideal is made of fresh air. Each in-spiration brings you truth. By contrast, the least of motor vehicles is a sort of original sin, or the reminder of an unrelenting decadence.

I would not wish to say that I have given humanity "the greatest gift." Is to compare not also to confuse? And a gift is never more than a gift. I would prefer to have unveiled a horizon for humanity. Not higher or lower, but hidden in the reality of the everyday. Perhaps I have opened humanity's eyes a little? Or its ears? Or other senses? Perhaps I have helped to bring everyone back to his or her life, to life? I hope I have taught them to renounce being this or that, more or less than, higher or lower. . . .

Ce que je transmets est imperceptible. Et beaucoup me tiennent rigueur de ne pas leur apprendre quelque chose.

Cela ne les empêche pas de m'annoncer, dans les mois qui suivent, qu'ils, ou elles, ont découvert l'amour, ont enfanté, ont écrit un livre ou réalisé quelqu'oeuvre d'art. Mais le rapport est rarement établi entre ces événements et notre rencontre. Néanmoins certain(e)s le font. Sinon, j'en douterais moi-même.

Assurément la fécondité spirituelle existe. Elle a lieu parfois en deça ou au-delà de tout discours. Et autant l'énoncé de certains dogmes stérilise, autant le vrai engendre à l'état libre.

Cela dit la moindre de mes paroles est exploitée avec un désir plus ou moins conscient de me surpasser. Pourquoi préférer la compétition au fait d'être soi? Voilà qui m'apparaît de mauvais augure pour la pensée. Et être ensemble n'est-il plus grand bonheur que posséder?

Ce que je dis est invite à être et non à avoir. M'écouter risque de laisser les mains et l'estomac vides à qui a déjà perdu le chemin de son devenir. Mais ce peut être lumière pour qui chemine dans la voie de la fidélité à soi.

Je n'aime ni les extrêmes ni les contraires. Y recourir est toujours, de ma part, une stratégie de libération. C'est pour échapper à un opposé qu'il m'arrive d'être absolue, non pour m'y tenir. Et—me croirez-vous?—renverser ne me sied pas. Seule la nécessité peut m'y contraindre. Presque tous les échafaudages ou perspectives déjà construits obscurcissent. Partir d'eux retarde l'avénement de la vérité. Pour en percevoir encore quelque chose, il n'est pas inutile de mettre quelques têtes sous les pieds. Ce qui signifie, entre autres, de remettre l'élémentaire terrestre en position de désirable. C'est l'indispensable à la vie qui doit être recherché. Le reste importe peu. Et s'il est un privilège qui ouvre à tout, n'est-ce pas celui de vivre?

On me prête volontiers une certaine méchanceté. Des années durant j'ai tenté de répliquer. Lasse de palabres inutiles, j'ai cherché à comprendre. Deux motifs me semblent expliquer ce malentendu. Qui soupçonne la douceur de mes poils d'angora? Et encore: Qui imagine, venant d'une

What I communicate is imperceptible. And many reproach me for not teaching them something.

This does not stop them from announcing to me, in the months that follow, that they have discovered love, given birth, written a book, or produced some work of art. But the connection between these events and our meeting is rarely drawn. Nevertheless, some do draw it. Otherwise, I would doubt it myself.

Certainly spiritual fecundity exists. It sometimes occurs before or beyond all discourse. And the statement of certain dogmas sterilizes as much as the true, in its free state, engenders.

This said, the least of my utterances is exploited in the more or less conscious desire to surpass me. Why prefer competition to being oneself? This is what, it seems to me, augurs ill for thought. And is not being together a greater happiness than possessing?

What I say is an invitation to be and not to have. Listening to me might leave anyone who has already lost the path of their becoming with empty hands and stomach. But it can be a light for those who walk in the path of fidelity to themselves.

I do not like extremes or opposites. When I have recourse to them it is always a strategy of liberation. When I happen to be absolute, it is in order to escape an opposite, not to espouse one. And—do you believe me?—inverting does not suit me. Only necessity can force me to. Almost all existing constructions and perspectives obfuscate. Taking them as a point of departure delays the coming of truth. In order still to catch a glimpse of truth, it is useful to stand some things on their head. Which means, among other things, making the earthly elemental desirable again. We should be looking for what is indispensable to life. The rest is of little importance. And if there is a privilege that opens everything up, is it not the privilege of living?

I have been readily credited with a kind of maliciousness. For years I tried to respond. Tired of the useless palaver, I tried to understand. It seems to me that two motives explain this misunderstanding. Who could

femme, une rigueur de pensée qui ne soit pas malignité? Notre tradition même nous l'interdit. Il est vrai que la chose est rare. Et cela ouvre à un troisième motif possible de ma soi-disant mauvaiseté: quand mes vertus sont reconnues, elles deviennent immédiatement égalables. Cette évidence s'accompagne d'une automatique dévalorisation de mon oeuvre et, surtout, de ma personne. Et j'entends argumenter devant moi, quand ce n'est pas chez moi, que je ne vaux pas plus que . . . mon interlocutrice, par exemple. Cela m'est encore arrivé pas plus tard que vendredi dernier. N'avait-elle pas écrit autant de livres que moi? Je n'aurais jamais imaginé que le mérite puisse se mesurer au nombre de pages imprimées. Sans parler de la valeur de la pensée, insoupçonnée sans doute de qui tient, sans rire, de tels propos.

Il en est d'autres: "Tout ce qu'elle fait, je puis le faire." Etonnant, non?

Ainsi, un homme qui a mérité est-il respecté, admiré, vénéré même, pour ses oeuvres. Une femme est plutôt réprimandée. Et la riposte de ses semblables (quel mot inadéquat!) est de la ramener au plus bas ou de s'élever elles-mêmes au plus haut sans discernement. Là où la qualité émergeait, la quantité la rabaisse et l'anéantit. Il n'est encore question que du même, quel que soit le véhicule sous lequel il se propage.

Quant à moi, vous comprendrez pourquoi je me cache volontiers. Outre que cela m'évite de fatigants reproches, je suis ainsi soustraite à l'imitation d'une part de moi-même. Car qui songerait à s'enquérir de l'autre? Celle qui, justement, permet de penser.

Qui n'a pas éprouvé ce qu'il en est de la transcendance entre femme et homme n'entend pas grand chose à ce que je dis. Car ce rien que je mets entre eux, entre nous, ce double rien même, le sien et le mien, contrarie toute compréhension. A moins d'un miracle? Je veux dire d'une rencontre inattendue.

Avec une arrogante surdité, l'un ou l'autre y va de ses jugements. Il ou elle ne condamne que soi. Entre nous, manque le silence qui autoriserait la question: Qui es-tu? Ou: Quelle est ta vérité? Et aussi: Quel jugement portes-tu sur toi-même?

Qui prétend décider de l'autre avant de telles interrogations en use comme d'un âne juste bon à porter les ignorances qu'il ne se reconnaît pas.

Dans ce défaut de perspectives, c'est toujours l'autre qui devient "moins quelque chose." Chacun(e) est bien plutôt "moins l'autre." Je suis une femme, tu es un homme: voilà notre chance. Entre nous se tient

suspect my soft angora hair? And then: Who could conceive of rigorous thought, coming from a woman, that was anything but malice? Our very tradition prohibits it. It is true that such thought is unusual. Which brings us to a third possible explanation for my supposed malice: as soon as my virtues are recognized, they become matchable. This is of course obvious, and it is accompanied by an automatic depreciation of my work and, above all, my person. And I hear it said in my presence, if not indeed in my own home, that I am no better than . . . the woman talking with me, for example. This happened to me again only last Friday. Hadn't she written as many books as I? I would have never imagined that merit could be measured by the number of printed pages. Not to speak of the value of the thought, which is doubtlessly undreamed of by anyone who could say such a thing seriously.

And there are others: "I can do everything she does." Astonishing, isn't it?

Thus a deserving man is respected, admired, even venerated for his works. A woman is reprimanded instead. And the riposte of her own kind (what an inadequate expression!) is to belittle her or to aggrandize themselves indiscriminately.[1] Where quality was beginning to emerge, quantity comes along to discount and destroy it. It's still just more of the same, no matter how it's being reproduced.

As for me, you understand why I willingly go into hiding. Apart from the fact that it spares me tiresome reproaches, I can avoid the imitation of a part of myself. For who would dream of inquiring about the other part? The very one that makes thinking possible.

Anyone who has not felt what is at stake in the transcendence between woman and man does not understand very much of what I say. For this nothing I place between them, between us, this double nothing, his and mine, thwarts all comprehension. Unless there should be a miracle? By which I mean an unexpected encounter.

With an arrogant deafness, one or the other will only pass judgment. He or she is judging only himself, herself. Between us, the silence is lacking that would allow the question: Who are you? Or: What is your truth? And also: What judgment do you pass on yourself?

Whoever claims to judge the other without first asking such questions treats the other like an ass that is only good for carrying the things he doesn't realize he doesn't know.

le néant d'être. Inutile donc de grimper ou de s'étendre en tous sens—l'irréductible se tient là, lieu encore à bâtir de la création humaine.

Que te dire? Comment t'écouter? Ces préalables demandent d'en revenir au suspens du jugement, d'apprendre à se taire.

Et ce d'autant plus que qui parle est hors du commun, étrange pour l'habitude. Encore futur(e)? Le goût faussement démocratique de tout ramener au même, entendez à soi, étouffe de nos jours les plus sublimes pensées, et dénie toute possibilité d'idéal aux humbles et aux enfants. Parmi nous fourmillent de petits légistes qui prennent leur ignorance pour la loi divine—que les fourmis m'excusent d'emprunter leur nom pour désigner de tels égoisme et paresse! A peine acquis quelques rudiments de connaissances, voilà donc ces universitaires nouveaux-nés—ne parlons pas des journalistes!—émettant des opinions sur des écrits dont la vérité leur échappe totalement. En quelques minutes, les pensées longuement méditées, les paroles mûries—en lumière, température, taux d'humidité—à travers quelques saisons, deviennent banalités ou redites à l'usage du commerce au jour le jour de publications médiatiques ou de livres à succès. Les espaces les plus transcendantaux s'y trouvent réduits à une atmosphère confinée où l'intoxication par des pouvoirs sociaux conjuguée à l'épuisement physique ne laisse plus filtrer aucune inspiration ni aucun rais de lumière. Ne restent qu'artifices fabriqués trop rapidement: ces machines à reproduire n'ont jamais de temps à perdre pour penser. Un coup d'oeil leur suffit pour ramener au déjà connu l'inouï d'une vérité nouvelle.

Et si une telle pensée s'exprime avec art, nos catégoriciens et synthétiseurs seront bien incapables de la concevoir comme philosophique, tant la sagesse est supposée devoir se dire sans grâce ni poésie. Il n'est pourtant aucun grand philosophe qui ne soit aussi un poète. Et ce double registre me semble même un critère pour distinguer la création du commentaire. Mais l'universitaire traditionnel voudrait nous faire croire que l'ennui est le signe infaillible de la vérité. Je n'étonnerai personne en disant que cet universitaire supporte mal de m'entendre et que, en France du moins, mes livres sont très rarement situés parmi les ouvrages de philosophie. Si cette erreur d'interprétation peut s'expliquer pour *Speculum,* célèbre pour une critique de Freud, bien que celle-ci n'ait pu se réaliser qu'à partir d'une démarche et d'une perspective de philosophe, si *Ce sexe qui n'en est pas un* comporte également des chapitres sur la psychanalyse qui peuvent entretenir l'aveuglement, il n'en va pas de même de la plupart de mes autres ouvrages qui ne parlent que de philosophie: *Amante marine, L'Oubli de l'air, Ethique de la différence sexuelle,* livres dès lors introuvables en

In this lack of perspectives, it is always the other that emerges as "less something." But rather, everyone is "less the other." I am a woman, you are a man: that is our fortune. Between us lies the nothingness of being. It is futile to climb or to stretch oneself in every direction—the irreducible is waiting there, as a site of human creation, yet to be built.

What can I say to you? How can I listen to you? These prerequisites necessitate returning to the suspension of judgment, learning to stay silent.

And all the more because the person speaking is out of the ordinary, strange in regard to the usual. Still in the future? Today, the falsely democratic taste for reducing everything to the same, in other words to oneself, smothers the most sublime thoughts and denies to the humble and to children any possibility of an ideal. Teeming among us are hordes of little jurists who take their own ignorance for divine law (may the ants excuse me for using their name for such egoism and laziness!).[2] So, having scarcely acquired a few rudiments of knowledge, these newborn academics—to say nothing of journalists!—start voicing opinions about works whose truth entirely escapes them. In a few moments, thoughts that have been carefully meditated, words ripened over several seasons—in sunlight, warmth, humidity—become banalities or clichés for the day-to-day commercial language of media publications or best-sellers. The most transcendental spaces are thus reduced to a confined atmosphere in which intoxication by social powers combined with physical exhaustion blocks out any in-spiration, any ray of light. All that remain are artifices produced too hurriedly: these reproduction-machines have no time to waste on thought. A single glance is enough for them to reduce the strangeness of a new truth to the already known.

And if such a thought is expressed artfully, our categoricians and synthesizers will be quite incapable of viewing it as philosophical, so strong is the assumption that wisdom cannot express itself with grace or poetry. Yet there is never a great philosopher who is not a poet as well. And this double register seems to me even a criterion for distinguishing creation from commentary. But the traditional academic would have us believe that boredom is the infallible sign of truth. I will not surprise anyone when I say that this academic does not like hearing me and that, at least in France, my works are rarely classed among the works of philosophy. If this error in interpretation is understandable in the case of *Speculum,* celebrated for its critique of Freud, even though this critique could not have come about had it not taken the method and perspective of a philosopher as its point of departure, and if *This Sex Which Is Not One* also contains chapters on

librairie. Et si j'étais homme, nul doute que *Parler n'est jamais neutre, Le Temps de la différence* et *Je, tu, nous* seraient reçus comme de la philosophie du langage ou de la philosophie politique. Ce qui serait simplement cohérent.

Mais voilà, je suis une femme. Et qui imagine qu'une femme puisse penser? Ce phénomène n'échappe-t-il à la conscience dans notre tradition? La femme peut enfanter, materner, aimer à la limite. Il lui sera même pardonné d'être une intellectuelle, à condition qu'elle s'en tienne au commentaire, éventuellement critique, des oeuvres des génies masculins ou qu'elle leur apporte des éléments plus ou moins expérimentaux, poétiques ou religieux susceptibles de contribuer à l'élaboration de leurs théories.

Mais une philosophe, qui plus est une philosophe qui prétend penser et créer sans soumission à l'ordre masculin, ce phénomène est encore irrecevable. Et il conviendrait que je raconte un jour toutes les paroles, comportements, sévices inimaginables que me vaut cette vocation de philosophe.

Ce genre d'écrit me rapporterait peut-être suffisamment d'argent pour poursuivre sans trop de peines mes recherches et méditations. N'est-ce pas le conseil que me donnait récemment un marxiste des plus sérieux? Il ajoutait que mes interprètes auraient besoin de précisions biographiques que je leur fournirais par la même occasion, ce qui allègerait leur travail.

Mais si je n'avais pu penser que selon mon histoire, aurais-je jamais pensé? Rien n'est moins sûr. Comment m'en expliquer auprès de cet honnête homme?

Je dois, peut-être, à mon père mon goût pour l'Italie. A peine franchie cette frontière, je ris, je pétille.

C'est depuis peu que je connais cette ascendance italienne. Et il me plaît d'y trouver l'origine de mes tendances aristocratiques. Une part de moi est une aristocrate italienne. Je ne m'en plaindrai pas. Même si j'y circule comme dans un labyrinthe.

Ainsi dans certains lieux d'Italie, brusquement me vient cette évidence: je suis chez moi. Et personne ne m'enlèvera cette certitude qu'il se passe là quelque chose d'une rencontre avec mes ancêtres.

L'attrait pour certains italiens a sans doute ce poids mystérieux. Quelque chose de nécessaire et d'infaillible y a lieu. Rien d'une séduction qui puisse se réduire, se résoudre. Il y est plutôt question d'une sorte d'attraction terrestre.

psychoanalysis that might be misleading, this is not the case for most of my other works, which speak of nothing but philosophy—*Marine Lover, L'Oubli de l'air, Ethique de la différence sexuelle,* books which for this reason cannot be found in bookstores. And if I were a man, *Parler n'est jamais neutre, Le Temps de la différence,* and *Je, tu, nous* would doubtless be taken as philosophy of language or political philosophy. Which would be entirely consistent.

But there it is, I am a woman. And who imagines that a woman is capable of thinking? Isn't this phenomenon beyond the ken of our tradition? Woman can give birth, mother, and, at most, love. She can even be pardoned for being an intellectual as long as she limits herself to commentary, perhaps even criticism, of the works of male geniuses, or brings in more or less experimental, poetic, or religious elements that might contribute to the elaboration of their theories.

But a woman philosopher—and moreover a woman philosopher who claims to think and create without submitting to the masculine order—is a phenomenon that is still inadmissible. One day I should really recount all the words, actions, and unimaginable ill-treatment this vocation for philosophy affords me.

Such a text would perhaps bring me in enough money to pursue my research and meditations without too much struggle. Isn't this the advice a very serious Marxist gave me recently? He added that my interpreters would be in need of biographical details, which I could supply at the same time, and which would facilitate their work.

But if I had only been able to think according to my personal history, would I ever have thought? Nothing is less certain. But how could I explain myself to this good man?

Perhaps I have my father to thank for my taste for Italy. As soon as I'm across that border, I'm laughing, sparkling.

It is only recently that I discovered this Italian ancestry. And I like to see in it the origin of my aristocratic tendencies. Part of me is an Italian aristocrat. I will not complain, although I move in it as in a labyrinth.

Thus in some places in Italy I suddenly have the feeling that I'm home. And no one can take from me the certainty that what is taking place is a kind of encounter with my ancestors.

There is no doubt that the attraction to certain Italians has this mysterious weight about it. Something necessary and infallible happens there.

Le rapport à mon père, loin d'être de pur langage, est de terre et de sang. N'allez pas y chercher un inceste. C'est plutôt sa différence, notre différence qui, enfin, me devient tangible dans certains lieux ou hommes italiens.

Si mon père n'était pour moi que langage, il ne me serait pas autre. Il serait plutôt désignation ou double de ma réalité. Je serais ma mère et le langage de mon père, le corps de l'une et la tête de l'autre, mais non le fruit de leur mutuelle fécondation.

Quand je rencontre des traces du sang de mon père, je sors de tout risque d'inceste, d'autisme, de symbiose, d'engloutissement. Je butte sur l'autre et sa réalité.

Cet autre, nul doute qu'il ne soit italien. Il est bon, chaleureux, artiste, plutôt gai et intelligent.

Certes, j'ai connu mon père triste. Je pense qu'il ne l'aurait pas été en Italie. Il était en exil.

J'ai cherché, pendant des années, le sens du visage de mon père. Etrange, sans ressemblance avec quiconque, il était attachant et effrayant à la fois. Après sa mort, arpentant l'Italie, j'ai cru me trouver face à lui. C'était sur une place de Vérone. L'homme était Dante. J'en suis restée sidérée. L'énigme du corps de mon père était sous mes yeux. A qui ne me croirait pas, je suis prête à envoyer une photo de lui. Mais, à vrai dire, le geste me déplaît. Je préfère l'envoyer à Vérone.

Par ma mère, je suis française du Nord. Ma mère était belle, élégante, plutôt réservée sauf avec les tout jeunes enfants. Rationnelle, dévouée, courageuse, ma mère a aussi une sorte de coquetterie centrifuge qui me déconcertera toujours. Elle imagine qu'elle intéresse, et se doit de s'exposer, du moins superficiellement. Il n'est pas exclu qu'il y ait là une forme de relation à l'aveu dont souffrent beaucoup de femmes. Par contre, ma mère semble ne se préoccuper en rien des autres. Si la remarque lui en est faite, elle rétorque que c'est par discrétion. Mais cela peut atteindre à des situations quasi burlesques.

Ma généalogie maternelle est faite de paysans. Les souvenirs que j'en ai sont toujours liés aux jardins, aux saisons, aux fruits, à la culture de la terre. A part les nourrissons, ma mère aime la nature, et surtout les plantes. Je pense qu'elle leur parle plus qu'elle ne l'a fait à ses enfants. Du moins réellement. Je n'en suis pas sûre. Elle ne m'en a jamais rien dit. Mais nul doute que celles-ci ne lui soient une compagnie importante.

Etrange couple. Entre eux. Et en moi. La France et l'Italie y sont en perpétuelles tractations. Et si l'essence de ces cultures et celle de leurs re-

It is nothing like a seduction that could be reduced or resolved. It is more like a sort of earthly attraction.

My relationship to my father, far from being one of pure language, is of earth and of blood. But don't start looking for incest. It is, rather, his difference, our difference that has finally become tangible to me through certain Italian places and men.

If my father were nothing but language to me, he would not be other to me. He would be more like the designation or the double of my reality. I would be my mother and the language of my father, the body of one and the head of the other, but not the fruit of their mutual fecundation.

When I come across traces of my father's blood, I escape all risk of incest, of autism, of symbiosis, of engulfment. I run up against the other and his reality.

No doubt, this other is Italian. He is good, warm, artistic, rather joyful and intelligent.

Of course, my father was sad when I knew him. I think he would not have been so in Italy. He was in exile.

For years I sought the meaning of my father's face. Strange, unlike anyone else, he was at once engaging and frightening. After his death, when I was roaming around Italy, I thought I found myself in front of him. It was in a piazza in Verona. The man was Dante. I stood frozen in my tracks. The enigma of my father's body stood before my eyes. I am prepared to send a photo of him to anyone who doesn't believe me. But to tell the truth, this gesture displeases me. I prefer to send them to Verona.

Through my mother I am a woman from the north of France. My mother was beautiful, elegant, and rather reserved, except with very young children. Rational, devoted, brave, my mother also has a sort of centrifugal coquettishness that will always disconcert me. She thinks she interests people and exposes herself, at least superficially, of her own volition. It may well be a case of that affinity for confession that plagues many women. By contrast, my mother does not seem at all concerned about others. When someone remarks on this, she replies that it is out of discretion. But it can create almost burlesque situations.

My maternal genealogy consists of peasants. The memories I retain of it always involve gardens, the seasons, fruits, the cultivation of the earth. Besides nurslings, my mother loves nature, and above all plants. I think she talks more to them than she did to her children. At least really talks. But I'm not certain. She has never said anything about it to me. But there is no doubt that for her they are important company.

lations me retiennent tellement, c'est pour une part que je m'y cherche. Les questions se focalisent surtout sur les harmonies entre le coeur et la raison. Mais elles ne sont pas simples à analyser. C'est tantôt plus haut ou plus bas, plus profond ou plus superficiellement que se manifeste l'un ou l'autre. Il en va de même pour le chaud et le froid. Quant à l'aristocratie et la paysannerie? Selon moi, les paysans sont des aristocrates. Mais il est vrai que si un citadin italien peut m'apparaître tel, les français de la ville sont trop vulgaires pour mon goût.

Puis-je trouver dans ces généalogies et caractères parentaux l'énigme de ma vérité? Une part, pas davantage. Et telle est bien une des limites du marxisme—il ne croit pas au hasard. Conjugué à la psychanalyse, autre lieu de réduction du mystère au connu, il rend l'Histoire irrespirable. Ces deux athéismes deviennent ainsi les plus sûrs chemins du retour au Dieu qui préside à notre destin séculaire. Ne nous a-t-il créés de son souffle? Et: Comment ne pas y faire recours pour qui n'interroge pas la grammaire comme ce qui règle traditionnellement notre être et notre devenir?

Pouvons-nous parler, nous parler différemment? Ne serait-ce l'aurore du siècle à venir? Car nous aurons beau fuir ici ou là, sans changement de code, les impératifs de l'ordinateur nous y rejoindront.

C'est plutôt du côté du *nous* que la question est à poser. De cet irréductible silence entre toi et moi qui dérange tout programme et déjoue toute intention unique.

Quand je te parle, qu'entends-tu? Et comment t'écouter, toi qui m'est et qui me restera toujours étranger? Et si je deviens et que tu deviens, ce que nous avons à nous dire n'échappe-t-il pas à tout code préalable. Même si nous sommes marxistes et psychanalystes, mon futur comme le tien ne dépendent-ils pas de l'imprévisible de nos rencontres? De l'improgrammable de nos échanges? Car, à moins d'être déjà asservis, qui peut décider de quoi sera fait notre demain? Et n'est-ce déjà mort que d'en rester aux partage et fractionnement de l'héritage paternel?

Et qui me veut parricide, ignore que mon goût de vivre me détourne d'un tel geste. Et ne pose, encore et encore, les demandes que d'un seul côté et selon une seule direction.

Pourquoi tuer l'autre me plairait-il plus que chanter ce que je vis? Que louer ma vie, la vie? Et comment ne pas se poser une telle question? Ne pas s'y arrêter, ne serait-ce déjà une forme de crime? Pourquoi devrais-

Strange couple. As a couple. And in me. Here France and Italy are in constant negotiation. And if I am interested in the essence of these cultures and their relations, it is in part because, in them, I am looking for myself. The questions mostly center on the harmonies between the heart and the mind. But they are not easy to analyze. Both can appear sometimes higher or lower, sometimes deeper or more superficially. It is the same with heat and cold. What about the aristocracy and the peasantry? For me, peasants are aristocrats. But it is true that even if an urban Italian may seem like one to me, French city dwellers are too vulgar for my taste.

Can I find the enigma of my truth in these genealogies and parental characters? A part of it, and no more. And this is certainly one of the limits of Marxism—it does not believe in chance. In conjunction with psychoanalysis, another place where the mysterious is reduced to the known, it makes History unbreathable. These two atheisms thus become the surest paths back to the God who presides over our secular destiny. Did He not create us out of His breath? And: How can anyone who doesn't examine grammar as that which traditionally orders our being and our becoming not have recourse to Him?

Can we speak, can we speak to each other differently? Would this not be the dawn of the new era? For no matter where we run to, unless we change the code, the imperatives of the computer will catch up with us.

The question should really be asked from the perspective of the *we*. From this irreducible silence between you and me, which upsets every program, thwarts every unique intention.

When I speak to you, what do you hear? And how can I listen to you, you who are, and will always be, foreign to me? And if I am becoming and if you are becoming, does not what we have to say to each other escape all predetermined codes? Even if we are Marxists and psychoanalysts, does not my future, like yours, depend on the unforeseeable in our encounters? On the unprogrammable in our exchanges? For unless we are already enslaved, who can decide what our tomorrow will be made of? And if we limit ourselves to the apportionment, the splitting of our paternal heritage, is this not already death?

And whoever wants to see me as parricidal does not understand that my taste for life bars me from such a gesture. And poses questions over and over from one side only and according to only one perspective.

je être débitrice et l'autre créancier? Cette croyance n'est-elle déjà secret détournement de qui donne vie et sagesse?

Et, à défaut d'y méditer, serons-nous jamais deux? Et quels silence ou parole objecterons-nous aux techniques de programmation si nous ne sommes pas tels—deux, irréductibles l'un à l'autre, dont le langage et le devenir sont encore pour une part futurs.

Car la loi du Père n'échappe pas aux codages. Elle en est même le prototype. Mais nos amours ne peuvent s'y soumettre. Et c'est bien plutôt à la rivailté entre mêmes qu'elle nous entraîne pour nous y enfermer. Il n'y a là que généalogies de pères et de fils. Ni femmes ni hommes encore. Et la guerre n'est pas entre les sexes mais entre les fils et leurs ombres.

Why would I prefer killing the other to singing what I live? To extolling my life, life? And how can one not ask oneself such a question? Not to hesitate over it, would not that itself be a form of crime? Why should I be the debtor and the other the creditor? Is this belief not already a secret deviation from the source of life and wisdom?

And if we do not reflect on this, will we ever be two? And with what silence or speech will we oppose the techniques of programming if we are not such—two, irreducible to one another, our language and our becoming still, in part, future?

For the law of the Father does not escape encoding. It is even its prototype. But our loves cannot submit to it. It pulls us instead toward a rivalry between sames and imprisons us there. Where there are only genealogies of fathers and sons. Still neither women nor men. And the war is not between the sexes, but between the sons and their shadows.

Translated by Madeleine Dobie
(Emended by Emery Snyder and Peter Burgard)

Notes

1. Cf. the French text. "Her own kind," her fellow women, in French is "ses semblables"—literally, "those who are like" or "the same" as her; it is this reduction to the same with which Irigaray takes issue. —Tr.

2. Cf. the French text. The French word for an ant, "fourmi," has given rise to the verb "fourmiller"—to teem or swarm. —Tr.

Bibliography
Contributors
Index

Bibliography

The following is a bibliography of work that addresses the question of Nietzsche and the feminine. Where treatment of the issue occurs in the context of a more general work, page numbers are provided.

Ackermann, Robert John. *Nietzsche: A Frenzied Look*. Amherst: Univ. of Massachusetts Press, 1990. 122–37.

Ainley, Alison. " 'Ideal Selfishness': Nietzsche's Metaphor of Maternity." In *Exceedingly Nietzsche: Aspects of Contemporary Nietzsche-Interpretation*, ed. David Farrell Krell and David Wood. New York: Routledge, 1988.

Allen, Christine. "Nietzsche's Ambivalence about Women." In *The Sexism of Social and Political Theory: Women and Reproduction from Plato to Nietzsche*, ed. Lorenne M. G. Clark and Lynda Lange. Toronto: Univ. of Toronto Press, 1979.

Ansell-Pearson, Keith. "Who is the *Übermensch?* Time, Truth, and Woman in Nietzsche." *Journal of the History of Ideas* 53 (1992): 309–31.

Baker, Lang. "Irigaray contre Bataille: Locating the Feminine in Nietzsche." *Discours social / Social Discourse: Research Papers in Comparative Literature* 2 (1989): 229–35.

Battersby, Christine. *Gender and Genius: Towards a Feminist Aesthetics*. Bloomington: Indiana Univ. Press, 1989. 119–23 and passim.

Behler, Diana. "Nietzsche's View of Woman in Classical Greece." *Nietzsche-Studien* 18 (1989): 359–76.

Behler, Ernst. *Derrida—Nietzsche / Nietzsche—Derrida*. Munich: Schöningh, 1988. 118–24 and passim.

Berg, Elizabeth L. "The Third Woman." *Diacritics* 12 (Summer 1982): 11–20.

Bergoffen, Debra B. "On the Advantage and Disadvantage of Nietzsche for Women." In *The Question of the Other: Essays in Contemporary Continental Philosophy*, ed. Arleen B. Dallery and Charles E. Scott. Albany: SUNY Press, 1989.

Bertram, Maryanne J. " 'God's *Second* Blunder'—Serpent Woman and the *Gestalt* in Nietzsche's Thought." *Southern Journal of Philosophy* 19 (1981): 259–77.

Blondel, Eric. "Nietzsche: Life as Metaphor." In *The New Nietzsche: Contemporary Styles of Interpretation*, ed. David B. Alison. New York: Dell, 1977.

Brann, Hellmut Walther. *Nietzsche und die Frauen*. Leipzig: Felix Meiner, 1931.

Burney-Davis, Terri, and R. Stephen Krebbs. "The Vita Femina and Truth." *History of European Ideas* 11 (1989): 841–47.

Cocks, Joan. "Augustine, Nietzsche, and Contemporary Body Politics." *Differences: A Journal of Feminist Cultural Studies* 3 (1991): 144–58.

Del Caro, Adrian. "The Pseudoman in Nietzsche: Or, The Threat of the Neuter." *New German Critique* 50 (1990): 135–56.

Derrida, Jacques. *Spurs: Nietzsche's Styles / Eperons: Les Styles de Nietzsche.* Trans. Barbara Harlow. Chicago: Univ. of Chicago Press, 1979.

——— and Christie V. McDonald. "Choreographies." *Diacritics* 12 (Summer 1982): 66–76.

Diethe, Carol. "Nietzsche and the Woman Question." *History of European Ideas* 11 (1989): 865–75.

Diprose, Rosalyn. "Nietzsche, Ethics, and Sexual Difference." *Radical Philosophy* 52 (1989): 27–33.

Doane, Mary Ann. "Veiling Over Desire: Close-ups of the Woman." In *Feminism and Psychoanalysis,* ed. Richard Feldstein and Judith Roof. Ithaca: Cornell Univ. Press, 1989.

Freydberg, Bernard D. "Nietzsche in Derrida's *Spurs:* Deconstruction as Deracination." *History of European Ideas* 11 (1989): 685–92.

Graybeal, Jean. *Language and "the Feminine" in Nietzsche and Heidegger.* Bloomington: Indiana Univ. Press, 1990.

Heath, Stephen. "Joan Riviere and the Masquerade." In *Formations of Fantasy,* ed. Victor Burgin, James Donald, and Cora Kaplan. New York: Methuen, 1986.

Irigaray, Luce. *Marine Lover of Friedrich Nietzsche.* Trans. Gillian C. Gill. New York: Columbia Univ. Press, 1991.

Jardine, Alice A. *Gynesis: Configurations of Woman and Modernity.* Ithaca: Cornell Univ. Press, 1985. 192–99 and passim.

Kennedy, Ellen. "Nietzsche: Women as Untermensch." In *Women in Western Political Philosophy,* ed. Ellen Kennedy and Susan Mendus. Brighton: Wheatsheaf, 1987.

Kofman, Sarah. "Baubô: Theological Perversion and Fetishism." In *Nietzsche's New Seas: Explorations in Philosophy, Aesthetics, and Politics,* ed. Michael Allen Gillespie and Tracy B. Strong. Chicago: Univ. of Chicago Press, 1988.

———. *Nietzsche et la scène philosophique.* Paris: Union générale d'éditions, 1979.

Krell, David Farrell. *Postponements: Women, Sensuality, and Death in Nietzsche.* Bloomington: Indiana Univ. Press, 1986.

Nill, Peggy. *Vita Femina: Nietzsches Konzeption des Selbst.* Frankfurt: Haag + Herchen, 1985.

Okhamafe, E. Imafedia. "Heidegger's *Nietzsche* and Nietzsche's Play: The Questions of Wo(man), Christianity, Nihilism, and Humanism." *Soundings: An Interdisciplinary Journal* 71 (1988): 533–53.

Oliver, Kelly. "Nietzsche's 'Woman': The Poststructuralist Attempt to Do Away with Woman." *Radical Philosophy* 48 (1988): 25–29.

———. "Who Is Nietzsche's Woman?" In *Modern Engendering: Critical Feminist Readings in Modern Western Philosophy,* ed. Bat-Ami Bar On. Albany: SUNY Press, 1994.

———. "Women as Truth in Nietzsche's Writings." *Social Theory and Practice* 10 (1984): 185–99.

———. "Woman's Voice, Man's Language: A Reading of Gender and Language in Nietzsche." Ph.D. diss., Northwestern University, 1987.

Ormiston, Gayle L. "Traces of Derrida: Nietzsche's Image of Woman." *Philosophy Today* 28 (1984): 178–88.

Platt, Michael. "Woman, Nietzsche, and Nature." *Maieutics* 2 (1981): 27–42.

Schlüpmann, Heide. "Zur Frage der Nietzsche-Rezeption in der Frauenbewegung gestern und heute." In *Nietzsche heute: Die Rezeption seines Werkes nach 1968,* ed. Sigrid Bauschinger, Susan L. Cocalis, and Sara Lennox. Bern: Francke, 1988.

Schulte, Günter. *Ich impfe euch mit dem Wahnsinn: Nietzsches Philosophie der verdrängten Weiblichkeit des Mannes.* Cologne: Balloni, 1989.

———. *Vielleicht ist die Wahrheit ein Weib: Anmerkungen zur Philosophie des Patriarchats.* Cologne: Balloni, 1984.

Schutte, Ofelia. *Beyond Nihilism: Nietzsche without Masks.* Chicago: Univ. of Chicago Press, 1984. 161–88 and passim.

———. "Nietzsche on Gender Difference: A Critique." *Newsletter on Feminism and Philosophy* 89, no. 2 (1990): 63–66.

———. "Nietzsche's Psychology of Gender Difference." In *Modern Engendering: Critical Feminist Readings in Modern Western Philosophy,* ed. Bat-Ami Bar On. Albany: SUNY Press, 1994.

Shapiro, Gary. *Alcyone: Nietzsche on Gifts, Noise, and Women.* Albany: SUNY Press, 1991.

Singer, Linda. "Nietzschean Mythologies: The Inversion of Value and the War against Women." *Soundings: An Interdisciplinary Journal* 66 (1983): 281–95.

Spivak, Gayatri Chakravorty. "Displacement and the Discourse of Woman." In *Displacement: Derrida and After,* ed. Mark Krupnick. Bloomington: Indiana Univ. Press, 1983.

Staten, Henry. *Nietzsche's Voice.* Ithaca: Cornell Univ. Press, 1990. 171–77 and passim.

Thiel, Manfred. *Nietzsche: Ein analytischer Aufbau seiner Denkstruktur.* Heidelberg: Elpis, 1980. 675–85.

Thomas, R. Hinton. *Nietzsche in German Politics and Society, 1890–1918.* Manchester: Manchester Univ. Press, 1983. 80–95 and 132–41.

Thompson, J. L. "Nietzsche on Woman." *International Journal of Moral and Social Studies* 5 (1990): 207–20.

Contributors

BENJAMIN BENNETT is William R. Kenan, Jr. Professor of German at the University of Virginia. He is the author of *Modern Drama and German Classicism, Goethe's Theory of Poetry, Hugo von Hofmannsthal: The Theaters of Consciousness, Theater as Problem: Modern Drama and Its Place in Literature,* and, most recently, *Beyond Theory: Eighteenth-Century German Literature and the Poetics of Irony.*

SUSAN BERNSTEIN is Assistant Professor of Comparative Literature at Brown University. She is currently completing a book on music and language in the nineteenth century; her articles include essays on Poe, on Fichte and the sublime, on Rousseau and harmony, and on Wagner and Heine.

PETER J. BURGARD is Assistant Professor of German at Harvard University. He is the author of *Idioms of Uncertainty: Goethe and the Essay* and articles on Lessing, Herder, Goethe, Nietzsche, Mann, Ibsen, Miller, Adorno, and Warhol.

LUCE IRIGARAY is a Director of Research in Philosophy at the Centre National de la Recherche Scientifique and a trained psychoanalyst. She is the author of *Marine Lover of Friedrich Nietzsche, Speculum of the Other Woman, This Sex Which Is Not One, Je, tu, nous, Sexes and Genealogies,* and numerous other works on philosophy, psychoanalysis, and feminism.

CLAYTON KOELB, Guy B. Johnson Professor of German and Comparative Literature at the University of North Carolina at Chapel Hill, has written widely on twentieth-century literature, intellectual history, and literary theory. His most recent books include *Inventions of Reading: Rhetoric and the Literary Imagination, Kafka's Rhetoric: The Passion of Reading,* and an edited volume on *Nietzsche as Postmodernist.*

SARAH KOFMAN is Professor of Philosophy at the Université de Paris I, Panthéon-Sorbonne. Among her many works on Nietzsche, Freud, and feminism are *The Enigma of Woman: Woman in Freud's Writing, Nietzsche and Metaphor, Nietzsche et la scène philosophique,* and, most recently, *Explosion I: De l'"Ecce Homo" de Nietzsche* (translation forthcoming 1995) as well as *Explosion II.*

Contributors

DAVID FARRELL KRELL is Professor of Philosophy at DePaul University. He is the author of *Daimon Life: Heidegger and Life-Philosophy, Of Memory, Reminiscence, and Writing: On the Verge, Intimations of Mortality: Time, Truth, and Finitude in Heidegger's Thinking of Being,* and *Postponements: Woman, Sensuality, and Death in Nietzsche.* He is editor and translator of a wide range of books and articles in German thought and literature, including *Exceedingly Nietzsche.*

JANET LUNGSTRUM, Assistant Professor of German and Comparative Literature at the University of Colorado, Boulder, has published a variety of articles on Nietzsche and theories of modernist creativity. She is currently preparing her dissertation on Nietzsche for publication and researching a future book project on architecture and film in German modernity.

KELLY OLIVER is Assistant Professor of Philosophy at the University of Texas at Austin. She is the author of *Reading Kristeva: Unraveling the Double-Bind* and has edited *Ethics, Politics, and Difference in Julia Kristeva's Writings.* She has recently completed a book entitled *Womanizing Nietzsche.*

ARKADY PLOTNITSKY is the author of *Reconfigurations: Critical Theory and General Economy, In the Shadow of Hegel: Complementarity, History, and the Unconscious,* and *Complementarity: Anti-Epistemology after Bohr and Derrida.* He has also published articles on romanticism, nineteenth-century philosophy, and modern critical theory. He teaches English and comparative literature at the University of Pennsylvania.

LAURENCE A. RICKELS is Professor of German and department chair at the University of California, Santa Barbara. He is the author of *Aberrations of Mourning: Writing on German Crypts, Der unbetrauerbare Tod,* and *The Case of California,* and editor of *Looking After Nietzsche* and Gottfried Keller's *Jugenddramen.* He is currently completing two books: *The Vampire Lectures* and *Nazi Psychoanalysis.*

ALAN D. SCHRIFT is Associate Professor of Philosophy at Grinnell College. Author of *Nietzsche and the Question of Interpretation: Between Hermeneutics and Deconstruction* and coeditor of *The Hermeneutic Tradition: From Ast to Ricoeur* and *Transforming the Hermeneutic Context: From Nietzsche to Nancy,* he is currently completing a manuscript on Nietzsche's influence upon recent French philosophy.

BIANCA THEISEN, Assistant Professor of German at The Johns Hopkins University, studied German and comparative literature at Bonn, Berlin, and Stanford. She has written on simulation and mimesis in Heinrich von Kleist and on mnemotechnique in Nietzsche. Her work focuses on late eighteenth- and early nineteenth-century literature and philosophy, particularly on early romanticism.

Contributors

LYNNE TIRRELL, Assistant Professor of Philosophy at the University of North Carolina at Chapel Hill, is currently completing a book entitled *Discursive Practice, Discursive Power: Derogatory Terms and Normative Ontology.* Her articles include essays on metaphor and philosophy of language, on storytelling and moral agency, and on feminist theory.

Index

Part I lists references to names and titles. Part II lists references to Nietzsche's works.

I

Index

II
Nietzsche's Works

Where there are numerous references to a particular work, part numbers and titles that could not be included with documentation in the text have been added.

Compositor: Tseng Informations Systems, Inc.
Text: 10.5 / 13 Sabon
Printer and binder: Braun-Brumfield, Inc.